21st Century Chinese Cybe

An examination of the Chinese Cyberthreat from fundamentals of Communist Policy regarding Information warfare through the broad range of military, civilian and commercially supported cyberattack threat vectors

21st Century Chinese Cyberwarfare

An examination of the Chinese Cyberthreat from
fundamentals of Communist Policy regarding
Information warfare through the broad range of
military, civilian and commercially supported
cyberattack threat vectors

WILLIAM T. HAGESTAD II

IT Governance Publishing

Every possible effort has been made to ensure that the information contained in this publication is accurate at the time of going to press, and the publisher and the author cannot accept responsibility for any errors or omissions, however caused. Any opinions expressed in this publication are those of the author, not the publisher. Websites identified are for reference only, not endorsement, and any website visits are at the reader's own risk. No responsibility for loss or damage occasioned to any person acting, or refraining from action, as a result of the material in this publication can be accepted by the publisher or the author.

Apart from any fair dealing for the purposes of research or private study, or criticism or review, as permitted under the Copyright, Designs and Patents Act 1988, this publication may only be reproduced, stored or transmitted, in any form, or by any means, with the prior permission in writing of the publisher or, in the case of reprographic reproduction, in accordance with the terms of licences issued by the Copyright Licensing Agency. Enquiries concerning reproduction outside those terms should be sent to the publisher at the following address:

IT Governance Publishing
IT Governance Limited
Unit 3, Clive Court
Bartholomew's Walk
Cambridgeshire Business Park
Ely
Cambridgeshire
CB7 4EH
United Kingdom

www.itgovernance.co.uk

First published in the United Kingdom in 2012
by IT Governance Publishing.

ISBN 978-1-84928-334-2

FOREWORD

'If you know the enemy and know yourself you need not fear the results of a hundred battles.'

Sun Tzu

Time is an interesting word. When we think about time and more specifically how cultures, countries, and technology evolve with time we realize the only certainty is the past. The author of this book has spent a lot of time, more than 27 years in fact, studying cultures in a military capacity. To know an adversary intimately is to respect their capability and understand their perspective. Lieutenant Colonel William Hagestad is considered an expert on the Chinese People's Liberation Army (PLA) because of the time he spent analyzing the capabilities of the PLA during his tenure in the United States Marine Corps. But his expertise also includes the culture of China and how the Chinese leverage technology. Bill has travelled extensively all over the world, served in many different military theaters and this book represents the nexus of his experiences.

21st Century Chinese Cyberwarfare is not just another text describing the information warfare capability of the Chinese. Moreover this book is about time, and also about understanding. Through the eyes of Lt. Col. Hagestad, the reader gains insight into the culture, history and language of the Chinese. These three things are significant drivers of ideology, military or otherwise, and the author educates the reader as to their importance in China. Ideology often inspires or determines a particular action and in terms of security, it is often helpful to understand the ideology of your adversary. Understanding information technology, information security, and the challenges an interconnected world face in the digital age are equally important. As readers, we have the unique privilege to benefit from Lt. Col. Hagestad's experience and through his analysis we gain a better appreciation for the driving forces behind many of the stories currently reported today regarding Chinese electronic warfare.

Finally, many people have a limited understanding as to the military capability of their country or other countries for that matter. The images of tanks, planes and troops marching across deserts can be found daily in a number of newspapers or magazines. If we think about time and the evolution of warfare, we realize that military strategy has changed but the tools used to accomplish the mission have evolved at a far greater pace. Knowing how to use the tools and knowing how to deploy the tools in the most appropriate manner are equally important. Behind the scenes, there are many critical functions that most people never see on CNN as the troops march by. Those critical functions for protecting the security of a nation are explored by the author and because of his experience in the United States Marine Corps we are provided rare insight to the most awesome of capabilities any military brings to bear.

I hope you enjoy reading *21st Century Chinese Cyberwarfare* and challenge yourself to keep an open mind as you turn the pages.

Mike

Michael L Kearn, CISSP

PREFACE

Future wars will not be kinetic. These conflicts will be waged in cyberspace; the opponents will rarely, if ever, meet each other face to face in the physical realm. Cyberwarriors will be the participants of future political will, just as warfighters since time immemorial have carried out the political instructions of their Government managers. Countries will cross digital boundaries to carry out the policy demands of their nation-state against other nation-states digitally, and not kinetically. Victims of future cyberwarfare will be a combination of traditional non-combatants – civilians, military personnel, their families – and every man, woman and child that resides within a geographical space now recognized as a country, or nation-state.

Cyberwarfare will be the new form of today's kinetic effects-based conflict. However, instead of physical destruction, these cyberincursions and attacks will be infrastructure-based. The targets will be the electrical grid, financial systems' networks, military information networks and security systems. The cyberattackers will be based in the People's Republic of China and they will be carrying out the political, economic and patriotic wishes of their Chinese Communist Party masters.

The 21st century Chinese cyberwarfare will be economically, societally and culturally changing, and damaging for the nations that the 'Middle Kingdom' chooses to cybertarget. The People's Republic of China will use its considerable military resources to carry out and execute plans for worldwide domination based upon its dynasties-old history and intention to never again be beholden to the vicarious wishes of an invading and colonizing foreign force.

ABOUT THE AUTHOR

Lieutenant Colonel Hagestad has a Master of Science degree in Security Technologies from the College of Computer Engineering, University of Minnesota, conferred in 2011. He also has a Bachelor of Arts in Mandarin Chinese, with minor emphasis in Classical Chinese and Modern Japanese, while also holding a second Master of Science degree in the Management of Technology from the Carlson School of Management, University of Minnesota.

William is an internationally-recognized expert on the Chinese People's Liberation Army & Government information warfare. He advises international intelligence organizations, military flag officers and multi-national commercial enterprises with regard to their internal IT security governance and external security policies. The linguistic, historical, cultural, economic and military aspects of Chinese cyberwarfare are his forte.

Lieutenant Colonel Hagestad's military experience spans over 27 years; enlisting in the United States Marine Corps in 1981 and having served in numerous command posts. During 2002-03, Lieutenant Colonel Hagestad was the Anti-Terrorism Officer for Marine Central Command during the initial build-up and subsequent operations in Iraq; and in 2006-07, he served with I and II Marine Expeditionary Force (MEF) and the US Army's 1st Armoured Division in Ramadi, Al-Anbar Province, Iraq. Currently he is in an advisory position as an Anti-Terrorism/Force Protection Officer. His personal decorations in the Marine Corps include the Navy Achievement Medal with Gold Star, the Navy Commendation Medal, Operation Iraqi Freedom Medal with single campaign star, the Global War on Terrorism Medal and the Selected Marine Corps Reserve Medal with 4 stars. He speaks both domestically and internationally on the Chinese cyberthreat.

ACKNOWLEDGEMENTS

Writing this publication has been a full-time job. There are so many people I would like to acknowledge and thank. To Mrs Libby Hallas-Muchow for showing me how easy it should be to write, a lesson I'll always be grateful for – thank-you Libby! Absolute undying gratitude goes to Mrs Victoria Loewengart for introducing me to my publisher, IT Governance. Of course, very great appreciation goes to the publishing team and Mr Alan Calder at IT Governance – thank you all for your vision, support and wisdom.

Grateful thanks are due to the reviewers of this book for their helpful insights: John Custy, Managing Consultant, Distinguished Professional in Service Management DPSM ^{TM}, JPC Group; Robin Smith, Head of Information Risk, UHL NHS; Antonio Velasco, CEO, Sinersys Technologies; Giuseppe G. Zorzino CISA CGEIT CRISC, Lead Auditor 27001, Security Architect.

It is imperative that I thank Mrs Wang Michaelson who got me started studying the Chinese language of Mandarin, the culture and history of China when I was a mere 16 years old –謝謝王老師.

To my written and spoken teachers at Nankai University, 南开大学, 謝謝老師.
我衷心祝愿你們倆最好的，你的家人和你的健康
感謝所有的知識，你跟我一起分享。I know my Mandarin Chinese is far from perfect – I have never claimed fluency in this wonderful language, for anyone to do so is ignorant, disrespectful and dishonest – but to both of my Chinese teachers in the People's Republic of China I owe so much gratitude and respect that I can only hope to repay in this lifetime or those that follow.

To gentlemen who have studied and continue to research the Chinese information warfare landscape – LTC (RET) Timothy L Thomas, US Army; Lt Col Mark A Stokes, US Air Force; Dr James Mulvenon; LC Russell Hsiao; Mr Desmond Ball, and many others I have never met – your dedication to this subject is truly inspiring – thank you.

Thank you to the few individuals who have reminded me that the language of China changes and my colloquial use is always up for review and correction – 因為我很少有機會練習口語 – 謝謝你，我的中文水平低.

A great deal of respect and gratitude goes to the many information security professionals around the world. At the top of that list is Mike Kearn who has taught me so much about securing the network and how to hack the network … thank you Sir.

To Mr Niels Groenveld, whose tireless news postings on Chinese information warfare have helped keep this publication as current as the next minute will allow – dank u meener! His counterpart at Cyber Warzone, Reza Rafati should also have recognition for the outstanding and similarly tireless efforts in educating the world about matters relative to international cyberwarfare – dank u meneer! Also... با تشکر از شما دوست من.

Mr Pierluigi Paganini at Security Affairs for his tireless efforts in the area of cybersecurity research – thank you so much Sir for being both a friend and a colleague.

To Mr Scot Terban, whose website Krypteia should be on everyone's essential cyber- and information security resource lists – thank you for your service to our country and your unabashed view of the People's Republic of China.

Recognition needs to go to Scott Henderson and his spectacular work about the Chinese hacking underground – thank you also for your service to our country. If you haven't read his book "The Dark Visitor" or visited Scott's website, I wholeheartedly encourage you to do so.

Anthony M Freed and his monumental information security website InfoSecIsland – you Sir, are an inspiration – thank you for all your contributions – they are and remain invaluable.

Least but certainly not last – to all of the Marines I have served with over the years, specifically Sergeant Major Duane Hauer; Master Gunnery Sergeant Bob Pederson; Gunnery Sergeant Chuck Elliott; Lieutenant Colonel Stephen Eastham – thank you for your service to our country – once a Marine always a Marine – Semper Fidelis.

To Marcia and Gerry for some of the most exhausting and rewarding miles on a road bicycle – keep the rubber side down, always. Those endless rides helped keep me focused on writing this manuscript.

My best friend and wife Andreé deserves the highest form of accolades and respect; for without her support this publication would have never materialized. Her tireless patience, encouragement and wisdom have been infinite, and I could never have accomplished this manuscript without everything she has done for me – thank you Andreé. To my children William, Zachary and Grace – I miss you all so much each day we are apart, please know my love for each of you is forever, always ... Love, Dad.

Semper Fidelis,

Bill Hagestad

CONTENTS

Contents

Contents

INTRODUCTION

The People's Republic of China is a vast and beautiful country with an eloquent language, a diverse culture and a rich history transcending any of the notions held by Western civilization. Trying to understand the vast panorama that is called China in the pages of one publication is impossible. Belief that one is a so-called expert on China is a fallacy; stating that one, who is a non-native speaker of Mandarin Chinese, is fluent, is similarly disrespectful.

The study of armed conflict, for any military professional, must include a reverent reflection on both works of the Ancient Chinese military philosopher Sun Tzu and of the 18th century Prussian General Carl Von Clausewitz. Those who have served in the armed forces may be all too familiar with both of these warrior scholars. The civilian, commercial world has tried to adapt the ethos of the warrior from Sun Tzu, and failed miserably, perhaps because an age-old Chinese military philosophy cannot transfer well to a "quarter by quarter" corporate mentality.

Understanding the concept of information technology and its vast taxonomy is also a lifelong task. Combining managing technology with a security element, one arrives at a far more focused and difficult endeavor, now called cybersecurity. Constructing a defensible position within the cyber realm can never be perfect – for those in the information security profession realize, know and attempt that, whilst educating both the innocent and the responsible alike, many organizations have already been compromised.

21st century Chinese cyberwarfare draws from a combination of business, cultural, historical, linguistic and personal experience, to attempt to explain China to the uninitiated. Chinese information warfare doctrinal development has been advanced by many notable senior officers within the People's Liberation Army, including Major General Dai Qingmin, Major General Wang Pufeng, and Senior Colonels Qiao Liang and Wang Xiangsui. These PLA officers have determined that warfare, via information networks, is the only methodology by which China can beat the United States, whom they fear, whilst also challenging the many other nation-states that China seeks to dominate as the new superpower. The reader will be forced to confront the Mandarin language and begin to understand the complexity of this wonderful foreign language. This publication also offers a rare insight

1

into the world of identifying physical and cyberthreats from a military perspective; drawing upon the theory of traditional kinetic warfare, as well as the use of historical examples of ancient and modern war.

Ultimately the objective of this title is to raise awareness that the People's Republic of China is using a combination of their unique culture, language and political will, known as Chinese Communism, to maintain their age-old heritage. The Chinese will also bring to bear upon their cybertargets the use of 21st century hacking technology to carry out a campaign of intelligence targeting and collection to support the information needs necessary to become the next superpower.

The 21st century is already here. The 'Middle Kingdom' which is China, 中國, is determined, and in their focus destined to achieve worldwide leadership through the use of their state-sponsored, military-developed and civilian-executed information dominance. The threat of Chinese cyberwarfare is no longer something that can be ignored; it is a clear and present danger to the experienced and innocent alike – confrontation of the red dragon rising is now necessary, as the existence of 21st century Chinese cyberwarfare is already here!

GLOSSARY

The Glossary provides a review of the definitions of cyberwarfare necessary to set the stage and context for the rest of this publication. The relevant historical, quantifiable facts and the figures surrounding China's cyberattacks against non-Chinese countries will also be introduced and examined.

Note: For this publication, the term cyberwarfare is defined as the calculated use of both offensive and defensive computer network attacks (CNA) and computer network exploits (CNE), to take advantage of computer network vulnerabilities (CNV) at the geo-political level, nation to nation, fighting in what is now defined as the fifth dimension – cyberspace. A military doctrine which includes the use of net centric warfare (NCW), including but not limited to the use of CAN and CNE as a part of computer network operations (CNO) is called information warfare (IW).

Cyberwarfare Definitions

Before examining the statistics of the threat in cyberspace by the People's Republic of China, a review of the different types of cybercombat and cyberwarfare, the essence of information warfare (IW), is necessary.

The Chinese cyberobjective when conducting (IW) will be to disrupt the availability of an adversary's information networks, corrupt the integrity and availability of information and access to these networks, whilst also dismantling and exploiting the confidentiality and privacy of information on the target information networks.[i]

The People's Republic of China has developed cyberwarfare doctrine which includes components of the following both offensive and defensive cyberoperations:

Cyberwarfare (CyW) – "Any act intended to compel an opponent to fulfill our national will, executed against the software controlling processes within

3

an opponent's system. CyW includes the following modes of cyberattack: cyberinfiltration, cybermanipulation, cyberassault, and cyber raid."[ii]

Information Assurance (IA) – (US) Department of Defense (DoD) "Information operations that protect and defend information and information systems by ensuring their availability, integrity, authentication, confidentiality and nonrepudiation. This includes providing for restoration of information systems by incorporating protection, detection, and reaction capabilities."[iii]

Information Operations (IO) – (US DoD) "Actions taken to affect adversary information and information systems while defending one's own information and information systems."

Information Superiority – (US DoD) "The capability to collect, process and disseminate an uninterrupted flow of information while exploiting or denying an adversary's ability to do the same."

An alternative and revised definition details, "That degree of dominance in the information domain which permits the conduct of operations without effective opposition."[iv]

Information Warfare (IW) – (US DoD) "Information operations conducted during time of crisis or conflict to achieve or promote specific objectives over a specific adversary or adversaries."[v] "IW is any action to Deny, Exploit, Corrupt or destroy the enemy's information and its functions; protecting ourselves against those actions and exploiting our own military information functions."[vi]

Network Centric Operations (NCO) – "Network Centric Operations (NCO) involves the development and employment of mission capability packages that are the embodiment of the tenets of Network Centric Warfare (NCW) in operations across the full mission spectrum. These tenets state that a robustly networked force improves information sharing and collaboration, which enhances the quality of information, the quality of awareness and improves shared situational awareness. This results in enhanced collaboration and enables self-synchronization, improving sustainability and increasing the speed of command, which ultimately result in dramatically increased mission effectiveness."[vii]

Psychological Operations (PYOPS) – (US DOD) "Planned operations to convey selected information and indicators to foreign audiences to influence their emotions, motives, objective reasoning, and ultimately the behavior, of foreign governments, organizations, groups and individuals. The purpose of psychological operations is to induce or reinforce foreign attitudes and behavior favorable to the originator's objectives."[viii]

Psychological Warfare (PSYWAR) – (US DoD) "The planned use of propaganda and other psychological actions having the primary purpose of influencing the opinions, emotions, attitudes, and behavior of hostile foreign groups in such a way as to support the achievement of national objectives."[ix]

(CNO) Computer Network Operations

(CNA) Computer Network Attacks

(CNE) Computer Network Exploits

(SIGINT) Signals Intelligence

(COMINT) Communications Intelligence

(EW) Electronic Warfare

(CDAA) Circularly Disposed Antenna Array

(HF) High Frequency

(VHF) Very High Frequency

(DF) Direction Finding

(ELINT) Electronic Intelligence

(ESM) Electronic Support Measures

(C3I) Command, Control, Communications and Intelligence

(UAV) Unmanned Aerial Vehicle

(SIGINT) Signals Intelligence

(C3ISR) Command, control, communications, intelligence, surveillance and reconnaissance

(C3ISREW) Integrated (or networked) command, control, communications, intelligence, surveillance, reconnaissance and electronic warfare

(C4I) Control, Communications, Computers and Intelligence

(C4ISR) Command, Control, Communications, Computers, Intelligence, Surveillance, Reconnaissance

(CMC) Central Military Commission

(GSD) General Staff Directorate

(ISR) Intelligence, Surveillance and Reconnaissance

(SATCOM) Satellite Communications

(PLAAF) People's Liberation Army Air Force

(CNEIEC) China National Electronics Import and Export Corporation

(SWIEE) Southwest China Research Institute of Electronic Equipment

(GHz) Gigahertz units of frequency

(dBW) dBW notation represents a power level in decibels relative to 1 Watt

(MIIz) Megahertz are units of frequency. Sound, light and radio frequencies are measured in MHz

(DDoS) Distributed Denial of Service

(IFF) Identification Friend-and-Foe

(GPS) Global Positioning System

Types of Hacker

A Hacker is an individual who uses computer technology in ways not originally intended by the vendor. Commonly, the term is applied to people who attack others using computers. Hackers are subdivided as follows:

Script kiddies: Unskilled attackers who do not have the ability to discover new vulnerabilities or write exploit code, and are dependent on the research and tools from others. Their goal is achievement. Their sub-goals are to gain access and deface web pages.

Worm and virus writers: Attackers who write the propagation code used in the worms and viruses, but not typically the exploit code used to penetrate the systems infected. Their goal is notoriety. Their sub-goals are to disrupt the networks and attached computer systems.

Security researchers and white hat operators: This group has two sub-categories, bug hunters and exploit coders.

Their goal is profit. Their sub-goals are to improve security and achieve recognition with an exploit.

Professional hacker-black hat: Individuals who get paid to write exploits or actually penetrate networks; this group also falls into the same two sub-categories as above. Their goal is also profit. "A black hat hacker, sometimes called a "cracker", is someone who breaks computer security without authorization or uses technology (usually a computer, phone system or network) for vandalism, credit card fraud, identity theft, piracy, or other types of illegal activity."[x]

Information Warfare Elements

Senior Management Scientist for the RAND Corporation, Martin C Libicki, further focuses IW within cyberwarfare doctrinal development of the Chinese People's Liberation Army (PLA), emphasizing that they are indeed developing "several distinct forms of information warfare". These cyberwarfare doctrinal developments include non-kinetic types of conflicts, involving those which include information network capability degradation, denial of service (DDoS), defensive and offensive protection of organic information networks and distributed network manipulation. Thus, each of these Chinese cyberwarfare doctrinal constructs is independently developed, with an overarching and suitable application to a true cybercombined arms effect on an adversary's information networks. This includes cybertargeting of economic, governmental and military network infrastructures. The Chinese cyberwarfare doctrine includes elements of:

1. A command-and-control type of warfare, effectively destroying the enemy's decision-making ability and command infrastructure;
2. Effects-based warfare. maximizing every conceivable form of intelligence, disabling the enemy's ability to react effectively through the denial of network infrastructure systems, denied access to any means from which an enemy can achieve information that will enable them success in the cyber realm, and confidence and superiority in protecting all systems;
3. All manner of current and future innovations relating to electronic warfare (EW), including cryptographic and stenographic techniques, space communications and all types of radio electronic methods of system access;
4. Creation of a strategic advantage over opponents through the use of psychological warfare, using information to advantage, to create confusion in the adversary's mind, essentially bending them to our will strategically;
5. Use of essential personnel who have the necessary skills to hack and attack networked information systems via the use of "hacker" warfare;
6. Creation of conditions of economic uncertainty, effectively putting the adversary at a disadvantage, thus disabling their ability to make strategic economic decisions through information denial activity;
7. The use of cyberwarfare, which is a combination of unrelenting attacks, using the Internet as an international avenue of approach to attack, deny and defeat the enemy's ability to co-ordinate or muster an effective defense through the use of their information network infrastructure. [xi]

It is within the framework and constructs of Libicki's research on information warfare (IW) and the People's Republic of China's ability to inculcate the full range of asymmetric cyberthreats that 21st century cyberwarfare begins.

CHAPTER 1: THE CHINESE CYBERTHREAT

We will begin with a summary of the convincing, credible data that exists regarding the Chinese cyberthreat. The frequency, tenacity and veracity of advanced, persistent cyberattacks from the Internet originating from within the People's Republic of China is undeniable and yet largely unexplained, as absolute, attributable evidence, directly leading to either the State, Communist Party or military within China, has yet to be conclusively demonstrated. However, reports of systematic, enduring cyberincursions borne from the People's Republic of China are irrefutable and absolutely undeniable.

The US Department of Defense (DoD) has been the subject of numerous cyberattacks and data exfiltration campaigns by Chinese based cyberattackers. In October 2011, the United States Office of the Counterintelligence Executive (ONCIX) released a comprehensive report, titled "*Foreign Spies Stealing U.S. Economic Secrets in Cyberspace*", documenting the quantified amount of economic loss attributable to nation-states such as China and Russia. The ONCIX report details how billions of dollars in intellectual property and classified information are being lost every year to cyberespionage and data exfiltration campaigns by cyberintruders from China. ONCIX states "Foreign economic collection and industrial espionage against the United States represent significant and growing threats to the nation's prosperity and security."[xii]

The US-China Economic and Security Review Commission, instructed Northrop Grumman Corporation (NGC) to prepare a report in 2009, titled "*Capability of the People's Republic of China to Conduct Cyber Warfare and Computer Network Exploitation*". This NGC report detailed China's capabilities to wage attacks using the Internet as a commercial and military avenue of approach, a strategic force multiplier for achieving superiority through computer network operations (CNO) in times of relative peace and harmony globally, with an eye on preparing for future conflict in cyberspace. Indeed the Latin saying "Si vis pacem, para bellum", "If you wish for peace, prepare for war", could perhaps never have a more appropriate and timely application to the Chinese concept of cyberwarfare than now in the 21st century! The NGC report states further that, as the Chinese pre-plan their targets using CNO in a potential war with the US, the West can fundamentally view the People's Liberation Army's (PLA) cyberwarfare doctrinal focus on achieving information superiority as being that of an enemy attempting to use the Internet in an advanced technological way to gain an advantage militarily.

Cyberattacks on North Atlantic Treaty Organization (NATO) countries are also cause for concern in Europe, as both military and commercial targets have been relentlessly violated, via cyberincursions from the Internet. Serious levels of cyberattack have taken place. During 2011, the cyberassaults were particularly significant. The hacking group "*Anonymous*" publicly took exception to NATO's report on hacktivism which mentioned the group. Subsequently, "*Anonymous*" compromised a NATO server, exfiltrating a significant amount of sensitive and classified data. In fact, in June 2011, "*The Register*" reported how NATO leaders had been given fair warning of the Anonymous threat to member states security.[xiii] A NATO-affiliated bookstore was also violated by the hacker group LulzSec in response to NATO's role in Libya; during this cyberattack, names, passwords and associated usernames of over 12,000 registered accounts were eventually posted online.[xiv] Norway, the third member country of NATO, had her military attacked by malicious software; a hacking group took exception to Norway's air campaign in Libya; although officially, only one computer was compromised, the distinct linkage between a nation-state's military offensive campaign and the subsequent violation of its official military network via cyberspace remains irrefutable.[xv]

Statistics of the Cyberwarfare Threat

The numbers surrounding the composite cyberwarfare threat to the US are daunting. In 2008, a total 54,640 total cyberattacks against US Department of Defense (DoD) took place[xvi]. However, a year later this number of incursions increased dramatically with 43,785 cyberincidents in the first quarter of 2009 alone, representing a 60 per cent increase over the whole of 2008[xvii]. Curiously, in response to this growing number of cyberattacks, the US military spent more than $100 million in the first six months of 2009, repairing damage caused by cyberattacks, according Army Brigadier General John Davis, deputy commander for network operations.[xviii]

In 2011, the US Federal Government was expected to spend $8.3 billion to protect and defend its networks and computers from hackers, a year on year budget increase of a staggering 60 per cent. A leading indicator of why the US Government and DoD are in the reactive mode – providing a proverbial "finger-in-the-dyke" to the seemingly exponentially growing spate of cyberattacks – is that both government entities, when considering and procuring cyberdefense technologies, are still living in the era of ensuring that such technology is designed to military specifications (MILSPEC). It takes the Pentagon 81 months to make a new computer system operational once it is first funded. Conversely, in the commercial world, the development of the iPhone from initial artist concept, to design and production models for sale to the public, took Apple Corporation just 24 months.[xix] The US Government and DoD could take a lesson from Apple's business handbook.

In a speech last year, Deputy Secretary of Defense William J Lynn said that at the Pentagon alone, there were an "estimated 90,000 people engaged in administering, monitoring and defending 15,000 networks connecting 7 million computers."[xx]

As if to answer the need for information security defense, the Pentagon's fiscal 2011 budget proposal, unveiled in January 2011, gave cybersecurity a $105 million increase on the previous year. The DoD's sub-command dedicated to cyberwarfare, located in a facility in Fort Meade, Maryland (known as 'US Cyber Command'), is slated for a fiscal 2011 budget of $139 million,[xxi] yet the pronouncements of additional money to a DoD command dedicated to defending the US against all cyberenemies, both foreign and domestic, did not deter hackers from offering US DoD websites for sale on the Internet, after they had been hacked.[xxii]

The North Atlantic Treaty Organization (NATO) began their implementation of a cybershield plan[xxiii] in response to the growing number of cyberhack attacks against their organization. Similarly, so have the UK, Germany, Australia, South Korea, Japan, Taiwan, France and many other nations, which have experienced an increase in cyber-related attacks on their networks.

This series of cyberattacks and violations would set the scene for the question: who is behind these attacks?

The popular press in the West has also highlighted the alleged attacks by China; even without direct Internet Protocol (IP) address attribution to the State in China, the inescapable conclusion to be drawn is that the People's Republic of China is attacking the West via the Internet.

'Operation Titan Rain'

From 2003, a team of Chinese government-sponsored researchers in Guangdong Province carried out a series of advanced, persistent cyberattacks on US Government information networks. Assisting a network intrusion at Northrup Grumman Corporation, Shawn Carpenter at Sandia National Laboratories completed an IP traceroute investigation of IP addresses that led him to these Chinese researchers. The Chinese intent behind the tremendous cyberespionage ring was to specifically target the information networks of several DoD military research laboratories, including the US Army Space and Strategic Defense installation in Huntsville, Alabama, Defense Information Systems Agency in Arlington, Virginia, National Aeronautics and Space Administration (NASA), the Naval Ocean Systems Center, a defense department installation in San Diego, California, US Army Information Systems Engineering Command at Fort Huachuca, Arizona, and the World Bank. The Chinese hackers were given the code name '*Titan Rain*' by the Federal Bureau of Investigation (FBI).[xxiv]

Information networks at the US State Department's East Asia Bureau suffered Internet violation via a backdoor method of intrusion. In July 2006, the State Department became a victim of cyberhacking, after an official in East Asia accidentally opened a malicious e-mail; by clicking on an attachment he allowed the cyberintruder into the State Department's networks. Once inside the network the cyberattackers navigated their way around the entire network infrastructure, hacking into computers at US embassies all over Asia, through persistent penetration of networked systems in Washington DC.[xxv]

In March 2009, researchers in Toronto concluded a 10-month investigation that revealed a massive cyberespionage ring they named '*Operation Ghost Net*'. The attackers used Chinese malware, and from IP addresses based in Beijing, penetrated more than 1,200 networked computer systems in over 103 countries. Victims included foreign embassies, non-governmental organizations (NGOs), news media institutions, foreign affairs ministries and international organizations. Almost all Tibetan-related organizations (which the People's Republic of China has taken significant issue with), were compromised, most notably offices of the Dalai Lama.

In April 2009, the *Wall Street Journal* reported that Lockheed Martin Corporation's F-35 program had been compromised by hackers operating from China. The significant data exfiltrations – of sensitive data related to the military's the F-35 program – took place over several years before ever being detected.[xxvi]

The People's Republic of China denies that anyone in an official capacity is doing any of the cyberattacking.

In January 2010, China vigorously denied being behind any cyberattacks on Google; the Chinese Government went on the offensive, accusing the US Government of engaging in cyberattacks, perhaps tired of being depicted as the international cybervillain.[xxvii]

During a June 2011 international security forum, Chinese Defence Minister Liang Guanglie told delegates that China was not behind any cyberattacks, further stating that the Government of China opposes any cybercriminal activity.[xxviii]

In August 2011, '*Operation Shady RAT*' was announced by anti-virus vendor McAfee. According to the company's analysis '*Operation Shady RAT*' pointed the finger at China, but also indicated that Russia could be behind cyberincursions which took place since 2006, and cybertargeted over 72 entities' information networks, including those of the UN, US Government agencies, multiple defence contractors and numerous high technology companies. Of course, in response, *The People's Daily*, the Chinese State run newspaper, quoted Chinese Government officials vehemently denying China's involvement, saying "It is irresponsible to link China to Internet hackers".[xxix]

In October 2011, Chinese Officials maintained China's innocence in the face of US allegations that two of its environmental monitoring satellites were cyberviolated and tampered with via a connection-based cyberintrusion from a ground-based satellite station in Norway.[xxx]

Statistics of the Chinese Cyberwarfare Threat

The threat of cyberbased warfare originating in the PRC has entirely different statistics. According to the Jamestown Foundation, a Eurasian think-tank founded by William Geimerk with Arkady Shevchenko, Beijing is rapidly improving its cyberwarfare capacity and has *"rapidly become the leading source of information about the inner workings of closed totalitarian societies."*[xxxi] During *'Operation Night Dragon'*, a MacAfee anti-virus company report detailed that Chinese hackers were allegedly targeting energy firms; this took place in the form of a cyberattack threat occurring over than four years, during which international oil and petroleum companies were attacked via sophisticated SQL injection attacks, allowing remote command and control of the target company servers and databases.[xxxii xxxiii]

Another report alleged Chinese cyberattacks, with hackers using spear-phishing to target source code and intellectual property.[xxxiv]

Other alleged Chinese hacking attacks included key employees at more than 20 companies worldwide, such as Adobe and Google, who received Adobe .pdf files; when the files were opened, the Adobe Reader program executed a zero day vulnerability[xxxv] and inserted a backdoor Trojan, which connected outbound traffic from the now infected laptop or desktop computer to the hackers on the other end of the digital connection.[xxxvi xxxvii]

Answering the claims that the PRC is behind these cyberattacks, a China military paper urged steps against the US cyberwar threat.[xxxviii xxxix]

Uniquely, a report by the US-China Economic and Security Review Commission (USCC) details Chinese conduct of "aggressive and large-scale" espionage against the US, [xl] but does not give specific evidence to support claims of Chinese cyberhacking. What is most compelling is that, besides the US, Australia, the UK and Germany are also very concerned about the Chinese use of espionage to harvest competitive business information, [xli] and have established their own national cyberdefense organizations.

According to a recent Reuters special report: (sic) "*cyberspy vs. cyberspy, China has the edge*"[xlii]; cyberattacks from China have been steadily increasing in frequency and velocity – all with the intent and purpose of gathering and harvesting economic information from foreign companies; however, yet again there is no specific attributable evidence supporting statements about factual cyberborne attacks from China, just that the PRC has a honed and distinct technological advantage when it comes to cyberespionage. Further information from this report by Reuters, indicated that US defense investigators had uncovered an alleged Chinese military hacking operation they aptly named '*Byzantine Hades*'; US investigators indirectly attributed this series of cyberattacks to the Chinese military. An April 2009 cable even pinpoints the attacks to a specific unit of China's People's Liberation Army.[xliii]

The British intelligence organization, MI5, accused China of cyberespionage in a leaked report titled "*The Threat from Chinese Espionage*"; in the report, which was sent to a variety of British corporate and governmental leaders,[xliv] it candidly details electronic espionage as a specific cyberattack threat vector.[xlv]

The Virtual Criminology Report found that attacks had progressed from initial curiosity probes into well-funded and well-organized operations for political, military, economic and technical espionage.[xlvi] Whilst not naming the PRC as the source of the cyberprobes, the report attempts to build a case for attribution to the PRC.

China says it is not involved in cyberwarfare with the US according to Chinese Vice Foreign Minister Cui Tian Kai.[xlvii] Yet, an academic paper by Wang Jianwei, a graduate engineering student in Liaoning, China, includes specific and explicit details of methods to hack the US energy grid. Subsequently, this research paper set off numerous DHS and DoD alarms in the US.[xlviii]

Statistics of the People's Republic of China cyberthreat to the US military are a small fraction of the overall known threat. This project examines the foundations of the Chinese Government's intent and motivation, through an examination of the People's Liberation Army (PLA), Commercial Enterprises, their theft of intellectual property, and the use of Chinese civilians to carry out a variety of cyberbased hacks and malware-based assaults. One statement is absolutely true: the statistics and facts surrounding the Chinese-based cyberthreats are evolving daily and are infinitely unceasing.

Figure 1: Heat map of inbound and outbound cyberattacks over a 48-hour period – South China Region [xlix]

Conclusions about the Chinese Cyberthreat

The conclusion could be reached that the People's Republic of China drives the intent to use information warfare in the cyber realm, and thus that the use of cyberwarfare is state-sponsored. Furthermore, the PLA has a unit assigned to carry out cyberwarfare, known as the *'Blue Army*[l]; they conduct both offensive and defensive cybermissions in support of President Hu Jin Tao's official edict that cyberwarfare is needed to secure China's infrastructure from foreign cyberthreats. There are significant cultural, economic, historical and linguistic threads which resonate throughout the decade, in addition to China's history of cyberwarfare: the Chinese have a desire to remain a pure culture without foreign influence, intervention or cyber-related direction; the Chinese economy is on fire, and growth is fueled by both internal organic growth and foreign investment in a 1.33 billion Chinese population market.[li]

Historically, the PRC has seen itself as the country, China, otherwise known as the 'Middle Kingdom'. However, foreigners have viewed China as a country full of unique culture and economic opportunity to be exploited; although advocates of citizen hacking, the CPC can no longer control the permeability of commercial enterprises worldwide by Chinese cyberhacking in all its forms and methods; similarly, the US Department of Defense cannot defend itself adequately from the various Chinese information warfare threats in the 5th domain of warfare; the composite People's Republic of China cyberwarfare threat is unending and will only become much, much worse.

For centuries there have been physical landscapes to discover, boundaries to push and new frontiers beckoning exploration. The cyber realm is no exception; from the moment when the first bulletin board services beckoned people to share ideas and communicate virtually, humankind was presented with a unique dimension.

With increasing frequency, news of cyberattacks by the People's Republic of China (PRC) intrude into our daily consciousness in the form of newspaper articles, magazine exposés and even via loose attribution by official government sources within many Western nations. However, since 1995, there have been no direct 100 per cent, proof-positive links of attribution or definitive evidence given to a cyberhack having originated within or from China. This publication seeks to define what organizations within the PRC may have the motive and opportunity to carry out cyberbased hacking attacks against other non-Chinese nation-states.

Detailed Statement of the opportunity and problem

Defining the Chinese cyberthreat is extraordinarily complex, because it is ever-changing and constantly evolving. A professional consideration and complete understanding of the distinct threat by the People's Republic of China (PRC) in cyberspace must include an examination of the Communist Party of China (CPC), the People's Liberation Army (PLA), commercial Chinese enterprises (CCE) and Chinese citizen hackers (CCH).

This use of information warfare by the People's Republic of China began in 1995. However, in the past 12-14 months the notoriety and significance of this issue has engulfed the US Government (USG) and the US Department of Defense (DoD), as well as British, German, French and US commercial businesses. The cyberwarfare threat from the PRC has created such a negative response amongst military officials worldwide that indirect and oblique references without careful attribution have mandated as necessary an official policy of defending and attacking those countries that would use cyberspace to attack them.[lii]

Furthermore, the examination of the cyberwarfare threat from China will include the Communist Party of China's formal legislation and edict regarding the use of information warfare, and the People's Liberation Army (PLA) understanding and intent for planning a distinct government-sponsored information warfare doctrine.

The Communist Party of China (CPC) – which is the Government, the People's Liberation Army (PLA), numerous state-owned enterprises (SOE), and Chinese civilians or hacktivists – are all involved in information warfare. The CPC, PLA, hacktivists and SOEs have developed a very sophisticated cyberwarfare capability; their methods are intentional and the targets of their computer network attacks (CNA) and computer network exploits (CNE) are as divergent as the Mandarin Chinese language. Cyberthreat vectors, used by the government, military, commercial enterprises and citizens to gain knowledge and sensitive information, include fundamental computer hacking methods, knowledge and sophisticated information warfare techniques, many of which leave no trace of their activities, and anger, puzzle and frustrate the most experienced IT security professionals in the world.

The Chinese have allegedly exploited weaknesses of nation-states including the US, Australia, England, Canada, France, Germany, India, Pakistan, Japan, Taiwan, South Korea and Vietnam, via the public Internet and World Wide Web. It is widely reported that the Chinese allegedly electronically invade countries worldwide for the purposes of data exfiltration and gaining competitive economic advantage, whilst inculcating disruptions in Internet service in countries and organizations who criticize the Chinese political system.

We must examine in detail the ways in which nation-state cyber- and information warfare is actioned by the People's Republic of China, including who is involved, and their organization, culture, history and motivations for carrying out this borderless information war. The distinct challenges that the Western World faces in terms of potential cyberattacks from the PRC are daunting, and include the facets of one-upmanship, similar to the nuclear threat faced by the former Soviet Union. However, the cost of conducting an adequate cyberdefense is now frustrated by the necessity to counter attack. Information warfare doctrine in the US, only consists of alerting and defensive measures[liii]. An effective cyberwarfare program consistently and effectively applies a cogent IW doctrine by identifying threats, mitigating these threats based upon risk, and then countering with a similarly proactive and effective IW offensive capability. This cyberthreat, of warfare threat mitigation methodology, is illustrated in Figure 2.

Figure 2: Information warfare (IW) power zone

Nation-states have the opportunity to mount effective cybercounter attack programs by incorporating in their IW doctrines three strategies: of identifying Chinese cyberthreats, mitigating the identified Chinese cyberthreats, and then counter-attacking with like or greater cyberweapons.

Based upon the current history and trends of Chinese cyberwarfare, the question must be asked as to whether or not there is a history of co-operation, confusion or complicity? According to blog authors, *Network World*, China has pledged to step up administration of Internet[liv], essentially stating to the world it will police its own civilian hacktivists – ensuring these cybervigilantes will not create conditions for forced cyber retaliation by commercial entities, nation-states or fellow hacking professionals.

Are economic ties between the US and the PRC greater than cyberdomination? Another aspect of potential Chinese co-operation by the US, and the seemingly unending stream of cyberattacks, is that perhaps the US does not want to end the cyberattacks. Two particular nefarious reasons come to mind: the US wanting to enter into a cyberwar situation, much like the nuclear arms race with the Russians. The PRC also holds a significant amount the US treasury bond market, and if these Chinese loan holders were angered, the implications for both the US and Chinese economies could be potentially devastating.[lv lvi] Perhaps even the military, the People's Liberation Army (PLA), is asserting itself as the power domain within the Central Communist Party (CPC) edicts and constructs for defending and protecting China.

Who are the PLA "princelings" and what is their importance and relevance to the cyberwarfare initiative in China? Vice President Xi Jinping [lvii] is a key figure in China's cyberdominance efforts. After the Eighteenth Party Congress in Beijing, Xi will wear three very important leadership hats in the People's Republic of China: General Secretary of the Chinese Communist Party, President of the People's Republic of China and, equally importantly, Chairman of the Central Military Commission, which controls the powerful People's Liberation Army. This significant leadership change will occur during the 2012 CPC plenum. Xi's history as a political leader in China is a curious one. He is the only Chinese to have publicly criticized Mao Tse Tung's economic reform ("the Great Leap Forward"). This criticism did not come without punishment, as he was sent to a rehabilitation program. However, what is remarkable and important to the current state of cyberwar in China is that Xi, after his "re-programming", was actually promoted under Deng Xia Peng's leadership and further economic reform. Thus, while Xi was seen by Mao as a mutinous Communist Party member, subsequent Chinese political and military leadership have had significant confidence in him as visionary, who has both mother China's well-being in mind and the ability to execute his strategic plans. What about the People's Liberation Army? Vice-President Xi Jinping is consolidating his hold over the military forces; while Xi, 57, was made a vice-chairman of the policy-setting Central Military Commission (CMC) only last October, the "crown prince" has successfully manoeuvred to expand his influence over the top general officers of the People's Liberation Army (PLA).[lviii]

The Chinese tradition is one of manipulation, encompassing all aspects of their culture, history, language, international policy and military strategy. Playing one party's side of an issue against another's, especially if it is in favor of the Chinese desired end-state, which usually includes economic bargaining and negotiating, is the ultimate grand game. A great example recently was the decision by the Central Chinese Government to entertain bids for the national airline aircraft purchase. This involved more than just winning a Chinese Government bid; according to a *BusinessWeek* article "the Chinese market is growing fast, and the company, Airbus, could achieve the greatest benefit from this opportunity. An aircraft business unit within the European Aeronautic Defense & Space (EADSY) is making significant China market entry progress by winning far more orders than industry competitor Boeing. Boeing is in the midst of a verbal tit for tat between Washington and Beijing that could ultimately cost Boeing more market share and put it even further behind its larger rival in this ever growing aircraft market.[lix] On January 29, the Obama Administration informed Congress of plans to sell $6.4 billion in weapons to Taiwan, and the following day the Chinese government said it would punish US companies involved in the sales. That could hurt Boeing, which makes the Harpoon missiles that Taiwan will be purchasing as part of the deal."[lx]

Another example of coercive co-operation by the People's Republic of China is one in which they have pitted the US against the European Union, openly criticizing both entities for their economic failings. Since President Obama signed the latest deficit budget, raising the debt limit, the Chinese have a "we told you so" attitude, stating their undisguised contempt and disgust for this Western nation's inability to manage their economy without help from China's financial bailout efforts and offers. The EU does not escape this withering condemnation from the People's Republic of China either. China cannot contain itself over the EU's failure to shore up the Greek economy.[lxi]

CHAPTER 2: EVOLUTION OF CHINESE CYBERWARFARE

In Chapter 2, the Eight Pillars of Unrestricted Warfare will be introduced and examined, followed by a review of the key motivators for nation-state sponsored cyberwarfare, from the Chinese perspective. An overview of the cyberattackers will also be examined: the Communist Party of China (CPC), People's Liberation Army (PLA), state-owned enterprises (SOE) and citizen hacktivists (CH) will all be briefly introduced as actors on the Chinese cyberwarfare stage.

Overview of the Attackers

Communist Party of China (CPC)

The CPC is the key governmental and political powerbase behind cyberwarfare in the People's Republic of China.[lxii] President Hu Jintao has made an official proclamation that the People's Liberation Army (PLA) is to conduct cyberwarfare in the name of Chinese self-preservation. Vice President Xi Jinping, President Hu's most likely successor, also has the strategic technical vision that information warfare will be carried out by distinct hacking entities, including the PLA, SOE and CH.

People's Liberation Army (PLA)

According to SinoDefence.com and a web post entitled "*Chinese Military Overview*" the armed forces within the People's Republic of China (PRC) maintain the world's largest military force, based on its troop number composition. The armed forces of the PRC comprise of three integral elements – the People's Liberation Army (PLA), the People's Armed Police Force (PAP), as well as the reserve forces and militia. The PLA, which encompasses the Army, the Navy, the Air Force, and the Second Artillery Corps (strategic missile force), is the regular army, totaling some 2.3 million troops. The PAP has a total strength of 660,000 troops. Additionally, there are also 800,000 men in the reserve forces and approx. 10,000 militia. The official defense budget for 2008 was RMB417.77 billion (US$59 billion), though many believed that the actual military expenditure could be two to three times higher.

The Chinese armed forces are given three fundamental roles: to defend the country against foreign invasions; to maintain internal security and stability; and to engage in the economic development of the country. Under the constitution of the PRC, the armed forces are under the absolute leadership of the Chinese Communist Party (CCP). The Party guarantees its control over the military through a political system consisting of Party branches, political officers, and the political department implanted in every level of the armed forces. The armed forces receive orders from the Central Military Commission (CMC) through the General Staff, General Political, General Logistics and General Armament Departments.

The Chinese leadership has been trying to modernise the country's military since the mid-1980s. The PLA has undergone three major force reduction programmes in 1984, 1997, and 2003, dropping its total strength from 4 million to the current level of 2.3 million. At the same time, older weapon systems and equipment that came into service in the 1960s and 1970s were gradually phased out and replaced by new designs. The PLA has also been reforming its organisational structure, doctrine, education and training, and personnel policies, in order to fulfil its initiative of *"fighting and winning a local war under the informationized condition"*.

The current military modernisation process has three main focuses. First, the PLA has paid close attention to the performance of the US ground forces in Afghanistan and Iraq, and is learning from the success of the US military in information-centric warfare, joint operations, C4ISR, hi-tech weaponry, etc. Second, the PLA is gradually building up its power projection capabilities, which will allow it to deploy forces not only within China, but also in peripheral regions. Third, the PLA is quietly developing the capability of rivalling a technologically-superior military power through so-called *"asymmetric warfare"*, in order to deter US intervention in case of war with Taiwan."[lxiii]

Until recently, there has been little information available on the information warfare (IW) operations of the PLA. Their official cybercommand was only started in 2010. Prior to 2010, the PLA's organizational structure for information warfare was fairly fractured and geographically separated amongst the seven regional military commands. Command structures within the PLA's information warfare mission were generally based around significant universities, who had developed computer science programs, significant bandwidth to the Internet and CPC over-watch in the form of political officers. Examples of the early information units were found at Bei Jing University, Tsing Hua University and many others, spread across the People's Republic of China.

State-owned Enterprises (SOE)

State-owned enterprises in the People's Republic of China were originally formed during the immediate post-Mao economic reform under Deng Xiao Peng, and were called collectives. This is an important nuance when it comes to understanding the commercial cyberthreat; these original collectives – supported by provincial governmental authorities – are now mature, successful multi-national commercial enterprises, which must now compete on the world stage, without the benefit of knowing how to compete fairly. As a result, these SOE's, who all have direct and indirect ties to the PLA, will use cyberespionage to gather corporate knowledge, giving them an unfair advantage over their competition.

Civilian Hackers (Hacktivists)

What is hacktivism and how does it apply to Chinese cyberwarfare? According to Dorothy Denning at Georgetown University "Hacktivism is the convergence of hacking with activism, where "hacking" is used here to refer to operations that exploit computers in ways that are unusual and often illegal, typically with the help of special software ("hacking tools"). Hacktivism includes electronic civil disobedience, which brings methods of civil disobedience to cyberspace."

This section explores four types of operations: virtual sit-ins and blockades; automated e-mail bombs; Web hacks and computer break-ins; and computer viruses and worms. Because hacking incidents are often reported in the media, operations in this category can generate considerable publicity for both the activists and their causes.[lxiv] Thus, hacktivists are a type of cyberattacker who practices hacktivism.

Chinese hacktivists are an interesting and very dangerous element of the Chinese cyberthreat personality parade. Currently, they are a very dire problem for the CPC and PLA alike, essentially uncontrollable. Hacktivists use very sophisticated hacking tools and methods in their efforts. Their original main purpose, which was supported by both CPC and PLA, was to keep the honor and pride of China pure. Taiwan and Japan have been repeated targets for Chinese hacktivists, reminding Taiwan, through web defacement, that they are still a province of China, albeit a runaway province, whilst Japan has never been forgiven by the Chinese for the crimes and atrocities they carried out against the Chinese people during the 1930s and World War II (specifically the rape and pillaging of Nan Jing and the series of chemical warfare attacks in the Inner Mongolian city of BaoTou).

Motivation of the People's Republic of China

The motivation of the People's Republic of Chinese to conduct cyberwarfare is comprised of fear, self-preservation and hegemony. China has a centuries-old history of being invaded by foreigners, or outsiders; the Chinese characters or symbols for foreigner are derogatory and mean outsider, non-Chinese. 外国人 literally means outsider, foreigner, and the English Pin Yin pronunciation is Wàiguó rén.

Thus, based upon a history of invasions, the Chinese have developed a very strong sense of defending themselves. From Sun Tzu's 'Art of War' treatise, which details how commanders in the Ancient Chinese armies were to conduct battle both tactically and strategically; to the Thirty Six Strategies of Ancient China, which explain economic, political and psychological tactics and strategies for dealing with Wàiguó rén; to Sun Pin's (great grandson of Sun Tzu's) which further elaborated on the Art of War, bringing more military clarity and definition of purpose to martial China; and finally Military Methods and the Seven Military Classics of Ancient China (of which the Art of War was the only one of the seven allowed to be seen outside of the Ancient Imperial Chinese Government); these classics explain in great detail how to overcome, through a combination of political, economic, espionage, military, psychological and strategic means, enemies of China, the Wàiguó rén, 外国人.

While the Chinese out-manoeuvered their opponents in the Forbidden City and on the battlefield, they were still subject to abject humiliation by foreign invaders. Over centuries they tried to stop the mass invasions by building one of the Seven Wonders of the World, the Great Wall of China. To no avail, the Mongols, Marco Polo and others simply went around the wall or through it at various geographic locations.

It is through an understanding of Chinese history, from 500 BC through the various dynasties, repeated invasions by the Mongols led by Ghengis Khan and his sons, to the Boxer Rebellions in 1910, and to the subsequent invasion by the Mao Tse Tung-supported and endorsed Japanese invasions of the 1930s and 1940s, that one starts to understand the People's Republic of China's motivations for carrying out cyberwarfare; wishing to be first to the cyberfight, demonstrating to the world that they have dominance and proactively defend their country against would-be cyberattackers. Today's Chinese cyberwarfare is borne of official CPC edicts that the PLA and others will conduct cyberwarfare in the form of hacking other nation-states to gain intelligence on possible operations which could harm China, and gathering economic information that will shed light on where natural resources such as oil, natural gas and rare earth minerals are to be found, to support China's economic and national interests. It is this last statement which is the underlying reason behind China's forays into cyberspace beyond their borders which is currently causing so much concern for world leaders and multi-national corporate leadership. No country or corporation is safe; those who think they have yet to be cybercompromised, already have been, and either cannot admit, or simply do not know, yet.

History & Origins of Information Warfare in the People's Republic of China

The history of cyberwarfare in the People's Republic of China is very mature in Internet terms. Beginning on May 03 2001, China warned the Western Hemisphere of massive hack attacks.[lxv] In 2002, – based upon the "informatization" proposal within the PRC – 信息化, the global energy industry saw an emergence of fundamental, targeted cyberattacks worldwide. During a speech before the 16th Party Congress, Chinese Communist Party (CCP) General Secretary and Central Military Commission (CMC) Chairman Jiang Zemin, stated two informatization edicts be undertaken by the Politburo and the PLA; these were[lxvi] Critical Infrastructure. The energy sector was a specific focus of China's information war and threats, given the connection and interdependence of information systems with the open Internet, making it an obvious target (the existing US power grid, or that of any foreign country, being a prime example). Why is the Grid such an invaluable target for the Chinese hacking efforts?

There are a number of examples of indirectly attributed Chinese cyberwarfare. In 2007, *'Ghost Net'* 幽灵网 was an international cyberespionage ring, based out of Ling Shui near Hai Nan Island. Over 18 months, a consortium of international law enforcement investigators and researchers from the Munk Institute in Toronto, Canada, uncovered deliberate cyberevidence, linking the PLA and the PRC government to cyberespionage.[lxvii] During 2007, *'Titan Rain'* 泰坦雨[lxviii] came into the popular information security consciousness when it was discovered that numerous US Government defense networks, their servers and computers, had been compromised by a foreign cyberthreat. The FBI called this massive hack attack *'Titan Rain'* because of the size, persistent nature and unceasing deluge of cyberexploitation. In 2008, *'Time Magazine'* reported that Asian web surfers were rated number one in the world for time spent online,[lxix] indicating in a general sense that Chinese hacktivists have more time to learn how to effectively hack and target nation-states and companies who might criticize the efficacy of Chinese nationalism.

According to a US DoD report called *"Pentagon: China Cyber Weaponry Poses Threat – Internet Gives China a Global Military Presence"*,[lxx] the Chinese military and civilian leaders may not have fully considered the global and systemic effects of the use of these information warfare capabilities. Pentagon officials assert that, last year, China apparently targeted computer systems around the world, including those operated by the US. government. "Although these intrusions focused on exfiltration of sensitive information, the accesses and skills required for these intrusions are similar to those necessary to conduct computer network attacks."[lxxi]

The Qílín operating system (QLOS), 麒麟, is an operating system developed by academics at the National University of Defense Technology in the People's Republic of China, and is approved for use by the People's Liberation Army. Based on Mach and FreeBSD, it is designed to add an extra level of security to the QLOS operating system. It is similar to Security-Enhanced Linux, which was originally developed primarily by the US National Security Agency. The first public version was called Kylin[lxxii]by the Western World; released in 2007.[lxxiii] 麒麟 – Qílín is a FreeBSD UNIX-based operating system that was developed in response to the Western World restricting export licensing of the Unix-based operating system. Qílín is in use by the Ministry of State Security, (MID), 3rd, 4th & 7th Bureaus, all of whom have responsibility for intelligence gathering, collecting and analyzing with the PLA.

The question of where the Chinese cyberwarfare threat is coming from then arises, and the answer is 'everywhere but nowhere', 它无处不在但无处, the Pin Yin pronunciation is Wú chù bùzài què wú chù. The Ling Shui Signals Intelligence Facility is run by the Third Technical Department of the PLA and operates very near to the infamous Hainan Island Airfield. Recall the captured US Navy P-3 Orion, during which a People's Liberation Army Air Force (PLAAF) crashed into a US Navy P-3 Orion reconnaissance aircraft operating out of Okinawa's Kadena airbase. Figure 3 shows a geographic representation of HaiNan Island.

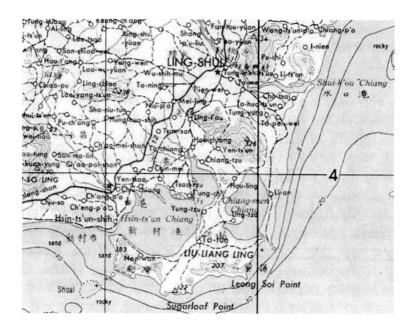

Figure 3: Map of Hai Nan Island, People's Republic of China
lxxiv lxxv

An Overview of Chinese Cyberwarfare

Origins of Chinese Cyberwarfare

The People's Republic of China's development of cyberwarfare doctrine has its origins in Ancient Chinese warfare philosophy. Sun Tzu's *'The Art of War'* has numerous anecdotal references to waging unconventional warfare. *"So in war, the way is to avoid what is strong and to strike at what is weak."*[lxxvi] Another historical reference to unconventional or guerrilla warfare comes from the profound speeches of Chairman Mao Tse Tung's concept of *'People's War.'*

Ultimately China's desired end state is one of cultural, historical, political and economic hegemony. The use of unconventional warfare waged through cyberspace will enable the PRC to realize its strategic focuses, which include survival of the Communist Party of China, in addition to economic, military and cultural leadership, if not dominance, in all of Asia including very close neighbors such as India, Burma, Japan, Singapore, Thailand, Afghanistan and even Russia. The Chinese also want to reign in their runaway province Taiwan and reintegrate it into the 'Middle Kingdom' once again. The imperative, overarching focus of the People's Republic of China is to be recognized and feared worldwide as a true superpower, transcending even the United States' ability to wield political influence.

Cyberwarfare has been the military doctrinal focus of Chinese military strategy since the early 1990s. The military leadership of China saw the distinct need to understand and execute military operations, involving information technology as a weaponized force. This was a unique lesson demonstrated by the US military during the first Gulf War; the United States effectively eliminated the Iraqi's ability to communicate, thus crippling their related ability to shoot and move as an effective army. The PLA and the CPC realized the significance of technological superiority, and how using the advantage of *'informationized'* forces could dominate any lesser technologically-capable adversary.

It was during the Chinese revolution in military affairs that PLA military strategists realized the importance that information technology would have in future Chinese military warfare success. Chinese military ability to quickly realize and create cyberweapons, led them to be increasingly dependent upon the PLA's effectiveness at both denying and defeating an adversary's ability to communicate electronically or via networked interfaces. As the PLA effectively destroyed and disabled the opponent's information flow, their ability to conduct military operations using traditional kinetic tactics and weapons would be a non-factor.

The PLA knows that its conventional ground forces could not be a factor in a regional war, given that they have an underdeveloped non-commissioned officer (NCO) corps.[lxxvii] In 1999, having realized this NCO shortfall, the People's Liberation Army Air Force (PLAAF) Senior Colonels, Qiao Liang and Wang Xiangsui, delivered their now famous manuscript "*Unrestricted Warfare*", which described and crystalized both unconventional warfare from Sun Tzu, and the tenets of guerrilla warfare from Mao Tse Tung, that the PLA should consider a form of asymmetric warfare that "transcends all boundaries and limits," and taking advantage of the possibilities that the fifth domain, cyberspace, will play in future PLA warfare.[lxxviii]

Since the early 1990s, the results of rapid Chinese military cyberwarfare doctrinal development have been impressive. In recent years, the PRC has steadily leveraged its rapidly growing economy to advance its capabilities to act in cyberspace. As Richard Lawless, then Deputy Undersecretary for Defense for Asian and Pacific Security Affairs, noted back in 2007, the Chinese have developed significant defensive and offensive cyberwarfare capabilities in order to enhance their economic espionage information collection initiatives. The Chinese intent is to maximize organic network vulnerability to achieve superiority over other nation-states in their cyberwarfare doctrine.[lxxix]

Because the People's Republic of China is a Communist country, there is no accountability to citizens regarding military spending. Thus, Western intelligence agencies, academics and governmental agencies, who are fearful of the Chinese ability to conduct cyberwarfare, are unable to determine the extent to which China's PLA are developed to carry out asymmetric computer-based attacks. However, a report issued in 2009, detailed how the People's Republic of China had developed significant capability, through distinct military doctrine, for cyberspace dominance and cyberwarfare.[lxxx] It is clear that, relative to other nations, the PRC is investing heavily in cyberwarfare.

A network-based cyberdoctrine has been developed in true Chinese style: slow, steady and certain. Initially, the PLA demonstrated cyberdoctrinal capabilities through the development of asymmetric disruptive network capabilities. According to *The Journal of International Security Affairs* "the People's Liberation Army had already task organized its first cyberwarfare tactical capabilities in 2003".[lxxxi]

From the early 2000s, the People's Republic of China mandated that foreign companies must provide their intellectual property for thorough examination, to ensure that it does not violate original Chinese company intellectual property. By mandating this technology transference, the Chinese Government has a record of the secret source for every foreign, technical company's software, hardware, cryptologic recipes, etc. With these unique technology designs, the PLA can deliberately create cyberweapons, to take advantage of the weaknesses posed by the foreign-registered designs. Given that the PLA has access to foreign technological network hardware and software designs, it is very easy to understand how they can create their own organic malware to infiltrate surreptitiously into any organizational network. Once delivered as dangerous payloads, the Chinese PLA cyberunits can exploit these remotely-planted command and control devices, to collect all manner of sensitive governmental, economic or confidential information.

'Operation Titan Rain' is the most infamous invasion of US Government computers and network. This nefarious Chinese cyberinvasion took place between November 1st 2004 and December 14th 2005. According to a story from Breibart, the *'Operation Titan Rain'* attacks have been traced to the Guangdong province of China. Techniques used by the infiltrators provide evidence that their methods were anything other than military in design and effort, according to Alan Paller, the Director of the SANS Institute, an education and research organization focusing on Cybersecurity.[lxxxii]

According to *Time Magazine* on *'Titan Rain'*, the purported Chinese cyberattacks targeted specific US Government entities. The cyberattackers found multiple information network system vulnerabilities at the US Army Information Systems Engineering Command at Fort Huachuca, Arizona. The US Defense Information Systems Agency in Arlington, Virginia was also a victim. Cyberattackers were relentless, proceeding to violate a defense department installation in San Diego, California, known as the Naval Ocean Systems Center. Huntsville, Alabama was the next cyberattack geo-location, with the US Army Space and Strategic Defense installation targeted. As with previous attacks, all the targeted information infrastructure networks were unclassified US Government systems.[lxxxiii]

Brian Manzac crystallizes the *'Titan Rain'* cyberincursion very eloquently, by saying that, essentially, the Chinese ability to plan and execute computer network attacks (CNA) for the purpose of economic espionage and national Chinese interests are less of a threat than the portent of Chinese military doctrinal development of cyberwarfare and informization, which will ultimately pose a threat to US national security.[lxxxiv]

Chinese cyberwarfare doctrine is a highly evolved form of Chairman Mao Tse Tung's military edict, that the People's Republic of China must "seal up the enemies' eyes and ears, and make them become blind and deaf, and … as far as possible confuse the minds of their commanders and turn them into madmen, using this to achieve our own victory."[lxxxv]

The Chinese PLA thus defeats the adversaries' ability to communicate and ultimately fight a network based war. Carl Von Clausewitz called this the "fog of war".

Ultimately, the People's Liberation Army could use its cyberwarfare capabilities to leverage neighboring nation's conventional military lapses and unpreparedness, thus maximizing the effect of a limited regional war.

Purpose behind Chinese Cyberwar Doctrine

The People's Republic of China's main reason for waging cyberwarfare is simply to discourage other nation-states from considering invading China, whether physically or via the Internet. "*China's interest in achieving military effects via cyberwarfare begins with deterrence.*"[lxxxvi] The People's Republic of China has political, military, economic, cultural and historic reasons for preventing other countries from invading it. Chinese history is replete with examples that the Communist Party of China would rather not see repeated. Thus "*the goal is not to deter other nations from conducting cyberwarfare against the People's Republic of China; rather, it is to use the threat of cyberwarfare to deter an actor from behaving in a manner that is in opposition to Chinese strategic interests.*"[lxxxvii]

The advantage gained by the People's Republic of China by "*threatening strategic cyberwarfare for a deterrence impact is that it is a more realistic threat when compared to the threat of other strategic weapons such as nuclear weapons*".[lxxxviii] Mazanec also contends that "*a strategic cyberwarfare attack*" by the People's Republic of China provides them "*with less international stigma and a likely more restrained retaliatory response, which is significantly more credible.*"[lxxxix] Furthermore, the challenge of attribution in cyberspace provides China with plausible deniability and makes cyberwarfare all the more attractive.

The military-strategic cyberthreat posed by the People's Republic of China is more than "the threat of counterforce/counter value cyberwarfare to deter an adversary such as the US"[xc] If the PRC is to negatively manipulate and convince other nations that their actions are not in line with China's strategic intents, then she must be prepared to follow-through with the threatened punishment or action, even if the targeted nation-state does not acquiesce. Ancient Chinese military strategy calls this tactic one of "*gaining mastery before the enemy has struck*".[xci]

Academics in the People's Republic of China wrote about a first strike cybercapability in their 2000 *Science of Campaigns Report*. The People's Republic of China will seek to use cyberwarfare confidently and overtly to attack US military networks and exfiltrate important salient technologies directly as a result. Chinese cyberattacks would clearly target systems which the US military rely upon to accurately deploy forces forward in time of crisis. "Timeliness and reliability of information upon which US forces depend (i.e. C4ISR systems)."[xcii]

According to Wang Houqing and Zhang Xingye of the Science of Campaigns of the National Defense University Press in Beijing, the goal of Chinese information warfare is to cut off the enemy's ability to obtain, control and use information, and when carried out at the critical time and region of the Chinese selection and determination, provides an effective overall campaign of information operations which will ultimately influence the adversary, reduce their ability to communicate and issue appropriate orders. The desired end state is to destroy the enemy's capabilities on the battlefield, so that observation, decision-making and command and control of troops are destroyed. The Chinese will maintain an organic ability to effectively command and control forces ahead of any disorganized enemy capability, in order to seize and gain information superiority, and ultimately set the conditions for military strategic and campaign superiority, thus achieving the desired end state of having created conditions for winning any decisive battle China that engages in.[xciii]

China's 'Cyber Command'

Perspectives on China's 'Cyber Command'

China's cyberwarfare program is capturing worldwide attention, especially in Australia, France, Germany, the UK and the US. Why are these nations so attentive to the 'Middle Kingdom's' cybercapabilities? Perhaps the most obvious is that they all have linguistically romance-based national languages. The not-so-obvious reason is less Occidental: Western nations share a majority of foreign threat intelligence amongst their various internal and external focused agencies. While evolving doctrines and incidents of cyberintrusions have helped China-watchers glean the development of China's growing cyberwarfare capabilities, far less certainty surrounds the command and control side of this enigmatic operation. This is partly because key tasks of China's computer network operations and information warfare had, until recently, been decentralized between different departments within PLA General Staff Headquarters and specialized bureaus located in the different military regions.

During July 2010, the People's Liberation Army newspaper, the *PLA Daily*, published a story on the PLA's General Staff Department (GSD) announcement of the formation of the Chinese 'cyber command'. This demonstrated how the GSD dictates operations doctrine for the entire PLA, across all operational units within the Chinese military. In true Communist Chinese fashion the GSD is led both organizationally and politically by the Central Military Commission (CMC). Thus, this is indeed an actual PLA military command.[xciv]

The *"Information Security Base"* was tasked with the mission to address potential cyberthreats and to safeguard China's national security. According to Chinese media reports, the establishment of the cyberbase was a strategic move ordered by President Hu Jintao to handle cyberthreats as China enters the information age, and to strengthen the nation's cyberinfrastructure.[xcv]

According to the *Global Times* article, which is associated with *the People's Daily*, the national paper of China, an unnamed PLA official of the General Staff Department was quoted as saying, "*the setup of the base just means that our army is strengthening its capacity and is developing potential military officers to tackle information-based warfare.*"[xcvi]

Other tasks will include online information collection and the safeguarding of confidential military information by "constructing walls." The officer emphasized that, "*it is a 'defensive' base for information security, not an offensive headquarters for cyber war*".[xcvii]

The stated missions of the new cyberbase appear to complement the PLA's information warfare (IW) units, which the PLA has been developing since at least 2003. The PLA's IW strategy was largely spearheaded by Major General Dai Qingmin, then-director of the PLA's electronic warfare department (Fourth Department), who advocated a comprehensive information warfare effort.[xcviii]

The high echelon of military officers from the General Staff Department represented at the unveiling ceremony seem to also reflect the importance that the leadership attaches to this newly organized 'cybercommand' initiative.

Held in Beijing, the Chinese 'cybercommand' was chaired by PLA Chief of General Staff General Chen Bingde, and attended by other top brass from the PLA General Staff Department. The entourage included four deputy chief of staffs: General Zhang Qinsheng, General Ma Xiaotian, Vice-Admiral Sun Jianguo and General Hou Shusen; and the two assistant chief of staffs: Major General Qi Jianguo and Major-General Chen Yong; as well as leaders from the other three General Departments – the General Political Department, General Logistics Department and General Armament Department.[xcix]

One attendee worth pointing out is Deputy Chief of Staff General Zhang Qinsheng, who is a member of the 17th CCP Central Committee and currently the commander of the Guangzhou Military Region. General Zhang previously served as director of the military training department of the Beijing Military Region, and deputy director of the military training department of the General Staff Headquarters.[c] While at the National Defense

University, he served as director of the Campaign Teaching and Research Office, dean of studies, and director of the operations department of the General Staff Department. Throughout his PLA career General Zhang has been recognized as a PLA expert on *'informationized warfare'*. In fact, General Zhang has conducted research on network command systems, further reinforcing his technical and operational expertise about China's *'informationized warfare'* doctrine.

In December 2004, then-Major General Zhang was elevated to chief of staff assistant of the General Staff Department, and was promoted to vice chief of staff in December 2006. In 2007, he was appointed commander of Guangzhou Military Region. Zhang was recently elevated to the rank of general by President Hu in mid-July 2010.[ci]

PLA responded with significant reflection and comment to the establishment of the US *'cyber command'*; Professor Meng Xiangqing from the PLA's National Defense University Institute for Strategic Studies stated:

"It is really hard to distinguish attacks and defenses in Internet war. In traditional wars, there was a definite boundary between attacks and defenses. However, in the war of internet, it was hard to define whether your action was an attack or a defense. If you claim to fight against hacker attack, it is hard to say that you are just defending yourself." Meng added, *"To fight against a hacker attack, you might attack other Internet nodes, which leads to the Internet paralysis in other countries and regions. Moreover, the Internet is a virtual world. It is hard to say that acquiring information from other countries is a defense".*[cii]

Formation and announcement of the PLA's 'cyber command' gives notice to the Western World that the Chinese military is intent on making cyberwarfare part of official military doctrine. Another indication of the extent to which the PLA is serious about *'informationized warfare'* is that traditional military commanders and strategists, such as the retired Lieutenant General Xiong Guangkai, are being relieved by the installation of military officers with a background and expertise in *'informationized warfare'*. General Zhang, taking over as deputy chief of staff of signals intelligence, is a foreshadowing of both the change in Chinese military command structure to one which is more technical and astute at information warfare, as well as the "*increasing influence of the cyber dimensions in Chinese decision-making on military strategy.*"[ciii]

Now that the PLA has fielded a '*cyber command*' within China's military organizational structure, countries such as the US should be wary. Richard Hsiao also wrote that the top echelon leadership within the People's Republic of China has seen the importance and significance of maximizing its own organic military and civilian networked information infrastructure. Thus, Chinese governmental and military bureaucracies focus on cybersecurity as a national means of defense and offense gives a strong indication that the Chinese leadership is serious in developing a cyberwarfare capability that furthers he interests of the State within China.[civ]

CHAPTER 3: CHINESE UNRESTRICTED WARFARE

War Without Limits

What is Unrestricted Warfare & who is behind it?

Unrestricted warfare, 超限戰 (traditional Mandarin Chinese) pronounced Chāo xiàn zhàn in Pin Yin, transliterated, means a war without limits or war beyond limits, thus the popular title in the West, *Unrestricted warfare*. Unrestricted warfare was published in Beijing, PRC by the PLA Literature Arts Publishing House, in February 1999.

"Unrestricted Warfare" was authored by two senior colonels, Colonel Qiao Liang, and Colonel Wang Xiang sui, who serves as the Director of the Strategy Center at the Beijing University of Aeronautics and Astronautics; both hold the rank of Senior Colonel in the People's Liberation Army Air Force (PLAAF).

Colonel Qiao Liang serves as a professor in the Strategic Studies Department of the Air Force Command College, according to a monthly journal of the State Council's Chinese Institute of Contemporary International Relations. Colonel Qiao was born 1955 in Xin County, Shanxi Province, PRC. A lineage of service to the Chinese military as a prerequisite in his family, Colonel Qiao has held various ascending positions in the PLAAF, including serving as the assistant director of the production office within the PLAAF's political department. Colonel Qiao's writings include articles that adopt the distinct view that the West should be regarded with deep suspicion. Following the 2008 Tibet riots, he argued that the world was headed toward a "soft war", such as a clash between Western and Chinese cultural values in the coming decade.[cv]

Senior Colonel Wang was born 1954 in Guangzhou Province. His family also had a tradition of military service; he entered the PLA in 1970 and was assigned to ascending positions of responsibility, including political instructor, group political commissar, section deputy head and regiment political commissar, as well as division deputy political commissar.[cvi] Prior to his academic career, Wang served as a political commissar in the PLA and is the author of several books on military history and military analysis.

The origins of "*war without limits*", 超限戰 Chāo xiàn zhàn, has its roots in the belief that the Western World, specifically the US, cannot be trusted militarily. The PLA's information warfare leadership, in particular the father of Chinese IW, Major General Wang Pufeng, has placed a strong emphasis in reinforcing this anti-Western view.

In his essay *The Challenge of Information Warfare* Major General Wang Pufeng wrote of how the Chinese military should and would conduct information warfare.

Eight Principles of Chinese Unrestricted Warfare

According to the internationally misunderstood treatise on the Future of Chinese Warfare, "*unrestricted warfare*", loosely attributed to what many protagonists call Chinese cyberwarfare, there are eight principles core to Chinese military thought.

They are the following;

全方位的方向性	– Omni-directionality
同步	– Synchrony
有限的目标	– Limited objectives
无限措施	– Unlimited measures
不对称	– Asymmetry
最小的消耗	– Minimal consumption
多维协调	– Multi Dimensional co-ordination
调整，全过程控制	– Adjustment, control of the entire process.[cvii]

The first principle of *"unrestricted warfare"* is *"omni-directionality"*. The Chinese authors, Senior Colonels Qiao Liang and Wang XiangSui defined it as *"360-degree observation and design, combined use of all related factors".* The Mandarin Chinese version

is "三百六十度的观察与设计，组合使用所有相关因素" and the Pin yin pronunciation is "Sān bǎi liù shí dù Guānchá hé shèjì, suǒyǒu xiāngguān yīnsù de jiéhé shǐyòng".

"Omni-directionality": this principle is the starting point of *"unrestricted war"* ideology. As such there is no longer any distinction between what is or is not the battlefield. Senior Colonels' Qiao and Wang stated that warfare can take a military focus, (kinetic in focus and effect), and/or quasi-military, or non-military in effort and effect. The senior colonels viewed China's entire combat power, from national combat power to encompass both intercontinental and worldwide confrontations. That *"unrestricted warfare"* should make the use of terrain and denial of terrain strategically, in order to achieve military objectives. Chinese military commanders and political leaders must look at every aspect, every possible avenue of approach or … cyberattack, to achieve the military or political end state desired by the People's Republic of China.[cviii]

The second principle of senior Colonel's Qiao and Wang's *"unrestricted warfare"* is called *"synchrony"*. The technical description the two PLA colonels used is *"conducting actions in different spaces within the same period of time".* The Mandarin Chinese version

is 内进行的同一时期在不同的空间操作 and the Pin Yin pronounciation is "Nèi jinxíng de tóngyī shíqí zài bùtóng de kōngjiān cāozuò".

Within *"synchrony"*, Colonel's Qiao and Wang describe the technical PLA military measures employed in modern warfare, paying particular attention to highlight the spread of information technology as an absolute strategy, which will enhance the emergence of long-range warfare technology for the People's Republic of China. This strategic use of information technology allows the use networks as battlefields.[cix] This is perhaps the first notion of asymmetric warfare outside of either counter-insurgency tactics or true guerilla warfare, of which the PRC's founding father Mao Tse Tung was both the father of and very fond of using to establish the People's Republic of

China in 1949. Next, the senior colonels of the PLA mention both military and non-military forces offering equal footing into the war; for example, the use of a hacker cadre, 黑客干部, Hēikè gànbù.[cx] One of the very egregious examples of how frail and target-rich Senior Colonel's Qiao and Wang see the United States military, is evident in the following quote: the "*US military's information campaign systems (yield) < 1 minute provides data on 4,000 targets & 1, aircraft*"[cxi] The culminating point of "*synchrony*" is that "*China will engage in a full-depth simultaneous attack – the United States unable to expand to battlefields such as the cyber-realm.*"[cxii]

Senior Colonels Qiao and Wang's third principle of "*unrestricted warfare*" is "*limited objectives*". Their military-oriented description is "*set a compass to guide action within an acceptable range for the measures*", the Mandarin Chinese version is 指南针设置可接受的范围内来指导行动的各项措施 and the Pin Yin pronunciation is Zhǐnánzhēn shèzhì kě jiēshòu de fànwéi nèi lái zhǐdǎo xíngdòng de gè xiàng cuòshī. They describe setting the compass to guide the PLA's actions to include one in which political and military objectives must always be smaller than the resources used: That the PRC and the PLA should not pursue objectives which are unrestricted in time and space, and that there should be a conscious effort to pursue limited objectives and eliminate objectives which are beyond one's abilities.[cxiii] From a Chinese perspective, Western political and military failures throughout history include the mistakes made by MacArthur in the Korean War, the American Army's failures in Vietnam and the ten year war experienced by the Soviets in Afghanistan. In fact, the Chinese also view the American experiences in both Iraq and Afghanistan as objectives that were set foolishly by vacillating political direction, with no certain military objective in mind other than appeasing US politicos prior to the 2012 election season; another example of not having certain achievable objectives is the United States' goal of becoming the world's number one superpower. The Chinese view isolationism from the rest of the world, such as experienced under the Clinton Administration, as leading to certain financial and moral bankruptcy.

"*Unlimited measures*" is the fourth pillar of "*unrestricted warfare*"; in Mandarin Chinese this

is 目前的趋势是朝着无限制就业的措施，但仅限于有限目标的实现 with a Pin Yin pronunciation of Mùqián de qūshì shì cháo zhe wú xiànzhì jiùyè de cuòshī, dàn jǐn xiànyú yǒuxiàn mùbiāo dì shíxiàn, which in English is *"the trend is toward unrestricted employment of measures, but restricted to the accomplishment of limited objectives".*[cxiv] In this fourth principle, the Colonels state that unlimited measures are necessary to accomplish limited objectives as the ultimate boundary (sic) objective. In this case, the PRC studied Western examples, such as General Sherman's advance toward Savanna, which had little military purpose; thus, it was a not combat mission, but one in which the advancing Union Army executed a "burn and plunder" or scorched earth campaign, during which they essentially burnt every building to the ground. The Communist Party of China (CPC) and the PLA also note successful unlimited measures to achieve limited political and military objectives. These include the Yom Kippur War in 1973; the occupation of the Sinai Peninsula was termed a failure by the Chinese, missing victory by stopping the military campaign at the Bar Lev Line in order to occupy the Sinai desert.

"Asymmetry" is the fifth principle of *"unrestricted warfare"*. *"Asymmetry"* is *"seeking nodes of action in the opposite direction from the contours of the balance of symmetry"*. The Mandarin Chinese translation is 在相反的方向寻找行动节点从对称平衡轮廓 while the Pin Yin pronunciation is Zài xiāngfǎn de fāngxiàng xúnzhǎo xíngdòng jiédiǎn cóng duìchèn pínghéng lúnkuò. They state that use of *"asymmetry"*, to accomplish the objective, manifests itself in every aspect of warfare; that the PLA should find and exploit enemy soft spots, both geographically, and in the cyber realm. A close model in Western military doctrine is the successful use of maneuver warfare by the US Marine Corps; this utilizes the discovery of an enemy's surfaces (which are either physical or seemingly impenetrable tactical features), while taking advantage of an enemy's gaps (which are the avenues of approach to be exploited), and taking advantage of an enemy's ill-prepared offense or defensive position. Again, the Chinese political and military establishment studies Western military for examples: Chechnya vs. Russia, Somalia vs. the US, Northern Ireland guerrillas vs. Britain, and Islamic Jihad vs. the entire West. In each of these political/military examples the Chinese observe a smaller factional force of irregulars, and their refusal of confronting the armed forces of nation-states head-on; instead fighting *"asymmetrically"* to achieve their objectives. One of the Chinese military's often-studied notions of irregular warfare is John Nagel and Peter Schoomaker's *Learning to Eat Soup with a Knife.*

"Unrestricted warfare's" sixth principle is *"minimal consumption"*. The Mandarin Chinese version of this is given as利用战斗资源最少数额足以完成目标 with an English translation of using (sic) *"the least amount of combat resources sufficient to accomplish the objective"*[cxv] Within *"minimal consumption"* they state that rationality is more important than thrift, and thus the "size of combat consumption is decided by the form of combat".[cxvi] Military commanders and political decision-makers must (sic) "use "more" (more measures) to pursue "less" (lower consumption)".[cxvii] The military tactic and strategy of proportionality is undertaken, which effectively means a combat commander should only use the appropriate number of personnel and combat power to achieve an objective. The Chinese cite the way in which the German Army was able to sweep away the joint British-French force after crossing the Maginot Line, effectively by-passing a seemingly insurmountable military force by simply choosing not to attack it, also another example of *"asymmetry"*.

The seventh principle of *"unrestricted warfare"* is *"multi-dimensional co-ordination"*: the *"co-ordinating and allocating all the forces which can be mobilized in the military and non-military spheres covering an objective"*. The Mandarin Chinese version

is 协调和分配所有的， 可在军事和非军事目标球占地动员 while the Pin Yin pronunciation is Xiétiáo hé fēnpèi suǒyǒu de, kě zài jūnshì hé fēi jūnshì mùbiāo qiú zhān dì dòngyuán. Their statements about *"multi-dimensional co-ordination"* include the requirement for a specific nature and duration objective; that while Chinese military and political decision-makers plan military campaigns, careful co-ordination and co-operation, among different forces in different spheres, must be observed, in order to accomplish an objective. In Western military doctrine, the Chinese have studied the very successful use of combined arms by the US Marine Corps, using their Marine Air Ground Task Force (MAGTF) Concept. The Chinese focus on the ability of a military unit to accomplish either a political or military-defined objective by bringing to bear the necessary components of success, such as ground combat, air combat and combat logistical support functions, to achieve the stated objective. The senior colonels decree that any sphere can become a battlefield, and any force can be used under combat conditions, including in the cyber realm. Thus, the use of inserted malware, to exfiltrate an enemy's critical and sensitive data, could be combined with social engineering via spear phishing attack. They continue to state that "*multi-dimensional co-ordination*" also involves the "employment of intangible "strategic resources" such as geographical factors, the role of history, cultural traditions, and sense of ethnic identity, dominating and exploiting the influence of international organizations".[cxviii]

The eighth and final principle "*unrestricted warfare*" is "*adjustment & control*" of the entire process; in Mandarin Chinese this is 在战争的全过程从它开始通过它的进步它的结论不断获取信息调节作用并控制局面, with a Pin Yin pronounciation of Zài zhànzhēng de quán guòchéng, cóng tā kāishǐ tōngguò tā de jìnbù, tā de jiélùn, bùduàn huòqǔ xìnxī, tiáojié zuòyòng, bìng kòngzhì júmiàn The English translation is "*during the entire course of a war, from its start, through its progress, to its conclusion, continually acquire information, adjust action, and control the situation*". Essentially, this is command and control. The Chinese military minds propose that "*warfare is dynamic process randomness & creativity prevail*"[cxix] This is akin to Clausewitz' "*fog of war*": that a greater use of intuition and creativity be used on the battlefield, and that "*today, with information technology welding the entire world together into a network, the number of factors involved in a war is much, much greater than in past wars*"[cxx], such that the "*shift of the battlefield to non-military spheres is inevitable.*"[cxxi]

Within the PLA military doctrine, the cyber realm + network infrastructure = cyberwarfare ... or '*informationized warfare*', war without limits and thus, '*unrestricted warfare*'.

The Challenge of Information Warfare

Major General Wang Pufeng wrote "*The Challenge of Information Warfare*" during the Spring of 1995, for the "*Chinese Military Science*" publication. The compelling reason why "*The Challenge of Information Warfare*" (the text of which is in Appendix D) must be considered and read, is that Major General Wang Pufeng is a former Director of the People's Liberation Army Strategy Department. Major General Wang is a credible author, and thus his theories and writings about the future of asymmetric warfare within the

Chinese military doctrinal development are based in his experience as a senior military officer, with a technical background in information warfare.

In this paper, General Wang presents several carefully articulated core beliefs, with accompanying historical antecedents. It is within these ideas that we begin to get to see how China has formulated, and will continue to mature, her cyberwarfare tactics and strategies.

The prophetic words about information warfare doctrinal development are remarkable in several ways. One of the most critical elements is the way in which *"The Challenge of Information Warfare"* examines the deficiencies in Chinese IW doctrine, attributing these shortcomings to a lack of advanced information technology, or the access to it within the PLA. The Chinese PLA concepts of IW include specific attributes as "combat secrecy, military deception, psychological warfare, electronic warfare, physical destruction of C2 infrastructure, and computer network warfare",[cxxii] to be developed in order to further modernize the PLA, so that it can effectively protect and defend China's national and international interests.

Another prescriptive detail is the study of Western military information operations and IW strategy, particularly the US during the first Gulf War, and the success in shutting down the Iraqi information networks prior to the ground invasion in 1991.[cxxiii] Additionally, General Wang observes the US Army's information technology modernization as a necessary pre-requisite for a successful revolution of military affairs (RMA) in the US; a technology foresight program which is also essential for the modernization of the PLA. Achieving cyberfirepower superiority is a corollary to the need for advancing China's military use of advanced information technologies; this is also stated as a necessary requirement for China's success as a superpower in cyberspace.

General Wang states that the PRC must grow militarily from the industrial age, with a more modern embrace of advanced information technology offered by the information age, so that China, through its military, can achieve and maintain a prominent position in the realm of IO and IW practice.

Another unique feature of General Wang's cyberdoctrine theory is deference to Chinese military history through the teachings of Mao Tse Tung and the ancillary Marxist teachings on which the PLA has been based since 1949. The quote he cites is very chilling to any military or cyberwarrior: ""using the inferior to overcome the superior" in information warfare is definitely much different in content and form from the techniques of war used in the past."[cxxiv]

The recurring theme of General Wang Pufeng's theory is that additional study by the PLA is necessary as a condition for success in mastering the 5th domain of cyberspace and cyberwarfare.

CHAPTER 4: PRINCIPLES OF WARFARE – WEST VERSUS EAST

Warfare – Mapping East to West

Before entering to the realm of the People's Liberation Army and how they dominate cyberspace with their version 21st Century cyberwarfare, one should have an understanding of how both Chinese and non-Chinese militaries conduct traditional kinetic effects-based warfare. It is necessary to map Western principles of warfare to Eastern principles; indeed it is essential, in that it lays a foundation for the principles of 21st century Chinese cyberwarfare to be discussed comparatively with the way in which the West intends to fight in the 5th domain. Only then can a better appreciation be achieved regarding PRC designs for cyberwarfare doctrine.

'On War' – Carl Von Clausewitz 1780–1831 A.D.

Anyone who has served in a military capacity has likely to have studied the principles of warfare. *On War* by Carl Von Clausewitz is considered by most Western military tacticians and strategists to be the bible on conducting warfare. Clausewitz has eight books covering the subject in *On War,* from the foundational treatise *On the Nature of War*, the purpose, genius, dangers and ubiquitous *Fiction in War* is covered in great detail. In his other books are presented the distilled Western principles of war, of which there are eleven. These are for the conduct of traditional symmetric warfare, applicable in a fundamental sense to the conduct of asymmetric and cyberwarfare.

The principles of Western warfare are:

1) Mass: When a military commander "*concentrate(s) combat power at the decisive place and time*"[cxxv]
2) Offensive: To "*seize, retain, & exploit the initiative*"[cxxvi]
3) Objective: "*Direct every operation towards a clearly defined, decisive, & attainable objective*"[cxxvii]
4) Surprise: "*Strike the enemy at a time, place, or manner for which they are unprepared*"[cxxviii]
5) Economy of force: "*Allocate minimum essential combat power to secondary efforts.*"[cxxix]

6) Maneuver: "*Place the enemy in a position of disadvantage through flexible application of combat power*"[cxxx]
7) Unity of command: "*For every objective, ensure unity of effort under one responsible commander*"[cxxxi]
8) Security: "*Never permit the enemy to acquire an unexpected advantage*"[cxxxii]
9) Simplicity: "*Prepare clear, uncomplicated plans concise orders to ensure thorough understanding*"[cxxxiii]

Carl Von Clausewitz has been a model for traditional and modern warriors, and how they conduct warfare. These guiding principles have given the British Army success in the Falkland Islands, Iraq and Afghanistan. The US and "*The War Against Terror*" have seen the successful application of Von Clausewitz in both Iraq and Afghanistan. However, these were conflicts of limited duration, fought on geographies that are physical and can be pointed to on a map. How then do these Clausewitzian principles of modern warfare apply to cyberwarfare in the non-physical 5th domain?

Before that question is answered a review of the Ancient Chinese military philosopher Sun Tzu is required.

'The Art of War' – Sun Tzu 544 – 496 B.C.

Both Western and Asian military warriors have studied Sun Tzu's *The Art of War*. This Ancient Chinese military treatise is comprised of thirteen chapters, which have guided Chinese military commanders to repeated victories across numerous Chinese dynasties and serve, even today, as a basis for Chinese cyberwarfare doctrinal development. Sun Tzu's principles of war are the following;

The first Sun Tzu principle of war is 始计 Shǐ jì, *Detail Assessment and Planning*.

This, Sun Tzu states "*explores the five key elements that define competitive position namely, political intelligence, climate, terrain, leadership and organization characteristics, and how to evaluate one's competitive strengths against one's adversaries.*"[cxxxiv]

The second principle is *Waging War* 作战 Zuòzhàn.

This principle *"explains the economic nature of competition and how success requires making winning pay, which in turn, requires limiting the cost of competition and conflict."*[cxxxv]

Sun Tzu's third principle is *Strategic Attack* 谋攻 Móu gong.

This *"defines the source of strength as unity, not size, and the five ingredients that you need to succeed in any competitive situation."* [cxxxvi]

The fourth Sun Tzu principle is *Disposition of the Army* 军形 Jūn xíng.

The meaning is one which *"explains the importance of defending existing positions until you can advance them and how you must recognize opportunities, not try to create them."*[cxxxvii]

The fifth principle of warfare according to Sun tzu is *Forces* 兵势 Bīng shì.

It is explained as *"expels the use of creativity and timing to build your competitive momentum."*[cxxxviii]

Sun Tzu's sixth principle *"explain how your opportunities come from the openings in the environment caused by the relative weakness of your competitors in a given area."*[cxxxix] 虚实 Xūshí has a meaning of *"Weaknesses and Strengths"*.

The seventh principle, *Military Maneuvers* 军争 with Pin Yin pronounciation Jūn zhēng *"explains the dangers of direct conflict and how to win those confrontations when they are forced upon you."*[cxl]

Variations and Adaptability, 九变 Jiǔ bià is the eighth principle from Sun Tzu' Art of War. This principle of war *"focuses on the need for flexibility in your responses. It explains how to respond to shifting circumstances successfully."*[cxli]

Sun Tzu's ninth principle *Movement and Development of Troops,* 行军 Xíngjūn *"describes the different situations in which you find yourselves when you move into new competitive arenas and how to respond to them. Much of it focuses on evaluating the intentions of others."*[cxlii]

Terrain 地形 Dìxíng is the tenth principle and is explained as the different types of physical and cerebral military uses of terrain. Sun Tzu wrote that *"There are different kinds of terrain, such as: communicative ground, entrapping ground, indifferent ground, constricted ground, key ground and distant ground."*[cxliii]

Sun Tzu said: *"In the deployment of troops, there is dispersive ground, frontier ground and key ground. There are also communicative ground, focal ground, serious ground, treacherous ground, constricted ground and death ground."*[cxliv] This is the eleventh principle of war which is *The Nine Battlegrounds* 九地 Jiǔ de.

Sun Tzu's twelfth principle of war, *Attacking with Fire,* 火攻 Huǒ gong, states *"there are five ways to use fire to attack the enemy. The first way is to burn the enemy soldiers in their camp. The second way is to burn enemy's stockpiles and provisions. Third way is to burn the heavy military equipment and supplies of the enemy. Fourth is to burn the armory and warehouses of the enemy. The fifth way is to torch the transportation trains of the enemy."*[cxlv]

And the last of Sun Tzu's Ancient Chinese principles of war is *Intelligence and Espionage* 用间 Yòng jiān. This is perhaps the most appropriate as it relates to the comparison of Chinese vs. non-Chinese principles of war, and *"focuses on the importance of developing good information sources, and specifies the five types of intelligence sources and how to best manage each of them."*

Sun Tzu can have had no idea that all his ancient principles would be applicable across all the future centuries. He certainly would have had no idea that his modern day warriors, the PLA, would use his ancient principles as a basis for 21st century Chinese cyberwarfare.

Principles of Chinese Cyberwarfare – 中国网络战的原则

The People's Republic of China has principles of cyberwarfare, 中国网络战的原则 – Zhōngguó wǎngluò zhàn de yuánzé. This is a brief review from Chapter 3, again, from "*War Without Limits*":

Omni directionality
Synchrony
Limited objectives
Unlimited measures
Asymmetry
Minimal consumption
Multi dimensional co-ordination
Adjustment and control of the entire process.

However, it is impossible to locate similar cyberwarfare principles for the non-Chinese or Western military. The Author chaired and presented an eight-hour seminar on Chinese cyberwarfare in at a European Conference, in Berlin, Germany during Sept/Oct 2011.

When the last slide in the seminar was presented, showing the Chinese People's Liberation Army cyberwarfare principles, alongside none for the West, there was outrage and anger, leading to surprise and embarrassment. The eventual acknowledgement and resignation, to this lack of Western cyberwarfare rules, was begrudgingly accepted by a senior US naval officer representing US 'Cyber Command', representatives from NATO, the EU, and proud members of the US Air Force Air Mobility Command and Cyberwarrior training squadron. Perhaps it was an unwelcome wakeup call, so exercising patience, during a subsequent London workshop, I asked a senior representative if US 'Cyber Command' (USCYBERCOM) had cyberwarfare laws, principles or rules of engagement. The gentlemen's response was an unequivocal "No. We, USCYBERCOM, cannot even define what cyberspace is!"

If you cannot define your military area of interest (AI) or area of operations (AO) in cyberspace, how can you effectively mount either a defensive or offensive campaign in this new dimension of warfare?

The PLA's 制信息权 Information Dominance

The PRC is at an introspective crossroads. Their political systems remain Communist, in both application and governed-thought; the collective economic system of the late 20th century has morphed within China into a decidedly (albeit begrudgingly-accepted) capitalist version; and yet the rich culture, language and history remain a foundation in everything Chinese.

Because the 'Middle Kingdom' has such a rich history, which has seen its share of foreign intrusions, invasions and problems, they want to develop their own organic IW doctrine. Chinese IW theory must include a recollection of the Chinese cultural, historical and linguistic past, whilst also including the current and future needs of the People's Republic of China. The political and economic focus of China will always be paramount. Should there be a real or imagined threat to this precarious Chinese balance, the Golden Emperor's sons and daughters will take the necessary proactive steps to eradicate any real or perceived threat.

Chinese Information War Theory and Implementation

The People's Liberation Army (PLA) has always been an advocate of using information technology and warfare thought, to become an even more effective policy instrument for the Communist Party of China (CPC). Based on the Chinese military need for an understanding of information war (IW), and how it will apply to their role in current Chinese society, several notable articles have been written by military theorists and civilian academics.

Significant IW theory and thought has crystallized and matured into Chinese doctrine since at least 1995, when Major General Wang Pufeng wrote *"The Challenge of Information Warfare"*. Other Chinese military strategists and technologists have also written about the merging of the art of war, incorporating information technology in Chinese military warfighting doctrine.

Current Chinese military IW concepts are based on the focus and idea of a 'People's War'. Yet this dichotomy, of the present Chinese state and the rich cultural history, is omnipresent. The use and application of Ancient Chinese military thought included in the *"Book of Qi"* details a variety of Chinese military strategies based upon the *I-Ching*'s notion of Yin and Yang. Regarding military strategy, Yin was the reference to six which is the square root of the I-Ching. Thus, in popular Western writings, these ancient military strategies are often called the *"Thirty Six Stratagems"*. The original text of these stratagems has a complicated and historically-flowing style that is common to Classical or Literary Chinese. Each proverb is accompanied by a short comment, no longer than a sentence or two, that explains how the proverb is applicable to military tactics. These Chinese proverbs are related to 36 battle scenarios in Chinese history and folklore, predominantly of the *"Warring States Period"* and the *"Three Kingdoms Period"*.

It is very important to read and reflect on these Ancient Chinese military stratagems as a necessary prerequisite for understanding 21st century Chinese IW and cyberwarfare doctrinal development. It is important that each of these stratagems be read with a focus on the use of information technology, ancient and modern Chinese warfare, and their intent of using these to craft Chinese computer network operations (CCNO) that include both computer network defense and computer network offensive capabilities.

The *"Thirty-Six Stratagems"* are divided into categories based on the use of espionage, offense, defense and deception.

Stratagems when in a superior position

The first of these Ancient Chinese proverbs is "*Fool the Emperor to Cross the Sea*", the Mandarin Chinese version is 瞞天過海 and the Pin Yin pronunciation is Mántiānguòhǎi which states that "*Moving about in the darkness and shadows, occupying isolated places, or hiding behind screens will only attract suspicious attention. To lower an enemy's guard you must act in the open hiding your true intentions under the guise of common every day activities.*"[cxlvi]

This, in the case of CCNO, means to "conceal the real objective; disguise the course being pursued; camouflage the real purpose."[cxlvii]

The second Ancient Chinese stratagem which applies to current Chinese information warfare is "*Besiege Wei to Rescue Zhao*", 瞞天過海 Pin Yin pronunciation is Mán tiān guò hǎi, and it is taken from the Chinese "Warring States Period". This parable reads "*When the enemy is too strong to attack directly, and then attack something he holds dear. Know that in all things he cannot be superior. Somewhere there is a gap in the armor, a weakness that can be attacked instead.*"[cxlviii]

Such that if one applies this to CCNO and current Chinese IW doctrinal development "*Subdue the enemy indirectly by threatening one of his unprotected weak spots.*"[cxlix] This can be interpreted technically to mean that the Chinese 'cyber command' will reconnoiter foreign networks, probing, looking for either an unprotected network segment or server, and exploiting it.

The third Ancient Chinese Stratagem is "*Kill with a Borrowed Sword.*" The Mandarin Chinese version is 借刀殺人 and the Pin Yin pronunciation is Jiè dāo shā rén. The third verse states "*When you do not have the means to attack your enemy directly, and then attack using the strength of another. Trick an ally into attacking him, bribe an official to turn traitor, or use the enemy's own strength against him.*"[cl]

Harod Von Senger's interpretation is "*Eliminate an opponent using an outside agency; harm someone else indirectly without exposing oneself*".[cli] This stratagem can clearly be translated into CCNO by understanding that the

Chinese IW practice could include the use of a virtual private server (VPS) re-direct tactic. Using this cyberhacking methodology, the Chinese could easily promote a website or an IP address other than their true origination, to deceive forensic analysis or advanced methods to geo-locate them during a cyberattack.[clii]

The fourth Ancient Chinese military strategy is "*Await the Exhausted Enemy at Your Ease*" and the Mandarin Chinese version is 以逸待勞 the Pin Yin pronunciation is Yǐ yì dài láo. The Literary Chinese translation of this stratagem reflects the following: "*It is an advantage to choose the time and place for battle. In this way you know when and where the battle will take place, while your enemy does not. Encourage your enemy to expend his energy in futile quests while you conserve your strength. When he is exhausted and confused, you attack with energy and purpose.*"[cliii]

Von Senger's version is much more concise and the application to Chinese IW doctrinal development is even more compelling; "*Preserve your own strength while maneuvering the enemy into exhausting himself.*"[cliv] The applications of this Chinese folk tale to 21st century Chinese cyberwarfare are very compelling; many nation-states are spending considerable time and resources reporting on and blaming the PRC for cyberexploits on their networks, yet nothing seems to be done to either finitely prove or disprove the veracity of the cyberattacks. This is the perfect storm of an infinite closed loop of the network admin chasing his tail to no end, which the cyberperpetrators can continue to exploit without worry.

Attributed to the "Warring States Period" in Chinese history, "*Loot a Burning House*" is the fifth Ancient Chinese military strategy. The Mandarin Chinese is 趁火打劫 with a Pin Yin pronunciation is Chèn huǒ dǎj ié. Von Senger's application of this phrase is "Exploit a fire to commit a robbery – exploit another's troubles or crisis for your own advantage; attack the enemy when he is in a state of chaos."[clv] Applying this parable of Ancient Chinese military history to the modern woes of the US economic crisis, it is very easy to see how the PLA will use the current problems in America to their cyberadvantage.

The sixth strategy is from the Chinese Song Dynasty *"Clamor in the East, and attack in the West"*, the Mandarin Chinese for this prose is聲東擊西 with a PinYin pronunciation hēng dōng jí xī. This stratagem reads *"In any battle the element of surprise can provide an overwhelming advantage. Even when face to face with an enemy, surprise can still be employed by attacking where he least expects it. To do this you must create an expectation in the enemy's mind through the use of a feint."*[clvi]

Harrod Von Senger applies this strategy as *"Announce an attack to the east but carry it out to the west, feint eastward but attack westward. Diversionary maneuver to mask the real direction of an attack."*[clvii]

Stratagems for confrontation

From the Chinese T'ang Dynasty comes the seventh Ancient Chinese military strategy,*"Create Something From Nothing"*, with Mandarin Chinese version 無中生有 and the Pin Yin pronunciation wú zhōng sheng yǒu. The Literary Chinese translation is *"You use the same feint twice. Having reacted to the first and often the second feint as well, the enemy will be hesitant to react to a third feint. Therefore the third feint is the actual attack catching your enemy with his guard down."*[clviii]

Von Senger calls this *"the creator stratagem"*[clix] During a PLA military channel, CCTV-7, broadcast on 16 July 2011, an 11-minute broadcast of 网络风暴来了, Wǎngluò fēngbào láile, Mandarin Chinese for *"the Internet Storm is Coming"*, the PLA showed a graphical user (GUI) hacking tool screenshot attacking a selected IP from the University of Arkansas. This was a fantastic cyberfeint by both the Chinese Government and the PLA. By showing an old GUI hacking tool attacking an inconsequential IP address formerly associated with the Falun Gong religious sect, it focused the entire world on a very old hacking tool.[clx] Thus, the PLA, by demonstrating an old capability, took the attention and resources away from their real intent and cyberefforts.

The eighth Ancient Chinese military parable is *"Openly Repair the Walkway, Secretly March to Chencang"*, 暗渡陳倉 with a Pin Yin pronunciation of Àndùchéncāng. This stratagem is fundamentally one of divide and conquering the enemy, and is succinctly stated from the original Literary Chinese as *"Attack the enemy with two convergent forces. The first is the direct attack, one that is obvious and for which the enemy prepares his defense. The second is the indirect, the attack sinister, that the enemy does not expect and which causes him to divide his forces at the last minute leading to confusion and disaster.*"[clxi]

The significant Chinese story "*Romance of the Three Kingdoms*" provides the ninth Ancient Chinese military philosophy, which is "*Observe the Fire on the Opposite Shore*", the Mandarin Chinese translation is 隔岸觀火 with a Pin Yin pronunciation of Gé'ànguānhuǒ. The plain English version of this parable is "*Delay entering the field of battle until all the other players have become exhausted fighting amongst themselves. Then go in full strength and pick up the pieces.*"[clxii]

The "*Warring States Period*" also offers the tenth stratagem, with "*Hide Your Dagger Behind a Smile*" in Mandarin Chinese, 笑裡藏刀while the Pin Yin pronunciation is Xiào lǐ cáng dāo. The Literary Chinese translation of stratagem number ten is "*Charm and ingratiate yourself to your enemy. When you have gained his trust, you move against him in secret.* "[clxiii]

Von Senger's translation of this parable is "*Speak flattery, but plan evil in your heart; mask evil intent with outward friendliness and fine sounding words.*"[clxiv] In March 2011, China announced that its defense budget would rise 12.7 per cent in 2011, to 601.1 billion Yuan ($91.7 billion), fuelling regional concerns about Beijing's military build-up, in addition to its worldwide economic clout. At the end of May 2011, China announced the formation of its '*Blue Army*' to carry out defensive responses to cyberattacks. Subsequently, on June 1st 2011, General Zhang Qinsheng, deputy chief of the PLA stated, in response to the Chinese military's development of an '*informationized*' force: "*China has always been embarking on peaceful development and the development of China is by no means a threat*".[clxv]

The eleventh stratagem is similar to the Western parable of the sacrificial lamb and reads "*Let the Plum Tree Wither in Place of the Peach*", the Mandarin Chinese is 李代桃僵Lǐdàitáo jiāng. From the "*Three Kingdoms Period*" in Ancient China, this stratagem states "*there are circumstances in which you must sacrifice short-term objectives in order to gain the long-term goal. This is the scapegoat strategy whereby someone else suffers the consequences so that the rest do not.* "[clxvi]

This philosophy is similar to the seventh stratagem, describing the PLA's 'accidental' disclosure of early 2000 GUI hacking tools. By acknowledging the fact the PLA has these hacking tools, they are drawing attention away from more advanced cyberhacking methodologies.

"Seize the Opportunity to Lead the Sheep Away" is the twelfth Ancient Chinese military strategy. The Mandarin Chinese version is 順手牽羊 with a Pin Yin pronunciation of Shùn shǒu qiān yáng. The Literary Chinese translation reflects thus *"While carrying out your plans be flexible enough to take advantage of any opportunity that presents itself, however small, and avail yourself of any profit, however slight."* "[clxvii]

Harod Von Senger's translation into English applies very directly to the Chinese PLA cyberwarfare doctrinal development in that *"Constant vigilance and psychological readiness to exploit opportunities to one's advantage, whenever and wherever they arise."* "[clxviii] This stratagem resonates daily in newsfeeds and was identified by the 2009 Northrup Grumman Corporation (NGC) report (detailing the Chinese Government's ability and propensity to conduct cyberespionage), which is commissioned by the US-China Economic and Security Review Commission. According to a *PCWorld* article titled *"Report Says China Ready for Cyber-war, Espionage"* the NGC report concluded in 2009 that *"China is likely using its maturing computer network exploitation capability to support intelligence collection against the US government and industry by conducting a long-term, sophisticated computer network exploitation campaign."* "[clxix]

Stratagems for attack

The thirteenth strategy comes from the Southern T'ang Dynasty of A.D 977 and is *"Beat the Grass to Startle The Snake"*. The Mandarin Chinese version is 打草驚蛇 with a Pin Yin pronunciation of Dǎcǎojīngshé. The Literary Chinese translation is *"When you cannot detect the opponent's plans launch a direct, but brief, attack and observe your opponent reactions. His behavior will reveal his strategy."* "[clxx]

This stratagem offers elements of both intimidation, firing a warning shot and provocation, agitating your enemy into revealing their plans. The Chinese have successfully applied this Ancient Chinese military strategy in 2010 and 2011. With so much unattributable news about cyberexploitation of networks worldwide, and many of the accusations leveled at the PRC, many Western nations are codifying the national cyberstrategies. As they announce their cyberpolicies, they have told a cyberadversary where the weaknesses in the network are; an invitation to attack and exploit.

From the Yuan Period, A.D. 1271–1368, the fourteenth stratagem is "*Borrow a Corpse to Raise the Spirit*", in Mandarin Chinese this is 借屍還魂 the Pin Yin pronunciation is Jièshīhuánhún. A Literary Chinese rendition reflects "*Take an institution, a technology, or a method that has been forgotten or discarded and appropriate it for your own purpose. Revive something from the past by giving it a new purpose or to reinterpret and bring to life old ideas, customs, and traditions.*"[clxxi] Harod Von Senger's explanation is to "Revive something from the past by infusing it with new purpose."[clxxii] This is a stratagem of "*renewal*".[clxxiii] This stratagem is indeed prophetic and is the essence thus far of 21st century cyberwarfare doctrine development – take Ancient Chinese military philosophy and apply it to today's technological situation, enabling successful Chinese PLA IW thought to develop and mature.

From the Journey of the Son of Heaven, during the "*Three Kingdoms Period*" of Ancient Chinese history, is the fifteenth strategy of to "*Lure the Tiger Down the Mountain*", the Mandarin Chinese version is 調虎離山 with the Pin Yin pronunciation of Diào hǔ lí shān. The Literary Chinese translation is "*Never directly attack a well-entrenched opponent. Instead lure him away from his stronghold and separate him from his source of strength.*"[clxxiv]

Harod Von Senger's application suggests a strategy of isolation for the enemy, "Weaken the enemy by separating him from his main supporters."[clxxv] Examples of this strategy being used can be extrapolated from the various US power grid failures over the past decade; in theory the PRC is probing the energy grid in the US looking for weaknesses. The PLA will accomplish this through reconnaissance as a prelude to large scale cyberattack, through which they will separate geographical areas within the US in order to extract trade or economic concessions, or perhaps even physically invade the weakened area to gain a foothold.

AD 223–225, also known as the Six Dynasties Period, offered the sixteenth strategy of *"To Catch Something, First Let it Go"*, the Mandarin Chinese version 欲擒故縱 pronounced in Pin Yin as Yùqíngùzòng. This is the proverbial cat and mouse strategy offered from the Literary Chinese version *"Cornered prey will often mount a final desperate attack. To prevent this you let the enemy believe he still has a chance for freedom. His will to fight is thus dampened by his desire to escape. When in the end the freedom is proven a falsehood the enemy's morale will be defeated and he will surrender without a fight."*[clxxvi]

The seventeenth stratagem is called *"give and take"* states *"Prepare a trap then lure your enemy into the trap by using bait. In war the bait is the illusion of an opportunity for gain. In life the bait is the illusion of wealth, power, and sex."*[clxxvii] The Mandarin Chinese translation is 拋磚引玉 and the Pin Yin pronunciation is Pāo zhuān yǐn yù.

The PLA has used this stratagem with particular success in the physical world via its international espionage efforts, and in Chinese IW doctrinal application this could be explained via the use of phishing attacks – the dispatch of seemingly authentic e-mails sent with a subject meant to generate a response. This would be especially important and useful prior to diplomatic talks, or in the event there are commercial discussions between a state-owned enterprise and a Western business.

During the Spring and Autumn period in Ancient China, the eighteenth military philosophy was created *"To Catch bandits First Capture Their Leader"* the Mandarin Chinese version is 擒賊擒王 while the Pin Yin pronunciation is Qín zéi qín wáng. This Archimedean point strategy is one in which the enemy is neutralized by taking out the leader. In this case the PLA would target the command and control of the adversary they are targeting, eliminating the opponent's ability to communicate with subordinate units, effectively destroying their ability to issue orders on the network in response to an attack. The Literary Chinese translation is *"If the enemy's army is strong but is allied to the commander only by money or threats then, take aim at the leader. If the commander falls the rest of the army will disperse or come over to your side. If, however, they are allied to the leader through loyalty then*

beware, the army can continue to fight on after his death out of
vengeance."[clxxviii]

Stratagems for attack

The nineteenth Ancient Chinese military philosophy is a strategy which is
taken from the Japanese historical annals, specifically the Legendary Era of
Japan's history which occurred from 660 BC–539 AD. This stratagem says
"*When faced with an enemy too powerful to engage directly you must first
weaken him by undermining his foundation and attacking his source of
power.*"[clxxix] The Mandarin Chinese for this strategy is 釜底抽薪 while Pin
Yin pronunciation is Fǔ dǐ chōu xīn.

The PLA's cyberstrategy application of the nineteenth stratagem is very
obvious indeed – fearing the cyberbuildup in the West, particularly the
announcement to create the US 'Cyber Command' in 2010, by General
Alexander[clxxx], and the statement by the US military that cyberattacks will be
considered acts of war, and that it will respond with kinetic force if
necessary[clxxxi], the PRC would most certainly fear this aggressive action from
the United States and take appropriate actions to design their cyberstrategy,
initiating DDoS attacks against the US 'Cyber Command' to forestall any
overt military action, should it be proven the Chinese have attacked via the
Internet.

The twentieth stratagem, "*Steal The Firewood From Under the Pot*", the
Mandarin version is, 混水摸魚 and is pronounced in Pin Yin as Hún shuǐ mō
yú, states "*Before engaging your enemy's forces create confusion to weaken
his perception and judgment. Do something unusual, strange, and unexpected
as this will arouse the enemy's suspicion and disrupt his thinking. A
distracted enemy is thus more vulnerable.*"[clxxxii]

This Spring and Autumn Period of China strategy is quite prophetic. The
PLA's IW doctrine would make use of this stratagem by divulging nascent
hacking skills via broadcast television (as the PLA did in 2011), so that the
enemy focuses their efforts from a cyberdefensive position of anticipating an
older hacking tool. In fact, the PLA would use significantly more modern
cyberoffensive capabilities and exploit the new weaknesses of the intended
cybertarget.

The "*Three Kingdoms Period*" of Ancient China provides the twenty-first stratagem "*Shed Your Skin Like the Golden Cicada*" which in Mandarin Chinese is 金蟬脫殼 with a Pin Yin pronunciation of Jīn chán tuō ké. The military philosophy of Ancient China reads "*When you are in danger of being defeated, and your only chance is to escape and regroup, then create an illusion. While the enemy's attention is focused on this artifice, secretly remove your men leaving behind only the facade of your presence.*".[clxxxiii]

The warlord Cao Cao of Wei thus provides the cyberdoctrine development of the PLA with a deception tactic. Perhaps the Chinese military is already using this tactic as certainly there has yet to be proof positive or direct IP address attribution that the Chinese PLA has inculcated attacks on any country via the Internet. Thus the confusion of who is to blame for cyberincursions is a mere false claim by the popular press.[clxxxiv]

"*Shut the Door to Catch the Thief*" is the twenty-second Ancient Chinese military stratagem, pronounced in Mandarin Chinese 關門捉賊 with a Pin Yin pronunciation of Guānmén zhuō zéi states "*If you have the chance to completely capture the enemy then you should do so thereby bringing the battle or war to a quick and lasting conclusion. To allow your enemy to escape plants the seeds for future conflict. But if they succeed in escaping, be wary of giving chase.*" [clxxxv]

Chinese military cyberdoctrine would make full use of this "*Warring States*" era strategy, which is one of not giving the enemy advantage nor taking any quarter from the cyberfoe; the Chinese military has already used this stratagem during the Korean Conflict, unofficially supporting the North Korean human wave attacks on the multi-national peacekeeping force. Application by PLA IW commanders of this twenty-second strategy in the fifth domain of warfare is one of overwhelming cybersuperiority, much like the alleged mapping of the US electrical grid in preparation for an invasion.[clxxxvi]

In 2008, Tom Donohue, with the Central Intelligence Agency (CIA) stated that "*a cyber-attack had taken out power equipment in multiple regions outside the US. The outage was followed with extortion demands,*"[clxxxvii]

The twenty-third Ancient Chinese military stratagem the PLA consider a part of the IW doctrine development is one in which they will "*Befriend a Distant*

Enemy to Attack One Nearby". The Mandarin Chinese version of this strategy is 遠交近攻 with a Pin Yin pronunciation of Yuǎn jiāo jìn gong, it states "*It is known that nations that border each other become enemies while nations separated by distance and obstacles make better allies. When you are the strongest in one field, your greatest threat is from the second strongest in your field, not the strongest from another field.*"[clxxxviii]

This Han Dynasty military strategy is already being used by the PLA cyberplanners, based on the philosophy of concentrating on the immediate threat. The Chinese Government announced the formation of the 'the Blue Army', whose mission is to "to ensure the security of China's military networks."[clxxxix]

The Government of the PRC is tasking its military with preparing for defense against cyberwars from other nation-states, via the task organization, and formation of this elite force of Chinese cyberwarriors.

The Ancient Chinese military strategy of 假途伐虢, pronounced in Pin Yin Jiǎ tú fá guó, is "*Borrow the Road to Conquer Guo.*" This is the twenty-fourth ancient stratagem of China's military forefathers and it states, "*Borrow the resources of an ally to attack a common enemy. Once the enemy is defeated, use those resources to turn on the ally that lent you them in the first place.*"[cxc]

In effect this strategy for PLA IW doctrinal development ties directly to the state-owned enterprises (SOE) within the oil and gas industry, and their initiatives to tie off both economically and natural resource affiliations with Canada, eliminating the possibility of the US taking advantage the oil sand fields in the Western province of Alberta, Canada. The state-controlled Sinopec is investing over $ 4.7 billion (US) in the Athabasca oil sands field project.[cxci] By solidifying a claim to these natural resources, the Chinese Government solidified its claim to a vast resource, placating Canada economically and further isolating the US, both politically and economically.

Stratagems for gaining cyberground

The twenty-fifth Ancient Chinese military strategy comes from the Six Dynasties Period of China and is called "*Replace The Beams With Rotten Timbers*" the Mandarin Chinese version is 偷樑換柱 with a Pin Yin pronunciation of Tōu liáng huàn zhù. This stratagem states *"Disrupt the enemy's formations, interfere with their methods of operations, change the rules in which they are used to following, go contrary to their standard training. In this way you remove the supporting pillar, the common link that makes a group of men an effective fighting force."*[cxcii]

The Chinese PLA use this stratagem in the cyberapplication via the Communist Party of China (CPC), during which they favor negotiations with a political intent in mind, creating a feint for the enemy to believe in, while the Chinese PLA uses cyberattacks to achieve the actual goal. In 2011, the Chinese Government openly criticized Japan's worries over the defense modernization occurring in the 'Middle Kingdom' in an official Japanese defense memorandum. China's state news agency *XinHua* reported that Japan was engaged in ""China bashing", warning that the document could jeopardize relations between the neighbors"[cxciii]. Later that year major Japanese defense contractors Mitsubishi Heavy Industries (MHI) and Kawasaki were both cyberviolated by a hacker who knew and used Mandarin Chinese.[cxciv]

The Han Dynasty of China provides the twenty-sixth Ancient military stratagem *"Point At The Mulberry But Curse The Locust Tree"* which in Mandarin Chinese is指桑罵槐 with a Pin Yin pronunciation of Zhǐ sang mà huái. This strategy says that in order to *"To discipline, control, or warn others whose status or position excludes them from direct confrontation; use analogy and innuendo. Without directly naming names, those accused cannot retaliate without revealing their complicity."*[cxcv]

This indirect confrontation tactic is distinctly codified with PLA espionage, and applies to their objectives in the cyber realm also. Specifically, in 1995, Burma and China signed a joint intelligence sharing agreement.[cxcvi]

"Feign Madness But Keep Your Balance" is the twenty-seventh stratagem of Ancient China from the Sui Dynasty Period. The Mandarin Chinese is假癡不癲 and the Pin Yin pronunciation is Jiǎ chī bù diān. This is a strategy which says *"Hide behind the mask of a fool, a drunk, or a madman to create confusion about your intentions and motivations. Lure your opponent into underestimating your ability until, overconfident, he drops his guard. Then you may attack."*[cxcvii]

This philosophy of feigning an ability to conduct cyberwarfare, is most certainly already part of the PLA's IW doctrine, denied numerous times by the Chinese Government in response to claims that the Chinese is behind cyberattacks.[cxcviii] By stating that they do not hack, they create an effective disinformation campaign to mask their true cyberintentions.

The twenty-eighth stratagem "*Lure Your Enemy Onto the Roof, Then Take Away the Ladder*" comes from the Han Dynasty and Mandarin Chinese is 上屋抽梯 with a Pin Yin pronunciation of Shàng wū chōu tī. This military philosophy of Ancient China states "*With baits and deceptions lure your enemy into treacherous terrain. Then cut off his lines of communication and avenue of escape. To save himself he must fight both your own forces and the elements   of   nature.*"[cxcix]
This strategy is another excellent use of deception in the PLA IW doctrine. In this way the Chinese cyberarmy maps out the opponent's information networks, makes plans for disruption through denial of service attacks and formulates plans for secondary attacks on critical infrastructure, while the nation's military is focusing on regaining command and control of its communications capabilities.

The Three Kingdoms Period in Chinese history provides the twenty-ninth strategy and reads "*Tie Silk Blossoms to the Dead Tree*" which in Mandarin Chinese is 樹上開花 with a Pin Yin pronunciation of Shù shàng kāihuā. This parable of military thought says "*Tying silk blossoms on a dead tree gives the illusion that the tree is healthy. Through the use of artifice and disguise make something of no value appears valuable; of no threat appear dangerous; of no use, useful.*"[cc]

Applying cyberwarfare tactics, the PLA use a form of "honeypots" to draw a cyberattacker to a site, so that the malicious attempts can be recorded, traced and mitigated. An example this is the Matrix Chinese Distributed Honeynet Deployment Project, which was initiated with the support of Chinese Computer Emergency Response Team.[cci]

According to the Institute of Electrical and Electronics Engineers (IEEE), a "honeypot is a prominent technology that helps learn new hacking techniques from attackers and intruders (sic)."[ccii]

The thirtieth stratagem of that China's cyberwarfare doctrine is based on is "*Exchange the Role of Guest for that of Host*" in Mandarin Chinese 反客為主, with a Pin Yin pronunciation of Fǎn kè wéi zhǔ. The Literary Chinese translation is "*Defeat the enemy from within by infiltrating the enemy's camp under the guise of co-operation, surrender, or peace treaties. In this way you can discover his weakness and then, when the enemy's guard is relaxed, strike directly at the source of his strength.*"[cciii]

This is another economic tactic that directly supports follow-on PLA cyberstrategies, one in which Chinese SOE's are establishing special economic security zones within the US under the full endorsement of local municipal governments, gain a physical presence and then exploit economically with a physical Chinese presence on the ground. The SinoMach Corporation, a wholly-owned Chinese Government SOE, has begun the process of establishing and building a significant private compound near Boise, Idaho for industrial purposes.[cciv] [ccv]

Stratagems for desperate situations

The thirty-first stratagem comes from the Han Dynasty and stated as "*The Strategy of Beautiful Women*". The Mandarin Chinese is represented as 美人計 with the Pin Yin pronunciation of Měirén jì. This Ancient Chinese military axiom is translated from Literary Chinese "*Send your enemy beautiful women to cause discord within his camp. This strategy can work on three levels. First, the ruler becomes so enamored with the beauty that he neglects his duties and allows his vigilance to wane. Second, other males at court will begin to display aggressive behavior that inflames minor differences hindering co-operation and destroying morale. Third, other females at court, motivated by jealousy and envy, begin to plot intrigues further exasperating the situation.*"[ccvi]

This strategy is self-explanatory, physical espionage, and perhaps even more nefarious, applying the PLA's cyberwarfare doctrine, using it to their advantage offensively. Military technology, law firms, oil and gas industries are among the many focus areas of interest in PLA cybertargeting.

"*The Strategy of Open City Gates*" is the thirty-second Ancient Chinese military stratagem. It comes from the "*Three Kingdoms Period*" in Chinese history, the Mandarin version is 空城計 with a Pin Yin pronunciation of

Kōng chéng jì. The Literary Chinese translation is "*When the enemy is superior in numbers and your situation is such that you expect to be overrun at any moment, then drop all pretense of military preparedness and act casually. Unless the enemy has an accurate description of your situation this unusual behavior will arouse suspicions. With luck he will be dissuaded from attacking.*" [ccvii]

The thirty-third stratagem of Ancient Chinese history is "*The Strategy of Sowing Discord*" with a Mandarin Chinese version of 反間計 and a Pin Yin pronunciation of Fǎn jiàn jì. This strategy comes from the Six Dynasties Period and related that one should "*Undermine your enemy's ability to fight by secretly causing discord between him and his friends, allies, advisors, family, commanders, soldiers, and population. While he is preoccupied settling internal disputes his ability to attack or defend, is compromised.*"[ccviii]

This stratagem is applicable to both the 5th domain of cyberwarfare, as well as the traditional battlefield; when an army is on the attack, the course of action should be aggressive, decisive and swift. And when pressing the cyberattack, do so in an unpredictable manner, using hacking methodologies and hours of operation which the enemy is unlikely to expect (a surprise attack). This particular cyberstrategy is difficult for the PLA to incorporate given that they are used to regimen order and discipline.

"*The Strategy of Injuring Yourself*" is the thirty-fourth stratagem. In Mandarin Chinese this is stated as 苦肉計 while the Pin Yin pronunciation is Kǔ ròu jì. This strategy says "*Pretending to be injured has two possible applications. In the first, the enemy is lulled into relaxing his guard since he no longer considers you to be an immediate threat. The second is a way of ingratiating yourself to your enemy by pretending the injury was caused by a mutual enemy.*"[ccix]

This is more a tactic of feigning injury to create an illusion of helplessness and therefore encourage the foe to come closer before counterattacking. The application to Chinese PLA cyberdoctrine is similar to the use of a honeypot methodology; enable the adversary to be drawn to an unprotected network segment, gain information on their Internet network connectivity and then pursue hem vigorously allowing no chance of a counter-attack.

The thirty-fifth strategy of Ancient China is more akin to a tactic, but at nation-state level it applies very well; the PRC incorporation of this stratagem into PLA cyberdoctrinal development has been successful. It reads "*The Tactic of Combing Tactics*" with the Mandarin Chinese version of this is stratagem is 連環計 and the Pin Yin pronunciation is Lián huán jì. The Literary Chinese translation is "*In important matters one should use several strategies applied simultaneously. Keep different plans operating in an overall scheme; in this manner if any one strategy fails you would still have several others to fall back on.*"[ccx]

This tactic applies to anyone who has served in a combat zone or demanding environment where the safety of oneself and the comrades served with is paramount, maintaining situational awareness or "SA".

The final Ancient Chinese stratagem that applies to Chinese cyberwarfare doctrinal development is from the Ming Dynasty and states "*If All Else Fails Retreat*". The Mandarin Chinese version of this strategy is 走為上計 and the Pin Yin pronunciation reflects as Zǒu wéi shàng jì. The Literary Chinese translation of this prose is "*If it becomes obvious that your current course of action will lead to defeat then retreat and regroup.*"[ccxi]

While this retreating strategy is not in the Marine Corps warrior ethos, the applicability to a non-kinetic environment of cyber is apropos, especially for Chinese military IW doctrine. Obviously in the 5th domain there is only keyboard, mouse and monitor interaction with one's foes, however the aspect of being P@wned, having ones cyberassets compromised and used against one's own efforts, is a real possibility.[ccxii]

The next step in reaching an understanding on how 21st century Chinese warfare has developed is through the lens of Chinese military theorists such Senior Colonels Wang Baocun and Li Fei Major General Wang Pufeng.

CHAPTER 5: NATURE OF INFORMATION WARFARE

Information Warfare

During 1995, Senior Colonels Wang Baocun and Li Fei, who serve at Academy of Military Science, Beijing Military District of the People's Liberation Army, wrote a series of articles for the June 13th and June 20th editions of the *Liberation Army Daily*.

The application of Information Warfare within Chinese military cyberwarfare doctrinal development is very important. The theories and statements from both Senior Colonels echo the PLA's frustration of not being able to compete on the international combat arms stage, and exemplify the need for action within the Chinese military leadership to develop a cogent cyberstrategy.

Use of this important document is provided Courtesy of the Federation of American Scientists (*www.fas.org*)

"While the military officials of all countries have not yet defined information warfare (IW) authoritatively, military experts in many countries have delimited its implications. While such definitions may be imperfect and even somewhat biased, they are certainly of great benefit to our understanding of the innate features of information warfare."

In *Army* magazine (1994), Lieutenant General Cerjan, former US National Defense University President, notes, *"Information warfare is a means of armed struggle aimed at seizing the decisive military superiority and focused on the control and use of information."* General Sullivan, US Army Chief of Staff, holds that *"information is the most crucial combat effectiveness,"* with the essentials of *"battlefield information warfare"* being to *"collect, process, and use enemy information, and to keep the enemy from acquiring and using our information."*

A US combat theory analyst sums up the substance of information warfare in six points:

To obtain intelligence on enemy military, political, economic and cultural "*targets*," and to keep the enemy from acquiring intelligence on one's own similar "*objectives*."

To destroy or jam the enemy's C3I system, and to protect one's own C3I system.

To ensure our use of outer space information and to keep the enemy from using space information.

To establish a comprehensive data processing system that covers everything from sensing to firing.

To establish a mobile and flexible information and intelligence data base.

To use simulated means to help commanders make decisions.

Chinese experts who are studying high-tech warfare have also defined information warfare:

Information warfare is combat operations in a high-tech battlefield environment in which both sides use information-technology means, equipment, or systems in a rivalry over the power to obtain, control, and use information. Information warfare is a combat aimed at seizing the battlefield initiative; with digitized units as its essential combat force; the seizure, control, and use of information as its main substance; and all sorts of information weaponry [smart weapons] and systems as its major means. Information warfare is combat in the area of fire assault and operational command for information acquisition and anti-acquisition; for suppression [neutralization] and anti-neutralization; for deception and anti-deception; and for the destruction and anti-destruction of information and information sources.

We hold that information warfare has both narrow and broad meanings. Information warfare in the narrow sense refers to the US military's so-called "battlefield information warfare," the crux of which is "command and control warfare." It is defined as the comprehensive use, with intelligence support, of military deception, operational secrecy, psychological warfare, electronic warfare, and substantive destruction to assault the enemy's whole information system including personnel; and to disrupt the enemy's information flow, in order to impact, weaken, and destroy the enemy's command and control capability, while keeping one's own command and control capability from being affected by similar enemy actions.

The essential substance of information warfare in the narrow sense is made up of five major elements and two general areas.

The five major elements are:

Substantive destruction, the use of hard weapons to destroy enemy headquarters, command posts, and command and control (C2) information centers

Electronic warfare, the use of electronic means of jamming or the use of anti-radiation [electromagnetic] weapons to attack enemy information and intelligence collection systems such as communications and radar

Military deception, the use of operations such as tactical feints [simulated attacks] to shield or deceive enemy intelligence collection systems

Operational secrecy, the use of all means to maintain secrecy and keep the enemy from collecting intelligence on our operations

Psychological warfare, the use of TV, radio, and leaflets to undermine the enemy's military morale

The two general areas are information protection (defense) and information attack (offense):

Information defense means preventing the destruction of one's own information systems, ensuring that these systems can perform their normal functions. In future wars, key information and information systems will become "combat priorities," the key targets of enemy attack.

Information offense means attacking enemy information systems. Its aims are: destroying or jamming enemy information sources, to undermine or weaken enemy C&C capability, and cutting off the enemy's whole operational system. The key targets of information offense are the enemy's combat command, control and co-ordination, intelligence, and global information systems.

A successful information offensive requires three prerequisites:
1) The capability to understand the enemy's information systems, and the establishment of a corresponding database system;
2) Diverse and effective means of attack; and,
3) The capability to make battle damage assessments [BDA] of attacked targets.

Information warfare in the broad sense refers to warfare dominated by information in which digitized units use information [smart] equipment. While warfare has always been tied to information, it is only when warfare is dominated by information that it becomes authentic information warfare.

The IW Impact on Combat Concepts

The IW proposition will have an impact on many aspects of combat concepts:

It will make the rivalry over "information dominance" particularly intense. Certain experts note, "information dominance can be defined most easily and accurately as knowing all enemy information, while keeping the enemy from learning one's own." In future wars, most participating troops in most situations will be dealing not with material, but rather with information. The formation and development of troop combat effectiveness will rely mainly on information collection, processing, transmission, control and usage. A superior force that loses "information dominance" will be passive, beaten and in trouble, while an inferior one that seizes the information advantage will be able to win the battlefield initiative. As future combat actions will all be dependent and focused on information, the struggle to wrest information dominance will permeate everything and will be exceptionally fierce and intense.

76

It will expand the implications of warfare. This will be manifested mainly in two areas:

1) It will make it harder to win wars. In the agricultural age, it was necessary only to exterminate the enemy's armed forces to win the war. In the industrial age, in addition to wiping out the enemy country's military, it has also been necessary to destroy its military-industrial base. However, in the information age, it will be necessary not only to eliminate the enemy country's war-making "material base," but also to control and destroy the enemy's information systems, which will be the primary assault targets.

2) It will expand the limits of war into outer space. That is because the key IW systems space monitoring, positioning, guidance and communications systems will all be deployed there.

It will shorten the time of battle. The institution of IW will shorten future wars for two reasons:

1) On one hand, attack means will be highly precise, with the strike targets also being key enemy military positions, such as "brain centers," which can be forced to submit very quickly.
2) On the other hand, in the information age (as compared to the industrial age), the combat objectives pursued by both belligerents will be more limited, not total surrender or extermination of the other side, but rather limited, political objectives.

The IW Impact on Organizational Structure

Because of the "effects" of IW and military spending shortages, developed nations are adopting an equipment establishment policy of "more research and new technology, and less production and arms purchases." To implement this policy, they are taking three steps:

Terminating and adjusting preset unit development projects and purchase plans:

For instance, the US has eliminated over 150 arms production plans, and delayed over 20 equipment purchase plans; Germany has eliminated and postponed over 40 arms purchase plans.

Increasing their research input:

In past decades, the defense research outlays of Japan, the US, France and Germany have increased, respectively, by 120 per cent, 67 per cent, 66 per cent, and 56 per cent. Most of this outlay is going to develop the "crucial technologies" of smart ammunition, smart weapons platforms, and the C3I system.

Upgrading existing weapons:

While the Western nations are slowing their rate of production of new weapons, they are paying more attention to the use of electronic information technology to modernize and upgrade their existing equipment.

To be able to fight IW in the 21st century, developed nations such as the US will place priority on the development of equipment such as the C4I system (command, control, communications, computers, and intelligence system), personal digitized equipment, and stealth weapons.[ccxiii]

Information Warfare: A new form of people's war

In 1996, PLA military theorist, Wei Jincheng, wrote *"Information War: A new form of People's War"*, published in the Military Forum column, in the June 25th edition of the *Liberation Army Daily*.

The entire work, in English, is presented here as further statement on PLA military thoughts about future wars and how information warfare would be a critical element of successful Chinese PLA doctrine. The access and ability to cite this work is appropriately acknowledged by Courtesy of the Federation of American Scientists (*www.fas.org):*

"A future war, which may be triggered by a disruption to the network of the financial sector, may be combat between digitized units or a two-man show,

with the spaceman (or robot) on the stage and the think tank behind the scenes. It may also be an interaction in the military, political, and economic domains, making it hard to define as a trial of military strength, a political argument, or an economic dispute. All this has something to do with the leap forward of modern technology and the rise of the revolution in the military domain.

The technological revolution provides only a stage for confrontations. Only when this revolution is married with military operations can it take on the characteristics of confrontation. Some believe that the information superhighway, the Internet, computers, and multimedia are synonymous with commerce, profit, and communications. In fact, this is far from true.

Thanks to modern technology, revolutionary changes in the information domain, such as the development of information carriers and the Internet, are enabling many to take part in fighting without even having to step out of the door. The rapid development of networks has turned each automated system into a potential target of invasion. The fact that information technology is increasingly relevant to people's lives determines that those who take part in information war are not all soldiers and that anybody who understands computers may become a "fighter" on the network. Think tanks composed of nongovernmental experts may take part in decision making; rapid mobilization will not just be directed to young people; information-related industries and domains will be the first to be mobilized and enter the war; traditional modes of operations will undergo major changes; operational plans designed for information warfare will be given priority in formulation and adoption; and so on and so forth. Because other technologies are understood by people only after they are married with information technology and because information technology is becoming increasingly socialized, information warfare is not the business of armed forces alone. Conditions exist that effectively facilitate the participation of the public in information warfare.

Ideas Guide Action

In the information age, an all-new concept of operations should be established. Information is a "double-edged sword." In the information age, information is not only a weapon of combat but also the object sought after by the warring parties. The quantity, quality, and speed of transmission of information resources are key elements in information supremacy. That is why information is not just a piece of news and information weapons do not refer only to such information-based weapons as precision-guided weapons and electronic warfare weapons. The most effective weapon is information itself. Information can be used to attack the enemy's recognition system and information system either proactively or reactively, can remain effective either within a short time or over an extended period, and can be used to attack the enemy right away or after a period of incubation. Therefore, good information protection and launching a counterattack with information weapons when attacked will become the main subjects of preparation against war during the information age.

Information is intercommunicative and therefore must not be categorized by sector or industry. It is very wrong to think that information in only the military field is worth keeping secret and that information for civil purposes does not belong to the category of secrecy. In fact, if no security measures are taken to protect computers and networks, information may be lost. Similarly, if we think it is the business of intelligence and security departments to obtain the enemy's information and that it has nothing to do with anyone else, we would miss a good opportunity to win an information war.

In March 1995, Beijing's Jingshan School installed a campus network with 400 PCs, an "intelligent building" design, and multimedia technology. The school runs 10 percent of its courses through computers; students borrow books from the library through a computerized retrieval system; and experiments are conducted with demonstrations based on multimedia simulation systems. This illustrates in microcosm the many information networks that our country has built with its own resources. More than one million PCs were sold in China in 1995, and the figure is expected to reach 2.7 million in 1996. Faced with the tendencies of a networking age, if we looked upon these changes merely from a civil perspective and made no military preparations, we would undoubtedly find ourselves biased and shortsighted.

Information War Depends on the Integrity of the Information System

Information warfare is entirely different from the conventional concept of aiming at a target and annihilating it with bullets, or of commanders relying on images and pictures obtained by visual detection and with remote-sensing equipment to conduct operations from a map or sand table. The multidimensional, interconnected networks on the ground, in the air (or outer space), and under water, as well as terminals, modems, and software, are not only instruments, but also weapons. A people's war under such conditions would be complicated, broad-spectrum, and changeable, with higher degrees of uncertainty and probability, which requires full preparation and circumspect organization.

An information war is inexpensive, as the enemy country can receive a paralyzing blow through the Internet, and the party on the receiving end will not be able to tell whether it is a child's prank or an attack from its enemy. This characteristic of information warfare determines that each participant in the war has a higher sense of independence and greater initiative. However, if organization is inadequate, they may each fight their own battles and cannot form joint forces. Additionally, the Internet may generate a large amount of useless information that takes up limited channels and space and blocks the action of one's own side. Therefore, only by bringing relevant systems into play and combining human intelligence with artificial intelligence under effective organization and coordination can we drown our enemies in the ocean of an information offensive.

A people's war in the context of information warfare is carried out by hundreds of millions of people using open-type modern information systems. Because the traditional mode of industrial production has changed from centralization to dispersion and commercial activities have expanded from urban areas to rural areas, the working method and mode of interaction in the original sense are increasingly information-based. Political mobilization for war must rely on information technology to become effective, for example by generating and distributing political mobilization software via the Internet, sending patriotic e-mail messages, and setting up databases for traditional education. This way, modern technical media can be fully utilized and the openness and diffusion effect of the Internet can be expanded, to help political mobilization exert its subtle influence.

In short, the meaning and implications of a people's war have profoundly changed in the information age, and the chance of people taking the initiative and randomly participating in the war has increased. The ethnic signature and geographic mark on an information war are more pronounced and the application of strategies is more secretive and unpredictable.

Information-based confrontations will aim at reaching tangible peace through intangible war, maintaining the peace of hardware through software confrontations, and deterring and blackmailing the enemy with dominance in the possession of information. The bloody type of war will increasingly be replaced by contention for, and confrontations of, information.

The concept of people's war of the old days is bound to continue to be enriched, improved, and updated in the information age to take on a new form. We believe any wise military expert would come to the same conclusion."[ccxiv]

CHAPTER 6: CHINESE CYBERWARFARE DOCTRINES

Chinese Cyberwarfare Doctrinal Development

The Chinese People's Liberation Army (PLA) has been sensitive to continuous changes in international geo-political and geo-strategic contexts, as well as the changing nature of warfare overall. The PLA has fashioned responses to these nation-state strategic civil-military-political changes by developing appropriate military doctrines and strategies to meet future threats and challenges.

The Chinese PLA military doctrine has undergone a transition from 'people's war' to "people's war under modern conditions"; this is a historical fact and pre-requisite. Subsequent tactical strategic references "limited local war" have changed similarly to "limited war under high tech conditions".

The PLA's doctrinal concept of limited war under high tech conditions was formulated as a response to what it learned from observing the US military during *'Operation Desert Storm'*. The PLA saw and realized particular tactical and strategic value, especially from the American military within the areas of information technologies and knowledge-based warfare.

During 2004, China published a white paper focused on the People's Republic of China's National Defense. The paper detailed the rapid promotion of a Revolution in Military Affairs (RMA) with Chinese characteristics through the construct and development of an *'informationized'* force.

The Chinese PLA concept of *"limited war under high tech conditions"*, a cornerstone of military doctrine for greater than 10 years, was being replaced by *"local war under informationized conditions."*[ccxv]

Within the People's Republic of China since 1998, every publication written on China's National Defense has declared that the PLA adheres to the '*strategic concept*' of 'people's war' as part of China's '*military strategy*' of active defense.[ccxvi]

Even after an updated war fighting doctrine was issued in 1999, the '*People's War*' concept has remained a basic tenet of Modern Chinese military thought.

The concept is prominent in authoritative works like "*The Science of Campaigns*" and "*The Science of Military Strategy*", where 'people's war' is described as "*a fundamental strategy ... still a way to win modern war.*"[ccxvii] The White Paper mentions the main objective of PLA as:

"*The PLA, aiming at building an informationized force and winning an information war, deepens its reforms, dedicates itself to innovation, improves its quality and actively pushes forward the RMA with Chinese characteristics with an informationization" focus at its core.*"[ccxviii]

The Chinese cyberwarfare term '*informationization*' has its roots in asymmetric warfare. It covers a very wide range of information warfare and information operations terms. The concept of Chinese '*informationization*' also covers other military doctrinal terms pertaining to computer attack-based tactics and strategy, including intelligence and counter-intelligence based weaponry (including all elements of command, control, networked computers, wire line and wireless communications, intelligence collection, surveillance and reconnaissance (C4ISR)); included in this definition are traditional components of information warfare.

While '*informationization*' is only a sub-set of the RMA with Chinese characteristics, information warfare is a sub-set of '*informationization*'. For the PRC, it transcends the military doctrinal necessities and becomes an important national and strategic tool for shaping perceptions and belief systems of adversaries and competitors. The 2004 White Paper makes certain observations and places emphasis and focus.[ccxix]

Magnus Hjortdal (University of Copenhagen) writes in his paper "*China's Use of Cyber Warfare: Espionage Meets Strategic Deterrence*":

"*Means of information operations and automated command systems, information measures, sound organizational structures and advance weaponry and equipment, which possesses an integrated and complete array of information support and operational means.*"

The PLA will also continue the "*promotion of 'Informationization' of missiles and equipment, and improvements in communications and reconnaissance capabilities, especially of the Second Artillery Force.*"[ccxx]

According to the 2010 report from the PRC, called "*China's Defense in 2010*", there have been "*A series of projects on military information systems have been completed and information technology elements have been incorporated into battle systems and development support to military information structure has been guaranteed*".[ccxxi]

The Information Office of the State Council of the PRC goes on to report that the "*Development of new military and operational theories and increased emphasis on training for information warfare. Integration of military and civil resources for efficient information mobilization mechanisms for exploiting (information warfare doctrinal) synergies.*"[ccxxii]

Importance of Information Warfare

"*Informization*", a fundamental aspect of Chinese cyberwarfare doctrine, gives a unique perspective into the evolution of Chinese theories and concepts on Information Warfare (IW). In keeping with the consistent development of Chinese military theories and strategic perspectives, Chinese traditional wisdom and strategic thought is applied to all new concepts and precepts originating from the US or other post-industrial nation-states.[ccxxiii]

The PLA was the first military to seriously apply military theory, strategy and practice with the concept of information technology to develop cogent theories of IW. They went further by adapting Western military concepts and tactics about IW to "*suit local conditions.*"[ccxxiv]

In 1995, PLA Major General Wang Pufeng observed:

"*In near future, Information warfare will control the form and future of war. We recognize this developmental trend of information warfare and see it as a driving force in China's military and combat readiness. This trend will be highly critical to achieve victory in future wars.*"[ccxxv]

Major General Wang Pufeng further emphasized that China must use a practical combination of IW and Maoist and Marxist military thought to guide IW issues under military doctrinal design. The Chinese military must study ways of using inferior equipment to achieve victory over the enemy's superior equipment.[ccxxvi] He further advocated study on how to conduct "*People's war in the IW domain*". The underlying theme of Chinese concepts on IW has been emphasis on devising ways and means to attack an enemy's weaknesses and vulnerabilities, and on exploiting own strengths.[ccxxvii] Another fundamental assumption of the Chinese is one in which superior military tactics can compensate for inferior technology.

Timothy Thomas writes further in his paper "*Behind the Great Wall*" that "*According to some Chinese military analysts, because of the increasing relevance of information technology to people's lives, individuals who take part in IW are not all soldiers and that anybody who understands computers may become a fighter.*"[ccxxviii]

IW is an inexpensive military tactic and weapon; the tactical or strategic military objective can be delivered a debilitating and paralyzing cyberattack through the network. So effective are these cyberweapons that the adversary will probably never know where the cyberattack came from.[ccxxix]

The opponent is faced with a tremendous amount of useless information, which can be created to block or stop the functioning of an adversary's information system, typically known as a Denial of Service (DoS) attack. In true form, and keeping with Mao Tse Tung's concept of a 'people's war' in context of a IW campaign a cyberattack on a distant target (on the information network) can be carried out by hundreds of millions of people, using open-type modern computers.[ccxxx] Even political mobilizations for war can be achieved via the Internet, sending patriotic e-mail messages and setting up databases for education.[ccxxxi]

The concept of a 'People's War' is further supported and evidenced by another Chinese author, who observes that *"even as ... government mobilized troops, the numbers and roles of traditional warriors will be sharply less than those of technical experts... since thousands of personal computers can be linked up to perform a common operation, to perform many tasks in in place of a large-scale military computer, an IW victory will very likely be determined by which country can mobilize the most computer experts and part-time fans ... That will be a real People's War."*

Preparing for 'people's war' is a recurring theme in Chinese writing. This concept has found practical expression in turning some of the 1.5 million reserve forces into mini-IW regiments.

The People's Armed Forces Department (PAFD) has reportedly organized militia/reserve IW regiments at district levels in many provinces. At the Echeng district of Hubei province, the PAFD has a network warfare battalion, as well as electronic warfare, intelligence and psychological warfare battalions, and also a training base for IW activities. The PAFD has also carried out an *"Informaticised People's Warfare Network Simulation Exercise"*.[ccxxxii] A version of this concept was also put into practice following the bombing of the Chinese embassy in Belgrade on May 8, 1999, during *'Operation Allied Force'*. The Chinese hacked a number of US political, military and diplomatic websites, and carried out a network battle, mobilizing thousands of net users to send e-mails and viruses, causing servers to crash, and paralyzing a large number of websites.[ccxxxiii]

Concerns about China's cyberwar capability were heightened after the *'Titan Rain'* attacks on US defense computer systems, and after the Chinese cybermilitia carried out IW exercises. The Chinese targeted countries including India, the US, Taiwan, Germany, England and Japan.[ccxxxiv] The aim was to disrupt critical infrastructure (banking, power supply and telecommunication networks) as part of China's strategy of asymmetric approach to warfare.

Chinese cyberdoctrine focuses on precise methods of targeting via connected networks. The first cyberweapon methodology is the use of e-mails for planting viruses; the second cybermethod is called 'phishing' and the third cyberweapon used is the introduction of "intelligent Trojan's" and "vacuum Trojans".[ccxxxv] Diverse routes of planting Trojans and viruses have been used to attack critical networked computers, which in turn send out the requested files or cause significant damage to the networked infrastructure, including malfunctions.[ccxxxvi]

Cyberthreats are becoming more automated and easy to implement and use; one such example is a vacuum Trojan, which extracts information from a pen drive automatically when connected to a USB port.[ccxxxvii]

Another example is in Nanjing, where the PLA has developed more than 250 Trojans and similar cyberhacking tools. Here, foreign companies were made to hand over 300 computer viruses by the Ministry of Public Security's lab in an effort to speed up the certification of antivirus products.[ccxxxviii] In 2004, the Chinese Academy of Sciences, which provides suggestions about national information security policy and law, established the State Lab for Information Security. The lab developed a "National Attack Project" as one of its focused research programs. Select professionals have also been inducted into militia organizations to boost cybercombat capabilities in future wars.[ccxxxix] Ultimately, the PRC has been developing offensive IW strategies for utility in future wars in cyberspace. No doubt, this offensive cybercapability will also be meted to a consistently developed defensive cybercapability.

Goals of Chinese Information Warfare

The Chinese understanding of IW, which was initially based on Western concepts, has increasingly moved towards evolving its own orientation.[ccxl] The goal is to "*force the enemy to regard their goal as our goal, to force the opponent to give up the will to resist and end confrontation and stop fight by attacking enemy's perceptions and belief via information energy.*"[ccxli]

In December 1999, Xie Guang, the then Vice Minister of Science and Technology and Industry for National Defense, defined IW as war via the use of information; an overall use of all manner of various types (of) information technologies, equipment and systems, particularly via command and control systems, to create friction within the determination of an adversary's policy makers; simultaneously, use of every means possible to ensure that that inherent network information systems remain undamaged and undisturbed, that C4SRI remains intact and usable in the face of a cyberattack. The Chinese regard this definition as one which includes all the necessary aspects of IW's goals at the strategic national level within China.[ccxlii]

Qiao Liang and Wang Xiang Sui, both PLAAF Senior Colonels wrote in "*War Without Limits*" that the elements of IW are:

"Substantive destruction, the use of hard weapons to destroy enemy headquarters, command posts, and command and control (C2) information centers;

Electronic warfare, the use of electronic means of jamming or the use of anti-radiation [electromagnetic] weapons to attack enemy information and intelligence collection systems such as communications and radar;

Military deception, the use of operations such as tactical feints [simulated attacks] to shield or deceive enemy intelligence collection systems; operational secrecy, the use of all means to maintain secrecy and keep the enemy from collecting intelligence on our operations;

Psychological warfare, the use of broadcast television, radio, and leaflets to undermine the enemy's military morale."[ccxliii]

The two main areas of Chinese IW are information protection (defense) and information attack (offense).

Information defense means preventing the destruction of one's own information systems, ensuring that these systems can perform their normal functions. In future wars, key information and information systems will become "combat priorities", the key targets of enemy attack. It also includes many other manifestations of IW, like computer virus warfare, precision warfare and stealth warfare, all dependent in some manner on information and software programs.^{ccxliv}

Information Operations (IO) are specific operations and are considered to be at the core of IW, in the same manner as IW is considered to be at the core of 'informization'. In fact, IO is a manifestation of IW on the battlefield. It can be both defensive and offensive, and can be conducted at the strategic, operational, campaign and tactical levels at times of peace, wars and crises.

Principles of IO have been defined by Chinese military authors to include centralized command, decentralized control (multi-level power delegation), multi-dimension inspection and testing, timely decision-making and integration of military and civil actions, with focus on key links. Major General Dai Qingmin, Director of PLA's General Staff responsible for IW and IO (and also ex-Commander of PLA's IW Centre in Wuhan) observes that integrated and joint information operations give more scope and purpose to 'people's war'. He defines IO as a series of operations with an *'informationized'* environment as the basic battlefield condition, with military information and information systems as the direct operational targets and electronic warfare (EW) and computer networks as the principal form. He has outlined various IO strategies because, according to the traditional Chinese approach, strategies can compensate for inferior equipment and technologies and, in the case of IO, it may also compensate for gaps in information or poor information about the enemy.^{ccxlv}

Significant tenets of Chinese military IO strategies:

1) Electronic jamming or executing sabotage directly against an enemy's network information infrastructures or "information systems".
2) Defeating via the use of combined sabotage the adversary's entire intelligence and information operational organization.
3) Rendering ineffective the adversary's ability to use any means of conducting information warfighting capabilities or capacities.
4) Wreaking disharmony and confusion within an enemy forces' planned air, land and sea force campaigns; ensuring the own organic-like capability to

warfight including a concentration on direct force control, arms fire direction and fire control measures.

5) Defining the adversary's battlefield picture so that a normative view of the combat operations is distorted, creating absolute confusion is mutually assured. The goal being one of diversion of an enemy so that the combat operational picture is only beneficial to one's own force composition.

6) Delivering a diversionary intelligence picture to the oppositional reconnaissance efforts through distinct diversionary preparation of an alternate battlefield picture.

7) Through the use of a successful disinformation campaign and assured false intelligence picture launch sufficiently successful counter attacks, so as to defeat an adversary's ability to conduct any offensive combat operations.

8) Through the use of all manner of technology including all possible spheres and avenues of approach "blind" and silence an enemy with "false" and fake operational information.

9) "Confusing an enemy or disrupting his thinking."

10) Delivering a manufactured operational perspective to an adversary who is absolutely wrong so that they make plans and preparations based upon an incorrect intelligence analysis.

11) "Causing an enemy to make a wrong judgment or take wrong action."[ccxlvi]

During Chinese military IW exercises, various methods of IO were practiced, and these can be viewed as tactics used within the electronic battlefield. These methodologies are:

1) Planting information mines
2) Conducting information reconnaissance
3) Changing network data
4) Releasing information bombs
5) Dumping information garbage
6) Disseminating propaganda
7) Applying information deception
8) Releasing clone information
9) Organizing information defense
10) Establishing network spy stations
11) Computer Network Operations.[ccxlvii]

Information warfare in Chinese cyberdoctrinal development has also included information technology networking. The PLA's RMA emphasis on military jointness and service integration also are unique to their integration of the various military and civilian information networks within the PRC, to achieve the combination of the 'People's War' and asymmetric warfare capabilities across the entire network infrastructure.

Timothy Thomas further exemplified the combination of military and civilian networks in his papers about Chinese cyberwarfare, in that the Chinese feel it necessary to prepare for a "*network people's war*".[ccxlviii]

In 2000, Major General Dai Qingmin had written about the distinct forms of IW as they apply to the Chinese military use of computer network operations (CNO).[ccxlix] According to Major General Dai the forms of information warfare include:

1) Operational security
2) Military deception
3) Psychological warfare
4) Electronic warfare
5) Computer network warfare
6) Physical destruction.[ccl]

Integrated Network Electronic Warfare (INEW)

Perhaps the closest true and legitimate Chinese cyberwarfare doctrine to date, developed by Major General Dai, is "*Integrated Network Electronic Warfare*" (INEW).

According to itlaw.wikia.com – INEW is defined as a true combined arms effect in cyberspace, including the use of "*traditional electronic warfare operations, such as the jamming of radar and communications systems,*" especially damaging to an adversary or enemy's networked information infrastructure when co-ordinated with deliberate computer network attack operations. INEW's goal is to deliver a decisive attack against an enemy's C4SIR, which creates a zero to none chance of a successful counterattack "in the early stages of a conflict."[ccli]

The PRC, which includes, when referring to network centric warfare (NCW), both the Communist Party of China (CPC) and the People's Liberation Army (PLA), involves both an offensive computer network attack (CNA) capability, as well as a computer network defensive (CND) parameter.[cclii]

In 2002, Major General Dai continued with his INEW theories and application towards Chinese cyberdoctrinal development when he wrote "*On Integrating Network Warfare and Electronic Warfare*".[ccliii] Thomas further reflected on Major General Dai's INEW & EW paradigm through the observation of what Dai considered most appropriate:

1) Achieving information superiority; definitions of information war and other terms, all with Chinese characteristics
2) Importance of information technology training
3) Information Operations (IO) centers of gravity
4) IO contradictions
5) Network weaknesses.[ccliv]

Thomas further stated that the Chinese definition of INEW, according to Dai, focuses on a series of both offensive and defensive combat operations that use the integration of electronic warfare and computer network warfare measures. These intentional disruption operations are focused on defeating normal operation of enemy battlefield information systems while protecting one's own, with the objective of seizing information superiority – similar to the US definition of IO. While network war disrupts processing and use of information, EW disrupts acquisition and forwarding of information. The core of computer network warfare is to "*disrupt the layers in which information is processed, with the objective of seizing and maintaining control of network space.*" EW is targeted at networked information systems and '*informationized*' weapons, in order to increase combat effectiveness. INEW is essential for the system-versus-system confrontation on the '*informationized*' battlefield.[cclv]

The annual report prepared by Northrup Grumman Corporation (NGC), "*Capability of the People's Republic of China to Conduct Cyber Warfare and*

Computer Network Exploitation", prepared for the US-China Economic and Security Review Commission, details how the PRC computer network operations (CNO) comprise network attacks, defense, and exploitation.[cclvi] In 2011, the DoD report "*Military and Security Developments Involving the People's Republic of China 2011*" detailed for the US Congress the People's Liberation Army military power capabilities; the PLA views CNO as critical to seize the initiative and "electromagnetic dominance" early in a conflict, and as a force multiplier.[cclvii]

The Chinese PLA's use of an '*informationized*' force multiplier demonstrates their effective integrated use of electronic warfare, computer network operations (CNO) and precision physical strikes against key C4ISR nodes to disrupt an enemy's battlefield network information systems.

The Chinese 'Cyber Command' capabilities with the PLA have established information warfare units to develop viruses to attack enemy computer systems and networks, and tactics to protect friendly computer systems and networks. Additionally, the PLA has increased the role of CNO in its military exercises.[cclviii] While the PLA initially constructed IW training standards to be defensive in nature, in keeping with President Hu Jintao's 2010 proclamation of defending the (Chinese) state and protecting its infrastructure, PLA military cyberexercises have included the use of offensive cybertactics and operations with the intent to be used as fundamental initial cyberstrikes against enemy networks.[cclix]

The 'Three Warfares' concept

The Chinese Communist party (CPC) and the Central Military Commission (CMC), issued approval of the '*Three Warfares*' concept, 三种战法, pinyin pronunciation, (san zhong zhanfa), in 2003. The '*Three Warfares*' is largely based on the PLA concept of cyberwarfare in their operational documentation known as "*Regulation on the Political Work*".[cclx]

The '*Three Warfares*' is the PLA information warfare concept, also known as "*informization*", aimed at influencing the psychological dimensions of military activity. The critical elements of the '*Three Warfares*':

Psychological Warfare seeks to undermine an enemy's ability to conduct combat operations through psychological operations aimed at deterring, shocking and demoralizing enemy military personnel and supporting civilian populations.

Media Warfare is aimed at influencing domestic and international public opinion to build public and international support for China's military actions and to dissuade an adversary from pursuing policies perceived to be adverse to China's interests.

Legal Warfare uses international and domestic laws to gain international support and manage possible political repercussions of China's military actions.[cclxi]

The PRC's concept of 21st century warfare

During the past quarter century, both civilian and military strategists within the PRC have debated the nature of modern warfare. Sources of these discussions are taken from PLA strategic traditions and its historical experiences to provide perspective on the *'revolution in military affairs,' 'asymmetric warfare,'* and *'informationization'* war.

These academic and military based viewpoints shed some enlightenment on PRC interest in not using traditionally kinetic warfare, instead focusing on the increased role of economic, financial, information, legal and psychological instruments of PLA *'informization'* theory and war planning.

PLA Academy of Military Science doctrinal publication, *Science of Military Strategy*, highlighted their holistic and multidimensional view of warfare. Of important note is that "*war is not only a military struggle, but also a comprehensive contest on fronts of politics, economy, diplomacy, and law.*"[cclxii]

These *'warfares'* are being developed for use in conjunction with other military and non-military operations, such as attempting to influence international organizations that have both judicial and non-judicial authority in the international arena.

China has incorporated its Legal Warfare concept into its attempts to shape international opinion and interpretation of the UN Convention on the Law of the Sea (CLOS), moving away from long-accepted norms of freedom of navigation and territorial limits toward increased sovereign authority out to the 200-nautical mile Exclusive Economic Zone, the airspace above it, and possibly outer space.[cclxiii]

Another example of China's application of Legal Warfare was September 12, 2011, when China along with Russia and several other nation-states, submitted "*the International Code of Conduct for Information Security*" to the United Nations. In this proposed treaty, "*it raises a series of basic principles of maintaining information and network security which cover the political, military, economic, social, cultural, technical and other aspects. The principles stipulate that countries shall not use such information and telecom technologies as the network to conduct hostile behaviors and acts of aggression or to threaten international peace and security and stress that countries have the rights and obligations to protect their information and cyberspace as well as key information and network infrastructure from threats, interference and sabotage attacks. They advocate establishing a multilateral, transparent and democratic international Internet governance mechanism, fully respecting the rights and freedom of information and cyberspace with the premise of observing laws, helping developing countries develop the information and network technologies and co-operating on fighting cyber-crimes.*"[cclxiv]

Secrecy and Deception in PLA Military Strategy

PLA doctrinal writings point to a working definition of strategic deception as "*[luring] the other side into developing misperceptions . . . and [establishing for oneself] a strategically advantageous position by producing various kinds of false phenomena in an organized and planned manner with the smallest cost in manpower and materials.*" In addition to information operations and conventional camouflage, concealment and denial, the PLA draws from China's historical experience and the traditional role that stratagem and deception have played in Chinese doctrine. Recent decades have witnessed within the PLA a resurgence of the study of classic Chinese military figures Sun Zi, Sun Pin, Wu Qi, and Shang Yang and their writings, all of which highlight the centrality of deception.

There is uncertainty regarding how the tendencies of China's military and security establishment toward secrecy will conflict with the demands of the integrated global economy, which depends upon transparency and the free flow of information for success. This contradiction notwithstanding, the CCP's institutional emphasis on secrecy, acting in tandem with the PLA's use of denial and deception to cover force modernization and disposition, supports opacity in national security affairs, which could lead to miscalculation or misunderstanding by outsiders of China's strategic intentions. Conversely, overconfidence among China's leaders in the uncertain benefits of stratagem and deception might lead to their own miscalculation in crises. In addition, the same skills commanders use against adversaries are often used to slow – or cover up – the revelation of bad news internal to the PLA. Secrecy and deception, therefore, may serve to confuse China's leaders as much as it does its adversaries.

Asymmetric Warfighting

Ancient Chinese military strategists Sun Tzu and his great grandson, Sun Pin remain filially connected to today's PLA and modern warfare strategy and tactics. China continues to search out methods of defeating an adversary, including "*by avoiding his strong points and attacking his weak points.*" PLA strategic and military writings focus on identifying military technologies and doctrines by which a weaker force could defeat one that is stronger.

In fact from the Ministry of National Defense of the People's Republic of China, the PLA has codified a study of several Ancient Chinese Military Strategists.

Sun Tzu explained in great detail the intricacies of his thinking on waging war. "*Weakness*" in military terms implies fragility, or areas of unpreparedness, and weak points. "*Strength*" in military terms means might or preparedness, as well as strong points.

Sun Tzu advocated that in warfare one must "*avoid what is strong and strike at what is weak*" to the greatest extent possible, thus avoiding the enemy's strong points and well-prepared areas, and attacking his weak points and unprepared areas.

The basis of this idea is to avoid meeting force with force, to compare strength and dissipate your resources. Instead, he emphasized discovering and accurately selecting your enemy's weakest points in order to strike at them, for the greatest effect and victory with the smallest cost. As has already been discussed, in military strategizing Sun Tzu believed in "*conquering an enemy easily conquered*". The way to achieve this is by enhancing self-development, increasing national strength, establishing yourself in an impregnable position, and waiting for the enemy to show his weaknesses.

Sun Tzu said: "*That you are certain to take what you attack is because you attack a place the enemy does not or cannot protect.*" He also said: "*Your offensive will be irresistible if you plunge into the enemy's weak points,*" as well as: "*Troops thrown against the enemy as a grindstone against eggs is an example of the strong beating the weak.*"

A Qi State militarist slightly after Sun Tzu's lifetime thoroughly explained: "*In any war, you will be rebuffed if you strike at strong points; striking at weak points will meet with great success. If you attack the strong points, even a weak enemy will become formidable. If you attack the weak points, even a strong enemy will become defeatable*". That is to say, if you attack its strengths or prepared points, a weak enemy will seem to be strong; if you attack its weaknesses or unprepared points, a strong enemy will become weak.[cclxv]

Looking at the famous Battle of Guandu, this point can be very well attested. In the late 2nd century AD and early 3rd century AD, during a chaotic time followiing the collapse of the Han Dynasty, there was a surge of outstanding politicians and militarists such as Cao Cao, Liu Bei, Zhu Geliang, Sun Quan and Zhou Yu; they all struggled to reunite the country. Every man, woman and child in China knows their heroic stories, of which the Battle of Guandu is one.

In 200 AD, when Cao Cao was working to unite Northern China, he came upon the fierce attack of a mighty enemy, Yuan Shao. They maintained a standoff in Guandu (located in Zhongmou County of today's Henan Province) for several months. Cao Cao's army was smaller in size and had few provisions. The soldiers were worn-out and could hardly hold on. Just at this time, Cao Cao happened to receive intelligence from one who had surrendered from Yuan's army. Over 10,000 chariots of supplies were stored in Wuchao. This was the Yuan army's last supplies, and there were no great numbers of troops to defend them.

Cao Cao acted immediately, personally leading 5,000 elite troops on a night mission to raid Wuchao, destroying all the provisions stored there. The morale of the Yuan army was shaken, there were internal rifts, and the Cao army jumped on this opportunity to attack. The core of the Yuan army was destroyed.

Cao Cao used this key moment to strike out at the enemy's weakest point, successfully changing the course of the war and obtaining a decisive victory.

This example illustrates that the key to "*avoiding what is strong and striking at what is weak*" is to discover, seize hold of, and accurately strike at the enemy's weakness to inflict a fatal wound. If you only strike at several nonessential weak points, this is not to "*avoid what is strong and strike at what is weak*"; rather, it is a passive war strategy and has no benefits, only detriments."[cclxvi]

Since the 1991 Persian Gulf War and '*Operation Allied Force*' (1999), PLA military strategists have emphasized using asymmetric approaches to level the playing field against technologically superior opponents.

"[A] strong enemy with absolute superiority is certainly not without weakness... [O]ur military preparations need to be more directly aimed at finding tactics to exploit the weaknesses of a strong enemy."[cclxvii]

"[The] application of non-nuclear high technologies can bring about strategic effects similar to that of nuclear weapons, and at the same time, it can avoid the great political risk possibly to be caused by transgressing the nuclear threshold ... Among other things, following the advent of cyber information age, information warfare and information warfare strategy are widely drawing attention."[cclxviii]

The components of China's approach to asymmetric warfare can be seen in its heavy investment in ballistic and cruise missile systems; undersea warfare systems, including submarines and advanced naval mines; counter space systems; computer network operations (CNO); special operations forces; and the non-kinetic elements of the '*Three Warfares*' concept.

The Chinese have closely examined and studied examples of US and coalition warfighting practices since 1991. Beijing hopes to develop approaches to waging future conflict by adapting and emulating lessons learned in some areas while seeking perceived vulnerabilities that could be exploited through asymmetric means in others. Examples of some current thinking in China on asymmetric warfare include:

Counterspace: The PLA has developed a variety of kinetic and non-kinetic weapons and jammers to degrade or deny an adversary's ability to use space-based platforms. China also is researching and deploying capabilities intended to disrupt satellite operations or functionality without inflicting physical damage. The PLA is also exploring satellite jammers, kinetic energy weapons, high-powered lasers, high-powered microwave weapons, particle beam weapons, and electromagnetic pulse weapons for counterspace application.

Missiles/C4ISR: By fusing advanced ballistic and cruise missiles with a modern C4ISR architecture, the PLA is seeking to build the capability to degrade a potential adversary's force generation and sustainment by holding at risk or striking aircraft carriers, logistics nodes, and regional bases.

"*Non-Contact*" Warfare: An example of China's current thinking on asymmetric warfare is encapsulated by a military theory termed "*non-contact*" which seeks to attain a political goal by looking for auxiliary means beyond military boundaries or limits.

Examples of "*Non-Contact Warfare*" include: cyberwarfare against civilian and military networks – especially against communications and logistics nodes; fifth column attacks, including sabotage and subversion, attacks on financial infrastructure; and information operations.

Assassin's Mace Programs

As part of China's asymmetric warfighting strategy, the PLA has developed capabilities, referred to as "*assassin's mace*" programs, designed to give technologically-inferior military advantages over technologically-superior adversaries, and thus change the direction of a war. Since 1999, the term has appeared more frequently in PLA journals, particularly in the context of fighting the US in a Taiwan conflict.

It is unclear what platforms are specifically designated as *"assassin's mace."* However, descriptions of their intended use and effects are consistent with PLA asymmetric warfighting strategy. In this context, systems designated as *"assassin's mace,"* are most likely a mixture of new technologies and older technologies applied in innovative ways.

Major General Dai Qingmin's Cyberwar

One of the most important treatises on Chinese cyberwarfare is a paper written by Major General Dai Qingmin, called '*Operation Strategies and a People's War*'. Major General Dai Qingmin was director of the Chinese People's liberation Army's (PLA's) Communications Department of the General Staff.

General Dai was responsible for information warfare and operations for the PLA. He was quoted saying: "*new technologies are likely to find material expression in informationized arms and equipment which will, together with information systems, with sound, light, electronics, magnetism, heat and so on, turn into a carrier of strategies.*"[cclxix]

Chinese IW strategies rely then on curious and unique ways to fulfill ancient military stratagems such as to "*kill with a borrowed sword*" or "*exhaust the enemy at the gate and attack him at your ease.*" The Chinese, in designing and crafting cyberwarfare, believe that superior strategies, based upon those of both Sun Tzu and Sun Pin, can help overcome technological deficiencies.[cclxx]

Major General Dai also wrote "*Innovating and Developing Views on Information Operations.*" General Dai communicates his definition of information operations as "*a series of operations with an information environment as the basic battlefield condition, with military information and an information system as the direct operational target, and with electronic warfare and a computer network war as the principal form.*"[cclxxi]

Timothy L. Thomas wrote of '*China's Electronic Strategies*' in the May-June 2001 issue of *Military Review*: "*Major General Dai's article is an important benchmark in PLA military philosophy. First, he is a very credible and responsible figure. Before his present job, Dai commanded the PLA's Information Warfare Center in Wuhan. Second, he defines IW and IO with Chinese characteristics that are different from US definitions. Third, Dai broke tradition and advocated pre-emptive attack to gain the initiative and seize information superiority. This offensive emphasis contradicts China's military strategy of active defense. Finally, he noted that integrated and joint IO gives more scope and purpose to a people's war. Dai's article also indicates that China is clearly developing strategies to implement IW with Chinese characteristics. Other writers support his view with their own approaches to strategic IW.*"[cclxxii]

Since these information warfare operations are trials of strength focusing on knowledge and strategies, General Dai recommends a "*focus on strategies*" in order to form a basic springboard towards successful IW campaigns. Thus, as information technology changes and attack methodologies become obsolete, the strategies he espouses will formulate the fundamental basis for every successful IW campaign which follows. Reliance on organic or "*borrowed*" information technology innovations are thus irrelevant.

Yet, scientific and information security technology developments have given IW strategies a new battlefield. For success as an IW strategy, the initiative may include and contain different foci depending upon the unique and varied information security and warfare conditions. This then allows room for traditional Chinese IW strategies and for the creation of new IW strategies to created and designed based upon new information technology innovations. Such strategy enablers would include new information-confrontation strategies, such as adding strategic wings to technology or applying IW strategies in light of technology.[cclxxiii]

Thus, Thomas continues, the Chinese military view and constructive use of information "*technology finds expression in arms and equipment, then information systems and even electrons can be strategy carriers.*"[cclxxiv] Thus a good IW "*strategy can serve as a type of invisible fighting capacity; may make up inadequate material conditions to a certain extent; may narrow a technological or equipment gap between an army and its enemy; and may make up for a shortage of information, fighting forces or poor information operational means.*"[cclxxv]

General Dai further theorizes and is convinced the integration of military and civilian hacking forces can be enabled boldly by information systems, thus they are able to participate in IW and act as the PLA's significant information warfare reserve cadre during any future cyberwars the PLA is asked to conduct by the CPC.[cclxxvi]

In 1995, General Wang Pufeng wrote of enhancing Mao Tse Tung's people's warfare by combining the martial aspects of a military force and the specific desired technical skills of the civilian workforce. General Wang Pufeng wrote that integrating civilian and military specialists would breathe new life into Mao Tse Tung's theory of 'people's war'.[cclxxvii]

Appendix D has General Wang Pufeng's complete manuscript, incorporating the nascent 'People's War' with the advent of modern technology. Thomas further writes that *"ideas for uniting a people's war with IW are finding fertile ground in China's 1.5-million reserve force. Several IW reserve forces have already been formed in the cities of Datong, Xiamen, Shanghai, Echeng and Xian. Each is developing its own specialty as well. For example, Shanghai reserve forces focus on wireless telecom networks and double-encryption passwords."*[cclxxviii]

Conclusions

The PRC has seen how Western militaries have modernized their IW efforts during limited scale conflicts such as the First Gulf War. The PRC has also seen failure, when they witnessed, via television broadcast, during the US Army's infamous *"Black Hawk Down"* incident, as CNN broadcast a US soldier's body being dragged through the streets of Mogadishu, which transformed perceptions of US foreign policy from one of victory into one of defeat.[cclxxix] Senior Colonels Liang and Wang, authors of the infamous Chinese military IW theory *"Unrestricted Warfare"*, reflected on this US debacle: *"Did CNN's broadcast of an exposed corpse of a US soldier in the streets of Mogadishu shake the determination of the Americans to act as the world's policeman, thereby altering the world's strategic situation? And should an assessment of wartime actions look at the means or the results?"*[cclxxx]

Magnus Hjortdal writes that Western military observers must examine the Chinese model of a PLA cyberwarfare capability based on their concept of a civilian cybermilitia, and determine whether this civilian-military concept, of a cyberforce in readiness, would be appropriate or operate as efficiently in the West. Currently, there are Computer Emergency Response Teams (CERT) operating within military cybercommands, at the national civilian, state and municipal levels, solely responding to cyberattacks on civilian infrastructure; the concept is more defensive in nature. Perhaps the use of a non-defensive civilian cybermilitia would be more effective and necessary given the plethora of cyberhack attacks emanating from the PRC.

According to the Cox Report, the People's Republic of China has, throughout recent history, acquired state-of-the-art technologies from the West and Israel, via information warfare techniques. The Chinese have pilfered and spied, to upgrade PLA's cyberarsenal.[cclxxxi]

The PLA has applied Mao's 'People's War' concept to modern Chinese military IW doctrine to maximize the availability of a large number of civilian information technology resources. China has a large reservoir of scientists and an overheating internationally-based economy, which will help it in acquiring improved capabilities in the sphere of IW.[cclxxxii]

The PRC has made rapid advances in the field of information technology and computer network-based systems. Both of these modernizations will enhance military efforts by the PRC in eliminating the technology chasm with its economic and military nation-state competitors. The Chinese are able to dominate, through technological advances, the strategic and operational realms of cyberspace.

For the People's Republic of China IW is an important focus and doctrinal necessity, for the Communist Party of China at the strategic level, and operationally for the People's Liberation Army. Militaries worldwide have embraced both the information environment and information warfare as force multipliers, and as key cyberwarfare battle winning methodologies.[cclxxxiii]

Richard Crowell writes that a key force multiplier of the Chinese cyberwarfare doctrine is the electro-magnetic (EM) spectrum. Within the need for superiority as an IW campaign, the PLA sees EM as the *'operational high ground'*; their key contributing factor for success as an *'informationized'* warfighting force.[cclxxxiv]

China's rising military power has created concerns, not only for the US, but also its neighbors, which are equally if not more concerned with the possible destabilizing effects of a likely assertive China.

All of China's Asian neighbors need to evolve organic information warfare strategies to ensure their national and international information networks are safe and secure against the onslaught of 21st century Chinese cyberwarfare attacks.

The PLA knows that cyberdoctrinal development requires asymmetric warfare strategies based upon Mao Tse Tung's 'People's War' and the Chinese military theorists of Major General Wang PuFeng, Senior Colonels Qiao and Wang, as well as the Ancient Chinese military dictums of Sun Tzu. This combination of Communist doctrine, traditional Chinese kinetic military theories and modern Chinese information warfare thoughts, will serve the People's Republic of China well as it conducts 21st century cyberwarfare. China knows that its version of cyberwarfare can be used to deter and beat its modern Western rivals, especially the ones with better technological capabilities.

Rules of Engagement: PLA's Information Dominance

When considering the threat posed by the People's Republic of China, the following Rules of Engagement should be considered:

1) Consider the improbable
2) Understand your foe
3) Minimize cybergaps, maximize surfaces – channel the enemy
4) Educate your forces who are engaged in cyberwarfare
5) The Chinese cyberthreat is asymmetric and unceasing
6) Realize your country's will to defeat the Chinese cyberthreat must significantly outlast theirs
7) You will have setbacks, but learn from them, adapt and overcome the cyberthreat vectors
8) Simply throwing money, e.g. hardware, software and personnel at the Chinese cyberthreat is ineffectual at best – combined arms is a start.

CHAPTER 7: CHINA'S SIGINT CAPABILITIES

China and information warfare (IW): Signals Intelligence (SIGINT), Electronic Warfare (EW) and Cyberwarfare (CW)

'By knowing the enemy and knowing yourself, you can fight a hundred battles and win them all'.

Sun Tzu, 'The Art of War'

China is actively and extensively engaged in signals intelligence (SIGINT), electronic warfare (EW) and cyberwarfare activities. It ranks as the leader in Asia, in some important information warfare (IW) areas. China maintains the most extensive SIGINT capabilities of all the Asian countries. China has more SIGINT ground stations. Most of these were obtained from the Soviet Union in the 1950s, such as the large Krug circularly disposed antenna array (CDAA), and the Moon systems used for strategic SIGINT and HF DF operations; many of them have been considerably up-graded in the subsequent decades. China probably has more facilities for intercepting foreign satellite communications than any other country in Asia. It has the most SIGINT collection ships, and rivals Japan for the largest number of SIGINT aircraft. It has more tactical/battlefield ELINT/EW systems than any other country, reflecting the magnitude of its conventional forces.

Again, these are mostly based on systems supplied by the Soviet Union in the 1950s, such as the Watch Dog Electronic Support Measures (ESM) system installed aboard many Chinese Navy ships and submarines, the Stop Light ESM system used on the Whiskey-class submarines, the HF DF loops on numerous ships and submarines, and the Sirena radar warning receivers installed on the Air Force's MiG-19, F-4 and F-6 fighters.[cclxxxv]

During the 1980s, the People's Liberation Army (PLA), including its Navy (PLAN) and Air Force (PLAAF) branches, began to deploy a wide range of new SIGINT and EW systems of indigenous design (although derived from the Soviet systems). The defense modernization program which began in the early 1980s under Deng Xiaoping, guided by the strategic policy of 'People's War' under modern conditions', emphasized the importance of both command, control, communications and intelligence (C3I) and EW capabilities.[cclxxxvi] Chinese strategists began to consider the development of doctrine and operational concepts for IW, with the first book called Information Warfare being published in 1985.[cclxxxvii] New tactical SIGINT, EW and electronic counter-measure (ECM) units were formed by the PLA, equipped with truck-mobile ELINT, DF and jamming equipment, and trained to disrupt 'the enemy's radars and radios' and to destroy 'the enemy's command system'.[cclxxxviii]

The sustained, rapid growth in China's defense budget, involving double digit increases every successive year since 1988, amounting to more than 200 per cent over the last 15-year period, has provided extensive resources for the continued modernization of the PLA's SIGINT and EW capabilities, particularly airborne and naval capabilities.

An energetic round of new thinking, doctrinal change and organizational reform concerning IW operations was prompted by the performance of US forces in *'Operation Desert Storm'* against Iraq in 1991. The Chinese military leadership was impressed by the US operation, and especially 'the ease with which [the US forces] destroyed Iraq's largely Soviet and Chinese equipment'.[cclxxxix] The intelligence and EW aspects of the Gulf War were closely monitored by a special SIGINT unit located in Kashi, 1,700 miles from Baghdad, which intercepted large amounts of US and Allied military communications.[ccxc]

Special SIGINT units in the Chinese Embassies in Turkey and Iraq also intercepted communications and collected electronic intelligence on US and Allied military activities. These units reportedly intercepted intelligence that the ground phase of the war was about to start five days beforehand.[ccxci] Chinese defense analysts quickly appreciated both the Revolution in Military Affairs (RMA) and its IW dimension.[ccxcii]

A series of publications by senior military officers concerning IW were published in 1993-95.[ccxciii] Implementation of an IW plan began in 1995, and since 1997, the PLA has conducted several exercises involving cyberwarfare activities. The Ministry of State Security and other civil authorities have also become well-versed in cyberwarfare, partly through their attempts to establish a 'great firewall' around China's computer networks, and to strictly control Internet usage,[ccxciv] and because China is home to the most virulent non-governmental computer hackers in the world. Chinese strategists and military planners thoroughly analyzed the NATO air war against Yugoslavia in March–June 1999 ('*Operation Allied Force*')[ccxcv], which forced the Serbian forces from Kosovo, and were impressed by the efficacy of precision air strikes, often targeted with real-time intelligence (including imagery and SIGINT provided by UAVs), against the Yugoslav C3ISR (command, control, communications, intelligence, surveillance and reconnaissance) systems, and by the uselessness of the Soviet-made air defense systems against NATO's EW capabilities.

A special 'high-tech electronic espionage unit' was reportedly established in the military attaché's office in the Chinese Embassy in Belgrade, to collect electronic intelligence on US and Allied military activities (until it was bombed by the US on 7 May).[ccxcvi] Chinese strategists also closely monitored the war in Afghanistan ('*Operation Enduring Freedom*') in 2001–02, appreciating the potency of network-centric warfare, with integrated (or networked) command, control, communications, intelligence, surveillance, reconnaissance and electronic warfare (C3ISREW) systems, as well as the susceptibility of network-based forces to cyberwarfare.

The Third and Fourth Departments of the General Staff Headquarters (the Chinese national-level SIGINT agency), are responsible for managing China's strategic SIGINT capabilities and operations.[ccxcvii]

The Third Department was established in the early 1950s, with equipment supplied by the Soviet Union, primarily to provide strategic communications for the General Staff. It soon acquired the responsibility for strategic SIGINT operations. The first SIGINT stations were established along the eastern provinces across the Formosa Strait and in the northeast, to monitor signals from Taiwan and from US forces stationed in South Korea and Japan; e.g. at Nanking and Shenyang.

The Central Military Commission's (CMC) Third or Technical Department of General Service Headquarters is responsible for strategic SIGINT and has established a number of monitoring stations to intercept signals from countries such as India, Taiwan, Japan and South Korea.

In 1990, the PRC also established a Fourth Armed Forces Department, to look after offensive and defensive IW activities. It has also built "an information warfare simulation center" for training its network warriors. The center uses high technology simulation skills and equipment, to simulate information warfare and its environment. The Fourth Department has special detachments and units to manage and direct SIGINT and EW operations at all levels and includes Air Force and Navy operations.[ccxcviii]

The People's Republic of China has completed over one million km of fiber optics line and communication infrastructure ("Eight Horizontal Grids and Eight Vertical Grids"), supported by satellite, ground mobile receiving stations and ground-to-air data links.[ccxcix]

The Chinese have emboldened their cyberwarfare and information warfare capabilities by utilizing technologies appropriated from Western countries. The PLA has also taken advantage of successful organic commercial information technology and telecommunications manufacturers, in order to maximize the overall quality of its military cyberdoctrinal development. The PLA has acquired and deployed a wide variety of air, sea and land-based intelligence, surveillance and reconnaissance (ISR) systems, to enhance its ability to detect, monitor and target military activities in Asia and the West Pacific Ocean. Some of the latest programs include electro-optics, synthetic aperture radar, over-the-horizon radars, and surveillance systems that can detect stealth aircraft.

Through the 1960s, stations were established in the north and west to monitor signals from the Soviet Union, with particular emphasis on Soviet strategic missile developments and deployments (station locations included Lanzhou, Julemutu, Hami, Urumqi and Lop Nor). Other stations were established in the south and southeast to monitor signals from India, Burma, Vietnam and elsewhere in Southeast Asia (with stations at Chengdu and Guangzhou).

The headquarters of the Third Department is located at Zianghongqi, in the Haidian District of Beijing, about 8 km from the Summer Palace, on the northwest outskirts of Beijing. The Department's SIGINT net control station is located at Xibeiwang, about 5 km northeast of the HQ. The Department's principal SIGINT collection and processing stations are operated by the Third Bureaus attached to the headquarters of each of the Military Regions (Beijing, Shenyang, Chengdu, Guangzhou, Lanzhou, Jinan and Nanjing). These Bureaus also control several subsidiary SIGINT stations in each of their respective Regions. In the late 1990s, it was estimated that the 3rd Department had a staff of about 20,000 personnel.[ccc]

The Third Department is led by a very powerful figure in the Chinese political/military/intelligence structure. The first (and longest-serving) head was Lt Gen Wang Jheng, who headed the Department through the 1950s and into the early 1960s. Wang had served as a PLA radio operator in the 1930s, and as the chief of the PLA's communications activities (an organizational unit responsible for the PLA's strategic communications, communications security, and SIGINT collection activities) through the 1940s. He subsequently became Minister of the Fourth Machine Building Ministry, responsible for military electronics research and development.

Through the late 1960s and 1970s, the head was Major General Xiong Xianghui, who served simultaneously during much of this period as head of the Second (or Foreign Intelligence) Department of the General Staff Headquarters, and who was a close confidant of Premier Zhou Enlai. Xiong was intimately involved in the development of the rapprochement with the US in 1971-72. He provided the technical support for Henry Kissinger's secret visit to Beijing in July 1991, his follow-up visit in October, and President Nixon's historical visit in February 1992.[ccci] He was also the only military person present at the "private talk" between Nixon and Mao Zedong.

The previous head was Maj Gen Yun Shenbao, who was succeeded by Maj. Gen. Wang Jianren in mid-1993. General Wang had previously served as the Commissar, or the most senior political officer, in the Third Department.

In 1990, a Fourth or Counter-Electronic Warfare Department was established, at the same level as the Technical Department and the Second (or Foreign Intelligence) Department, reflecting the upgrading of China's tactical SIGINT and EW capabilities over recent years. EW was previously the responsibility of a branch in the Second Department. The HQ of the new Counter-Electronic Warfare Department was initially located with that of the Third Department (and that of the Second Department) at Xianghongqi, but in 1991 it was transferred to new facilities at Tayuan, southeast of the Summer Palace.

The Fourth Department has two major Special Detachments located at Xibiewang and Yangfang, which are responsible for the electronic warfare (EW) defense of key state and military headquarters and facilities in Beijing. Besides these two Special Detachments, which are run directly from the Fourth Department headquarters, units of the Department manage and direct SIGINT and EW operations for the Army through Military Region to Divisional levels.

There are, for example, several Counter-Electronic Warfare Department units in the Beijing Military Region, including a major unit at Xishan, in the western mountain area which has a general responsibility for the EW defense of the Beijing region. The Department also manages and directs SIGINT and EW operations for the Air Force and Navy.

The PLA SIGINT ground stations

There are several dozen SIGINT ground stations deployed throughout China, concerned with monitoring signals from Russia, the central Asian states of the former Soviet Union, Japan, Taiwan, Southeast Asia and India, in addition to internal communications. The two largest SIGINT stations are the main Technical Department SIGINT net control station at Xibeiwang, on the northwest outskirts of Beijing; and a large complex near Lake Kinghathu, in the extreme northeast corner of China.[ccii]

Another large SIGINT station in the Beijing area is in Nanyuan, just south of the urban area. There are also the Counter-Electronic Warfare Department's stations at Xibeiwang, Yangfang and Xishan, in the Beijing area. The large ground stations operated by the Third Bureaus of the Third Department, and attached to the headquarters of the seven military regions have different functional and geographic responsibilities. The Third Bureau's station at Lanzhou is responsible for monitoring Russian signal traffic and has the critical mission of providing strategic early warning of Russian missile attack. The station at Shenyang covers signals from Russia, Japan and South Korea; the station at Chengdu, controls Third Department SIGINT operations against India, and also has geographic responsibility for covering Pakistan, Tibet, Burma and some Vietnamese traffic. The Nanjing station has responsibility for monitoring Taiwanese signals; and the station at Guangzhou covers Southeast Asia, including part of Vietnam and the South China Sea.

Another large SIGINT station is located in the very northeast of the PRC, near Jilemutu, across from the Sino-Soviet border. Another monitoring facility is near Erlian, just off the Sino-Mongolian border. Near Hami, south of the Mongolian border is a third SIGINT monitoring facility. There are several other signals monitoring stations in the northwest, including those stations located at Urumqi, Zhaosu, Kashi and Luóbùpō, which are distinctly concerned with monitoring signal traffic responsibility in Russia, Kazakhstan and the various other central Asian republics of the former Soviet Union.

There is a large complex near Kunming, north of Indochina. There is also a large SIGINT complex on Hainan Island, mainly concerned with monitoring the South China Sea and the Philippines particularly when the US military bases were operational at Subic Bay, Capas Tarlac, Cubi Point and Clark Air Base. There are at least two major SIGINT stations in Shanghai, one of which is operated by the Navy and is concerned with monitoring naval traffic in the Yellow Sea and the East China Sea.

Additional SIGINT stations are located in the Jujian and Guangdong military districts opposite Taiwan. The Chengdu station, which controls SIGINT operations against India, is assisted by a sister station at Dayi, some 50 km west of Chengdu. Several stations are also located in the area along the border with Vietnam.

A large ELINT intercept station was built at Tachiu in the 1960s. The station is situated on a headland at 25°25'N and 119°37W, about 140 km from

Taiwan, and consists of an operations area atop a 1,368-feet-high coastal area, with a support area located at the base of the hill. In January 1969, there were 42 antennas in the operations area, including one VHF rhombic system, two Yagi antennas, eight discone antennas, 12 'mattress' arrays, seven solid parabolic dish antennas, six other parabolic dish antennas, one cut parabolic antenna, and two vertical arrays.[ccciii]

Many of the SIGINT monitoring stations were expanded during the 1990s. The large SIGINT complex at Lingshui has the responsibility for monitoring signals from the South China Sea, Vietnam and the Philippines. This monitoring station was 'vastly expanded by 1995'.[ccciv] The monitoring site at Lingshui, where more than 1,000 SIGINT analysts work, is located about 1.5 km west of the Lingshui military airfield, where the US Navy's stricken EP-3 SIGINT aircraft landed on 1 April 2001.[cccv]

Two large stations in Xinjiang (with one monitoring site at Dingyuanchen, used for monitoring communications in Russia and the Central Asian states, and the other monitoring facility at Changli, near Urumchi, used primarily for intercepting satellite communications) were both significantly improved and expanded during the 1999-2000 timeframe.[cccvi]

In 1978, the US reached tentative agreement with China to 'set up, install, man, equip and service a series of SIGINT sites along Urumchi, border with the Soviet Union'.[cccvii]

In April 1979, Vice Premier Deng Xiaoping indicated that these stations would have to be operated by China and that the data collected would have to be shared with China.[cccviii] Final agreement was reached in January 1980 to construct two stations, at Qitai and Korla in Xinjiang. Operations began in late 1980. The stations were constructed with equipment provided by the CIA's Office of SIGINT Operations (OSO), who trained the Chinese technicians that operate the stations, and periodically visited the stations to advise the Chinese operators and to service the equipment.[cccix]

Technicians from the PLA's Technical Department were trained at a SIGINT training center in Silicon Valley near San Francisco under the agreement.[cccx] Equipment originally installed at Qitai and Korla was designed to intercept telemetry from Soviet missile tests and space launches conducted from

Tyuratam near the Aral Sea, and anti-ballistic missile (ABM) and nuclear weapons tests in the Sary Shagan/Semipalitinsk area. Other COMINT and ELINT activities are also undertaken at these stations. It is believed that the US ceased its involvement in these stations in the early or mid-1990s.

Outside of the People's Republic of China, there is a SIGINT station established on Rocky Island (Shi-tao), near Woody Island (Lin-tao) in the Paracel Archipelago, in the early 1980s; the site is one of the highest points in the area, and provides excellent coverage of signal activity in the northwestern part of the South China Sea.[cccxi]

In 1993–94, China began to construct military structures on Mischief Reef in the South China Sea. These structures, including communications facilities, have been substantially expanded over the past decade. The communications systems include a small satellite communications dish and several HF and VHF antennas; the HF and VHF systems are capable of intercepting communications in these bands. It is also likely that the station is equipped 'to intercept radar signals'.[cccxii]

In 1991–92, Chinese technicians constructed a large SIGINT station at Great Coco Island, a Burmese island located just 50 km north of India's Andaman Islands, on the western side of the entrance to the Straits of Malacca. The station, which is operated by the Chinese PLA, provides intelligence on air and naval movements in the eastern Indian Ocean, and is able to intercept telemetry associated with Indian ballistic missile test launches over the Bay of Bengal.[cccxiii] A former Indian Defense Minister, George Fernandes, described this signal intercept facility as a "massive electronic surveillance establishment which is monitoring everything in India".[cccxiv]

Chinese technicians also assisted with the construction of six electronic surveillance stations along Burma's coastline, monitoring shipping between the Indian Ocean and the Straits of Malacca. These stations are located at Ramree Island, southeast of Sittwe, off the coast of Arakan; Hainggy Island, in the estuary of the Bassein River; Monkey Point, on the southeast side of Rangoon; Kyaikkami, south of Moulmein; Mergui; and Zadetkyi Kyun (or St Matthew's Island), off Burma's southernmost point, Kawthaung (or Victoria Point).[cccxv]

Three SIGINT stations were established in Laos in early 1994. The stations are in the southern province of Champasak, and monitor communications in Cambodia and Thailand.[cccxvi] The first Chinese SIGINT facility which is known to have been established outside China was a station near Sop Hau in Laos, in the mountains about 150 km west of Hanoi, which China maintained throughout the 1960s and into the early 1970s.[cccxvii]

In early 1999, following an agreement signed between China and Cuba, Chinese personnel began operating two SIGINT stations in Cuba. One is a large complex at Bejucal, just south of Havana, which has 10 SATCOM antennas. This signal intercept facility is primarily concerned with intercepting telephone communications in the US;[cccxviii] a cyberwarfare unit focuses on computer data traffic. The second, located northeast of Santiago de Cuba, at the eastern-most part of the country, is *"dedicated mainly to intercepting U.S. military satellite communications"*.[cccxix]

The People's Republic of China has developed extensive SATCOM SIGINT capabilities for monitoring international satellite communications. In December 1968, reports indicated that China had established *"a ground station for intercepting signals transmitted through US and Russian communication satellite systems"*, together with an associated decryption capability, on Hainan Island.[cccxx] The station is situated at the Lingshui, SIGINT complex.[cccxxi]

A second SATCOM SIGINT station is located outside Beijing. On 4 June 1989, Chinese authorities intercepted unedited video relating to the Tiananmen massacre, which was transmitted by the American Broadcasting Corporation via satellite. This video transmission intercept was then used by the Chinese authorities to track down and arrest a leading dissident.[cccxxii]

A third station is located at Changli, in western China, for monitoring satellite communications in central Asia.[cccxxiii] China has also established a SATCOM SIGINT station at Santiago de Cuba, at the eastern end of Cuba, to intercept US satellite communications.[cccxxiv]

116

A satellite tracking and control station at Kiribati, which sits astride the equator in the central Pacific, is also capable of intercepting selected (S-band) satellite communications in the mid-Pacific.[cccxxv] In addition, the four Yuan Wang and the Shiyan space event support ships are also equipped with extensive SATCOM monitoring equipment.[cccxxvi]

Airborne SIGINT capabilities

The Chinese Air Force (PLAAF) has more than 20 dedicated ELINT collection aircraft. This includes an assortment of HD-5s, at least one EY-8, eight HD-6s, and five Tu-154M aircraft. The HD-5, Hong Dian, or 'bomber electronic', ELINT aircraft, which entered service in the early and mid-1980s, are modified versions of the H-5 light bomber which is designed and based on the Soviet Il-28 Beagles, designed in the 1950s. In addition to ELINT collection operations, some HD-5s were configured for EW missions, including the provision of ECM support to the PLAAF's bomber fleet.[cccxxvii] It has not been a satisfactory system – it has limited range, and its EW equipment is old (mainly analogue).[cccxxviii]

More than a dozen HD-5s have been thought to be converted to the ELINT/EW role; these aircraft are being phased out as further HZ-6 and Tu-154M ELINT aircraft enter PLAAF EW service.[cccxxix]

In the late 1980s, at least one EY-8 ELINT aircraft was produced. The Y-8 four-engine turboprop is an indigenous development of the Soviet An-12 Cub. It was equipped with a BM/KZ-8608 ELINT system, developed by the Southwest China Research Institute of Electronic Equipment (SWIEE) in Chengdu, Sichuan, which is able to monitor the frequency spectrum of 1 to 18 GHz. It is designed to detect, identify, analyze and locate land-based or ship-borne radar emitters with a high probability of intercept, and with high sensitivity (-100 dBW) and accurate measurement of parameters. Frequency measurement is accurate to 5 MHz; and bearing accuracy varies from 5° for the 1-8 GHz range to 3° for the 8-18 GHz range.[cccxxx]

The HZ-6 SIGINT aircraft are converted H-6 bombers, the Chinese version of the Tu-16 Badgers, capable of a range of some 4,300 kilometers and an airborne dwell time of nearly six hours. These aircraft are reportedly equipped with the EL/L-8300 SIGINT system, produced by Elta Electronics

Industries in Israel, and consists of several elements: the EL/L-8312A ELINT section, the EL/K-7032 COMINT section (covering the HF, VHF and UHF communications bands), the EL/L-8350 command and analysis station, which fuses the COMINT and ELINT and reports to a ground station (EL/L-8353) in real-time, and an EL/L-8352 post-mission analysis station.[cccxxxi]

The People's Liberation Army Air Force (PLAAF) currently operates four Tu-154M Careless long-range transport aircraft modified for SIGINT collection.[cccxxxii] The first two of these were based at Nan Yuan airfield, south of Beijing.[cccxxxiii] Another Tu-154M SIGINT aircraft is operated by China United Airlines (CUA), the commercial arm of the Air Force; it uses civil markings (CUA B-4138), but was equipped in 1995 with a synthetic aperture radar (SAR), as well as COMINT and ELINT equipment for covert SIGINT operations.[cccxxxiv]

The development of PLAAF SIGINT systems is the responsibility of the Sixth (Telecommunications Technology/Intelligence) Research Institute, which is functionally subordinate to the PLAAF's Scientific Research Department, but is administratively subordinate to its Second (or Intelligence) Department, and which is located in northern Beijing. The primary missions of the Sixth Research Institute are development of telecommunications equipment for SIGINT collection, including both ground-based and airborne systems. A division within the Institute is responsible for the development of equipment for PLAAF SIGINT ground facilities along China's borders.[cccxxxv]

Chinese Naval SIGINT Activities

In addition to equipping some of its frigates for SIGINT operations, in the mid-1980s the Navy launched a series of new vessels for dedicated SIGINT missions. The first of these new SIGINT ships became operational in 1987–88. There are now more than a dozen of them, constituting the largest SIGINT collection fleet in Asia. They include the Xiangyang Hong 09 (V 350) 'oceanographic research' ship; the Xiangyang Hong 10, which is equipped with several large log-periodic antennas usable for COMINT purposes; the Xiangyang Hong 14; the Xing Fenghan (V 856); the Dadie class No. 841, which displaces some 2,300 tons, and which has been used to monitor US-South Korean Team Spirit exercises; the Yanbing (pennant number 723); and the three armed Yanha (pennant numbers 519, 721 and 722), which were completed in the late 1980s and which operate in the North China Sea.[cccxxxvi] Several 'trawlers' have also been configured for SIGINT operations (e.g. AGI 201).[cccxxxvii] In addition, the four Yuan Wang and the Shiyan space event support ships are capable of collecting missile and satellite telemetry and monitoring satellite communications.[cccxxxviii] One noteworthy naval SIGINT operation was the use of the Xiangyang Hong 09 (V 350) and an accompanying 'environmental research ship', Xiangyang Hong 05, in preparation for the Chinese actions in the Vietnamese-occupied area of the Spratly Islands in the South China Sea in March 1988. In October 1987, the two vessels began a careful survey of the Yongshu (Fiery Cross) Reef, obtained all the data needed for the pre-emptive seizure of the reef in March 1988, before Vietnamese forces could react.[cccxxxix]

Since 1999, Chinese spy ships have regularly been probing the waters off Japan. According to the Japanese Foreign Ministry, the number of instances in which Chinese spy ships intruded into Japanese waters, approaching to within 30-40 nautical miles of the coast, increased from four in 1997 to 30 in 1999.[cccxl] There have been numerous deployments of 'oceanographic research' ships to the area around the disputed Tiao Yu Tai Islands, as well as the waters around Okinawa.[cccxli]

In May 2000, the Yanbing AGI (No. 723), in an unprecedented move, passed through Japan's two most important straits, the Tsugaru Strait between Honshu and Hokkaido, and the Tsushima Strait off Kyushu. Interestingly, the vessel did not violate Japanese territorial waters by transiting through the Straits.[cccxlii] In August 2000, a Chinese spy ship 'equipped with sophisticated electronic monitoring devices' penetrated inside the 12-mile limit during a Chinese Navy war game.[cccxliii]

There are almost continuous SIGINT collection operations around Taiwan. The Ziangyang Hong 14, which "operates in the Taiwan Strait all year around", was found in Taiwanese waters and driven away by Taiwanese warships on three occasions in 2002.[cccxliv] In May, during Taiwan's Hankuang ('Han Glory')-18 military exercises, it was spotted off Chinpeng naval base. On both 9-10 October and 3 November, it was chased away from Lanyu

('Orchard Island'), 60 km southeast of Taiwan proper. The vessel's mission is believed to be one of 'intercepting Taiwan's communications'.[cccxlv]

Chinese PLA Electronic warfare

The People's Liberation Army has significantly, enhanced its mobile battlefield ELINT capabilities since the mid-1980s. In August 1987, it was announced that the Central Military Commission had implemented a large-scale restructuring of the PLA, including the formation of new electronic countermeasures (ECM) units. These units were evidently elements of six new combined group armies (CGAs) – the 39th and 64th Armies in the Shenyang Military District, the 38th Army in the Beijing MD, the 63rd in the Taiyun MD, the 67th in the Jinan MD, and the 12th in the Nanjing MD.[cccxlvi] They were equipped with truck-mobile ELINT, DF and jamming equipment.[cccxlvii] The mission-oriented task was one "disrupting the enemy's radars and radios, and of destroying the enemy's command system".[cccxlviii]

An example of the PLA's tactical SIGINT and EW capabilities was given by the Deputy Commander of the Chengdu Military Region in early 1986, when he recounted incidents from recent fighting on the Sino-Vietnamese border. In these incidents, the PLA SIGINT/EW units had been able to intercept and read Vietnamese Army radio transmissions, and to isolate and jam the radio net of the particular Vietnamese Army headquarters.[cccxlix]

The establishment of the Counter-Electronic Warfare Department in 1990 reflected a further enhancement of the PLA's tactical SIGINT and EW capabilities. As a result of Chinese assessments of the Gulf War in January-February 1991, the Department received additional funding and skilled personnel. The PLA has several different types of indigenously-produced ELINT and EW systems for tactical/battlefield purposes. These include the DZ 9001 ground-mobile ELINT system, the man-portable ZJ 9301-1 ESM system, the truck-mobile BM/DJG 8715 and Model 970 radar jamming systems, the WZ 551 radio intercept and radio/radar jamming system, and various HF/VHF radio intercept and DF systems, as well as EW systems, designed for use by PLA Special Forces.

The DZ 9001 ELINT system, produced by China National Electronics Import and Export Corporation (CNEIEC) in Beijing, covers the D- through J-bands (i.e. 1-18 GHz). It consists of a three-truck convoy, in which two vehicles carry deployable (scissors-lift) antenna radommes with the third being configured as a control center. A trailer carries a generator and other support equipment. The system has a DF accuracy of >3° RMS.[cccl]

The ZJ 9301-1 battlefield ESM system, also produced by CNEIEC in Beijing, provides a man-portable capability across the same frequency range. It has two configurations: one covers the D- through H-bands (i.e. 1-8 GHz), and the other the I- through J-bands (i.e. 8 to 18 GHz). This EW system is "able to handle between three and five detected radars simultaneously", with a Direction Finding (DF) accuracy of >4° RMS.[cccli]

The BM/DJG-8715 vehicle-mounted radar intercept and jamming system, produced by the Southwest Institute of Electronic Engineering (SWIEE) in Chengdu, operates in an air defense network, and is aimed at airborne radars, including missile guidance radars, missile seekers, navigation radars and terrain-following emitters. The system consists of one ESM station and up to eight ECM sites, integrated by means of data links to ensure automatic control, direction of jamming, and feedback of ECM data. Both the ESM and the ECM stations are mounted on self-propelled vehicles "to ensure high mobility". The system features a wide frequency coverage (I/J-bands, or 8-18 GHz), automatic classification and identification of a variety of radar threats, monopulse auto-angular tracking with high DF accuracy (5-8°), and a multi-threat jamming capability.[ccclii]

The Model 970 mobile radar jamming system, produced by CNEIEC, is primarily designed to protect high-value ground targets from air attack by interfering with airborne surveillance and navigation radars and radar-guided missiles. The system covers the I/J-bands (8 to 20 GHz). It has a receiver for measuring the bearing, frequency and other parameters (such as antenna rotation speeds) of hostile radars, which can be used in conjunction with a pulse analyzer to measure parameters such as pulse widths, pulse repetition frequency (PRF), radar illumination, etc. The equipment is contained in a trailer for rapid mobility, with the antenna system mounted on the roof. Operationally, a number of Model 970 units are placed some 3-5 kilometers from the protected area.[cccliii]

A variety of HF/VHF radio interception, DF, ELINT and jamming systems have been developed for use by PLA Special Forces. These light-weight, man-portable systems are used to conduct interception, jamming and deception missions against communications and radar systems.[cccliv]

The Chinese electronics industry has also produced a Radar Signal Environment Simulator, which can reportedly simulate 100 radar signals in order to deceive adversary ELINT collection and EW systems.[ccclv]

Since at least 1997, EW and counter-command and control missions have been regularly conducted as part of the PLA's large-scale exercises. In an exercise in Chengdu Military Region in October 1997, an EW scenario included both standard EW actions, such as distinct intercept, jamming, and electronic protection measure capabilities, and physical and electronic attacks by Special Forces against enemy command posts and communications facilities.[ccclvi]

Airborne EW systems

The PLAAForce has a limited range of EW systems, including tactical ELINT, ESM and ECM systems for air support operations, radar jamming systems for strike and fighter aircraft, and self-protection radar warning receivers (RWRs) for a wide variety of combat aircraft. All of them are produced by the SWIEE. The SWIEE also produced the BM/KZ 8608 ELINT system installed on the EY-8 aircraft, and used for both strategic and tactical ELINT operations. The PLA has also equipped some Z-9 helicopters for EW missions.[ccclvii]

The development of China's airborne SIGINT/ELINT/EW capability has been greatly assisted by Israel. The EL/L-8300 SIGINT systems installed on the HZ-6 aircraft were acquired from Israel.[ccclviii] The BM/KZ-8608 airborne ELINT system is a derivative of the Elistra CR-2800 ELINT/ESM system;

and the BM/KJ-8602 RWR "bears a strong resemblance in appearance and capability to Elistra's SPS-1000 RWR".[ccclix] In addition, China has reportedly also acquired other advanced airborne ELINT and EW equipment from Israel.[ccclx]

CHAPTER 8: CHINESE IW CAPABILITIES

Assessing China's IW Capabilities

China is the leader in IW in Asia, at least according to more quantitative measurements. It has the most SIGINT ground stations in the region, and the most EW sets installed aboard combat aircraft and naval combatants. The People's Republic of China collects voluminous diplomatic and military COMINT, facilitating crypt-analytical processes and providing invaluable strategic and military intelligence. It comprehensively monitors electromagnetic emissions from around its borders, collecting a massive amount of ELINT about the radars, EW systems and electronic sub-systems aboard weapons platforms maintained by neighboring defense forces. Its EW systems have been tested in large-scale field exercises more often than in most regional defense forces. Chinese mathematicians, linguists, electronics technicians and cryptologists are clever and accomplished. China has the largest number of practicing cyberwarriors, including both those employed in official defense, intelligence and state security agencies, and private citizens or citizen hacktivists.

Chinese strategists and military planners vigorously debate the latest technological developments and operational concepts, and the Central Military Commission and the PLA institute progressive doctrinal changes and organizational reforms.

But how good are China's IW capabilities? How well would they perform in either large-scale or intensive military operations? How do they compare with those of its neighbors? Could China be expected to achieve 'information superiority' over its potential adversaries in contingent circumstances?

Most of China's IW equipment is technologically obsolescent. Much of the EW equipment is still based on the Soviet systems of the 1950s, and although it has been substantially up-graded by the Chinese manufacturers, most of the EW sets currently in service incorporate technology available to China as of the 1980s. In the case of the Navy, the quest for modernization has involved the acquisition of numerous sorts of EW and combat information systems from abroad, sometimes accessing more modern European technology (including technology such as the Dutch Signaal Rapids EW suite installed on the Harbin, the lead ship of the Luhu-class destroyers, and the Italian Elettronica Newton Beta ESM/ECM system on the Jianghu-class frigates), but resulting in major inter-operability and logistics problems. In the case of the Army and Air Force, only a relatively few units have new equipment, and there is a dearth of state-of-the-art EW systems in production.

China's defense strategists have a thorough understanding of the theoretical aspects of IW, and appreciate the fundamental requirements of an effective IW strategy – including the need for doctrinal innovation, recruitment and training of sufficient technically-adept personnel, and drastic reorganization of command structures at both the High Command and operational levels, as well as the requirements for broadband, digitized and smart technical systems. The PLA has successfully accomplished the transformation of some of its conventional military conscripts into a network warfare saavy, cybercombat smart and networked war-fighting military.

The personnel challenges are tremendous if not impossible to overcome. Chinese military strategists have noted that:

"In the final analysis, information warfare is conducted by people. The basic great plan is to cultivate talented people suited to information warfare. One aspect is to cultivate talent in information science and technology ... The second aspect is talented people in command and control. The leaders especially need to have the ability to conduct comprehensive analysis and policy-information processing, to understand themselves and the enemy, as well as the battlefield, and also have a capacity for scientific strategic thinking and a comprehensive point of view. [They must also] be adept at using information technology to organize and command warfare."[ccclxi]

While the PLA has announced the 20 soldier strong"'Blue Arm" in 2011, there is very little evidence of any 'great plan' being implemented to cultivate such talented people, or to transform the informational and technical abilities of the PLA's senior commanders. There is no recognition of the potential long-term fundamental inconsistency between the demands for a liberally-educated, technically-adept and well-informed populace, and the constraints on imaginative thinking and the free flow of ideas imposed by the authoritarian Communist dictatorship.

Success in IW ultimately requires fundamental political, social, cultural and educational changes which will take China generations. Anyone who has studied Chinese history and political regime changes knows that as long as the Chinese people accept the Chinese Communist Party's edicts, then the long-term goal of utilizing information warfare without limits will be successful.

The PLA itself must be thoroughly reorganized and transformed. Chinese strategists appreciate that a digitized defense force "is a pre-requisite for information warfare", enabling transmission of information such as voice, graphics, text and data, producing a transparent battlefield and a "supreme battlefield knowledge-base";[ccclxii] that overall co-ordination of all defense combat and support services is imperative, and that IW operations are invariably joint Service operations. With respect to 'overall co-ordination', Chinese strategist General Wang Pufeng wrote: "Overall co-ordination is another feature of information warfare. The building of the battlefield information superhighway will mean that all operational systems such as combat forces, combat support units, and combat logistics support units, as well as all operational functions such as battlefield intelligence, command, control, communications, and assaults, will be linked into an organic whole".[ccclxiii]

Regarding greater PLA joint service integration the basic feature of future operations within the Chinese military will be joint operations with integrated services capabilities. Air strikes are no longer only attacks by the Air Force. Naval and Army Air Forces can also play very important roles. Missile attacks can be from aircraft, cruise missiles or land [units]; information war, electronic wars and psychological war are usually combined actions of all services together.[ccclxiv]

The PLA increasingly stresses joint-Service operations, as well as EW activities in its large-scale exercise, with joint maneuvers between Navy, Air Force, infantry, Marine infantry, paratroop, armored and missile units. In June 2001, the PLA conducted a large-scale amphibious exercise on

Dongshan Island, in Fujian province and abreast of the southern entrance to the Taiwan Strait. It involved "advanced fighter planes, warships, missiles and electronic warfare equipment", as well as use of reconnaissance satellites and satellite navigation systems.[ccclxv] Curiously these are not true joint-military exercises. Rather, they involve large elements from various Services and support units, conducting pre-arranged missions in a multi-Service environment. There is no capacity for joint-operational command or for pooling the information collected by the disparate sensors to conduct joint intelligence analysis or real-time mission planning. There is too little digitization and too few common data links. There are no really integrated operations, with field units networked to common data bases or exchanging tasks in response to changes beyond the set-piece scenarios. The ability to conduct truly integrated operations is at least a decade away.

Chinese strategists are quite aware of their own deficiencies and vulnerabilities with respect to cyberwarfare. In June 2000, "*a series of high-technology combat exercises*" being conducted by the PLA "*had to be suspended when they were attacked by a computer hacker*".[ccclxvi]

The People's Republic Of China's telecommunications technicians have been largely unsuccessful in defeating the random and infrequent hijacking of the Sinosat-1 national communications satellite by technically savvy Falun Gong practitioners; this is especially frustrating, since the media interruption has occurred since June 2002.[ccclxvii]

The SINOSAT-1 satellite was launched in 1998, and carries 24 C-band and 14 Ku-band signal transponders, providing telecommunication services, data transmission and TV broadcasting capabilities for all of China and a majority of the Asia-Pacific. SINOSAT-1 carries the signal of 45 television stations and 43 radio stations throughout the People's Republic of China.[ccclxviii]

According to the Xinhua News Agency, the SINOSAT-1 also carries data transmissions for the People's Bank of China, China's National Air Traffic Control System, and the Global Satellite Data Broadcasting System. Earlier in 2002, the Falun Gong wreaked havoc electronically, when they disrupted television services in China, effectively taking broadcasting down for over a week.[ccclxix]

The People's Liberation Army offensive cyberwarfare capabilities appear to be fairly elementary. Hackers of Chinese origin have been able to conduct adequate simultaneous "*pings*" to crash targeted web servers, carrying out denial of service (DOS) attacks.

Chinese-based cyberwarriors have been able to penetrate various nation-state websites, carrying out all manner of cybernefariousness, such as defacing them and erasing published data, while even posting different information, such as propaganda slogans, nationalistic pride and derisive slander.

The PLA has also developed various fairly simple viruses for spreading by e-mail, to disable targeted computer network systems. They also use Trojan Horse programs, which are capable of delivering, via e-mails, a program, which when opened within the e-mail essentially "*exfiltrates*" harvested information.

The PLA, has demonstrated very little proficiency with more sophisticated hacking techniques, such as remote file include (RFI), SQL injections, and cross-site scripting. The viruses and Trojan Horses have usually been fairly easy to detect and remove before any damage has been done or data stolen. There is no firm evidence that China's cyberwarriors can penetrate highly secure networks or covertly steal or falsify critical data. They would probably be unable to systematically cripple selected command and control, air defense and intelligence networks and data bases of advanced adversaries, or to conduct deception operations by secretly manipulating the data in these networks. The gap between the sophistication of the anti-virus and network security programs available to China's cyberwarriors (as compared to those of their counterparts in the more open, advanced IT societies), is immense.

The People's Republic of China's cyberwarfare leadership are frustrated by the technological innovations and rapid development of both commercially-available and clandestinely-designed information security, communications systems and very developed technical expertise, all of which are available to other nation-states.

The conclusion is virtually inevitable, if only partly stated; Chinese cyberwarfare, offensive organizational focus is condemned to inferiority in IW capabilities for probably several decades. At best, it can employ asymmetric strategies designed to exploit the dependence on information technology by their potential adversaries – both the C3ISREW elements of adversary military forces and the vital telecommunications and computer systems in the adversary's homelands.

Specifically, attacks on US information systems relating to military command and control, transportation and logistics could "*possibly degrade or delay US force mobilization in a time-dependent scenario*", such as US intervention in a military conflict in the Taiwan Straits.[ccclxx]

The unstated element of Chinese IW doctrine is that this involves a policy of striking first. The extensive Chinese IW capabilities, and the possibilities for asymmetric strategies, are only significant and effective if the PLA employed these first.

Cybersecurity professionals seem to suggest that Chinese researchers are incapable of organic malware design; the PLA is considering obtaining 0-day attack tools from independent malevolent sources, of which there many such repositories are available on the Internet. "*Zero day exploits are bought and sold in numerous public and private markets without the involvement of the victim software's vendors, often for tens of thousands of dollars per vulnerability.*"[ccclxxi] This revelation should give implicit concern and pause to any commercial enterprise or nation-state that has their network connected to the Internet.

Regarding hacking attacks which have emanated from the PRC, an unnamed source at the MITRE Corporation said that the hackers seemed to be consistent in their attack methodologies. These Chinese hackers worked during a single eight-hour shift, issuing reconnaissance commands identical to those observed and reported in previous attacks against the network. There was no originality or uniqueness to these threats other than they were persistent in their efforts to compromise an undisclosed US Government network.

When significant differences were recognized between this computer and previously compromised systems on the same network, the attack team extracted small amounts of data to determine the configuration of security software installed, and their ability to access targeted data on the company's network. The operators installed a rootkit, which gives the attacker privileged access to a victim computer, whilst remaining undetectable, suggesting the attackers intended long-term covert use of the victim computer.

The attackers configured the rootkit to execute upon the next system reboot, effectively hiding the operators' files, programs, network connections and registry settings. However, according to forensic analysis, operator-error caused a problem in the rootkit execution, and locked the attackers out of the targeted computer, ending the operation. The rootkit code is still not publicly-available, suggesting that the attacker obtained it directly from the coder, or from someone with direct access to them.

It is likely that the overall effort consists of multiple groups and skilled individuals, operating against different targets. The adversaries are successful because they are able maintain a presence on a targeted network for extended periods, enabling them to establish a connection to a compromised computer on the network.. This information is exploited most frequently to craft specific, seemingly legitimate-looking, e-mails to targeted users, often referencing a current project or meeting with which the recipient is involved. The e-mails usually contain either malicious software embedded in an attachment, or links to malicious websites.

The scale and complexity of such targeting suggests that it is probably backed by a mature intelligence collection management bureaucracy, able to collate and disseminate collection priorities to diverse teams of operators, intelligence analysts and malware developers. These individuals may be a mix of uniformed military personnel, civilian intelligence operators, and freelance high-end hackers known as cybermilitias. These Chinese hacking efforts are a type of attack which often begins with an e-mail message containing a malicious file attached, with both an exploit code and remote control connection to another networked infrastructure.

The overall PRC hacking effort is likely to consist of multiple groups and skilled individuals, operating against different targets. They will use software to give the attacker control of the victim's computer. When these files (usually an image, document or spreadsheet) are opened by the vulnerable program on the victim's computer (e.g. PowerPoint, WordPad, Adobe Acrobat) the backdoor program executes. *"E-mail is the most common entry vector because the operators are often able to learn an employee's (or group of employees') trust relationships (i.e. their professional networks) by analyzing who they frequently e-mail. The intruders then craft credible looking e-mails from members or groups within an individual's network that the target will likely open."*[ccclxxii]

The Chinese computer hackers often reuse the same targeted employee profiles generated by earlier reconnaissance, in multiple targeting attempts, either because the user failed to open the attachment the first time, or because they are a gullible soft target who may open e-mails randomly, allowing the executable attachment to open a communication channel back to the Chinese perpetrator. This inconsolable chain of cyberactivities represents a clear and present danger, and also a very reliable entry point for the cyberhacker onto the unsuspecting and ill-prepared networked infrastructure.

This initial penetration, utilizing e-mail and malicious attachment, is frequently only the first phase of an advanced operation; the users targeted first, and the data on their computers, may not be the actual target of collection.

Targeting the data owners of the attacker's real collection objective increases the risk of detection, and the possible implementation of tighter controls around the data they are seeking to exfiltrate, making later attempts more difficult.

Analysis of forensic data associated with penetrations attributed to sophisticated state-sponsored operators suggests that multiple individuals are sometimes involved; they may be responsible for specific tasks, such as gaining and establishing network access, surveying portions of the targeted network to identify information of value, and organizing the data exfiltration.

One role is an entry or "breach team" tasked only with gaining entry and maintaining a flexible, redundant presence in the target network (essentially "picking the lock" and ensuring, not only that the door stays open, but that there are multiple doors available if the one being used is "closed").

Once the breach team has successfully established access to the network, a second team or individual may conduct the data reconnaissance, and locate and exfiltrate targeted data. Different individuals or groups could be utilized for the specialized skills required for each phase of an intrusion. Additionally, much like any terrorist organization, they operate as independent units; the first cell has no idea about the objective which is being targeted by tertiary units. In effect, the hacking operation is both more successful and secure from possible detection and causal linkage.

These explanations are, however, largely speculative; the fidelity of data on such incidents almost never provides insight into the internal communications, identity or relationship dynamics of the actual people behind these intrusions. This type of task-oriented structure utilizes multiple skill sets, possibly requiring several individuals to complete one operation. This model, if accurate, also implies some means of recruiting, organizing and managing such a team, to ensure proper completion of a given mission. If this model is indeed accurate, and it is being replicated across dozens of intrusions over time, then that oversight structure must also be proportionately larger and more complex.

Additional individuals or teams, probably tasked with the collection of the actual targeted information, have demonstrated greater skill and highly detailed knowledge of the targeted networks. Their efforts to locate and move data from the network often involves techniques that place a premium on redundancy, stealth, comprehensiveness of preparation and attention to detail. Using network intelligence gathered during earlier reconnaissance efforts, these collection teams may have copied the data from the servers and workstations to a secondary server. This acts as a "staging point" where they compress, encrypt, segment and replicate the data, before distributing it through encrypted channels, out of the targeted organization, to multiple external servers that act as "drop points". These drop points may also play an obfuscation role, ensuring that investigators are unable to identify the data's final destination.

CHAPTER 9: THE CHINESE IW ORGANISATIONAL STRUCTURE

To set the stage for an understanding of China's intelligence organizational structure (particularly within the People's Liberation Army), and the ability to conduct espionage and cyberespionage, a snapshot of the PLA's state-ordered budget is necessary.

In 2011, China's defense budget grew 12.7 per cent to $91.5 billion, the largest in the world after the US. The importance of this increased Chinese military spend has certainly not been lost on the many nation-states who felt their information networks probed – allegedly by IP addresses associated with the People's Republic of China.

The PLA's capacity to increase its weapons platforms comes directly from the Chinese Government's coffers; if the Communist Party of China (CPC) receives a military budget increase request, it fulfills it without either legislative oversight or Chinese population curiosity as to what the additional money will be spent on.

The People's Liberation Army (PLA) considers active offense to be the most important requirement for information warfare to destroy or disrupt an adversary's capability to receive and process data. Launched mainly by remote combat and covert methods, the PLA could employ information warfare pre-emptively, to gain the initiative in a crisis. Specified information warfare objectives include the targeting and destruction of an enemy's command system, shortening the duration of war, minimizing casualties on both sides, enhancing operational efficiency, reducing effects on domestic populations, and gaining support from the international community. The PLA's Information Warfare (IW) practices also reflect investment in electronic countermeasures and defenses against electronic attack. The Chinese have adopted a formal IW strategy called "Integrated Network Electronic Warfare" (INEW) that consolidates the offensive mission for both

Computer Network Attack (CNA) and Electronic Warfare (EW). China's Computer Network Operations (CNO) includes computer network attack, computer network defense and computer network exploitation. The PLA views CNO as critical, to seize the initiative and achieve "electromagnetic dominance" early in a conflict, and as a force multiplier.

Although there is no evidence of a formal Chinese CNO doctrine, PLA theorists have coined the term "Integrated Network Electronic Warfare" to outline the integrated use of electronic warfare, CNO, and limited kinetic strikes, against key command and control, communication and computers nodes, to disrupt the enemy's battlefield network information systems. The PLA has established information warfare units to develop viruses to attack enemy computer systems and networks, and tactics and measures to protect friendly computer systems and networks.

The PLA is training and equipping its force to use a variety of IW tools for intelligence gathering, and to establish information dominance over its adversaries during a conflict. PLA campaign doctrine identifies the early establishment of information dominance over an enemy as one of the highest operational priorities in a conflict; INEW appears designed to support this objective.

The PLA is reaching out across a wide swath of the Chinese civilian sector, to meet the intensive personnel requirements necessary to support its burgeoning IW capabilities, incorporating people with specialized skills from commercial industry, academia and possibly select elements of China's hacker community.

Little evidence exists in open sources to establish firm ties between the PLA and China's hacker community.

However, research has uncovered limited cases of apparent collaboration between more elite individual hackers and the PRC's civilian security services. The caveat to this is that amplifying details are extremely limited and these relationships are difficult to corroborate.

The Chinese People's Liberation Army (PLA) is actively developing a capability for computer network operations (CNO) and is creating the strategic guidance, tools and trained personnel necessary to employ it in support of traditional warfighting disciplines. Nevertheless, the PLA has not openly published a CNO strategy with the formal vetting of either the Central Military Commission (CMC) – China's top military decision-making body, or the Academy of Military Sciences (AMS) – its leading body for doctrine and strategy development. The PLA has developed a strategy called "Integrated Network Electronic Warfare" to guide the employment of CNO and related information warfare tools. The strategy is characterized by the combined employment of network warfare tools and electronic warfare weapons against an adversary's information systems in the early phases of a conflict.

Chinese information warfare strategy is closely aligned with the PLA's doctrine for fighting "*Local Wars Under Informationized Conditions*", the current doctrine that seeks to develop a fully networked architecture capable of co-ordinating military operations on land, in air, at sea, in space and across the electromagnetic spectrum. China's military has shifted from a reliance on massed armies of the Maoist Era 'People's War' doctrine, and is becoming a fully-mechanized force, linked by advanced C4ISR technologies.

'*Informationization*' is essentially a hybrid development process, continuing the trend of mechanization; it retains much of the current force structure, whilst overlaying advanced information systems on it, to create a fully networked command and control (C2) infrastructure.[ccclxxiii]

The concept allows the PLA to network its existing force structure without radically revising current acquisition strategies or order of battle. PLA assessments of current and future conflicts note that campaigns will be conducted in all domains simultaneously – ground, air, sea and electromagnetic – but it is the focus of the latter domain in particular that has driven the PLA's adoption of the '*Informationized Conditions*' doctrine.[ccclxxiv]

Network-Centric Warfare (NCW), now commonly called Network-Centric Operations (CNO), is a universal military doctrine or theory of war. It seeks to translate an information advantage, enabled in part by information technology, into a competitive war fighting advantage, through the robust networking of well-informed geographically-dispersed forces. To achieve tenants of NCW, a robust and reliable multi-layered communication network for flow of information and integration of sensors, shooters and command and control elements, is an essential requirement of any force of the future.

The Government of the People's Republic of China (PRC) is a decade into a sweeping military modernization program, to fundamentally transform its ability to fight high-tech wars. The Chinese military, using increasingly networked forces capable of communicating across service arms and among all echelons of command, is pushing beyond its traditional missions focused on Taiwan and toward a more regional defensive posture. This modernization effort, known as '*informationization*', represented in Mandarin Chinese as 信息化 and pronounced in Pin Yin as Xìnxī huà, is guided by the doctrine of fighting "*Local War Under Informationized Conditions.*"

The Chinese formal IW strategy consolidates the offensive mission for both CNA and EW under 4th Department (Electronic Countermeasures) of PLA General Staff Department (GSD).

The Computer Network Defense (CND) and intelligence gathering responsibilities are likely to be with the GSD 3rd Department, 总参三部, Zǒngcān sān bù (Signals Intelligence), and possibly a variety of the PLA's specialized IW militia units.

The PLA Science and Engineering University provides advanced information warfare and networking training, whilst also serving as a center for defense related scientific, technological and military equipment research.[ccclxxv]

Recent IW related faculty research has focused largely on rootkit design and detection, including rootkit detection on China's indigenously and organically developed Kylin operating system (OS).

PLA Information Engineering University provides PLA personnel in a variety of fields advanced technical degrees and training, in all aspects of information systems, including information security and information warfare.[ccclxxvi]

Key PLA Departments: Integrated Network Electronic Warfare (INEW)

General Staff Department Third Department总参三部

The GSD Third Department, represented in Mandarin Chinese as 总参三部 and pronounced in Pin Yin as Zǒngcān sān bù deals in signals intelligence (SIGINT). The location and structure of GSD was described in Chapter eight.

Task organized as the PLA's most capable cryptologic resource, the GSD Third Department, with its large staff of trained linguists and technicians, also has a role in foreign language signals interception. Combining the crypto and linguistic experience and capability make it well suited for oversight of both the computer network defense (CND) and computer network exploit (CNE) missions within the PLA. The GSD Third Department maintains an extensive system of signals collection stations throughout China, with collection and processing stations co-located within each of the PLA's Military Region Headquarters.[ccclxxvii] The GSD Third Department is tasked with the foreign signals collection, exploitation and analysis, in addition to communications security for the PLA's voice and data networks, a responsibility that encompasses military and civilian network defense.[ccclxxviii]

According to a Chinese newspaper report 'Lantern Through the Night', the Central Military Commission Second Bureau (now known as the GSD Third Department, and also represented as the Technical Reconnaissance Bureau or TRB) grew out of the Second Bureau of the PLA's Central Military Commission (CMC) after the end of the Chinese Civil War.

The PLA played a key role in the Chinese Civil War, 1945–49. According to the Encyclopedia Britannica, "in a little more than four years after Japan's surrender, the CCP and the People's Liberation Army (PLA; the name by which communist forces are now known) conquered mainland China, and, on Oct. 1, 1949, the People's Republic of China was established, with its capital at Beijing (the city's former name restored). The factors that brought this about were many and complex and subject to widely varying interpretation, but the basic fact were a communist military triumph growing out of a profound and popularly based revolution. The process may be perceived in three phases: (1) from August 1945 to the end of 1946, the Nationalists and communists raced to take over Japanese-held territories, built up their forces, and fought many limited engagements while still conducting negotiations for a peaceful settlement; (2) during 1947 and the first half of 1948, after initial Nationalist success, the strategic balance turned in favour of the communists; and (3) the communists won a series of smashing victories beginning in the latter part of 1948 that led to the establishment of the People's Republic."[ccclxxix]

After the Chinese Civil War, the Second Bureau of the PLA's Central Military Commission (CMC), which had adroitly and effectively helped Mao Tse Tung's Red Army to intercept, decrypt and take advantage of the enemy's military signals traffic, was renamed the GSD Third Department.

In its present, modern PLA form, the GSD Third Department retains some of the original signals intelligence duties of the CMC Second Bureau, including those tasks associated with intelligence collection and translation of foreign signals material, along with deciphering and encryption.

In the 21st century, the GSD Third Department, and her sister services located in the PLA's Seven Military Regions (MRs), the People's Liberation Air Force (PLAAF), the People's Liberation Navy (PLAN), and the Second Artillery Corps (SAC), all have responsibility for overseeing a vast telecommunications infrastructure, monitoring data and voice communications traffic. Collection sites operate within the PRC, and from embassies and other foreign facilities of interest overseas. This communications and signals monitoring capability and infrastructure is not limited to terrestrial-based sources; space-based data and voice targets are currently vectored.[ccclxxx] The People's Republic of China has confidently demonstrated their technological parity with both US and Russian global positioning satellite efforts, with the launch of the 10th Beidou Compass Navigation Satellite System (CNSS), appropriately named Beidou 2, on the 6th of December 2011.[ccclxxxi]

Monitoring of most radio communication or voice phone calls within line of sight of Third Department signals intelligence (SIGINT) stations is a developed capability of the Department's data and voice network infrastructure. However, as long as the CPC and PLA are adequately interested, and the targeted data or voice traffic lacks highly complicated or eloquently developed data encryption, foreign data and voice transmissions are susceptible to interception.

The People's Republic of China, much like the US and other nation-states, are confronted with increasing cyberthreats and related challenges to their data and voice communication system infrastructures. The GSD Third Department has also been tasked with the mission of gaining and maintaining security of PLA computer systems. The Chinese military strategy and tactic of 技術偵察, pronounced in Pin Yin as Jìshù zhēnchá, is technical reconnaissance, and contains both defensive and offensive military cybercapabilities. [ccclxxxii]

The PLA's GSD Third Department also conducts missions of Jìshù zhēnchá, as a requisite technical measure to deny foreign adversaries from either accessing or defeating China's civilian and military data network infrastructures. This is the basis and foundation for China's information warfare in the 21st century, now known as '*informationization*'.

Similar to its American counterpart (the National Security Agency, NSA), the GSD Third Department has been increasing the scope of its original signals intelligence (SIGINT) mission. Cybersurveillance (or computer network exploitation (CNE) in the US DoD vocabulary) represents the cutting edge of SIGINT, and the GSD Third Department executes the Chinese PLA's national strategy of CNE. Within the Chinese military, the GSD Third Department serves as the only unit to carry out the national PRC authority mission of cybersurveillance. This is because of the GSD Third Department's:

(a) historical leadership and task competency in SIGINT;
(b) high performance computing and encryption / decryption technical capabilities;
(c) reputation as the PRC's single source provider of highly skilled foreign language linguists. [ccclxxxiii]

In China, computer network operations (CNO) are often referred to as both network attack and defense, represented in Mandarin Chinese as 网络功防 and pronounced in Pin Yin as Wǎngluò gōng fang; this is based on the premise that "without understanding how to attack, one will not know how to defend."[ccclxxxiv]

Technical Reconnaissance Bureaus (TRB)

The GSD Third Department People's Liberation Army has two different task-organized technical reconnaissance bureaus (TRB), which are based upon a specific military branch (within the PLA), and those associated with military region areas of operation (AO) (MR) geography.

Military Branch Technical Reconnaissance Bureaus (MB TRB)

Military Branch technical reconnaissance bureaus (TRB) are task-organized within both the People's Liberation Air Force (PLAAF) and Navy (PLAN), to plan for and carry out both data and voice network infrastructure monitoring. The PLAAF is mission-oriented towards monitoring data and voice communications, related to the foreign civilian and military aviation operations around and within flight reach of the PRC.[ccclxxxv] The TRBs within the PLAAF are relegated to three specific units, whose primary task organization is that of a "unit" and are assigned to the specific geographies of Beijing, Nanjing and Chengdu. While PLAAF TRBs have the stated mission of carrying out signals intelligence activity from the air, using both civilian and military airframes, they also have an indirect computer network infrastructure reconnaissance mission.[ccclxxxvi], [ccclxxxvii]

Headquartered and located in the City of Beijing's Huangsi District is the PLAAF's First TRB. The First TRB is also known as Unit 95830. Unit 95830 operates within a network of tunnels within the western hills of the Chinese capitol city. A task-organized sub-unit within Unit 95830 is in direct support of the TRB's headquarters, conducting research and creating reports regarding data and voice network infrastructure security.[ccclxxxviii] The PLAAF's Nanyuan Airbase is used by the Chinese Air Force for extensive signals intelligence missions.[ccclxxxix]

142

PLAAF's Second TRB operates out of Nanjing, providing operational oversight of SIGINT collection and direction-finding locations, on the Fujian coastline and in the city of Guangdong. The Second TRB's primary mission is actively monitoring the Taiwanese (Republic of China) Air Force (ROCAF) data, and voice communication network infrastructure on Taiwan. This stated communications intercept mission includes all cellular tower, ground control intercept, and air-to-air communications. Since Taiwan has deployed advanced tactical data links as part of the Posheng program, this has created operational havoc for the PLAAF technical reconnaissance mission.^{cccxc} A main Second TRB facility, PLAAF, is in city of Fúqīng in the Dōng hàn zhèn area, on Dǒng jìng Mountain. Subordinate direct support (DS) PLAAF Second TRB sub-units may be based in the Chinese Provinces of Fúzhōu and Guǎngzhōuas, well as the Chinese cities of Shànghǎi and Xiàmén. The PLAAF Second TRB also trains new SIGINT personnel at a facility it shares with the 7th Bureau's Third Department, at satellite ground station in northwest Běijīng. ^{cccxci}

Chéngdū Fènghuáng Mountains are the operational home and headquarters of the PLAAF's Third TRB. PLAAF Third TRB units, created in July 2004, have subordinate units task-oriented to conduct monitoring aircraft activity and air defense communication networks along China's southwestern, western and northwestern borders. Because of the geographic operational area, the Third TRB has approximately 13 direct support (DS) regimental-level located units.

The Chinese Navy, PLAN, commands two TRBs, which are geographically task-organized. During a PLAN reorganization, the fleet operation of the TRBs was restructured under PLAN headquarters as direct support (DS). PLAN's First TRB, known as the 91746 Unit, is task-organized and operates out of Běijīng. 91746 Unit operates 10 sub-units throughout northern China, including facilities in Húnchūn, Qīngdǎo and Yāntái. PLAN's Second TRB operates out of the Xiàmén's Xīmén District. Sub-units operate out of Níngbō, Wēnzhōu shì, Shàntóu shì and Hǎikǒu.^{cccxcii}

Second Artillery Corps (SAC)

Second Artillery Headquarters Department TRB, also known as 96669 Unit, has a base of operations in Běijīng's, Huílóngguān. According to

SinoDefence.com, the Second Artillery Corps (SAC) is designated as the Strategic Missile Force (SMF). SinoDefence.com provides this description:

"The Strategic Missile Force (SMF), also known as the Second Artillery Corps, is the strategic missile branch of the People's Liberation Army (PLA), controlling all of PRC's land-based strategic missile assets as well as the majority of its conventional theatre missile assets. The force is estimated to have a total strength of 90,000~100,000 personnel, most of which are in engineering and construction units. Actual missile operators and guards are probably less than half of the total strength. All SAC units are subject to strict command and control from the CMC. Orders are passed down to operational units via a four-level chain of command: CMC, missile bases, missile brigades, and launch battalions."

"The SMF is believed to be equipped with 110~140 nuclear-armed strategic missiles, including 15~20 DongFeng 3 (CSS-2) IRBMs, 15~20 DongFeng 4 (CSS-3) IRBMs, about 20 DongFeng 5 (CSS-4) ICBMs, and 60~80 DongFeng 21 (CSS-5) MRBMs, all of which carry a single warhead. The new-generation DongFeng 31 (CSS-9) began deployment in 2007, and its improved variant DongFeng 31A is also close to operational deployment. Additionally, the SAC is equipped with 900~1,000 conventional theatre missiles, including the DongFeng 15 (CSS-6) and DongFeng 11 (CSS-7) SRBMs. In recent years, the SMF has also began the deployment of the DongFeng 21C (CSS-5 Mod-3) conventionally-armed MRBM and the DH-10 land-attack cruise missile (LACM)."

"Currently the SMF has six operational missile bases, which are numbered from 51st to 56th. Four of these bases (51st, 52nd, 55th and 56th) are "Army Level" units, while the other two (53rd and 54th) are "Sub-Army Level" units, which are half grade lower in PLA's hierarchy. The 22nd Base, also "Army Level", located in Baoji, Shaanxi Province is officially known as the "Training and Experimental Base". Western intelligence suggested that this base may also serve as a warhead storage facility." [cccxciii]

Military Region (MR TRB)

The GSD Third Department's 12 operational bureaus are task-organized differently, and operate separately as Military Region Technical Reconnaissance Bureaus (MR TRB) and direct support (DS) units within each of the seven MR headquarters. The seven PLA military regions (MR) are known operationally as the Běijīng MR, Chéngdū MR, Guǎngzhōu MR, Jǐnán MR, Lánzhōu MR, Nánjīng MR and Chényáng MR. The Chief of Staff (COS) within MR Headquarters Department has administrative (ADCON) and operational command (OPCON) authority over a TRB within their AO.

However, Third Department command direction in Beijing and issue policy guidance and commander's intent for TRB collection, analysis and reporting.

TRB missions may parallel those of the Third Department, and include communications intelligence, direction finding, traffic analysis, translation, cryptology, computer network defense and computer network exploitation. However, their primary role is to support each of the seven MR commands. Military Region TRBs also support border security forces.

Beijing Military Region TRB Unit 66407

The operational command headquarters of the Běijīng MR TRB is Xiāngshān Mountain. Běijīng MR TRB is also known as an operational PLA unit, Unit 66407. Another PLA MT TRB subunit, which conducts cyberreconnaissance, is Unit 61580. "Headquartered in Beijing, the bureau's engineers specialize in computer network defense and attack, and have conducted joint studies with the PLA Information Engineering Academy Computer Network Attack and Defense Section. The bureau has been known to conduct research outlining US network-centric warfare and dense wavelength-division multiplexing."[cccxciv]

Beijing MR TRB is also assigned Russian linguists; sub-units operate out of garrisons along the border, in Inner Mongolia.

Chengdu MR TRB

There are two TRBs which operate out of the Chéngdū MR; the First TRB, also known as Unit 78006, has its headquarters in the city of Chéngdū. The PLA's Senior Colonel Guǎn yán serves as the First TRB Political Commissar of the Chéngdū MR. Unit 78006 is task-organized and has the mission statement of conducting CNE operations. The Second TRB in the Chéngdū MR, is also known as 78020 Unit, and is headquartered in northern Kūnmíng. 78020 Unit has sub-units in the border cities of Bǎoshān, and the county of Málìpō Xiàn, as well as other border locations within Yúnnán Province.

Guangzhou Military Region (75770 Unit)

Located in the outer area of the city of Guǎngzhōu, this MR TRB is also known as Unit 75770. Unit 75770 has operational control (OPCON) of eight sub-units located throughout southern China. Hú fùhuī is the Political Commissar and was transferred to the Guǎngzhōu MR TRB, where he heads the Second MR TRB Office.

Jinan Military Region

The Jǐnán MR TRB is also recognized as Unit 72959, and is headquartered and functions out of the city of Jǐnán. Unit 72959 is task-organized with 670 technical specialists. According to the Jǐnán Military Grand Technology Co., Ltd:

"the military record also known as the Military Technology Development and Technology Bureau is the unit of Jinan Military Region and Technology Bureau, Bureau of Jinan Military Region, Jinan Military technology the most intensive areas of technology, there are more than 70 senior engineers, 200 engineers, assistant Nearly 400 engineers. They have the last century 60's, 70's army, to all kinds of famous universities (Tsinghua University, Harbin Military Engineering Institute, Western military power, Fudan University, Tianjin) graduates, there eighties and nineties from the Military Academy (Information Engineering College), local prestigious university graduates, as well as recent graduates of the new force, there is no lack of them graduate students, recent years have almost a hundred technological innovations to contribute to PLA forces. Since 1984 the Technology Development Department (established in 1998 after the technology is limited in case of

Jinan companies, mainly to the production, installation of monitoring equipment, in 2003, changed its name to create the Jinan Military Technology Co., Ltd), participation in local construction work in various industries, focusing on satellite communications, computer networks, cabling, monitors sound engineering Construction of the weak play to their strengths for the socialist economic construction, with concrete actions to promote the construction of two civilizations. Main business scope: satellite ground receiving station systems engineering, microwave communications, cabling, system integration, cabling, CCTV and other systems engineering project design, installation and maintenance."[cccxcv]

Lanzhou Military Region

The Lánzhōu MR has operational control (OPCON) of two TRBs within its MR. The First TRB is called Unit 68002 and is in the south. Unit 69010 is the second TRB and is critical to the PLA's signals intelligence capability. The Lanzhou MR Second TRB is headquartered in Wūlǔmùqí's Shuǐmó gōu. Unit 69010 was originally task-organized under the Third Department's Second Bureau based in Xīnjiāng, and after being reconstituted within the Xīnjiāng MR, it was redesignated as Lánzhōu Unit 69010 during 1984. Unit 69010's area of operations (AO) includes vast reaches, monitoring military activities in India, Pakistani, Afghanistan, Tajikistan, Kyrgyzstan, Kazakhstan, Russia and Mongolia.[cccxcvi]

Nánjīng Military Region

The Nánjīng MR Headquarters is commanded by Major General Yáng huī. His former billet was that of the Director, GSD Second Department. Major General Yáng huī's AO includes administrative control (ADCON) and operational control (OPCON) of two TRBs (Units 73610 and 73630), monitoring the military and other communications and computer networks throughout Taiwan. Major General Yáng huī also has the responsibility for monitoring all US military activity in the Western Pacific area of operations, focused primarily on US Pacific Command (PACOM) and its subordinate units located on Hawaii.

Unit 73610 is Nánjīng MR's First TRB and it operates out of Nánjīng. Shàobǎoxiáng is the Commander of Unit 73610 and his Political Commissar is Píng xīngzhōng.

Unit 73630 is headquartered out of an underground bunker complex in the Zhèng jìnzhǐ cún neighborhood of Fúzhōu shì, Nanjing. MR's Second TRB was founded upon the Fuzhou MR's Third Bureau, and its AO appears to be the monitoring of voice and data network communications from Taiwan.

Shényáng Military Region

Unit 65016 is based out of Shényáng MR. Unit 65016's mission is comprised of data and voice infrastructure targets in Japan, Korea and Russia. The northeastern Chinese cities of Dàlián, Hā'ěrbīn, Jiamusi; the counties of Dōng níng, Hēilóngjiāng, Fúyú Qíqíhā'ěr; and the cities of both Hūlúnbèi'ěr and Húnchūn in Inner Mongolia, Nèiménggǔall, all have sub-unit garrisons for monitoring signals out of these bordering countries.

General Staff Department Fourth Department

The GSD 4th Department, also referred to as the Electronic Countermeasures Department (ECM), oversees both operational ECM units, and Research and Development (R&D) institutes, conducting research on a variety of offensive IW technologies. The 4th Department's oversight of IW dates back to at least 1990.

The GSD Fourth, or Counter-Electronic Warfare Department was established in 1990; it was given the same command and operational level responsibility as both the Technical Department and the Second (or Foreign Intelligence) Department. This task organization demonstrated China's strategic intent of upgrading its tactical SIGINT and EW. (Previously EW was the responsibility of a branch in the Second Department.)

The headquarters of the new Counter-Electronic Warfare Department was initially co-located with that of the Third Department (and that of the Second Department) at Xiāng Hóngqí. However, in 1991, the Counter-Electronic Warfare Department was transferred to new facilities at Tǎ yuàn, southeast of the Summer Palace.

The Fourth Department has two major Special Detachments located at Xībĕi wàng and Yáng fang, both of which are responsible for the electronic warfare (EW) defense of key state and military headquarters and facilities in Bĕijīng.

Additionally, while run directly from the Fourth Department headquarters, these two Special Detachments units manage and direct SIGINT and EW operations for the PLA, throughout the Military Regions down to the operational Divisional levels. There are several Counter-Electronic Warfare Department units in the Beijing Military Region, including a major unit at Xīshān, in the western mountain area of Beijing, which has a general responsibility for the EW defense of the Beijing Military Region. The Department also manages and directs SIGINT and EW operations for both the PLAAF and PLAN.

The Fourth Department's responsibility of electronic warfare (EW) uses the Chinese military cyberdoctrine concept of integrated network and electronic warfare, which defines the military operational concept of computer network attack and jamming.

Established in 1990, the Fourth Department has overall responsibility for electronic warfare (EW), including ELINT and tactical electronic support measures (ESM).

The Fourth Department is task-oriented to carry out computer network attack (CNA) operations, and is comprised of, at least, four bureaus, one brigade and two regiments. The Fourth Department's primary training and education organization for junior officers is the PLA Electronic Engineering Academy in the city of Héféi.[cccxcvii]

The GSD 54th Research Institute provides engineering support to the GSD Fourth Department. This sub-unit maintains very close relationships with a variety of China Electronic Technology Corporation (CETC) organizations, such as the 29th Research Institute in Chéngdū, and the 36th Research Institute in Jiā xīng shì.

Operational Fourth Department units include an ECM brigade, with headquarters in Langfang, Hebei Province, and subordinate battalion-level entities located in Anhui, Jiangxi, Shandong, and other locations in China. At least two Fourth Department units are on Hainan Island, with one apparently dedicated to jamming US satellite assets. A regimental-level unit located on Hainan Island appears to have either operational or experimental satellite jamming responsibilities. Military Regions, Air Force and Navy have at least one ECM regiment. The Third Department and GSD Fourth Department are said to jointly manage a network attack/defense training system.

Recent academic research reflects that Dài qíngmǐn's original work on Information Warfare (IW) was reviewed and approved by the 4th Department, prior to publication in 1999, thus indicating that it had organizational oversight of this military cyberdoctrine topic. The GSD's decision in 2000, to promote Dài qíngmǐn to head the 4th Department, vetting his advocacy of the INEW strategy, further consolidated the organizational authority for the IW and the CNA mission, specifically in this group. Dai's promotion to this position suggests that the GSD may have endorsed his vision of adopting INEW as the PLA's IW strategy.

PLA Information Warfare Militia Units

Since 2002, the PLA has been creating IW militia units, comprising of personnel from the commercial information technology sector and universities.[cccxcviii] These units represent an operational nexus between PLA CNO operations and Chinese civilian information security professionals.

In 2003, a political commissar for the Guangzhou People's Armed Police (PAP) garrison advocated the direct involvement of urban militia units in information warfare, electronic warfare and psychological warfare. He also proposed that militia reform efforts should focus on making information warfare one of the Guangzhou militia's primary missions.[cccxcix] PLA media reporting indicates that IW militia units are tasked with offensive and defensive CNO and EW responsibilities, psychological warfare and deception operations, although the available sources do not explain the lines of authority, subordination or the nature of their specific tasking. A militia battalion in Yongning County (Ningxia Province, Lanzhou Military Region) established an IW militia group in March 2008, and tasked it to conduct network warfare research and training, and to "attack the enemy's wartime networks" according to the unit's website.

Ministry of State Security

Within the PRC, the state organization for civilian intelligence collection (which is similar to the US Central Intelligence Agency, the CIA), is the Ministry of State Security. The Ministry of State Security was the result of a wholesale Chinese intelligence reorganization which took place during June 1983. The intelligence activities of the former Ministry of Public Security (MPS), which encompassed counter-intelligence, espionage and security activities, were included with the Investigative Department of the Chinese Communist Party central committee, and were combined following excessive Chinese Communist Party power plays and disagreements.[cd]

(MID) Second Department – Intelligence

The Military Intelligence Department (MID) of the People's Liberation Army's General Staff Department (GSD) is the second most significant human intelligence (HUMINT) collection organization within the People's Republic of China. The MID is also known as the Second Department David Finkelstein states that "the mission of the Second Intelligence Department of the PLA (GSD) is collecting military information."[cdi] Additional Second Department intelligence collection activities include work by military attachés at Chinese embassies overseas, clandestine special agents sent to foreign countries to collect military information, and the analysis of information publicly published in foreign countries."[cdii]

The Second Department oversees military human intelligence (HUMINT) collection, widely exploits open source materials, fuses HUMINT, signals intelligence (SIGINT), and imagery intelligence data, and disseminates finished intelligence products to the CMC and other internal People's Liberation Army intelligence customers.

Preliminary intelligence fusion is completed by the Second Department's Analysis Bureau, which resides in and is task-organized to operate the National Watch Center. The National Watch Center has a focal point for national-level intents and warning. Further in-depth intelligence analysis is also completed by the PLA's regional bureaus.[cdiii]

Although traditionally, the Second Department of the General Staff Department was responsible for military intelligence, it is increasingly focusing on scientific and technological intelligence in the military field; this follows the example of Russian agencies, in increasing the necessary tasks of collecting scientific and technological information from the West.[cdiv]

The research institute under the Second Department of the General Staff Headquarters is publicly known as the Institute for International Strategic Studies; its internal classified publication "Movements of Foreign Armies", is published every 10 days and transmitted to units at the division level within the People's Liberation Army.[cdv]

According to Nicholas Eftimiades, the Second Department has the following intelligence collection and analysis responsibilities:

The Enemies Order of Battle: The listing of armed military forces geographically close to the People's Republic of China, including both uniformed and insurgent types of military capabilities; specifically, the armed forces size, unit, location, activity, time and expectations for future operations. The Second Department focuses on Afghanistan, US Forces stationed in the Asia Pacific Rim and Southwest Asia areas of operation (AO), Burma, Cambodia, India, Mongolia, Taiwan, Thailand, both South and North Japan, Korea and Vietnam.

Biographical Intelligence information: Information pertaining to the key military leadership, including both senior officers and staff non-commissioned officers, making meticulous annotations regarding all aspects of both their personal and professional lives; intentions of both current and potential adversaries military operations and activities; military doctrine, including an adversary's operational philosophy, their battle plans, as well as targets of both existing and future nation-states, which be operating contrary to the People's Republic of China's national and international interests.

Military Economics: Details focused on the commercial and industrial capabilities, agricultural production capability, level of technical knowledge within the nation's military, as well as the quantity and capability to mass a strategic reserve; military geography of neighboring countries, including the terrain features specific to military operations;

Military Intelligence Watch Centers: Locations where a current and potential adversary will gather intelligence on the political, military and economic capabilities of the People's Republic of China.[cdvi]

Nuclear targeting: Details for the People's Liberation Army operational nuclear forces, with an inherent focus on foreign military centers of gravity, population centers and relevant civil and military areas of influence.

Chinese PLA soldiers: Both officer and enlisted soldiers, serving in professional work in Chinese military academies under the Second Department of the PLA General Staff Headquarters, usually have a chance to go abroad, either for advanced studies or as military officers working in the military attaché's office of Chinese embassies in foreign countries.[cdvii]

Chinese nationals: Personnel working in embassy military attaché's offices conduct military information collection activities, operating under the clandestine cover of "military diplomacy". As long as they refrain from directly subversive activities, they are considered as well-behaved "military diplomats."[cdviii]

The GSD's Second Department: The Department has units which also have geographical responsibility. The First Bureau has responsibility for intelligence collection among five distinct areas: Beijing area of operations, the Guangzhou region, Nanjing area, Shenyang and Shanghai regions. The First Bureau's primary areas of responsibility are the former British protectorate of Hong Kong, and Taiwan.[cdix]

According to several independent indigenous intelligence reports from the Hong Kong region, a People's Liberation Army intelligence unit from the GSD's Second Department, First Bureau, was called the "Autumn Orchid". The Chinese military intelligence agents were "assigned to Hong Kong and Macao in the mid-1980s, mostly operating in the mass media, political, industrial, commercial and religious circles, as well as in universities and colleges."[cdx] Main intelligence collection targeting responsibilities of the

"Autumn Orchid" intelligence group were also focused on three main information gathering tasks which included:

"Finding out and keeping abreast of the political leanings of officials of the Hong Kong and Macao governments, as well as their views on major issues, through social contact with them and through information provided by them."

"Keeping abreast of the developments of foreign governments' political organs in Hong Kong, as well as of foreign financial, industrial and commercial organizations."

"Finding out and having a good grasp of the local media's sources of information on political, military, economic and other developments on the mainland, and deliberately releasing false political or military information to the media to test the outside response."[cdxi]

(MID) Third Department – Intelligence

The Third Department of the General Staff Headquarters is responsible for monitoring the telecommunications of foreign armies, and producing finished intelligence based on the military information collected.

The communications stations established by the Third Department of the PLA General Staff Headquarters are not subject to the jurisdiction of the provincial military district and the major military region of where they are based. The communications stations are entirely the agencies of the Third Department of the PLA General Staff Headquarters, which have no affiliations to the provincial military district and the military region of where they are based. The personnel composition, budgets and establishment of these communications stations are entirely under the jurisdiction of the Third Department of the General PLA General Staff Headquarters, and are not related at all with local troops.

The Third Department has a manning estimated at approximate 20,000 PLA soldiers. The following figure details the People's Liberation Army information warfare table of task organization.

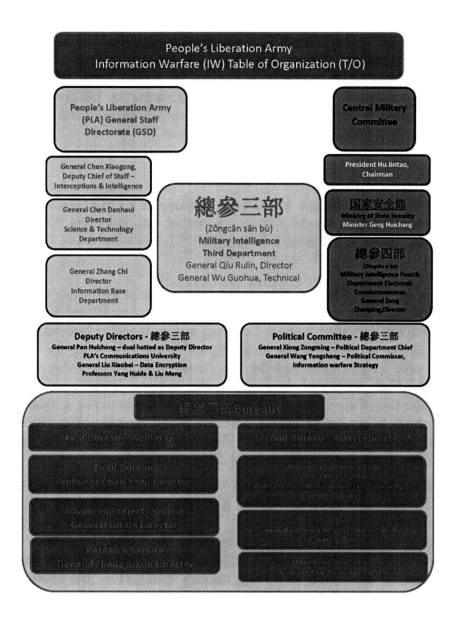

Figure 4: PLA information warfare table of task organization

Most of the GSD's Third Department linguists are trained at the Luoyang PLA College of Foreign Languages. This PLA military language school employs native English speakers from Australia, the UK and the US.

The following Reuters article exemplifies the US cautionary and perhaps displaced view of the Chinese PLA intelligence apparatus and how it applies to cyberincursions; "Secret US State Department cables, obtained by WikiLeaks and made available to Reuters by a third party, trace systems breaches – colorfully code-named "Byzantine Hades" by US investigators – to the Chinese military. An April 2009, cable even pinpoints the attacks to a specific unit of China's People's Liberation Army."[cdxii]

US Government efforts to halt the Byzantine Hades hacks are ongoing. In the April 2009 cable, officials in the State Department's CyberThreat Analysis Division noted that several Chinese-registered websites were "*involved in Byzantine Hades intrusion activity in 2006.*"[cdxiii]

Chinese hacking originated from several cities within the People's Republic of China, including websites whose IP addresses were registered in the city of Chengdu, the capital of Sichuan Province in central China (according to the cable). A person named Chen Xingpeng set up the sites using the "precise" postal code in Chengdu used by the People's Liberation Army Chengdu Province First Technical Reconnaissance Bureau (TRB), an electronic espionage unit of the Chinese military. "Much of the intrusion activity traced to Chengdu is similar in tactics, techniques and procedures to (Byzantine Hades) activity attributed to other" electronic spying units of the People's Liberation Army, the US Government cable states.

Ever since the 1950s, the Second and Third Departments of the PLA General Staff Headquarters have established a number of institutions of secondary and higher learning, for advancing "special talents." The PLA Foreign Language Institute at Luoyang comes under the Third Department of the General Staff Department, and is responsible for training foreign language cadres for the monitoring of foreign military intelligence. The Institute was formed from the PLA "793" Foreign Language Institute, which moved from Zhangjiakou after the Cultural Revolution, and split into two institutions based at Luoyang and Nanjing.

Though the distribution order they received upon graduation indicated the "PLA General Staff Headquarters," many of the graduates of these schools found themselves being sent all over the country, even to remote and uninhabited mountain areas. The monitoring and control stations under the Third Department of the PLA General Staff Headquarters are scattered in every corner of the country.

The communications stations located in the Shenzhen base of the PLA Hong Kong Garrison started their work long ago. In normal times, these two communications stations report directly to the Central Military Commission and the PLA General Staff Headquarters. The communications stations established in the garrison provinces of the military regions are the units responsible for co-ordination.

By taking direct command of military communications stations based in all parts of the country, the CPC Central Military Commission and the PLA General Staff Headquarters can not only ensure a successful interception of enemy radio communications, but can also make sure that none of the wire or wireless communications and contacts among major military regions escape the ears of the communications stations. This effectively achieves the desired goal; imposing a direct supervision and control over all major military regions, all provincial military districts, and all group armies.[cdxiv]

Eleventh Bureau – Electronic Computers Bureau

The Eleventh Bureau, the Electronic Computers Bureau, is responsible for analyzing intelligence gathered with electronic computers, and operating the computer network of the Ministry of State Security. It also collects information on advanced electronic systems from the West, and protects the information systems of the Chinese secret service from attacks by foreign intelligence agencies.

In Hong Kong, agents are recruited by the MSS' Third Bureau, which handles Chinese intelligence operations in Taiwan, Hong Kong and Macao. One of their major tasks is purchasing targeted technologies through "front" companies. These businesses are not usually run by intelligence officers themselves, but by people who have connections, sometimes overt, to the MSS.

One startling example of the Eleventh Bureau's intelligence connection with the Chinese commercial world is with the 88 Queensway Group. This unique Chinese business entity is named after the address of an office building in central Hong Kong, which was involved in a case of corporate espionage. This particular location is also home to several Chinese state-owned enterprises (SOE). The 88 Queensway Group, and the China Investment Corporation, the PRC's sovereign wealth fund were reported to be an authentic link between Chinese commercial interests and their vast intelligence organizations.[cdxv]

PLA Information Engineering University

The multi-disciplinary PLA Information Engineering University was created by merging the Institute of Surveying and Mapping, and the Institute of Electronic Technology, directly under the General Staff leadership. It provides a single telecommunications engineering path for professional development in electronics and information science and technology.

The PLA Information Engineering University's Institute of Surveying and Mapping is an operational command for the Army, providing military training and scientific research training. It is approved by the State Council, and is one of China's major institutions of higher learning.

The People's Republic of China uses its vast network of spies to augment and support its cyberwarfare initiatives, using a clandestine methodology of espionage. Indeed, the Ministry of State Security, in tandem with Military Intelligence Departments, all have one common goal, of supporting the State's intent of gathering confidential commercial, governmental and military data that is confidential, propriety and often classified information.

CHAPTER 10: CHINESE COMMERCIAL ENTERPRISES

The PRC's Economic Leadership

Who are the key decision makers from an economic policy perspective in the People's Republic of China? According to the *China Business Review* in 2008, Mr Cheng Li reported that "most of the major economic decisions in the country are subject to final approval by the nine-member Politburo Standing Committee (PSC) of the Communist Party of China."[cdxvi]

Only four members of the PSC, which includes President Hu Jintao, Premier Wen Jaiobao, Vice President Xi Jinping, and Executive Vice Premier Li Keqiang, are partially or primarily responsible for economic affairs within the People's Republic of China. Additionally, only three of 16 non-standing members of the Politburo oversee economic matters within China, these key players, "Hui Liangyu, Zhang Dejiang and Wang Qishan – are considered to be leading economic decision makers."[cdxvii]

What is a Chinese State-owned Enterprise (SOE)?

The People's Republic of China issued a "*Communiqué on Major Data of the Second National Economic Census (No.1)*"http://www.stats.gov.cn/english/newsandcomingevents/t20091225_40 2610168.htm on 25 December 2009.[cdxviii] According to the National Bureau of Statistics of China, this economic census yields very interesting statistics about Chinese SOEs. The census reveals that of all the 208 trillion RMB total assets of the secondary and tertiary sectors, which includes both industrial and service sectors, 63 trillion, or thirty per cent of total was held by SOEs.

In the People's Republic of China, SOEs are state sole-funded corporations and enterprises, with the state as the biggest shareholder. Relative to the number of enterprise numbers, there were 154,000 SOEs at the end of 2009, only accounting for 3.1 per cent of the total enterprise number. In the People's Republic of China, SOEs control a substantial part of total commercial enterprise assets, despite reporting that their total number is not very large.

China's SOEs

Many observers define a Chinese state-owned company as one of the 150 or so corporations that report directly to the central government. Thousands more fall into a grey area, including subsidiaries of these 150 corporations, companies owned by provincial and municipal governments, and companies that have been partially privatized, yet retain the state as a majority or influential shareholder.

The Chinese oil company China National Offshore Oil Corporation (CNOOC) and the Chinese utility State Grid Corporation of China (SGCC), are clearly state-owned enterprises under the first category. Yet personal computer maker Lenovo, and the home appliance giant Haier, are not such obvious examples of Chinese state-run companies. In both cases, the People's Republic of China is the dominant shareholder. A majority of the equity in the Chinese automaker Chery Automobile Co Limited belongs to the municipal government of Wuhu in Anhui Province. According to its 2009 financial report, Chery Limited posted revenues of ¥23.96 billion RMB (US$3.75 billion). Among these revenues, only ¥20.7 billion RMB (US$3.23 billion) were from sales of cars, which represented a net profit of only ¥66 million RMB (US$10.31 million), or a profit margin of 0.27%. Even more startling is that, during the three years from 2007 to 2009, Chery Limited depended heavily on government subsidies, which came to ¥285 million RMB (US$44.53 million), ¥470 million RMB (US$73.44 million) and ¥633 million RMB (US$98.91 million).[cdxix]

It is no surprise that, when the Chinese Politburo examines balance sheets similar to those of the Chery Group Limited, State-owned enterprises – in all economic sectors – are no longer granted economic immunity as they once were with the Chinese state authorities. Since the 1980s, the Chinese government and the ruling party have followed a policy of 正氣奮啟Pin Yin pronunciation Zhèngqì fèn kai. This policy mandates a formal separation of government functions from commercial business operations.

Western Perspectives on Chinese SOEs

Examples of the Western perspective on Chinese SOEs are not without suspicion and apprehension.

According to Carol Wickencamp, a Washington State based freelance writer and researcher, China's vast state-owned industries, with their hundreds of subsidiaries, pose two increasing threats to Western countries as they enter the bidding on infrastructure projects: threats to the domestic economy, and threats to internal security.

As China's state-owned enterprises (SOEs) enter the west's competitive bidding structure, with all the resources of the Communist dictatorship behind them, Western companies in on the bidding are out-gunned from the start. The SOE will handle its own financing though one of its many subsidiaries; it may manufacture the required heavy equipment or infrastructure components in one of its prison factories using cheap prison labor; it may even bring its own construction workers thousands of miles to accomplish the project. The Western company, on the other hand, will absorb its own expenses for financing and equipment expenditures, and employ workers according to fair labor practices.

Additionally, the SOE may be heavily subsidized as part of a long-range government goal to gain entry to strategic industries or infrastructure. Profit is not the motive for the SOE, though it will be essential for the company. The Communist Party, which fills the boards of directors in all SOEs with party secretaries, will absorb great losses in order to achieve their goals. Domestic industries and domestic employment are too often heavy losers, as many countries have already learned, when dealing with China.

Along with each project won by a Chinese SOE, is an increased security risk, as Chinese-manufactured electronic equipment becomes integrated with domestic industrial and infrastructure networks, and the internet. As the US Government recently observed, Chinese company Huawei's networking equipment could be used by China to spy on US activities; so too could devices manufactured by one of the many electronics companies operating as subsidiaries of the giant SOEs. Electronics that control industrial processes, infrastructure operations and communications can be built with "back doors" that may be used by Chinese operators, via the internet, to control operations, eavesdrop, collect information, or shut down vital domestic interests. The cost of domestic security losses may far outweigh any savings gained by employing low cost Chinese infrastructure development.

Ms Wickencamp, a uniquely qualified duty expert, addresses Chinese security threats and human rights abuses, with a focus on state-owned enterprises and their use of forced labor.

Carol also contributed the following, very precisely-worded, expert opinion on SOEs in the People's Republic of China, and how they manage themselves on the world stage, in every imaginable corner and artifice of the globe:

"China's explosion of investment in Africa and South East Asia has startled Western governments and analysts around the world. Leveraging the power and money of the gigantic SEOs to accomplish huge infrastructure and hydropower projects, mining developments, and resource extraction, Chinese investment has undoubtedly wrought some improvement in these less-developed and often impoverished countries. What the true cost has been to these countries bears examination now that there is room for gaining perspective over time.

Europe and the United States experience the impact of low cost green power products that are manufactured and subsidized by massive SOEs which sell them under slick Western names at far less than what domestic manufacturers can sell their products. Even the most developed and wealthy of countries feels the bruises that come from contact with China's government strategies to expand influence and market share around the entire world.

Africans are not happy with the big infrastructure projects across the continent. Often there is an expectation that Chinese infrastructure investment will bring more jobs for their citizens than materialize, and there is resentment when the Chinese company imports Chinese laborers. There are other issues too. Africans complain that Chinese companies destroy national parks in their hunt for resources and that they routinely disobey even rudimentary safety rules. Workers are killed in almost daily accidents. Some are shot by managers. Where China offers its companies preferential loans, African businesses struggle to compete. Roads and hospitals built by the Chinese are often faulty, not least because they bribe local officials and inspectors."

The Economist, April 20, 2011

China and Africa

Chinese Telecommunications Companies in Africa

Alcatel Shanghai Bell (ASB)

Alcatel-Shanghai Bell (ASB) is one of the biggest telecommunications equipment and solution suppliers in Asia. ASB is the Chinese flagship company of Alcatel-Lucent in Asia Pacific. It is the first foreign invested company limited by shares in China's telecommunications industry, with extensive global resources. ASB benefits from Alcatel-Lucent's comprehensive next-generation (NGN) portfolio. In 2007, ASB teamed up with Datang Mobile (which initially developed TD-SCDMA network solutions) to provide TD-SCDMA to Chinese service provider, China Mobile. Datang and ASB deployed TD-SCDMA for China Mobile in Shanghai, and in the southern city of Guangzhou. ASB provided the Node B equipment to be used in the network.

China Mobile

China Mobile Limited, China's largest telecoms company, was listed on the New York and Hong Kong Stock Exchanges in 1997. As the leading mobile services provider in China, the group boasts the world's largest unified, contiguous all-digital mobile network and the world's largest mobile subscriber base. In 2006, the Company was once again selected as one of the 'FT Global 500' by *The Financial Times*, and in the '*The World's 2000 Biggest Public Companies*' by *Forbes Magazine*. In April 2007, China Mobile indicated that it planned to buy companies in Africa and Southeast Asia as growth accelerates in those regions. It denied reports that it was planning to buy a stake in South African-based mobile player, MTN Corp. However, sources confirm that for a period, MTN was the target of some sort of Chinese acquisition attempt.

Huawei Technologies

Huawei is the main supplier to telecommunication giants China Telecom and China Unicom, and one of the world's ten-largest producers of telecom equipment. Its main products include switching systems, intelligent networks,

Synchronous Digital Hierarchy (SDH) transmission networks, wireless, datacoms, broadband integrated services (BISDN), power supplies, and freespace optical systems. Company sources claim that "only" one per cent of sales involve military customers, although this likely deflated number still represents more than US$30 million per year in equipment sales and service.

Huawei's products and solutions are deployed in over 100 countries, and serve 31 of the world's top 50 operators, as well as over one billion users worldwide. In 2006, it had an annual revenue of US$8,2 billion, and over 44,000 employees; over half its revenue came from overseas sales (US$ 4, 8 billion).

Huawei is often described as "*a Chinese firm with close ties to Beijing's military and a history of illicit exports and industrial espionage*", an allegation it vehemently rejects.

ZTE Communications

Originating from the Number 691 electronics factory under the China Aerospace Industry Corporation (CAIC), Zhongxing Telecom (ZTE) has grown to become China's largest listed telecommunications equipment manufacturer and wireless solutions provider. It lists shares in Hong Kong and Shenzhen, and is China's second-biggest telecom equipment vendor after Huawei Technologies Co. The company develops and manufactures telecommunications equipment for fixed, mobile, data and optical networks, intelligent networks and next-generation networks, as well as mobile phones.

The company has aggressively expanded in developing markets by exporting networking products, establishing joint ventures and investing in local communication operations. In October 2006, ZTE Chairman Li Taifong publicly confirmed that the African market has been targeted by the company as its "next business hub." ZTE has established three WiMAX R&D centers in America and China since its WiMAX operations began in 2002. With more than 400 R&D personnel dedicated to WiMAX operations, ZTE owns a growing patent portfolio in the WiMAX field.

China's increased involvement in the African telecommunications industry is part of a multidimensional engagement in the continent, to serve its broader strategy to enhance its global standing, counter Western influence, and to obtain resources and new export markets to feed its rapidly-expanding economy.

Alongside construction, energy and mining, telecommunications is one of the four strategic pillars underpinning China's economic development, and providing the necessary platform from which to challenge the West for global hegemony.

It is regarded as a vital industry for Chinese strategic interests from several approaches:

1) Acquisition of foreign
technology
2) Dual use military application
3) Reinforcing China's space and satellite development programme
4) Breaking into new markets.

Such assessments are closely driven by the Communist Party of China (CPC), and related ministerial and strategic planning institutions, which have as their primary mandate, the emergence of competitive international companies aligned with the strategic political considerations of the motherland. Importantly, Chinese telecom companies do not operate in isolation, but operate in tandem with Chinese geo-strategic objectives. This makes the need for effective countervailing strategies all the more important in dealing with the Chinese telecommunications challenge in Africa.

Initial assessments suggest that China has chosen several hubs from which to roll-out its telecommunication strategy on the continent. These include Egypt, Algeria, Tunisia, Kenya, Nigeria and South Africa.

Leading the pack are Chinese heavyweight companies such as Huawei Technologies and Zhongxing Telecom Ltd (ZTE) (both linked to the Chinese military and intelligence establishments), China Telecom and Alcatel Shanghai Bell (ASB). Improving technical capacity, linked to low costs of production, access to cheap state-subsidized funding sources and state political support, provide such companies with an important competitive edge which is not available to independent telecom companies.

The links between telecom deals and China's African strategy are not new.

The Chinese government's role was underlined in 2004, when Deputy Minister of Commerce Chen Jian stated: "*China will further expand telecom co-operation with African nations in line with mutual benefits and common development. Moreover, the Chinese government will support its telecom enterprises to run more telecom services in Africa.*" This, in a nutshell, explains the core of the Chinese telecommunication strategy in Africa. A number of important strategic indicators underline the business threat posed by Chinese telecoms companies:

As a result of Chinese Government support for the Chinese telecommunication companies, Chinese flagship companies, Huawei Technologies, ZTE and ASB can keep their prices extremely low, and tailor-make solutions for poor African countries. Critics of ZTE and Huawei point out that they sell cheaply to troubled governments like the regimes in Algiers or the Sudan, in deals that effectively amount to foreign aid, and with the full support of the Chinese Government. Because of its "*national champion*" status in China, ZTE can obtain low cost money that it can then lend to its own customers. Loans for African contracts are being encouraged, via preferential loans from government banks, which amount to a defacto subsidy. Money is funneled through lending channels, via preferential loans from the China Ex-Im Bank (EXIM), through the China Development Bank.

According to Chinese officials from the Ministry of Information Industry (MII), China, as a developing country, has similarities with developing countries in Africa, and enjoys a rich experience in ICT development from the perspective of a developing country. The director said that Africa needs all kinds of capacity building (such as the training for both students and teachers), and capacity building and e-learning are key factors to promote development in the continent.

In West Africa, companies in the area say that they find procuring equipment from Chinese companies attractive for a number of reasons. For instance, ZTE offered the best proposal in terms of price when Kasapa Telecom Ltd, a subsidiary of Hutchison Telecom, and one of four mobile operators in Ghana, wanted to procure equipment.

The Chinese Government's increasing financial support to African countries is giving a boost to the establishment to telecom infrastructure. The Export-Import Bank (EXIM) of China granted ASB financial assistance of US$63,3 million in 2004, to aid its overseas expansion. "*As China and African countries build solid political mutual trust, African countries are willing to get Chinese companies involved in more infrastructure projects*," said Zhou. "*We believe Chinese telecom equipment makers will have even bigger business opportunities in Africa in the future.*"

According to Christopher Wang, an analyst with an international securities firm in Shanghai: "*Doing business in China has taught ZTE and Huawei to focus on keeping their products simple and cheap. People in developing markets, such as Africa, don't need fancy or elaborate phones – they simply want something that works.*"

According to Charles Grosvenor, chairman of a consulting firm based in Shenzhen: "*ZTE is willing to forgo its branding, go the white label approach and customize to what operators and customers want.*"

According to Shi Lirong, senior vice president of ZTE, one reason why a growing number of service providers in Europe and North America are forging new partnerships with Chinese suppliers is because their relationships with traditional partners are failing to deliver:

"*R&D cost-cutting exercises over recent years may have lost Western-based telephony equipment manufacturers-including Lucent/Alcatel, Nortel, Siemens-their technological edge in the market place,*" he says. "*However, the story is radically different for Chinese equipment manufacturers that have so far concentrated sales efforts on developing areas. We haven't had those problems,*" he says."*There was no bubble to burst in these countries, so the trading environment is normal. Market investment is still increasing. For R&D investment there is no problem; we are still increasing budgets.*"

Finally, China is always careful to engage potential clients at the highest possible level. A macro-strategic intervention approach is key to winning over the power elites, which will buy into any proposed business plan. Only then do Chinese officials work down the food chain, to engage with local government-controlled mining companies and businessman, unless they are also well connected to the power elites.

Rare Earth Minerals (REM)

The People's Republic of China is the world leading holder of rare earth minerals (REM). According to *The Diplomat Blog "China Power"* the REM market is China's supply to control for the whole world; "*From 2009 to 2010, Chinese mines accounted for 259,000 tonnes out of a total global production of 263,000 tonnes of rare earth oxide.*"[cdxx] Currently REMs such as "*dysprosium, terbium, neodymium, europium, yttrium and lanthanum are a class of 17 chemical elements that play a critical role in modern technology including cancer treatment, cruise missiles, iPods, flat screen TVs, hybrid cars, wind turbines, solar panels and oil refineries to mention some applications.*"[cdxxi]

The People's Republic of China also produces 97 per cent of the world's REMs, even though the country has only 37 per cent of known global reserves of the metals. Given China's non-existent environmental regulations, low wages, and masterful understanding of what natural resources such as REM mean to the rest of the world, China has achieved a dominant position with rare earth resources, to the point of being classified as a monopoly.[cdxxii]

Why should countries worry about rare earth mineral production? The US was once the world's leading producer of rare earths, with California's Mountain Pass Mine. However, Mountain Pass ceased operating in 2002, because of declining prices for REM and the expiration of its environmental operating permits after a series of mine tailing spills, containing traces of radioactive uranium and thorium.[cdxxiii] Both Canada and Australia also stopped mining them in the 1990s, as lower cost Chinese rare earth minerals flooded the world market.[cdxxiv]

World prices for rare earth minerals soared significantly when China reduced its export quotas by 40 per cent in 2010, and by a further 35 per cent in the first half of this year, seeking to build a stronger domestic industry. It has also introduced an export tax on some rare earth products.[cdxxv]

During June 2010, the US uncovered an Afghani rare mineral discovery, containing gold, iron, copper, cobalt and lithium. Geologists in Afghanistan, accompanied by US Marines, found the mineral deposit estimated to be worth approximately one to three trillion US dollars! First to begin taking advantage of this natural resource "mother lode" was the People's Republic of China, who does not have one single soldier from the PLA deployed to Afghanistan. In his Foreign Policy article, *"Chinese Takeout"*, Aziz Huq points out that *"China, which has a narrow land border with Afghanistan, already invests heavily in the war-torn Central Asian state. The state-owned China Metallurgical Group has a $3.5 billion copper mining venture in Logar province."*[cdxxvi]

According to a letter to the editor of the *New York Times* by Mahmood Elahi, "While the American troops are being killed by the Taliban, China is quietly developing the Loghar copper mines. Why is the Afghan government, considered an American puppet by many, allowing a Chinese state-owned company to develop these resources? The answer: With the Chinese economy booming and the United States mired in a prolonged recession, the demand for copper and other minerals is coming from China."[cdxxvii]

In 2011, China announced that its biggest producer of rare earths was suspending production for one month in hopes of boosting the slumping prices of these exotic minerals.[cdxxviii] In late October 2011, besides limiting its export of REM to Japan, China also decided to reduce its exports of these crucial minerals to other Western countries, including the US and all of Europe. Since the Central Committee of the Communist Party had recently met, there are concerns that a nationalistic sense of China's economic dominance may be the new party line, further asserting its perceived and intended Chinese leadership over the world of rare earth minerals.

Sinomach

Sinomach is a significant, Chinese state-owned enterprise, located in Beijing, with global tentacles, and according to its corporate profile has "the approval of the State Council. China National Machinery Industry Corporation (SINOMACH) was established in January 1997. SINOMACH is a large scale, state-owned enterprise group under the supervision of the State Assets Supervision and Administration Commission.

SINOMACH has the most diversified business coverage, a complete business chain, and the strongest R&D capabilities in China's machinery industry. Under its portfolio, there are 50 wholly-owned and holding subsidiaries, including 6 listed companies and more than 70 overseas offices and branches. There are close to 80,000 employees working for SINOMACH around the world. For years, SINOMACH has sustained over 30 per cent annual growth, with main business revenue reaching 15 billion US$ in 2009.

Main businesses of SINOMACH focus on R&D and manufacture of machinery and equipment, project contracting, trade and services. Its service covers a wide range of key national economic sectors, including industry, agriculture, communication and transportation, energy, building, light industries, automobile, ship-building, mining, metallurgy and aerospace industries. SINOMACH has provided professional services for over 140 countries and regions around the world."[cdxxix]

What is really unique about Sinomach is the 50 square-mile Chinese city, called a special economic trade zone, which it is building in Boise, Idaho. The state constitution of Idaho was amended to allow Boise airport to borrow money to build facilities, which allow landing rights to foreign-flagged air carriers.[cdxxx]

Network Security & Chinese Telco Manufacturers

There are several Chinese SOEs that may be benefitting from economic and classic espionage: telecommunications equipment providers Huawei and ZTE; and telecommunications operators such as China Mobile (the world's largest mobile phone company based upon number of subscribers); BaoShan

Steel, and China National Petroleum Corporation. Chinese companies ZTE and Huawei are building digital telephone switches, providing roughly 200,000 subscriber lines in Afghanistan.[cdxxxi]

Huawei also installed, operates and owns the entire telecommunications infrastructure in Iraq. According to a *Washington Times* story, Huawei "*has won hundreds of contracts in Iraq since the 2003 US-led invasion, some paid in part with US tax dollars, and now effectively owns the country's phone system.*"

Huawei Technologies has won more than 600 telecommunications infrastructure contracts since Iraqi reconstruction began in 2004, said Robert C Fonow, the State Department's senior adviser to Iraq's Telecommunications Ministry from 2006 to 2008.

"*No other company comes close to*" that number, said Mr Fonow, now a consultant and managing director of the business-turnaround firm RGI Ltd. He said that Huawei "*controls the market for the national fiber-optic grid, and much of the mobile-phone and wireless fixed-line equipment markets in Iraq, which is just about everything.*"[cdxxxii]

When stocks in SOEs that are listed on the Shanghai Stock Exchange (SSE) are purchased, these purchases are ultimately financing the Chinese Government. Seven of the ten largest stocks on the Shanghai Stock Exchange are nothing but state-controlled companies: PetroChina; Industrial and Commercial Bank of China; Sinopec; Bank of China; China Shenhua Energy Company; China Life Insurance Company; and Bank of Communications.

Examples of Chinese business consortiums purchasing US companies include Chinese computer manufacturer Lenovo and Chinese telecommunications manufacturer Huawei. China's Lenovo Group, on May 1, 2005, purchased International Business Machines' (IBM) personal computer division for $1.75 billion. As part of the transaction according to CNET news:

"*IBM takes an 18.9 per cent stake in Lenovo. Lenovo paid $1.25 billion for the IBM PC unit and assumed debt, which brought the total cost to $1.75 billion.*"

Based on both companies' 2003 sales figures, the joint venture will have an annual sales volume of 11.9 million units and revenue of $12 billion, increasing Lenovo's current PC business fourfold."[cdxxxiii]

What is remarkable about the Lenovo purchase of IBM's personal computer division is the fact that they are selling x386 motherboards, made in China, in personal computers and servers worldwide. While that may not be unique, the Mandarin-based operating systems create a potential cybersecurity threat vector from the People's Republic of China.

As of October 1, 2011, 55.1 per cent of Lenovo stock was held by the general public, 41.5 per cent by Legend Holdings Limited, and 3.4 per cent by other entities including TPG Capital, General Atlantic and Newbridge Capital LLC. The Chinese Academy of Sciences owns 36 per cent of Legend Holdings.[cdxxxiv]

The chairman of Legend Capital, which owns Legend Holdings, is Mr Liu Chaunzhi. His biography and responsibilities, reported on the Legend Capital website, offers some very curious information and draws the correlation between Lenovo and the People's Liberation Army.

The Team bio page states:

"Mr Liu is president of Legend Holdings Ltd, non-executive director of Lenovo Group, and chairman of Raycom Real Estate Co and Hony Capital. Mr Liu is a member on the Investment Committee of Legend Capital.

In 1984, with initial capital of RMB200,000 (less than 25,000 US dollars then), funded by the Chinese Academy of Sciences (CAS), Mr Liu, together with 10 other staff members of the Institute of Computing Technology of CAS, established the New Technology Developer Inc (the predecessor of Lenovo Group of which he had served as president and Board Chairman until 2005). Mr Liu graduated from Xidian University (formerly Xi'an Military Institute of Telecommunications and Engineering). He is a senior engineer.

Mr Liu is also Vice Chairman of All China Federation of Industry and Commerce, a delegate to the 16th National Congress of the Communist Party of China, and a deputy to the 9th and 10th National People's Congress."

The Chinese Academy of Sciences (CAS) is a science and technology organization, run and administered by both the Communist Party of China and the People's Republic of China. The CAS owns Legend Holdings.

Mr Liu, having graduated from a PLA military university in Xi'an with an educational emphasis on telecommunications and engineering, is able to facilitate a distinct relationship between his holding company Legend and the PLA. Such linkage would allow the PLA to plan and carry out cyberwarfare through the sales of potentially infected personal computers and servers with pre-installed malware.

As a delegate to the Chinese Communist Part National Congress, and previous deputy to the People's Congress, he is in a very unique leadership position to receive mandates from President Hu Jintao when it comes to supporting the official Chinese Government edict of carrying out Chinese cyberwarfare through management and leadership of Legend Holdings who owns Lenovo.

On February 5th 2008, American-based Symantec, a security-focused technology company located on 350 Ellis Street, Mountain View, California, announced via a press release that they were entering into a joint venture with Chinese-based Huawei, which is located in Chéngdū, China. The joint Huawei-Symantec Press Release was as follows:

"CUPERTINO, Calif. and SHENZHEN, China – Feb. 5, 2008 – Symantec Corp (Nasdaq: SYMC) and Huawei Technologies Co Ltd. (Huawei) today announced that they have commenced their joint venture, which was announced in May 2007. The new company will develop and distribute world-leading security and storage appliances to global telecommunications carriers and enterprises. The transaction has satisfied all closing conditions,

received all required government and regulatory approvals and officially closed on Feb. 5, 2008.

The joint venture company is headquartered in Chengdu, China, with Huawei owning 51 per cent and Symantec owning 49 per cent. John W Thompson, chairman and chief executive officer of Symantec, has been named chairman of the board and Ren ZhengFei, chief executive officer of Huawei, has been named chief executive officer.

Huawei is licensing certain technology and Symantec is licensing certain storage and security software to the joint venture company. Symantec is also contributing US$150 million to the joint venture."

The Huawei-Symantec joint venture's website specifically says; "*Huawei Symantec Technologies Co. Ltd. (Huawei Symantec) is a leading provider of network security and storage appliance solutions to enterprise customers worldwide. Our solutions are developed to keep pace with evolving risks and demanding availability requirements facing enterprises. As a joint venture, Huawei Symantec combines Huawei's expertise in telecom network infrastructure and Symantec's leadership in security and storage software to provide world-class solutions that address the ever-changing needs in network security and storage for enterprises.*"

A Huawei corporation briefing, regarding the JV with Symantec identifies specific benefits of the merger and the persistent investment which followed: [cdxxxv].

"*Total investment amounts to US $157 million:*

- Over 1,000 full-time dedicated security and storage professionals.

- Set up storage and security R & D centers in India and four Chinese cities: Shenzhen, Beijing, Chengdu and Hangzhou.

- Set up China's first laboratory of attack and defense networks and applications ..."[cdxxxvi]

Jeffrey Carr wrote an article for *The Diplomat Blogs* called "*China's Silent Cyber Takeover?*" In the April 2011 blog, Mr Carr also detailed the Huawei-

Symantec joint venture and two other cybersecurity-related company mergers within the Western corporate cybersecurity and networking technology world, by People's Republic of China SOE's. In the first example, the joint venture of Huawei-Symantec signed a distributorship agreement with SYNNEX Corporation to distribute information technology and domain name service (DNS) security services throughout North America.[cdxxxvii] What is very interesting and strange about the Huawei-Symantec-Synnex relationship is the obvious ability for Huawei to enter into the cybersecurity market in the US without anyone questioning it, least of all the corporate management at either Symantec or Synnex.

We should not forget that Huawei has been trying very diligently to gain a foothold in the US, by building out a major telecommunication's provider 4G network. However, each time Huawei reaches the final selection they are ousted by the US Government, stating that there is a clear and present danger to the Homeland security of the United States. According to Karl Bode, of DSL Reports, there is much ado about Huawei and their ties to the People's Republic of China military, the PLA.

"Last month the National Preparedness Group released a report stating that national US emergency networks still aren't up to snuff a decade after the events of 9/11 and recommendations by the 9/11 Commission. Several Congressional efforts to build a nationwide LTE network have stumbled over the last few years, with partisan bickering, funding concerns, and carrier lobbyists all muddying the water and leading to productivity gridlock. If and when the United States' nationwide LTE emergency network gets built there's one thing that's clear: it won't be Huawei that winds up building it. The government has blocked all LTE build bids by Huawei due to the company's "close ties" with the Chinese government. Huawei "will not be taking part in the building of America's interoperable wireless emergency network for first responders due to US government national-security concerns," Commerce Department spokesman Kevin Griffis told The Daily Beast."

Griffis declined to elaborate on those concerns. But current and retired US intelligence officials tell *The Daily Beast* the longstanding concern about Huawei is that the company's chips, routers and other technical equipment will be bugged in a way that gives China's government a cyberbackdoor into sensitive information networks.

This is only the latest in a series of US obstacles imposed on Huawei, who continues to insist security fears are "*unsubstantiated.*" Meanwhile, first responders in some markets are tired of waiting for Congress and the FCC, and cities like Charlotte, North Carolina are building their own emergency LTE networks. On a national scale, it appears we may be in for another decade of ham operators continuing the heavy lifting when mainstream networks collapse during emergencies.[cdxxxviii]

Also according to Mr Carr's report, is the merger between Huawei-Symantec and Force-10 Networks. As a Michael Dell Company they definitely have sale initiatives with the US Government as their corporate web page describes:

"*Government enterprises are complex, geographically dispersed collection of networks delivering on operationally diverse missions.*

As agencies begin to evaluate and deploy the next generation of Internet Protocol (IPv6) technologies and security applications, now is the time to strategically migrate to a unifying infrastructure that delivers high speed, reliability and security within a single high-performance Ethernet network.

Force10 Networks works with defense, intelligence and civilian agencies to advance the bandwidth needs and reliability demands of government IT infrastructure while ensuring the economics and performance of mission critical networks."[cdxxxix]

So, if Force10 Networks caters to the US defense, civilian and intelligence agencies, what makes a logical person believe that this is indeed not the backdoor that Huawei, a Chinese-based company, needs to surreptitiously enter the United States cybersecurity realm? Is the economic joint venture between Huawei, Symantec, Synnex and Force10 a concern for the cyberdefenders of the United States?

Out of fairness to the Chief Executive Founder of Huawei, Ren Zhengfei, he was indeed a telecommunications officer in China's military, the People's Liberation Army. He joined the Communist Party of China in 1978, and is member of the 12th National Congress of the Communist Party of China. He has been involved in the General Staff Department's Information Engineering Academy. Ren himself was described in a 2005 *Time Magazine* profile as "*a former soldier who fashions himself after Chairman Mao*".[cdxl]

Huawei, while successful under a former PLA telecommunications officer's reign, has earlier business dealings with another US Government telecommunications provider, Level 3. In July 2009, Huawei won a competitive deal to provide Level 3 with effective but inexpensive optical networking switches for its 40-Gbits optical equipment needs. According to a report by *Optical Networking Industry* magazine, as for the potential security concerns about Level 3 running US federal government traffic over a network built with equipment from a Chinese vendor, "*Level 3 could get around the national security issue by guaranteeing that government traffic stays on Infinera (the incumbent optical provider) equipment while new, non-governmental traffic rides on the Huawei gear.*"[cdxli]

Conclusions about Chinese SOEs & the Cyberthreat

This chapter has only provided a sampling of Chinese Government owned, operated and managed state-owned enterprises. One consistent fact and direct correlation is that there is a link between potential cyberthreat vectors from these SOEs to non-Chinese companies, organizations and nation-states that purchase, install, use and maintain their products.

Does this necessarily mean that all of Symantec's security products and services are compromised? No, not uniquely so; but it should give pause to international governments who purchase their products, ultimately wondering if once a Symantec product is installed will their enterprise's information security program already be compromised?

Does the Force10 relationship with Huawei automatically mean that the US Government's purchase of information and security products are at risk?

Perhaps not yet. After the sales are made, and quotas met, who then remembers the relationship, potential cybersecurity risk and inherent threat that Force10 information security products might have?

However consider this, as the US Department of Homeland security purchases Force10 products, what are the second and third order effects for safeguarding the US critical infrastructure? Are these critical networks then already compromised? Perhaps when there are no more reports of Chinese cyberattacks, the knowledge that the critical infrastructure of the nation has already been compromised will be a precursor to something much larger.

CHAPTER 11: COMMERCIAL OBJECTIVES OF CHINESE CYBERATTACKS

China: industry infiltration or data exfiltration?

According to the 2010 US-China Economic and Security Review Commission, there are several reasons to be concerned about the People's Republic of China. Although these are cautionary words, they are not alarmist, or are they? The US-China Economic and Security Review Commission has a legislatively-mandated mission to "*monitor, investigate and submit to Congress, an annual report on the national security implications of the bilateral and economic relationship between the United States and the People's Republic of China (PRC), and to provide recommendations, where appropriate, to Congress for legislative and administration action.*" Public Law 108–7, the amendment to the initial authorization, charges the Commission to focus on the following areas: economic reforms, proliferation practices, energy, US capital markets, corporate reporting, regional and economic security impacts, US-China bilateral programs, WTO compliance, and media control by the Chinese government.^{cdxlii}

What is really remarkable about the fine work of the Commission is the fact that they use US tax dollars to pay Northrup Grumman to evaluate the People's Republic of China's ability to carry out cyberwarfare. The Commission's report comes out annually in the Fall; it is a wealth of information and is appropriately called "*Capability of the People's Republic of China to Conduct Cyber Warfare and Computer Network Exploitation.*"

Commercial Victims of Chinese Cyberattacks?

The cybervictims of the People's Republic of China's intent to carry out attacks through the cyberspace of the Internet include multi-national corporations of every conceivable market vertical and industry. Governments and their military bodies have been the victims of both direct and indirect cybertargeting by the Chinese.

'Operation Ghost Net' 幽靈網

Cybersecurity researchers at the Munk Center for International Studies based in Toronto, Canada, coined the phrase *'Operation Ghost Net'* (Mandarin 幽靈網) after tracking a significant worldwide cyberespionage effort, which was directly attributed to the People's Republic of China. Over 103 countries worldwide had their information technology infrastructures infiltrated, servers exploited and data exfiltrated, from almost 1,300 personal computers connected to these organization networks. All of the computer infrastructure hacking was controlled by cyberwarfare command and control, located in the People's Republic of China. According to the *New York Times* the main target of *'Ghost Net'* were the offices of the Dali Lama, with secondary and tertiary targets focused on embassies, governments and corporate infrastructure.

John Markoff of the *New York Times* wrote an exceptional story on *'Ghost Net'*, reporting that the researchers at the Munk Institute *"found that three of the four control servers were in different provinces in China – Hainan, Guangdong and Sichuan – while the fourth was discovered to be at a Web-hosting company based in Southern California."*[cdxliii]

According to the Markoff story, the Munk researchers determined from a set of computer logfiles that the attacks had perhaps commenced almost two years earlier, on May 22nd, 2007.[cdxliv] In conjunction with *InfoWar Monitor* (IWM), the SecDevGroup, a cybersecurity firm also based in Canada, released a very good in-depth analysis of *'Ghost Net'*. While a cyberenthusiast might find the *New York Times* article on *'Ghost Net'* sensational, the *IWM* report is significantly detailed and a must-read for anyone interested, even vicariously, in the importance and significance of 21st century Chinese cyberwarfare efforts. *IWM* states that *'Ghost Net'* was *"a suspected cyberespionage network of over 1,295 infected computers in 103 countries, 30% of which are high-value targets, including ministries of foreign affairs, embassies, international organizations, news media, and NGOs."*[cdxlv]

Information Warfare Monitor is an independent, public-private research venture, focused on the emergence of cyberspace as a strategic domain. It is operated by two Canadian institutions: the Citizen Lab at the Munk School of Global Affairs, University of Toronto and the SecDev Group, an operational think-tank based in Ottawa (Canada). The Secdev Group conducts field-based investigations and data gathering. IWM's advanced research and analysis facilities are located at "*the Citizen Lab.*"[cdxlvi]

Scott Henderson's "*The Dark Visitor*" website provides an incredible amount of detail on tracking the hacker from the city of Chengdu, People's Republic of China. In his summary of the Chinese hacker associated with '*Ghost Net*' Mr Henderson writes, regarding direct attribution to a Chinese hacker using the pseudonym "*lost33*": "*there are other lost33 websites out there, such as myspace/lost33, these do not meet the profile of our hacker. It would be a very unusual set of circumstances that would lead to such a bizarre set of coincidences coming together as we have here:*

The 'Ghost Net' websites list Chengdu, Sichuan under organization and the pseudonym losttemp33 as the contact e-mail address.

The e-mail address losttemp33@hotmail.com has been posted on at least two websites dealing with computer programming. The post on hacking Windows shows that the person also uses the alias lost33 as an alternative to the full e-mail address.

An individual using the lost33 signature has posted on several Chinese hacker forums including Xfocus and Isbase (the Green Army). He may even have been a student under Glacier.

The first lost33 website shows a birth date of 24 July 1982 and current address as Chengdu, Sichuan. The website motto is, "The bored solider sways on the empty battlefield."

The second "bored soldier" website is clearly owned by the same person as the first lost33 website. The owners were born on the same date; both live in Chengdu, Sichuan and use the same motto. The new website has links with known hacker websites (Xfocus, NSfocus and Eviloctal), links to hacker programs, and demonstrates an education in technology (University of Electronic Science and Technology of China).

Obviously the weakest link in the analysis is the jump between losttemp33 and lost33 but we feel the weight of the evidence shows a connection. We do not conclusively claim this person is involved but we think further inquiry is needed."[cdxlvii]

'Shadows in the Cloud'

The researchers at the Munk Institute successfully concluded another cybercounterintelligence coup against Chinese-based cyberwarriors, when on Monday 5th April 2010, they released a report called '*Shadows in the Cloud: An investigation into cyber espionage 2.0*'. During this Chinese cyberattack, the targets were explicitly classified Indian Government documents of a "RESTRICTED", "CONFIDENTIAL" and "SECRET" nature. The Munk Institute researchers, in conjunction with the SECDevGroup, were able to successfully recover documents, a feat they were unable to accomplish during their efforts associated with '*Ghost Net*'.

According to the *IWM* report, the Canadian cybersecurity researchers discovered and logged "a complex and tiered command and control infrastructure." The cyberattackers misused a variety of services, including those of *Twitter, Google Groups, Blogspot, Baidu Blogs, blog.com* and *Yahoo! Mail,* designing an advanced, persistent cyberincursion, whose focus was to maintain persistent control over the compromised computers. "This top layer directed compromised computers to accounts on free web hosting services, and as the free hosting servers were disabled, to a stable core of command and control servers located in China."[cdxlviii]

Additional notes from the '*Shadows in the Cloud*' report indicate that "*based on the character of the documents (and not IP addresses) we assessed that we recovered documents from the National Security Council Secretariat (NSCS) of India, the Embassy of India, Kabul, the Embassy of India, Moscow, the Consulate General of India, Dubai, and the High Commission of India in Abuja, Nigeria. In addition, we recovered documents from India's Military Engineer Services (MES) and other military personnel as well as the Army Institute of Technology in Pune, Maharashtra and the Military College of Electronics and Mechanical Engineering in Secunderabad, Andhra Pradesh. Documents from a variety of other entities including the Institute for Defence Studies and Analyses as well as India Strategic defence magazine and FORCE magazine were compromised.*"[cdxlix]

The Canadian researchers indicated that, in the case of the cyberintrusions associated with '*Shadows in the Cloud*', the cyberattacks were most likely to have come from the Chinese province of Sìchuān.According to a *New York Times* report on '*Shadows in the Cloud*', "*as with all cyberattacks, it is easy to mask the true origin, the researchers said. Given the sophistication of the intruders and the targets of the operation, the researchers said, it is possible that the Chinese government approved of the spying.*"[cdl]

With the discovery of the cyberespionage activities of the People's Republic of China as part of the '*Shadows in the Cloud*' report, it is quite evident that the Chinese are actively conducting government-condoned cyberattacks, to gather data and intelligence on the activities of foreign governments and their militaries.

'Operation Aurora'

'*Operation Aurora*' was a series of cyberattacks thought to have originated from the People's Republic of China. These hacking attacks started around the middle of 2009, and concluded in or around December 2009. Interestingly, Google was the first to disclose the cyberattacks that were part of '*Operation Aurora*', on January 12, 2010. In the following post on a Google's official blogsite, called "*A new approach to China*".

"Like many other well-known organizations, we face cyber-attacks of varying degrees on a regular basis. In mid-December, we detected a highly sophisticated and targeted attack on our corporate infrastructure originating from China that resulted in the theft of intellectual property from Google. However, it soon became clear that what at first appeared to be solely a security incident – albeit a significant one – was something quite different.

First, this attack was not just on Google. As part of our investigation we have discovered that at least twenty other large companies from a wide range of businesses – including the Internet, finance, technology, media and chemical sectors – have been similarly targeted. We are currently in the process of notifying those companies, and we are also working with the relevant U.S. authorities.

Second, we have evidence to suggest that a primary goal of the attackers was accessing the Gmail accounts of Chinese human rights activists. Based on our investigation to date we believe their attack did not achieve that objective. Only two Gmail accounts appear to have been accessed, and that activity was limited to account information (such as the date the account was created) and subject line, rather than the content of emails themselves.

Third, as part of this investigation but independent of the attack on Google, we have discovered that the accounts of dozens of U.S.-, China- and Europe-based Gmail users who are advocates of human rights in China appear to have been routinely accessed by third parties. These accounts have not been accessed through any security breach at Google, but most likely via phishing scams or malware placed on the users' computers."[cdli]

Besides Google, at least twenty other firms were cybertargeted by the Chinese during 'Operation Aurora'. Notable among the companies hacked via these Chinese operations were Adobe®, Dow Chemical, Juniper Networks, Morgan Stanley, Northrop Grumman, Symantec, Rackspace and Yahoo®.

The objective of the Chinese hackers during 'Operation Aurora' was to specifically target the e-mail accounts of human rights activists, known to be active and vocally criticizing the People's Republic of China and her human rights violations record.

According to McAfee, who produced a very detailed and substantial report, the cyberthreat methodology consisted of extremely complex and sophisticated hacking capabilities and tools. *Techie Buzz* offered the following after-action report of the *'Operation Aurora'* hack, "*hackers used multiple levels of encryption and took unprecedented precautions to avoid detection. An unknown exploit in Internet Explorer was utilised by the hackers to gain control of target systems. The exploit affects all versions of Internet Explorer since IE 6 and can be exploited on Windows 2000, XP, Server 2003, Vista, Server 2008, Windows 7 and Server 2008 R2.*"[cdlii]

Techie Buzz also went on to mention that "*Internet Explorer was not the only vector used by the hackers. Vulnerabilities in Adobe's Reader and Acrobat were also among the weaknesses utilised by 'Operation Aurora'.*"[cdliii]

Google, Inc.

During most of 2010, China and the US have been at odds over claims of violations of each other's cybersecurity posture. Google had stopped serving up Internet searches for its Chinese search engine, google.cn and redirected the Internet search traffic to servers in Hong Kong.[cdliv] This is illogical, as Hong Kong has been part of the People's Republic of China since 1999, when the British lease expired. Google has simply had enough of China's demands, particularly following the suspected cyberattacks from within the PRC, and related Chinese censorship edicts. The PRC has denied that the cyberattacks on Google have come from within China, and says that Internet regulation control is required to preserve a stable Chinese society.

The real crux of Google's issues in China started back on January 12th 2010, when the international search engine discovered that very sophisticated cyberhack attacks from inside the PRC had stolen Google's search engine source code. According to John Markoff of the *New York Times*, "*... a person with direct knowledge of the investigation now says that the losses included one of Google's crown jewels, a password system that controls* *access by millions of users worldwide to almost all of the company's Web services, including e-mail and business applications."*

What is particularly interesting about the cyberattacks on Google is that, besides the hacking being traced back to the PRC, the main competitor of Google in China, Baidu, has a distinct, if albeit loose link to the two information technology schools where the hacking was thought to have originated. The two Chinese universities, where the Google hacks are said to have come from, are the Shànghǎi jiāotōng dàxué and the Lán xiáng zhíyè xuéxiào.

The Google Hacking Plot Thickens

Shànghǎi jiāotōng dàxué is one of the People's Republic of China's premiere information technology and computer science higher education universities. It also calls itself a School of International Education, and, according to its website, sees itself as the "oriental MIT".[cdlv] The linkage to information technology, between Shànghǎi jiāotōng dàxué and the needs of the Chinese State, are quite clear. This was evidenced by computer science students from the university winning IBM's *"Battle of the Brains"* contest in 2010. In Harbin, China, during February 2010, Shànghǎi jiāotōng dàxué students solved all seven computer programming problems competing against a number of Asian and Eurasian technical universities. What is unusual about the Shanghai University is that it actually has a "School of Information Security Engineering".

The Information Security Engineering School of the Shanghai Jiaotong University School has unique Chinese state-sponsored projects focusing on information security technology. One of these projects is the *"National Information Security Application Demonstration Project"*, which has a Chinese Government Research code name of S219.

Lán xiáng zhíyè xuéxiào is less certain. Jonathon Watts of the British *Guardian* wrote of the dissimilarity between what was reported by the *New York Times* and the *Washington Post* on this subject, albeit not directly. His opening paragraph sums up the confusion, but also points to the potential

Chinese hacking conspiracy theory linking to this Chinese vocational school. In his story from June 2nd 2011, he writes "*depending on your perspective, Lanxiang vocational school is either the heart of a secretive global hacking conspiracy or a second-rate educational factory that is best known for churning out hairdressers and cooks.*"cdlvi

There is certainly controversy, in newspapers and in the blogosphere, as to whether or not the Google attacks really did originate in the PRC. *The People's Daily*, the Chinese government newspaper, certainly took issue with Google's accusation that it had traced cyberattacks on Gmail accounts to the People's Republic of China, claiming that Google was simply still angry over previous issues with doing business in the 'Middle Kingdom'.

'Night Dragon'

What was '*Night Dragon*'? And how does it fit into the cyberattack taxonomy of the People's Republic of China and 21st century Chinese warfare? '*Night Dragon*' was a series of cyberhack attacks, originating from within the PRC, whose targets were global energy companies worldwide. Although McAfee's report on this attack says that they only have circumstantial evidence pointing to the 'Middle Kingdom', they claim that the Chinese cyberperpetrators ran command and control (C&C) operations, on leased server infrastructure purchased from Internet hosting companies in both the Netherlands and the US.

The McAfee report on '*Night Dragon*' is quite illustrative of what took place, how the hackers performed their cybermanipulation, and accomplished their various energy firm information and data exfiltration. Here is an excerpt:

"The Night Dragon attacks work by methodical and progressive intrusions into the targeted infrastructure.

The following basic activities were performed by the Night Dragon operation:

• *Company extranet web servers compromised through SQL-injection techniques, allowing remote command execution*

• *Commonly available hacker tools are uploaded on compromised web servers, allowing attackers to pivot into the company's intranet and giving them access to sensitive desktops and servers internally*

• *Using password cracking and pass-the-hash tools, attackers gain additional usernames and passwords, allowing them to obtain further authenticated access to sensitive internal desktops and servers*

• *Initially using the company's compromised web servers as command and control (C&C) servers, the attackers discovered that they needed only to disable Microsoft® Internet Explorer® (IE) proxy settings to allow direct communication from infected machines to the Internet*

• *Using the RAT malware, they proceeded to connect to other machines (targeting executives) and exfiltrating email archives and other sensitive documents.*

Details of the Attack

Attackers using several locations in China have leveraged Command & Control servers on purchased hosted services in the United States and compromised servers in the Netherlands to wage attacks against global oil, gas, and petrochemical companies, as well as individuals and executives in Kazakhstan, Taiwan, Greece, and the United States to acquire proprietary and highly confidential information. The primary operational technique used by the attackers comprised a variety of hacker tools, including privately developed and customized RAT tools that provided complete remote administration capabilities to the attacker. RATs provide functions similar to Citrix or Microsoft® Windows® Terminal Services, allowing a remote individual to completely control the affected system.

To deploy these tools, attackers first compromised perimeter security controls, through SQL-injection exploits of extranet web servers, as well as targeted spear-phishing attacks of mobile worker laptops, and compromising corporate VPN accounts to penetrate the targeted company's defensive architectures (DMZs and firewalls) and conduct reconnaissance of targeted companies' networked computers. [cdlvii]

Multi-National Energy Companies

Chinese cyberattacks against oil and gas companies have focused on exfiltrating important proprietary drilling and necessary competitive bids, architectural plans, project definition documents, and functional operational aspects of future natural resource discovery efforts. The Chinese intent is two-fold, as the hack and attack through the vacuous oil company's networks, gain competitive pre-advantage when negotiating with the countries that have oil and gas resources, before the original oil company can achieve success; thus "Win competitive bids Siberia to China."[cdlviii] Baker Hughes Inc. said it was hacked recently as part of a wide assault on energy companies. "*Baker Hughes provides advanced drilling equipment & proprietary techniques – assessing the quality and accessibility of oil reserves…*"[cdlix]

'Operation Night Dragon' is one of several notorious international cyberattack and hacking excursions, thought to have been carried out by cybermilitias enlisted by the PLA, to illegally obtain information about the current and future activities of multi-national energy firms. The proprietary information exfiltrated by these Chinese hackers could then be used to provide an economic advantage to Chinese energy firms, seeking to utilize the same intellectual property to serve the natural resources requirements of the PRC.

'Operation Shady RAT'

On the 2nd of August 2011, Mr Dmitri Alperovitch, vice president of threat research at anti-virus manufacturer McAfee, discovered the commercial and government targeted cyberespionage activity now known as *'Operation Shady RAT'*. According to Alperovitch, the cyberespionage attacks are "*the most comprehensive analysis ever revealed of victim profiles from a five year targeted operation by one specific actor – 'Operation Shady RAT', as I have named it at McAfee*" (RAT is a common acronym in the industry which stands for Remote Access Tool).[cdlx]

What is interesting about the cyberattacks associated with the latest incursions over the Internet, and loosely attributed to the People's Republic of China, is that some of the cybervictims are repeat targets of some of the previous cyberattacks, such as *'Night Dragon'*, *'Aurora'*, and those associated with *'Ghost Net'*. Alperovitch goes on to report on the length and duration of *Shady RAT*: *"this is not a new attack, and the vast majority of the victims have long since remediated these specific infections (although whether most realized the seriousness of the intrusion or simply cleaned up the infected machine without further analysis into the data loss is an open question). McAfee has detected the malware variants and other relevant indicators for years with Generic Downloader.x and Generic BackDoor.theuristic signatures (those who have had prior experience with this specific adversary may recognize it by the use of encrypted HTML comments in web pages that serve as a command channel to the infected machine).*[cdlxi]

Alperovitch's report is filled with significant details of the cybervictim's locations and organizational attribution, as well as possible motives for the hacking by the Chinese. According to a *Vanity Fair* article, written on the McAfee discovery and the apt naming of *'Operation Shady RAT'*, the *"victims include government agencies in the United States, Taiwan, South Korea, Vietnam, and Canada, the Olympic committees in three countries, and the International Olympic Committee. Rounding out the list of countries where Shady Rat hacked into computer networks: Japan, Switzerland, the United Kingdom, Indonesia, Denmark, Singapore, Hong Kong, Germany, and India. The vast majority of victims – 49 – were U.S.-based companies, government agencies, and nonprofits. The category most heavily targeted was defense contractors – 13 in all."*[cdlxii]

These various institutes all seem to agree that commercially sponsored cyberattacks are originating from within the PRC. The Chinese Government, the Chinese Military, and state-owned enterprises all appear to have a common cyberespionage goal in mind, which is to attack soft cybertargets of foreign governments, gather information about their confidential and proprietary information networks, and exfiltrate data to benefit the People's Republic of China. This is the commercial and government sponsored face of 21st century Chinese cyberwarfare.

Apple®

Apple has also had its share of misadventures in the People's Republic of China. Three particular incidents should be recognized as overt attempts by the Chinese to simply copy Apple technology outright and claim the "knockoffs" as their own.

In July 2011, *IT Pro Portal* reported "*Fake Apple Stores Mushrooming In China; No iPhone 5 Inside*".[cdlxiii] This very obvious intellectual property fraud went beyond merely copying the technology. Entire stores located in Kunming, which is in Southwestern Yúnnán Province, were made to look exactly like Apple stores located anywhere else in the world. The article continues: "*A new worrying phenomenon has cropped up in China and Apple has been its first victim; meet the first fake Apple Stores, entire buildings that have been designed to look like the real thing.*

Chinese companies have long been known for being master copiers but this takes the concept of plagiarism and copying to a whole new level. As expected, everything, from the architecture of the building, to the products, the T-shirt worn by the staff down to the logo and the badge design come from Cupertino."[cdlxiv]

Three months later, Apple, through its legal efforts in China, was able to enforce the intellectual property and the stores were closed by the Kunming municipal government. *The Financial Times* story headline read "*Apple secures patents on China stores*"[cdlxv] They also reported on 21st September 2011, that Apple was successful and had "*been granted patents on some of the distinctive elements of its store designs in China as the US company moves to better protect itself against rampant copying of not only its products but also its sales channels on the Chinese mainland.*"[cdlxvi]

What is unusual about this outright fraudulent activity is that while Apple, at the time, had no stores in the City of Kunming, it did have 13 authorized resellers legally authorized to sell Apple products. Interestingly, according to a Reuters story, the fake shops were not closed down because of IP infringement, but rather because they did not have an appropriate business license.[cdlxvii]

According to an *International Business Times* article "*Apple Wins 40 Patents in China to Counter Piracy,*"[cdlxviii] the efforts to actually secure the uniqueness of its technology designs were also part of the victory over IP infringement in China. According to Dave Smith's story "*The patents, granted to Apple on Sept. 9, mostly cover aspects of Apple's mobile devices relating to user interface and speaker technology. However, the patents apply to 37 of Apple's most popular products, including the iPhone, iPad, and Macbook Air.*

The patents also include the architecture and design of its three Apple Stores in Shanghai, according to the IP blog Patently Apple. Many stores in China have been found to copy Apple's storefront, and according to the China Daily, 22 of these copycat shops have already been shut down."[cdlxix]

Healthcare and Pharmaceutical Products

The People's Republic of China is obviously a huge marketplace for healthcare and pharmaceutical companies. Entry into this 'Middle Kingdom' market is also not without its perils for these types of companies as well.

Pharmaceutical manufacturer Pfizer found illegally manufactured versions of its male libido-enhancing drug Viagra in China. Merck's Lipitor has also been illegally produced in China. AstraZeneca, listed as one of China's top employers, [cdlxx] discovered counterfeit versions of its drug Nexium.

All three of these pharmaceutical companies have significant long-term research and development facilities in China. Pfizer has had a relationship with China since 1989, while Merck Sharp & Dohme (MSD), known in the

US as Merck, has been there since 1992, and the relative newcomer, Astra Zeneca has had a presence since 1999.[cdlxxi]

International Governments

Since 2006, companies in Germany, Canada, Denmark, Indonesia, Singapore, South Korea and Vietnam have all been cybervictims via *'Operation Shady RAT'*.

Germany

Germany has been repeatedly cyberattacked from within the People's Republic of China. Here is a brief dateline of these reported cyberattacks:

27 AUG 2007 – According to a *Der Speigel* report "*China has hacked into the computers of Angela Merkel's Chancellery and three other German ministries in an extraordinary economic espionage operation.*"[cdlxxii] Chancellor Merkel held Chinese Premier Wen Jibaoto to account for the fact that "*a large number of computers in the German chancellery as well as the foreign, economy and research ministries had been infected with Chinese spy software.*".[cdlxxiii]

7 DEC 2010 – "*Germany reports 'sharp rise' in cyber attacks*".[cdlxxiv] According to the *Cyber Wars* report, and German Interior Minister Stefan Paris: "*in the first nine months of 2010 there were some 1,600 such attacks recorded, compared to around 900 for the whole of 2009, plus most likely a considerable number that went undetected*".

4 JAN 2011 – "*Chinese agencies double cyberattacks on Germany*".[cdlxxv] According to a *Rapid7* blog, "*the Bundesamt für Verfassungsschutz (Federal Office for the Protection of the Constitution, or BfV*" in response to cyberattacks emanating from the People's Republic of China,"*is founding the National Cyber Defense Center, a joint venture of the BSI, BfV, BND, and other agencies,*"[cdlxxvi] to protect against this threat.

29 JUN 2011 – "*Chinese cyberattacks target German ministers*".[cdlxxvii] This particular report quantifies what an attacked nation-state feels is in jeopardy,

should the People's Republic of China continue its cyberattacks on Germany.

The Bundesverfassungsschutz's latest report says the number of "*electronic attacks*" on German federal officials in 2010, was 2,108, which is about 600 more than the previous year. "*Most of the attacks aimed at federal officials and German business, because of their characteristics, can be assigned an origin in China*", the intelligence report says.[cdlxxviii]

France

7 MARCH 2011 – Paris G20 files stolen in cyberattack. The headline read "*Cyber-attack on France targeted Paris G20 files*".[cdlxxix] "*More than 150 of the French Budget Ministry's 170,000 computers were affected*"[cdlxxx] by the first cyberattack of this size and scale against the French government.

4 APR 2011 – "*Hackers break into French defense industry, Chinese link unearthed*".[cdlxxxi] Information networks of Safran subsidiary Turbomeca, which makes helicopter engines, were targeted by Chinese cyberhackers. The Chinese hacks allegedly took place over the first eight months of 2010. According to the TechEye story "*Turbomeca happens to be a supplier to China, with one in two helicopters there equipped with one of its engines. It also business partners with various Chinese companies including the helicopter-making divisions of China's Aviation Industry Corp, the state-owned aircraft maker*".[cdlxxxii] French intelligence believes that the hackers might have had help from company insiders.

United Kingdom

The UK's intelligence organizations, military and international businesses have certainly not been immune to the effects of China's cyberincursions.

As part of a contract with British Telecom (BT), Huawei was awarded a significant telecommunications infrastructure project in the UK in 2005.

In April 2007, the newly-appointed head of England's super-secret MI5, Jonathon Evans, had already begun warning financial institutions within the

UK of the serious threat posed by hackers based in the PRC. Mr Evan's letter to English industry further identified the links between the economic information needs of Chinese state-owned enterprises and the diligent efforts of the Chinese cybermarauders.[cdlxxxiii]

And if Jonathon Evan's prognostications were not taken seriously by the captains of England industry, almost exactly a year later, in 2008, he issued an open letter to over 300 banks, accountants and legal firms, warning them of the dire threat of Chinese economic espionage via the use of what he termed "*Internet spying*".[cdlxxxiv]

During a meeting with the British Home Secretary, Alex Allan, chairman of the Joint Intelligence Committee, said that while British Telecom (BT) had taken steps to secure its network, "*we believe that the mitigating measures are not effective against deliberate attack by China*", as reported by the *Sunday Times* in 2009.[cdlxxxv]

Again in 2010, MI5 warned UK businesses that Chinese security officials were offering free computer appliances as a ruse to deliver malevolent and damaging software, known as Trojans, to unsuspecting VIPs "*in the banking, defence and even the energy industries.*"[cdlxxxvi]

MI5 has continued to warn industry in England that economic espionage from the Chinese is, indeed, a clear and present danger to national security and the economy.[cdlxxxvii]

Conclusions

There many reasons why the PRC would sponsor cyberattacks via its state-owned enterprises. From gaining economic advantage through business intelligence and data exfiltration, to achieving dominance in the manufacturing sector, the bounds of China's Government-sponsored hacking initiatives are wide. Evans was quoted by *The Financial Times* as saying

11: Commercial Objectives of Chinese Cyberattacks

"A number of countries continue to devote considerable time and energy trying to steal our sensitive technology on civilian and military projects, and trying to obtain political and economic intelligence at our expense. They do not only use traditional methods to collect intelligence but increasingly deploy sophisticated technical attacks, using the internet to penetrate computer networks."

CHAPTER 12: CHINESE CIVILIAN HACKERS

The People's Liberation Army is not very different, in doctrinal terms, from any professional army. The concept of future operations is extremely important to the PLA. The need to integrate future operations is a prerequisite for any military operations planning and strategy.

This need for military operational foresight was not lost on General Dai, as he wrote of his Information Warfare strategies. He stated that they "*must be integrated.*"[cdlxxxviii] An example of integrated future operations includes the integration of both "*military and civilian information fighting forces.*"[cdlxxxix] An example of this IW operational concept is seen in the recruitment of civilian hackers by the PLA.

Chinese Cybermilitias

"*The United States for the first time is publicly warning about the Chinese military's use of civilian computer specialists in clandestine cyber-attacks aimed at American companies and government agencies.*"[cdxc]

According to the online *HackerJournals,* which provides a variety of technical news for the hacking community: "*the U.S. for the first time is publicly warning about the Chinese military's use of civilian computer experts in clandestine cyber-attacks aimed at American companies and government agencies. In a move that is being seen as a pointed signal to Beijing, the Pentagon laid out its concerns this week in a carefully worded report. The People's Liberation Army, the Pentagon said, is using "information warfare units" to develop viruses to attack enemy computer systems and networks, and those units include civilian computer professionals.*"[cdxci]

Associated Press reported on August 19, 2010, that when asked about the civilian hackers, a Defense Department spokesman said the Pentagon is concerned about any potential threat to its computer networks. The Pentagon, said Commander Bob Mehal, will monitor the army's buildup of its cyberwarfare capabilities, and "will continue to develop capabilities to counter any potential threat."[cdxcii]

"The Chinese government, particularly the PLA, has sought to tap into the hacker community and take advantage of it," said James Lewis, a Cybersecurity specialist and a senior fellow at the Center for Strategic and International Studies. *"One of the things that the Defense Department has been looking for is a way to start signaling potential opponents about activities that might cross the line in cyberspace."*[cdxciii]

In 2008, a Beijing Hacking show, *"Chinese Hackers Talk Hacker,"* was an event which attracted approximately 80 delegates. Very few of the hackers attending had actually ever met each other in person; in fact, many of the hackers had previously only communicated over the Internet. One of the more well-known attendees was Frankie Zie, of ShenZhen, PRC, who is currently chief technology officer of a network security company located in China. Mr Zie is a well-known former black-hat hacker, using the Hacker nom-de-guerre *r00t*, and claims to have hacked numerous websites in the US. Meanwhile, according to the Dell Secureworks interview report, the Hacker *"netcc, claims to possess the ability to hack a thousand websites per month."*[cdxciv]

Cyberattacks by the technically savvy entities within the People's Republic of China are certainly *"focused on exfiltrating information, some of which could be of strategic or military utility."* This statement is based on the US Department of Defense Report *"Military and Security Developments Involving the People's Republic of China 2010"*.[cdxcv]

While the People's Republic of China uses civilian hackers (although these technical skills are not yet developed in the People's Liberation Army), this naturally allows China the ability to claim cyberinnocence and to point the finger at other possibly malevolent countries, such as Iran or Russia.[cdxcvi]

In fact, China regularly claims that it is itself under attack. As reported by the *Wall Street Journal,* a senior Chinese official has accused foreign intelligence agencies of causing "*massive and shocking*" damage to China, by hacking into computers to ferret out political, military and scientific secrets.[cdxcvii]

This claim of China's innocence was made by Vice Information Industry Minister Lou Qinjian, in a Communist Party magazine, and appeared designed as a response to recent reports that Chinese hackers had infiltrated high-security computers at the Pentagon, the British Foreign Office and the German Chancellor's headquarters, among other targets.

Lou, writing in the September issue of the *Chinese Cadres Tribune*, did not specifically name the countries carrying out what he described as "*external espionage activities against our core, vital departments.*" But he said that 80 per cent of the computers used to hack into other systems are based in the US.[cdxcviii] According to US Navy Commander Bob Mehal, the civilian Chinese hackers or front companies "*often may have particular expertise, such as knowledge about certain defense contractors, critical industries, or government agencies.*"[cdxcix]

Defacement of US Government websites was the RHA's response to the NATO-led airstrike on the Chinese embassy in Belgrade.

There are an extraordinary number of sites that a neophyte or experienced Chinese hacker can go to for information on how to hack computer network systems; further details are listed in Appendix F.

Chinese Cybersecurity Professionals

As if to confirm the suspicions about Chinese civilians having the technical experience and ability to aid their government, on September 28, 2011, the *People's Tribune Magazine* published approximately a dozen articles, from both civilian and military academics, espousing the virtues of why it is necessary to develop advanced cyberhacking techniques. These authors (who come from such Chinese institutions as the People's Liberation Army Defense University, the Network and Digital Media Research Office at the China Academy of Social Sciences, Fudan University's Department of International Politics, and the Institute of Information and Social Development Studies at the China Institute of Contemporary International

Relations) all have the common opinion and viewpoint that it is the PRC who is threatened and under cyberattack from the US and many other countries.

Potential Chinese Cyberwarfare TTPs

So what does the PRC have in its arsenal of cyberwarfare tactics, techniques and procedures (TTP)? In 2007, the US Government Accounting Office identified possible TTPs, most of which have now become common place:

Type	Description
Spamming	Sending unsolicited commercial e-mail, advertising for products, services and websites. Spam can also be used as a delivery mechanism for malware and other cyberthreats.
Phishing	A high-tech scam that frequently uses spam or pop-up messages to deceive people into disclosing their credit card numbers, bank account information, Social Security numbers, passwords or other sensitive information. Internet scammers use e-mail bait to 'phish' for passwords and financial data, from the sea of Internet users.
Spoofing	Creating a fraudulent website to mimic an actual, well-known website run by another party. E-mail spoofing occurs when the sender address and other parts of an e-mail header are altered, to appear as though the e-mail originated from a different source. Spoofing hides the origin of an e-mail message.
Pharming	A method used by phishers to deceive users into believing that they are communicating with a legitimate website. Pharming uses a variety of technical methods to redirect a user to a fraudulent or spoofed website, when the user types in a legitimate web address. For example, one pharming technique is to redirect users – without their knowledge – to a different website from the one that they intended to access. Also, software vulnerabilities may be exploited or malware employed, to redirect the user to a fraudulent website when the user types in a legitimate address.
Denial of Service attack	An attack in which one user takes up so much of a shared resource that none of the resource is left for other users. DS attacks

Type	Description
	compromise the availability of the resource.
Distributed Denial of Service attack	A variant of the DS attack that uses a co-ordinated attack from a distributed system of computers, rather than from a single source. It often makes use of worms to spread to multiple computers that can then attack the target.
Viruses	A program that "infects" computer files, usually executable programs, by inserting a copy of itself into the file. These copies are usually executed when the infected file is loaded into memory, allowing the virus to infect other files. A virus requires human involvement (usually unwitting) to propagate.
Trojan horse	A computer program that conceals harmful code. It usually masquerades as a useful program that a user would wish to execute.
Worm	An independent computer program that reproduces by copying itself from one system to another across a network. Unlike computer viruses, worms do not require human involvement to propagate.
Malware	Malicious software designed to carry out annoying or harmful actions. Malware often masquerades as useful programs, or is embedded into useful programs, so that users are induced into activating them. Malware can include viruses, worms and spyware.
Spyware	Malware installed without the user's knowledge to surreptitiously track and/or transmit data to an unauthorized third party.
Botnet	A network of remotely-controlled systems used to co-ordinate attacks and distribute malware, spam and phishing scams. Bots (short for 'robots') are programs that are covertly installed on a targeted system, allowing an unauthorized user to remotely-control the compromised computer for a variety of malicious purposes.

Table 1: Chinese hacker tactics, techniques & procedures (TTPs) used to commit cyberattacks[d]

CHAPTER 13: THE CHINESE CYBERTHREAT: CONCLUSIONS

The central thesis of this book is that the People's Republic of China has a comprehensive cyberwarfare strategy that has both offensive and defensive objectives, and which encompasses government, military and commercial spheres. The question, for non-Chinese organizations, is: "how does one protect oneself against such attacks?"

Protection of an enterprise IT network must be based, in the context of 21st century Chinese cyberwarfare, on the concept of "realization": the realization that the organization's network and intellectual property has already been compromised.

Computer Security Reference Materials

NIST

Every information security professional should have the NIST's special publication, *NIST SP: 800-12 An Introduction to Computer Security: The NIST Handbook*. It is the cornerstone of computer network security guidelines, and is freely available for download: csrc.nist.gov/publications/nistpubs/800-12/handbook.pdf

Originally published in 2006, *NIST SP 800-100 Information Security Handbook: A Guide for Managers* contains information security management truisms that remain salient even in the 21st century.

Enterprise information security, planning for protection against 21st century Chinese cyberthreats, should consider the NIST Risk-Based Approach methodology. This multi-tiered risk management framework is designed for all types of organizations, including the intelligence community, Department of Defense, and US Federal civil agencies. It is equally applicable to the private sector, with their unique commercial enterprise information security needs.

NIST's Unified Information Security Framework (UISF)

The generalized model of the NIST Unified Information Security Framework (USIF) states that there are unique information security requirements for different types of organization, such as the intelligence community, defense departments, government civil agencies and the private sector. NIST's common information security requirements form the foundation for a set of information security standards and accompanying guidance. These security standards and guidance include:

> Organizational risk management, including the needs of the specific organization, based upon their mission and information systems;
> Categorization of information technology security, including both the criticality and sensitivity;
> Security controls for information technology, such as safeguards and countermeasures;
> Security assessment policies and procedures; and,
> A process for information security authorization.

Enterprise-Wide Risk Management (EWRM)

The NIST Enterprise-Wide Risk Management Model (EWRM) is effective, very straightforward and will serve any organization's information security planning requirements well. EWRM is a three-tiered model, which offers information security practitioners and managers both a tactical and strategic focus, planning an effective organizational information security program. EWRM is implemented by the executive level cybersecurity risk managers within an organization.

While EWRM is best-suited for an enterprise cybersecurity program (and its accompanying information network architecture and cybersecurity requirements), it does contain a life cycle development (SLDC) aspect, which means that any size of organization might find EWRM beneficial. EWRM is both flexible and agile, so the implementation – whether strategic or tactical – can begin at any level within the organization, in order to maximize its effectiveness and speed to implementation.

Tier 1 of the EWRM deals with the Governance aspect of an organization, and provides a strategic cybersecurity risk focus. The Mission of the organization and the critical business processes are dealt with in Tier 2, and are focused on the enterprise's information and associated information pathway flows. Tier 3 is Foundational. It is entirely tactical in its application and focus, with an emphasis on the actual information systems of the organization, and the mission-critical operational environment.

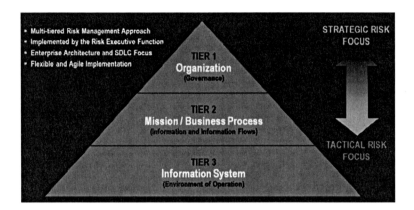

Figure 5: NIST enterprise-wide risk management

Further supporting the NIST EWRM are the risk-based approaches. The first element of a cybersecurity risk-based approach is that it integrates information security more closely into the overall enterprise architecture and system life-cycle. Next, it promotes near real-time risk management and ongoing system authorization, through the implementation of significant and robust IT network continuous monitoring processes. Thirdly, the risk-based approach provides senior leaders and management within the organization with necessary information, to assist delicate and needed risk-based decisions, so that affected information systems support the core business, and the organizational missions and business functions. Next, a risk-based approach links the risk management activities at, not only the organizational level, but also the mission and system levels, via a risk function at the executive level. The sixth element is the notion that it establishes both responsibility and accountability for cybersecurity controls deployed within an organization's information systems. Finally, a risk-based approach encourages the use of automated tools, to act as a force multiplier within the organization's cybersecurity team, to increase consistency, effectiveness and, of course, timeliness of information security controls implementation.

Risk Management Process

The cybersecurity planning and process also requires a fundamental understanding of both the process and framework for risk management within an organization's information and cyberinfrastructure. An effective risk management process also determines governmental regulations related to the business, in terms of potential for information loss. Certainly, within many countries, a company's market sector is driven by specific risk management legislation. The US, like other countries, passes laws with an eye on customer confidentiality and privacy protection. The next considerations are the enterprise business drivers and objectives.

After determining the governmental regulations, and appropriate standards for compliance and the critical business processes, a company should establish an enterprise-wide minimum level of acceptable risk. First step is to conduct a risk and threat analysis of the organization's information technology architecture and policies.

An enterprise risk management and analysis process should contain the following:

> Identify organization assets;
> Determine and assign a numerical value to each of these assets;
> Identify the vulnerability of each asset and the potential or possibility of an associated cyberthreat; and,
> Finally calculate the risk for each of the organization's assets previously identified.

Having completed the risk management process necessary, cyberprotection countermeasures are then determined and provided to the organization's management team. It is important to have established a cost benefit analysis for each of the recommended threat mitigation findings, so that leadership can act quickly and decisively, in deciding which cybersecurity procedures are most affordable and effective given the company's acceptable level of risk. Remember, not every cyberthreat from the Chinese can be mitigated every time.

Risk Management Framework (RFM)

One of the most effective risk management frameworks (RFM) is based upon the Security Life Cycle (SLC). The NIST special publication "*800-6 Revision 2 Security Considerations in the System Development Life Cycle for Information Security*" provides a wealth of information regarding security education and training, organizational security assessments, design, deployment and ongoing maintenance of the related security program, through management and support. Figure 6 provides a fundamental diagram of security life cycle management.

Figure 6: Fundamental diagram of security life cycle management

The RFM is then incorporated into the SLC management process, with the following cyclical steps, based on the NIST risk management framework: categorization of the information systems, selection of the security controls, implementation of the security controls, assessment, operational authorization within the information systems, and monitoring of these assigned security controls.

The first step of the NIST RMF is categorization of the information systems, during which the cyber risk assessment team defines the criticality and sensitivity of the information systems, according to the potential of cyberthreats and vulnerabilities, considering those cyberthreats which are the most severe and would have, if they occurred, a significant impact on the organization's mission or business operations.

The second step is to select baseline information security controls. Guidance for these cybersecurity controls must be appropriate and fitting for the identified cyber risks. Additional or supplemental information security controls are implemented based on the initial cybersecurity and vulnerability assessment.

Implementation of the security controls is the next step, such that the enterprise information technology architecture is based upon and uses proven, understandable and sound information systems security engineering practices. The information security configuration control settings are then applied across the enterprises architecture.

The fourth step of the NIST RMF is assessment. Organizational cybersecurity controls are assessed, to determine their relative effectiveness within the requirements of the operational information technology environment. Specifically, that the cybersecurity controls, which have been designed and implemented, were done correctly, that these cybersecurity controls are operating as engineered and intended. Determine that cybersecurity requirements for information systems within the organization are being met without exception.

Authorization is the next and fifth step in the NIST risk management framework. Enterprise information systems are then reviewed to determine if the cyber risks, and associated threats from Chinese hacking attacks, are sufficiently severe for the organization's operational information technology assets, staff and other linked organizations, to be protected via the authorization of the necessary information technology security systems.

The sixth and last step of this fluid, dynamic and ongoing NIST RMF, is monitoring of security controls. Changes to the information security architecture are logged and tracked to assess their impact on the information technology architecture. Reassessment of these security control changes is paramount, to ensure effectiveness of cyber risk management.

Once the cybersecurity education, risk and threat assessments are complete, and approved by the organizational leadership and management, the next step is designing a cybersecurity defense-in-depth, to ensure that the enterprise effectively defeats and denies Chinese cyberhacking efforts.

Cybersecurity Defense-in-Depth

An effective, enterprise-wide, cybersecurity defense-in-depth has specific linkages to ensure a comprehensive effort is affected. A successful cybersecurity methodology should include linkages between operational cybersecurity management, operational security processes and very specific technical security engineering controls. Chinese cyberadversaries will, most certainly attack the organization's soft spots; the most vulnerable areas of a network will be targeted and selected for exploitation.

A comprehensive list for creating an effective defense-in-depth should include the following cybersecurity items:

- Risk assessment
- Security planning, policies, procedures
- Configuration management and control
- Contingency planning
- Incident response planning
- Security awareness and training
- Security in acquisitions
- Physical security
- Personnel security
- Security assessments and authorization
- Continuous monitoring
- Access control mechanisms
- Identification and authentication mechanisms (biometrics, tokens, passwords)
- Audit mechanisms
- Encryption mechanisms

- Boundary and network protection devices (firewalls, guards, routers, gateways)
- Intrusion protection/detection systems
- Security configuration settings
- Anti-viral, anti-spyware, anti-spam software
- Smart cards

Once the elements of a successful cybersecurity defense-in-depth are implemented, a defense across the organization should be designed, implemented and publicized. Thus, everyone within the enterprise, regardless of role, can be aware of, and can contribute to, the cybersecurity plan effectiveness. Figure 7 is a variation on the NIST "Defense-in-Breadth" and is called an enterprise cyber-defense.

Enterprise Cyber-Defense

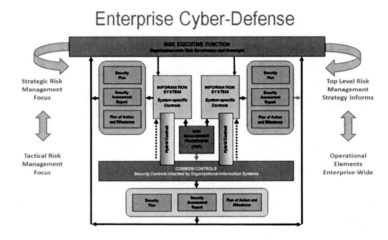

Figure 7: NIST enterprise cyber-defense flow

ISO/IEC 27001 Information Security Management

Another significant information security reference is ISO27001 which, together with ISO27002, is an internationally-recognized Information Security Management Standard.The latter was first published by the International Organization for Standardization, or ISO, in December 2000, as ISO17799. It was renumbered in 2007, as ISO/IEC 27002, and is part of the ISO/IEC 27000 Information Security Management Systems (ISMS) Series of Standards. These two standards are high level, broad in scope, and conceptual in nature. This approach allows them to be applied across multiple types of enterprises and applications. It has also made the standards controversial among those who believe that standards should be more precise. In spite of this controversy, ISO27001 is the only "specification" devoted to Information Security Management in a field generally governed by "Guidelines" and "Best Practices."

ISO27002 defines information as an asset that may exist in many forms and has value to an organization. The goal of information security is to suitably protect this asset, in order to ensure business continuity, minimize business damage, and maximize return on investments. ISO27002 defines information security as the preservation of:

Confidentiality – ensuring that information is accessible only to those authorized to have access;

Integrity – safeguarding the accuracy and completeness of information and processing methods; and,

Availability – ensuring that authorized users have access to information and associated assets when required.

ISO27002 addresses the following twelve areas: risk assessment; system policy; information security organization; asset management; human resources security; physical and environmental security; communications and operations management; access control; information systems acquisition, development and maintenance; information security incident management; business continuity management; and compliance.

The objectives of each section are:

1. Risk Assessment and Treatment
a) Risk assessment is fundamental to ISO27001, and security risk analysis must precede control selection.

2. System Policy

a) To provide management direction and support for information security.

3. Organizing Information Security
a) To manage information security within the organization.
b) To maintain the security of information and processing facilities, with respect to external parties.

4. Asset Management
a) To achieve and maintain appropriate protection of organizational assets.
b) To ensure that information receives an appropriate level of protection.

5. Human Resources Security
a) To ensure that employees, contractors and third parties are suitable for the jobs for which they are considered, understand their responsibilities, and to reduce the risk of abuse (theft, misuse, etc).
b) To ensure that the above are aware of IS threats and their responsibilities, and able to support the organization's security policies.
c) To ensure that the above exit the organization in an orderly and controlled manner.

6. Physical and Environmental Security
a) To prevent unauthorized physical access, interference and damage to the organization's information and premises.
b) To prevent loss, theft and damage of assets.
c) To prevent interruption to the organization's activities.

7. Communications and Operations Management
a) To ensure the secure operation of information processing facilities.
b) To maintain the appropriate level of information security and service delivery, aligned with third-party agreements.
c) To minimize the risk of systems failures.
d) To protect the integrity of information and software.
e) To maintain the availability and integrity of information and processing facilities.
f) To ensure the protection of information in networks, and of the supporting infrastructure.
g) To prevent unauthorized disclosure, modification, removal or destruction of assets.
h) To prevent unauthorized disruption of business activities.

i) To maintain the security of information and/or software, exchanged internally and externally.

j) To ensure the security of e-commerce services.

k) To detect unauthorized information processing activities.

8. Access Control

a) To control access to information.

b) To ensure authorized user access.

c) To prevent unauthorized access to information systems.

d) To prevent unauthorized user access, and compromise of information and processing facilities.

e) To prevent unauthorized access to networked services.

f) To prevent unauthorized access to operating systems.

g) To prevent unauthorized access to information within application systems.

h) To ensure information security, with respect to mobile computing and tele-working facilities.

9. Information Systems Acquisition, Development and Maintenance

a) To ensure that security is an integral part of information systems.

b) To prevent loss, errors or unauthorized modification/use of information within applications.

c) To protect the confidentiality, integrity or authenticity of information, via cryptography.

d) To ensure the security of system files.

e) To maintain the security of application system information and software.

f) To reduce/manage risks resulting from the exploitation of published vulnerabilities.

10. Information Security Incident Management

a) To ensure that security information is communicated in a manner allowing corrective action to be taken in a timely fashion.

b) To ensure a consistent and effective approach is applied to the management of IS issues.

11. Business Continuity Management

a) To counteract interruptions to business activities, and protect critical processes from the effects of major failures/disasters.

b) To ensure timely resumption of the above.

12. Compliance
a) To avoid the breach of any law, regulatory or contractual obligation, and of any security requirement.
b) To ensure systems comply with internal security policies/standards.
c) To maximize the effectiveness of, and minimize associated interference from and to, the systems audit process.[di]

Conclusions

The People's Republic of China has asked its military, the People's Liberation Army (PLA), to develop and demonstrate advanced, offensive cyberwarfare capabilities. PLA cyberwarfare capabilities are both offensive and defensive in their nature. In conjunction with the PLA's mandates from the Communist Party of China (CPC), to conduct cyberwarfare under the guise of defending China's Internet infrastructure, the PLA have also enlisted the capabilities of civilian hackers, essentially creating cybermilitias. State-owned enterprises help focus these cybercapabilities, with the intent of appropriating, collecting and acquiring proprietary commercial intellectual property.

Thus, the PLA, with its technically-capable cybermilitias, assists in both discovering and gathering sensitive military, economic and political information. Ultimately, the hegemony of the People's Republic of China is the underlying motivation for these cyberincursions, intrusions and attacks, on non-Chinese nation-states, companies and organizations. China still stings from the embarrassing history of foreign invasions, and is now embarked on a cyberpolicy of domination.

As the PLA, civilian hackers and SOE's collect this critical information, the PRC is purposefully determined on achieving cybereffects capable of influencing the outcome of conventional armed conflicts, damaging a foreign nation's critical infrastructure, in order to create economic harm prior to an invasion.

The People's Republic of China is interested in cyberwarfare as a tool of national power, and is continually improving its capabilities, to conduct offensive, military cyberoperations in the fifth domain, the cyber realm. In its 2010 report to Congress on China's military power, the US Department of Defense reported that "*China's strategic strike capabilities ... are expanding from the land, air, and sea dimensions of the traditional battlefield into the ... cyber-space domains.*" [dii]

Recommendations for Next Steps

There is no silver bullet in understanding the 21st century Chinese cyberwarfare threat. The Lone Ranger is dead, and we have no cybercavalry coming to meet the enemy at the Great Firewall of China. Indeed, we have met the enemy, and he is us. Our cultural, historical and linguistic ignorance of the People's Republic of China has been our own undoing.

Dealing with the 21st century Chinese cyberwarfare threat will require everyone, within every organization, who deals with any elements of security, to recognize that the threat is imminent and ceaseless.

After recognizing the threat, it will be absolutely mandatory to ensure that representatives of the business community, those involved in corporate security policy and governance, research scientists, entrepreneurs from the technical innovation marketplace, and all levels of an effective national government, participate in defining both what they consider to be near and longer term methods, of dealing with the clear and present danger which is the 21st century Chinese cyberwarfare threat.

Cybertargeting: People's Republic of China

If I were a cybertargeting officer, and wanted to deny the People's Republic of China the ability to conduct or wage cyberwar, how would I do that?

Internet Exchange Points (IXP) would be a great place to start. On the periphery of the People's Republic of China, there are several of these IXPs, which bring, from a variety of international commercial telecommunications carriers, Internet access to the vast array of netizens in China ... including the Communist Party of China, the People's Liberation Army and state-owned enterprises.

Notable IXP's include:

EQIX-HKG – Equinix Exchange Hong Kong
HKIX – Hong Kong Internet exchange.

Besides the Network Access Points (NAP), where the undersea cables enter China, one could look at targeting specific cable networks:

Qingdao, China: EAC-C2C and Trans-Pacific Express (TPE) Cable System;
Chomgming, China: APCN-2, Asia-Pacific Gateway (APG), China-US cable Network (CHUS) and Trans-Pacific Express (TPE) Cable System;
Shanghai, China: EAC-C2C, FLAG Europe-Asia (FEA) and SeaMeWe-3;
Nanhui, China: Asia Pacific Gateway (APG);
Fuzhou, China: Taiwan Strait Express-1 (TSE)-1;
Lantau Island, Hong Kong: APCN-2, Asia-America Gateway (AAG) Cable System and FLAG Europe -Asia (FEA);
Taipa, China: SeaMeWe-3;
Shantou, China:
1) Russia-Japan Cable Network
2) Matrix Cable System; APCN-2,China-US Cable Network (CHUS), SeaMeWe-3 and Southeast Asia Japan (SJC)
3) PIPE Pacifica Cable-1
4) Asia-America Gateway
5) Unity North
6) Telestra Australia-Hawaii.

The cyberwarriors from many nation-states may have already thought of these Internet connections, and have cyberweapons to target these international Internet connections to the People's Republic of China.

Alternatively, the major Internet players within the People's Republic of China may be targets; this cyberdenial would certainly impact the significant state-owned enterprises (SOE), who are benefiting from data ex-filtration through various cyberattacks on international companies and governments.

Short-term moves

It should be ensured that nation-state governments at the highest level of leadership take the Chinese cyberthreat seriously: This serious task, of dire importance, does not rest on the shoulders of government alone, it cannot. Recognition, definition and publicity of a nation-state cyberthreat must be the responsibility of everyone within a society.

Short-term move # 1

It should be mandatory that commercial enterprises educate all employees on the possibility of data exfiltration, by internal and external, human and automated, cyberborne, advanced and persistent Chinese cyberespionage threat vectors. A fantastic, albeit, damaging example of the inside threat by Chinese foreign nationals, which underscores the importance of this short-term move, occurred on October 20th 2011, at the Cargill Company, based in Minneapolis, Minnesota. The Human Resources "experts" at Cargill, so diligent at wanting to improve equal opportunity and diversity among their workforce, ignorantly and unknowingly hired a spy from the PRC.

The Human Resources department at Cargill refused to comment for the record "*because the matter is under investigation*" by the Federal Government.

Short-term move # 2

United States Executive Order 12829, National Industrial Security Program (NISP). Continued application and review of NISP in accordance with Department of Defense Instruction Number 5220.22 dated March 18, 2011:[diii] The Defense Security Service states that "*The NISP was established by Executive Order 12829 to ensure that industry safeguards the classified information in their possession or to which they have access while performing work on contracts, programs, bids or research and development efforts. The Defense Security Service (DSS) administers the NISP on behalf of the Department of Defense as well as 23 non-DoD federal agencies. Presently, DSS has Industrial Security oversight responsibility for over 13,000 cleared companies participating in the NISP. To have access to U.S. classified information and participate in the NISP, a company or other designated operating entity in private industry or at a college/university, must have a legitimate U.S. Government or foreign government requirement for such access. Once this requirement has been established, a company can be processed for a Facility Security Clearance (FCL). An FCL is an administrative determination that the company is eligible to access classified information at the same or lower classification category as the FCL being granted. The FCL may be granted at the Top Secret, Secret or Confidential level. When a determination has been made that a company meets the eligibility requirements for a FCL, the company must execute a Defense Security Agreement which is a legally binding document that sets forth the responsibilities of both parties and obligates the company to abide by the security requirements of the National Security Industrial Program Operating Manual (NISPOM)."*[div]

Short-term move # 3

It is important to define specific economic targets that the Chinese may pursue as part of their need to gain and maintain competitive economic leadership over foreign businesses. Within the US, this is the responsibility of the International Undersecretary at the Department of Commerce. They can assist, with aid of corporate management, and identify what companies and industries are most likely to be the targets of economic espionage. It will be critical for the government to work with commercial industry, to assist in defining possible loss of business if intellectual property is lost to China. All concerned and affected organizations, both private and public, must begin this process immediately upon receipt of this recommendation, and then continue quarterly, based upon business cycles and the advent of new innovations. The cost of this recommendation will be nominal, given the number of personnel required from both the government and private industry, yet it must be done to prevent further exfiltration of proprietary and confidential information to the People's Republic of China.

Short-term move # 4

All private and public organizations must educate their employees regarding the possibility of both cyber- and physical data theft and exfiltration. Simply turning a blind eye in the name of political correctness (as was the case with Cargill's Chinese espionage experience) is unacceptable. Corporate management, at all levels of an organization, is responsible for creating a culture of awareness, and enforcing operational security. Chief Information Security Officers (CISO) must make cybersecurity the paramount responsibility of everyone, within every organization. CISO's must immediately design educational awareness programs, to address identifying, reporting and mitigating foreign information exfiltration threats. Once established and mandated across every private and public organization, refresher training must occur monthly. The cost of this recommended course of action is nominal, but in comparison to the loss of corporate or organizational secrets, it is relatively inexpensive.

Short-term move # 5

The information security profession must design a universal, defense-in-depth policy; it must be applicable to all sizes of organization as standard, and be easily understood and implemented. The cyberdefense-in-depth architecture must be designed in conjunction with the information security industry, specifically the anti-virus, anti-malware and cybersecurity software manufacturers. Hardware manufacturers of intrusion detection and prevention (IDS/IPS) devices, firewall manufacturers, and network access control (NAC) design engineers must all participate in this cybersecurity defense-in-depth solution architecture. This cybersecurity standard must be applicable and scalable to the protection of a nation's critical infrastructure. It is vital that policy-makers enable civilian cybersecurity professionals to be successful at designing a solution for defense-in-depth, which inherently mitigates all Chinese cyberthreats, effectively protecting both economic and critical infrastructure information networks and capabilities. This needs to be undertaken and completed immediately. The cost of this will be expensive, but will be offset by the eventual hardware and software products and services necessary to meet this universal cyberdefense-in-depth standard.

Short-term move # 6

On the global-political stage, bodies such as the US Department of State, and the US Agency for International Development (USAID), need to work on an international basis, with organizations such as the Association of Southeast Asian Nations (ASEAN), to hold the People's Republic of China accountable for these cyberattacks. Barring the exertion of political will, the US Military, the North Atlantic Treaty Organization (NATO), and their associated cybercommands, need to immediately implement a cyberattack doctrine.

Short-term move # 7

The cybercommands of every nation need to understand the aspect of cybertargeting. If you have never pre-planned kinetic targets in a tactical or strategic manner, yet call yourself a member of the military, please allow the branches of the military – who understand targeting – to lead the way and execute their plans. Commonsense indicates that we should target (either through cyberattacks or kinetic-based impacts) the three network access points (NAP) feeding the People's Republic of China.

Short-term move # 8

Open the Internet to military personnel involved in combating and fighting the cyberthreat. A significant amount of the information about the publicly-known Chinese cyberthreat is available through the Internet; civilians can access this material, which is also known as open source information (OSINT). The armed forces of many countries, including the US and UK, may not, for fear that the information will present a cyberthreat vector and compromise vital national defense interests. This is incorrect, patently false, and guided by misinformed military leadership. The civilian world is as threatened (and has much, if not more to lose), yet they use commercially-available technology to restrict cyberthreats from causing wholesale damage to their information networks.

Short-term move # 9

In 2008, NATO established the "*Cooperative Cyber Defense Center of Excellence*" in Tallinn, Estonia. This organization should be allowed to take the lead in the worldwide development of strategies and tactics for mitigating Chinese cyberwarfare in the 21st century. They have the experience and knowledge base, and are pre-disposed to think in terms of both tactical and strategic offensive and defensive cybercountermeasures.

Short-term move #10

Begin teaching Mandarin Chinese in our public and private school. Like it or not, there is no other language which is currently as important to the future of our world as Modern Chinese.

Long-term moves

Kinetic effects-based warfare will continue to be a dangerous and violent clash, while improved information will tend to facilitate a more economical use of force. Obtaining information is not an end in itself. Rather, it is a means to an end, and increasingly, nations will view that end as the achievement of an effect, whether it be diplomatic, military, economic, informational, societal, technological, or a combination of these instruments of national power. In a war fighting sense, sensor technologies have extended the engagement envelope; computers and communications technologies have led to an increase in the tempo of operations; and the integration of sensors into weapons has made them more precise and lethal. The real transformation has not been in sensor, cyberweapons or information technology tools used by Chinese hackers, but in shifting the focus from the physical dimension to the fifth dimension of information.

As China's cyberattack capability becomes even more defined and refined, there is a need to acknowledge the vulnerability of national security information infrastructure, and commercial, financial and energy information networks. We, therefore, need to initiate requisite actions to mitigate the threat. The threat is global, and the entire computing industry needs to work together, to improve security of information networks, as businesses continue facing cyberattacks by the People's Republic of China.

There is no need to suggest long-term moves, because the threat of 21st century Chinese cyberwarfare is already here. The mandatory requirement is that corporate managers, on the private side of the issue, work in a co-operative manner with public officials, to act upon every one of the short-term moves listed here, such is the dire threat of Chinese cyberincursions. Without action, the only long-term plan will involve learning how to speak Mandarin Chinese.

APPENDIX A: CHINA & THE INTERNET – A HISTORY

The People's Republic of China has been on a significantly rapid economic growth trajectory since mid-1988; a growth that, for now, seems unending. And while China's two decades of history, with almost double-digit economic growth, has impressed the world, China's telecommunications sector has progressed even more rapidly than the rest of the 'Middle Kingdom's' economy. According to Milton Mueller and Siziang Tam, the telecommunications market in China has been expanding annually by 30–50 per cent.[dv] The Chinese Publicly Switched Telephone Network (PSTN) adds approximately 10 million phone lines to the nation's public network each year.

As of 2004, the People's Republic of China led worldwide broadband adoption, with 13 million users, effectively doubling the number of DSL subscribers in only a year.[dvi] And while China has more DSL subscribers than any other country in the world, DSL penetration in China only reaches 1 per cent of the population. China installed more than 73 million phone lines between 1999 and 2004. This is more than the rest of the developing world combined. More than 84 per cent of China's long distance networks are digitalized. 4,000 digital satellite communications circuits now link approximately 19 of China's provinces.[dvii]

Development of the Internet & Usage Statistics in the People's Republic of China

The People's Republic of China is successfully developing and adapting cutting edge information technology, to promote and stimulate the economy. Responding to National Information Infrastructure (NII) initiatives similar to those in the US, Japan and Europe, China is building out its own ubiquitous Internet effort, affectionately referred to as the "*Golden Projects*".

During 1993, the People's Republic of China initiated the "Golden Projects", as a co-ordinated NII policy. The end state for the national infrastructure ambitions was in 2020. The Golden Projects had three substantive phases:

Broadband telecommunications network, able to deliver in excess of one million telephone lines, and more than 10,000 television channels, to homes, businesses and government audiences;

Establishment of an information service and support services industry, supporting connectivity, and ensuring economic growth to all sectors of the economy of the People's Republic of China;[dviii] and

Telecommunications and information technology manufacturing industrial base.[dix]

Consistently, the Central Communist Party has provided a dichotomy regarding Internet access and content delivery; as a result confusing signals emerge. In the midst of its ambitious expansion, China's Government is trying to impose stricter controls on content and access. In January 1996, China's top civil authority, the State Council, announced regulations to consolidate the administration of all computer network-building activities, and international interconnections, under four government agencies.[dx]

During February of 1996, all Internet users were required to register with the Ministry of Public Security (MPS), an uncomfortable reminder to users that their activities could be monitored by police.[dxi] More currently, on July 26, 2011, the Chinese Government required all Wi-Fi providers, including those who operate within hotels, Internet cafes, bars, restaurants, and even bookshops with Internet access, to install very expensive web- and user-access monitoring software, all under the direction of the local Chinese security bureau.

What is quite interesting about all this monitoring and censorship, is that the end-users, who access the Internet, will be have personal information passed directly, to not only the local security offices, but also police and other Chinese State Security Services.[dxii], [dxiii] Of course, Wi-Fi operators, who fail to comply with Chinese State Regulations, will face the prospect of closure, and a 15,000 Ren Min Bi (RMB) fine for non-compliance. Meanwhile, the mandated Internet user monitoring software installation project will cost approximately 3,000 RMB or $ 466.14. At time of writing, the rate of the

Chinese Yuan Ren Min Bi (CYN RMB) to the US Dollar is .155 fen (Chinese cents), thus 1 USD = 6.43 CYN RMB.[dxiv]

The Internet Timeline of the PRC from 1986-2009 is graciously provided by the staff at the China Internet Network Information Center (CNNIC). The transliteration of annual Internet development events from the CNNIC is in chronological order.[dxv]

In Geneva, Switzerland, at 4:11 on August 25, 1986: Chinese Academy of Sciences Institute of High Energy Physics in Beijing, Professor Wu Wei min for Institute 710, via an IBM-PC machine, sent an e-mail to a Geneva-based Professor Steinberger, via a satellite link.[dxvi]

During September 1987, with the support from a scientific research group, led by Professor Werner Zorn of Karlsruhe University in Germany, Mr Qian Tianbai successfully sent out the e-mail to Germany, titled "*Across the Great Wall we can reach every corner in the world.*"[dxvii] , [dxviii]

```
(Message # 50: 1532 bytes, KEEP, Forwarded)
Received: from unika1 by irau11.germany.csnet id aa21216; 20 Sep 87 17:36 MET
Received: from Peking by unika1; Sun, 20 Sep 87 16:55 (MET dst)
Date:    Mon, 14 Sep 87 21:07 China Time
From:    Mail Administration for China <MAIL@ze1>
To:      Zorn@germany, Rotert@germany, Wacker@germany, Finken@unika1
CC:      lhl@parmesan.wisc.edu, farber@udel.edu,
         jennings%irlean.bitnet@germany, cic%relay.cs.net@germany, Wang@zc1,
         RZLI@ze1
Subject: First Electronic Mail from China to Germany

"Ueber die Grosse Mauer erreichen wie alle Ecken der Welt"
"Across the Great Wall we can reach every corner in the world"
Dies ist die erste ELECTRONIC MAIL, die von China aus ueber Rechnerkopplung
in die internationalen Wissenschaftsnetze geschickt wird.
This is the first ELECTRONIC MAIL supposed to be sent from China into the
international scientific networks via computer interconnection between
Beijing and Karlsruhe, West Germany (using CSNET/PMDF BS2000 Version).
    University of Karlsruhe        Institute for Computer Application of
 -Informatik Rechnerabteilung-    State Commission of Machine Industry
        (IRA)                         (ICA)
 Prof. Werner Zorn             Prof. Wang Yuen Fung
 Michael Finken                Dr. Li Cheng Chiung
 Stefan Paulisch               Qiu Lei Nan
 Michael Rotert                Ruan Ren Cheng
 Gerhard Wacker                Wei Bao Xian
 Hans Lackner                  Zhu Jiang
                               Zhao Li Hua
```

Figure 8: E-mail "Across the Great Wall we can reach every corner in the world"[dxix]

The initial origins of the Internet connectivity within the PRC came from significant science and technology universities throughout the 'Middle Kingdom'. These Chinese institutions of higher learning included the High Energy Physics network (IHEP), and the China Science Academy, also known as the China Academic Network (CANET), both of which are located in Beijing, the capital city.[dxx]

In 1990, Professor Wang Yunfeng and Professor Werner Zorn were successful with the registration of China's country code top-level domain – .CN; Mr Qian Tianbai was registered as the administrative contact. From then on, China had its own Internet identity. Since China had yet to achieve full functional connection to the Internet, the .CN top level domain (TLD) name server was temporarily established in Karlsruhe University in Germany.[dxxi]

During March 1991, the Institute of High Energy Physics of Chinese Academy of Sciences established connection to the computer network of the Stanford Linear Accelerator Center (SLAC).[dxxii]

In December 1992, Tsinghua University Network (TUNET) was set up and went into service. TUNET wass the first college network to adopt TCP/IP structure in China. Fiber Distributed Data Interface (FDDI) technique was successfully adopted for the first time, contributing very fast interconnection network capabilities within China.[dxxiii] Currently TUNET has 1,200 kilometers of dark fiber, a 10 Gb/second network backbone capability with an external network connectivity rate of 2 Gb/second. TUNET has 48,000 end users connected via 40,000 host machines. As recently as 2004, TUNET upgraded their network to accommodate 10 KM Ethernet at the network core, producing significant, high-speed internetworked capabilities. TUNET's connection to the China Education and Research Network (CERNET), is via two 1000 Mb/second connections.[dxxiv]

Also during 1992, the College Network construction was completed. CASNET connects over 30 education and research networks, including many institutions in the Zhong Guan Cun area, as well as the CASNET headquarters infrastructure in San Li He, Project NCFC, TUNET (Tsinghua University Net), and PUNET (Peking University Net).

On March 2nd, 1993, a 64KDECnet fixed line to the Stanford Linear Accelerator Center (SLAC) was officially opened.[dxxv] In May of 1995, China

Telecom started working on increasing Internet bandwidth within China, by building up the national Internet backbone network for CHINANET, one of two major commercial networks approved by the State Council to be a national Interconnecting Network in 1996.

During July of the same year, China's first 128K leased line connecting to the US was opened by China Education and Research Network (CERNET). CERNET is funded by the Chinese Government and directly managed by the Chinese Ministry of Education. It is constructed and operated by Tsinghua University and other leading Chinese universities.

In terms of Internet connectivity, early Chinese Internet users were educators wanting to share communication, and learn from fellow academicians around the globe. In response to the internal Chinese Internet connectivity from scholars, CERNET opened a series of digital data network (DDN) channels for its backbone network, connecting with eight cities – Beijing, Shanghai, Guangzhou, Nanjing, Shenyang, Xi'an, Wuhan and Chengdu. This initial inter-city connectivity occurred at a connecting speed of 64Kbps, a little greater than a plain old telephone system (POTS) line; basically dial-up. Given that the CERNET DDN network was up and operational, demand for faster Internet connectivity speeds was driven by university Internet users.

In August 1995, to answer the demand for more Internet speed, the primary phase of the "Golden Bridge Project" was completed, achieving internal Chinese connectivity via a satellite network, between 24 provinces and main hub cities, throughout the People's Republic of China.[dxxvi] High-speed Internet connectivity from the "Golden Bridge Project" soon followed. This gave both educators, and neophyte Internet users in China, the ability to access the World Wide Web.

During January 1996, CHINANET backbone network completed its construction and began to provide network services throughout the country.[dxxvii] Additional high-speed Internet connectivity between China and the World Wide Web, as the China "Golden Bridge Network" (China GBN), opened a 256K leased line connected to the US. In 1996, the operators of the China GBN also announced the decision to provide an Internet access service, primarily for institutional users through dedicated lines, such as E-1's, and Internet access to individual Internet users, through telephone lines via dial-up.

In September 1996, the Chinese State Development Planning Commission formally approved the start of the first stage project of "the Golden Bridge". Curiously, the "Golden Bridge Project" was a PRC joint venture with the Finnish Ministry of Employment and the Economy (MEE). The purpose of this joint Chinese and Finnish project was to set up the China-Finland Innovation Centre (CFIC) in Helsinki, facilitating market entry for Chinese companies to Finland and/or to Europe, and providing a platform to boost bilateral technology and innovation transfer.[dxxviii]

In December 1996, the China Public Multimedia Communication Network, known as Net 169, began its operations. A preliminary group of connected websites, Guangdong Shilingtong, Tianfu Hotline and Shanghai Online, officially opened for connectivity business.[dxxix]

In January 1997, *the People's Daily* newspaper established an online presence, by registering *http://peopledaily.com.cn/* [dxxx]; the English language version of this website is located at *http://english.peopledaily.com.cn/*. Interestingly, *the People's Daily* was the first online news outlet for the Communist Part of China (CPC).[dxxxi] A month later, during February 1997, the Information Highway Network (IIN) began operation.[dxxxii] The IIN was a critical development of Chinese Internet connectivity; within three months, the connection of eight cities (Beijing, Shanghai, Guangzhou, Fuzhou, Shenzhen, Xi'an, Shenyang and Harbin) was accomplished. It became the earliest and largest private ISP/ Internet Content Provider (ICP).[dxxxiii]

In October 1997, China's first national Internet backbone (ChinaNet)made the Internet connection with three backbone networks within China: China Science and Technology Network (CSTNET), China Education and Research Network (CERNET) and China Golden Bridge Network (CHINAGBN). In November of the same year, CNNIC published the first "*Statistical Report on Internet Development in China*". By October 31, 1997, there were 299,000 computer hosts and 620,000 Internet users in China; 4,066 domain names were registered under .CN.[dxxxiv] China had about 1,500 WWW websites and 25.408M of the international bandwidth[dxxxv]. On December 30, 1997, the Ministry of Public Security (MPS) issued an edict regarding further Internet control legislation, which the State Council approved: "*The Management of the Security of International Computer Network Information Networking*".

During November 1996, the Shihuakai Corporation built the Shihuakai Internet Café near to the Beijing Capital gymnasium; it was the first Internet café in China, essentially opening access to a then, unfiltered and content unrestricted Internet to the Chinese around Beijing.[dxxxvi] In the same month, CERNET opened the 2M international data line, connecting the People's Republic of China to the US. During the German President's visit, also in November, CERNET opened an educational Internet link between China and Germany, called CERNET-DFN; this Internet network connection was the first Internet connection to Europe from the Chinese mainland.

The People's Republic of China started constructing what they called the "*China Great Wall Network*", which was, naturally, approved by Central Government. Indeed, the "*China Great Wall Network*" was one of the four state-run ISPs, providing Internet access to regional downstream Internet providers; the critical point of this ISP approval by the Central Government was that it now had a mandated and official policy on regulating what was accessed within the People's Republic of China, via a state-owned enterprise (SOE).

In September 2000, Tsinghua University finished constructing DRAGONTAP, the first domestic exchange center of the next generation Internet. Through DRAGONTAP, the three domestic backbone networks (CERNET, CSTNET and NSFCNET) were connected to STARTAP, an American exchange center of the next generation Internet located in Chicago, and an exchange center of Asia Pacific Advanced Network (APAN) in Tokyo, Japan. The connecting speed of the two lines was 10Mbps. The project built up the connection of many scientific networks, such as Abilene, vBNS and CA*net3l; it also achieved the connection of the next generation Internet throughout the world.

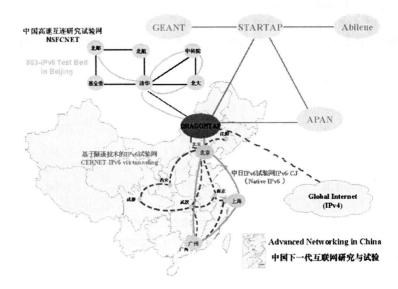

Figure 9: Next generation internet topology in the People's Republic of China[dxxxvii]

On January 17, 2001, China Internet Network Information Center (CNNIC) published "*the 7th Statistical Report on the Development of the Internet in China*". By the end of December 31, 2000, there were approximately 8.92 million computer hosts in China, about 22.5 million Internet users. 122, 099 domain names were registered under .CN. China had approximately 265,405 WWW websites, and 2,799Mbit/s of international bandwidth.[dxxxviii]

On January 16, 2003, China Internet Network Information Center (CNNIC) published the 11th "*Statistical Report on the Development of the Internet in China*". By the end of December 31, 2002, there were about 20.83 million computer hosts and 59.10 million Internet users in China; 179 thousand domain names were registered under .CN. China had about 371 thousand WWW websites and 9380M of the international bandwidth.[dxxxix]

China Netcom (CNC) announced in Beijing that it was officially independent from CHINANET, the ISP organization of China Telecom, and with this divesture, launched its new Internet service called "*Broad Band CHINA 169*".[dxl]

During July 2003, the Internet information office of the State Council issued the "*Survey Report on China Internet Information Resources*" in Beijing. By the end of December 31, 2002, the total number of domain names in China reached 940,300. China had 371,600 websites, 157 million web pages and 82,900 online databases.[dxli]

In August, 2003, the State Council authorized the launch of the model project for China's next generation Internet – CNGI (China Next Generation Internet); CNGI was the initiative project for implementing the development strategy of next generation Internet in China. The project was led by eight ministries: the National Development and Reform Commission, the Ministry of Science and Technology, the Ministry of Information Industry, the State Council Informatization Office, the Ministry of Education, the Chinese Academy of Science (CAS), the Chinese Academy of Engineering, and the National Natural Science Foundation of China.[dxlii]

During January 2004, the three nations' project (China–US–Russia) also known as the "*Global Ring Network for Advanced Applications Development*" (GLORIAD) was established. GLORIAD was funded and constructed by CAS, the National Science Foundation (US) and the Russian Ministry and Science Group Alliance.[dxliii] GLORIAD supports these three countries and their global advanced scientific and educational applications. The representative organizations included the Computer Network Information Center of CAS (PRC), the National Supercomputing Application Center of Illinois University (US) and the Kolchatov Institute of Russia.[dxliv]

CNNIC published the 13th "*Statistical Survey Report on the Internet Development of China*". By the end of December 31, 2003, there were approximately 30.89 million computer hosts, 79.50 million Internet users in China; 340,040 names were registered under .CN domain. China had about 595,550 WWW websites, and 27,216Mbps of international bandwidth.[dxlv]

By the end of December 2003, the total number of domain names in China had reached 1,187,380. China had had 311,864,590 web pages and 169,867 online databases.[dxlvi]

The Internet Engineering Task Force (IETF) formally issued RFC 3743[dxlvii] with the title of "*Joint Engineering Team (JET) Guidelines for Internationalized Domain Names (IDN) Registration and Administration for Chinese, Japanese, and Korean*" also known as CJKV. Together with JPNIC and KRNIC, CNNIC submitted RFC 3743 to the IETF, the purpose of which was to standardize conversion and translation of different forms of Chinese characters, such as traditional, simplified, and variants thereof, when using as IDN identifiers on Internet websites.[dxlviii]

As of December 2005, registrations of websites using the .CN domain name extension exceeded one million, comprised of 1,096,924 web domains that were .cn specific. Interestingly, China became ranked first among all country-specific top level domains (TLD) throughout Asia, and sixth in the world.[dxlix] Subsequently, it was no surprise that, when in January, 2006, the Chinese Government registered its own official domain, as the People's Republic of China officially opened up shop on the Internet, by launching the Central People's Government website at *www.gov.cn*; the English language version of the website is still posted and frequently updated, at *http://www.gov.cn/english/* .[dl] The Central Chinese Government's web interface details everything, from the various aspects of the Chinese State Structure, to a veritable "who's who" in the Government. Also included are categories for facts about China, an e-commerce help center, as well as a services portal for "non-residents".[dli]

Basic Principles & Practices of Chinese Internet Admin

The following is an official statement by the People's Republic of China Government, regarding their administration of the Internet within the 'Middle Kingdom':

"*China adheres to scientific and effective Internet administration by law, strives to improve an Internet administration system combining laws and regulations, administrative supervision, self-regulation, technical protection, public supervision and social education. The basic goals of China's Internet administration are to promote general and hassle-free Internet accessibility, and sustainable and healthy development, guarantee citizens' freedom of speech online, regulate the order of Internet information transmission, promote the positive and effective application of the Internet, create a market environment for fair competition, guarantee the citizens' rights and interests vested in the Constitution and law, and guarantee safety for Internet information and state security.*

China regulates the Internet by law

Since 1994 China has enacted a series of laws and regulations concerning Internet administration, including the Decision of the National People's Congress Standing Committee on Guarding Internet Security, Law of the People's Republic of China on Electronic Signatures, Regulations on Telecommunications of the People's Republic of China, Measures on the Administration of Internet Information Services, Regulations on the Protection of Computer Information System Security of the People's Republic of China, Regulations on the Protection of the Right to Online Dissemination of Information, Provisions on the Administration of Foreign-funded Telecommunications Enterprises, Measures on the Administration of Security Protection of the International Networking of Computer Information Networks, Provisions on the Administration of Internet News Information Services, and Provisions on the Administration of Electronic Bulletin Services via the Internet, among others. Relevant provisions of the Criminal Law of the People's Republic of China, General Principles of the Civil Law of the People's Republic of China, Copyright Law of the People's Republic of China, Law of the People's Republic of China on the Protection of Minors, Law of the People's Republic of China on Punishments in Public Order and Security Administration and other laws are applicable in the case of Internet administration.

China adheres to rational and scientific law-making, and reserves space for Internet development. Relevant laws and regulations pertaining to basic Internet resource management, information transmission regulation, information security guarantee and other key aspects define the responsibilities and obligations of basic telecommunication business operators, Internet access service providers, Internet information service

233

providers, government administrative organs, Internet users and other related bodies. The citizens' freedom and privacy of correspondence is protected by law, which stipulates at the same time that while exercising such freedom and rights, citizens are not allowed to infringe upon state, social and collective interests or the legitimate freedom and rights of other citizens. No organization or individual may utilize telecommunication networks to engage in activities that jeopardize state security, the public interest or the legitimate rights and interests of other people.

The Chinese government plays the leading role in Internet administration. Relevant government bodies, according to their statutory duties, safeguard Chinese citizens' rights and interests, public interests and state security by law. The state telecommunications administration department is responsible for the administration of the Internet industry, including the administration of basic resources of the Internet such as domain names, IP addresses within China. Abiding by the Measures on the Administration of Internet Information Services, the state practices a licensing system for commercial Internet information services and a registration system for non-commercial Internet information services. According to the Measures, state press, publication, education, health and other administrative departments practice licensing systems for "Internet information services concerning press, publication, education, medical care, medicines and medical instruments." Public security organs and other state law-enforcement agencies bear the responsibility for Internet security supervision and administration, and investigate and punish all types of network crimes.

The Chinese state proactively promotes industry self-regulation and public supervision. The Internet Society of China (ISC) was founded in May 2001. It is a national organization of the Internet industry with a remit for serving the development of that industry, netizens and the decisions of the government. The ISC has issued a series of self-disciplinary regulations, including the Public Pledge of Self-regulation and Professional Ethics for the China Internet Industry, Provisions of Self-regulation on Not Spreading Pornographic and Other Harmful Information for Internet Websites, Public Pledge of Self-regulation on Anti-malicious Software, Public Pledge of Self-regulation on Blog Service, Public Pledge of Self-regulation on Anti-Internet Virus, Declaration of Self-regulation on Copyright Protection of China's

Internet Industry, and other regulations, which greatly promote the healthy development of the Internet.

The ISC makes unremitting efforts to counter spam, reducing the global spam percentage of Chinese e-mails from 23% in 2002 to 4.1% in 2009. In order to strengthen public supervision of Internet services, the state has established the China Internet Illegal Information Reporting Center (CIIRC), Network Crimes Reporting Website, 12321 Harmful and Spam Internet Information Reporting and Reception Center, 12390 Pornography Crackdown and Press and Publication Copyright Joint Reporting Center and other public reporting and reception organizations since 2004. The Society issued the Measures for Encouraging the Reporting of Pornographic and Vulgar Information on the Internet and Mobile Media in January 2010. The Chinese government will further support the work of Internet industry self-disciplinary organizations, provide services to facilitate the organizations' roles and protect the public's legitimate rights to online reporting of illegal information and acts.

China advocates the rational use of technology to curb dissemination of illegal information online. Based on the characteristics of the Internet and considering the actual requirements of effective administering of the Internet, it advocates the exertion of technical means, in line with relevant laws and regulations and with reference to common international practices, to prevent and curb the harmful effects of illegal information on state security, public interests and minors.

The Decision of the National People's Congress Standing Committee on Guarding Internet Security, Regulations on Telecommunications of the People's Republic of China, Measures on the Administration of Internet Information Services, Measures on the Administration of Security Protection of the International Networking of Computer Information Networks, and other laws and regulations clearly prohibit the spread of information that contains contents subverting state power, undermining national unity, infringing upon national honor and interests, inciting ethnic hatred and secession, advocating heresy, pornography, violence, terror and other information that infringes upon the legitimate rights and interests of others. According to these regulations, basic telecommunication business operators and Internet information service providers shall establish Internet security

235

management systems and utilize technical measures to prevent the transmission of all types of illegal information.

The state advocates strengthening Internet legal and ethical education. The level of legal and ethical education of the whole society is closely connected with the construction of the Internet environment. It supports the work of Internet legal and ethical education, encourages the active participation by various media and social organizations, and proactively pushes forward the inclusion of Internet legal and ethical education in the curriculums of primary and middle schools. It attaches great importance to youth and women's organizations in their roles of elevating national network morals, and encourages relevant organizations to carry out activities for the public good to spread Internet knowledge and promote the correct use of the Internet.

The state guarantees online safety for minors. Minors have become China's biggest online group. By the end of 2009, a third of the country's 384 million Internet users were minors.

The Internet is playing an increasingly important role in the development of minors. Meanwhile, online pornographic, illegal and harmful information is seriously damaging the physical and psychological health of young people, and this has become recognized as a prominent issue of public concern. The Chinese government attaches great importance to online safety for minors, and has always prioritized the protection of minors in the overall work of Internet information security programs. The Law of the People's Republic of China on the Protection of Minors stipulates that the state shall take measures to prevent minors from overindulging in the Internet; prohibit any organization or individual from producing, selling, renting or providing by other means electronic publications and Internet information containing pornography, violence, murder, terror, gambling or other contents harmful to minors. The state encourages research and development of Internet tools that are conducive to the online protection of minors, as well as Internet products and services suitable for minors. Families, schools and all other social units shall work together to protect minors online and create a healthy online environment for the development of minors. The Chinese government will actively push forward the "Mothers' Education Program" to help parents guide their children in using the Internet correctly.

The state proactively protects digital intellectual property. Since 2000 China has revised the Copyright Law of the People's Republic of China, promulgated the Measures for the Administrative Protection of Internet Copyright and offered relevant judicial interpretations for the trial of cases involving computer and network copyrights disputes, thus providing a legal basis for digital intellectual property protection. The state copyright administrative department is in charge of the investigation and punishment of Internet copyright infringement and pirating activities. To combat repeated copyright infringement, group infringement and large-scale pirating activities, relevant government organs have taken a series of administrative actions. China will continue to explore intellectual property protection work in the Internet environment, and strive to realize a balance between public interest protection and the promotion of innovation.

The state protects citizens' online privacy. The protection of online privacy is closely connected with the people's sense of security and confidence in the Internet. The Chinese government proactively promotes the improvement of relevant legislation and Internet corporate service regulations, in order to steadily enhance online privacy protection systems. The Decision of the National People's Congress Standing Committee on Guarding Internet Security stipulates that illegal interception, tampering with or deletion of others' e-mails or other data and infringement upon citizens' freedom and privacy of correspondence that constitutes a crime shall be investigated for criminal liability. According to the self-disciplinary public pledges of the Internet industry, Internet service providers are responsible for protecting users' privacy. The providers shall announce their relevant privacy protection commitment when providing services, provide reporting and reception channels for privacy infringement and take effective measures to protect users' privacy.

The Chinese government actively explores channels and methods of scientific and effective Internet administration by law, and has formed a preliminary Internet administration model that is suitable for China's conditions and consistent with international practices. Internet administration is a process of continuous practice, and the Chinese government is determined to further improve its Internet administration work."[dlii]

Chinese Internet Regulatory Organizations

The Internet in China is regulated by many competing agencies, which have, since the birth of the Internet in China, aggressively parried with one another over who is actually in charge. Further exacerbating legislative control of the Chinese Internet is the fact that each organization sees a vested economic profit center, based upon which vertical of the Internet industry they wish to regulate, and derive taxation from. This is, in a sense, the truest form of the Chinese economic collective model, in which the PRC mandates control, and receives payment based upon required laws. Making bureaucratic matters more of a mess is the Chinese penchant for re-naming legislative control organizations.

Specifically beginning in 1993, the Economic Information Joint Committee was created as the authority on Chinese Internet control. As the Internet phenomena in China grew, the agency was renamed three years later, to become the State Council Steering Committee on National Information Structure (SCSNII). SCSNII has the following high-level responsibilities regarding governance of the Internet in the People's Republic of China: These mandates are the formulation of strategy, principles, rules and regulations in developing national informatization, co-ordinating projects and establishing standards.[dliii]

In 1997, the Ministry of Post and Telecommunications (MPT) merged with the Ministry of Electronic Industry, to form the Ministry of Information Industry (MII). MII was assigned as the PRC's Internet gatekeeper, and thus had daily regulatory responsibility for the Chinese Internet. MII was assigned with the authority as the lead organization responsible for issues related to telecommunications and high tech industry in China. However, during the 2008 People's Congress, MII was renamed the Ministry of Industry and Information Technology (MIIT).[dliv dlv]

The original functions of MII carried forward with the creation of MIIT, and include core focused responsibilities of:

"*Regulation of electronics and information product manufacturing and oversight of the development of the telecom and software industries, including pricing of telecom. These functions also include project planning, development, and regulatory management of China's radio and television (including cable) transmission networks, as well as satellite telecom networks.*"[dlvi]

The People's Republic of China has had a "circle and envelope" strategy for controlling the Internet since 1994. This information containment strategy has included two consistent focuses, (one) controlling Internet access and, (two), restricting content. The "*Rules of Security Protection of Computer Information Systems*" was the bedrock of Chinese control and surveillance of the Internet. These Rules had two specific focus areas: security protection of systems and security surveillance.[dlvii]

Important Timeline of Internet Censorship & Content Control in China

In 1995, ChinaNet, China Telecom's ISP, was given authority by the Chinese Government's State Council under Order No. 195, to operate a China national interconnected Internet network under "*Interim Regulation on International Interconnection of Computer Information Networks in the PRC*". What is unique about this first piece of Chinese Internet control legislation is that it occurred almost eight years after the first Internet network connectivity occurred.

In February 1996, the State Council issued "*the Interim Regulations of the People's Republic of China on the Management of International Networking of Computer Information*". These first Internet censorship regulations had three edicts.

The first Internet censorship was called the "*Temporary Regulation for the Management of Computer Information Network International Connection.*"

Within this regulation it decreed that:

"No units or individuals are allowed to establish direct international connection by themselves." (Item 6) *"All direct linkage with the Internet must go through ChinaNet, GBNet, CERNET or CSTNET. A license is required for anyone to provide Internet access to users."*

(Item 8) The second regulation was the *"Ordinance for Security Protection of Computer Information Systems"*. Issued on February 18th, 1994, by the State Council, it gave the responsibility of Internet security protection to the Ministry of Public Security, which is entitled to *"supervise, inspect and guide the security protection work"*, and to *"investigate and prosecute illegal criminal cases"* (Item 17)[dlviii]

On April 9, 1996, the Ministry of Posts and Telecommunications issued *"Rules for Administration of China's Public Computer Networks and International Connection"*, providing further direction on the developing control of the Chinese Internet by the Central Government of China. Subsequently, on June 3, 1996, the Electronics Industry Administration, published *"the Relevant Decisions on Administering the International Connection of Computer Information Networks"*.[dlix] *"China GBN"* was renamed *"China Golden Bridge Information Network"*.

Internet network standardization mandated by the Information Office of the State Council, required Internet network administrators to investigate current technical techniques of network implementation and administration of the four major networks, and nearly 30 ISPs, in the People's Republic of China. Thus, the second major series of Internet control was enacted officially with China. This Internet network investigation mandated a standardization of Internet connectivity administration throughout all of China.[dlx]

On May 20, 1997, the Chinese State Council reinforced *"the State Council's Decision on Revising the Provisional Regulations of the People's Republic of China on Managing Computer Internet Information Networks"* and amended this to the *"the Provisional Regulations of the People's Republic of China on Managing Computer Internet Information Networks"*.[dlxi]

During May 1997, the Informatization Leading Group Office of the State Council issued "*Interim Policies on the Administration of Internet Domain Names in China*". It then accredited CAS as the institute for founding and administering China Internet Network Information Center (CNNIC), while it gave the authorization to the center of CERNET, for managing "*.edu.cn*" through a contract with CNNIC.

Later in 1997, Mr Zhu En tao, China's Public Security Minister, announced a number of Internet acceptable use policies for Internet users in China, based upon Section Five of the Computer Information Network and Internet Security, Protection, and Management.

Regulations approved by the State Council:

"*No unit or individual may use the Internet to create, replicate, retrieve, or transmit the following kinds of information:*
Inciting to resist or breaking the Constitution or laws or the implementation of administrative regulations;
Inciting to overthrow the government or the socialist system;
Inciting division of the country, harming national unification;
Inciting hatred or discrimination among nationalities or harming the unity of the nationalities;
Making falsehoods or distorting the truth, spreading rumors, destroying the order of society;
Promoting feudal superstitions, sexually suggestive material, gambling, violence, murder;
Terrorism or inciting others to criminal activity; openly insulting other people or distorting the truth to slander people;
Injuring the reputation of state organizations;

Other activities against the Constitution, laws or administrative regulations."[dlxii]

In March 1998, the PRC directed another set of Internet access control policies by the Informatization Steering Group of the State Council, who, in turn, issued "*Implementing Rules for Interim Regulations of the People's Republic of China on the Management of International Computer*

Information Networking". These Internet network access rules came into effect immediately.[dlxiii]

Then, during May 1998, the Chinese Government started, but did not implement, official Internet content blocking and Internet filtering. This project was called the *"Golden Shield Project"* and is also known as the *"Great Firewall of China"*. Under the direct policy enforcement of the Ministry of Public Security of the People's Republic of China (MPS) *"Golden Shield"* provides the People's Republic of China with Internet censorship at the Internet backbone and ISP level. *"Golden Shield"* is widely known in the popular media as the *"Great Firewall of China."* This official Chinese censorship project primarily targets the movement of information between the global Internet and the Chinese Internet. Fang Bin xing, President of the Beijing University of Posts and Telecommunications, is widely known as the architect of the *"Golden Shield"* and started the initial design planning in 1998.[dlxiv] Mr Fang stated that that the creation and design of *"Golden Shield"* took five years, and was eventually launched in 2003.[dlxv]

China's Golden Shield

Behind China's *"Golden Shield"* project is the interesting figure of Mr Li Run sen. Since 1996, Mr Li has been Head of the Commission of Science and Technology of the Ministry of Public Security of the People's Republic of China. Since 1998, Mr Li has been group leader and chief technical advisor for China's *"Golden Shield Project"*, a communication network and computer information system operated by the Ministry of Public Security of the People's Republic of China. Mr Li was selected to serve as a Director on the Board of China Security & Surveillance Technology Incorporated, based upon his experience of over 40 years in the surveillance and safety industry in China. Mr Li has been involved in Chinese public policy matters, having served in several high-level positions within China's Ministry of Public Security.[dlxvi] As Technology Director at MPS, and a direct participant in the technology leadership of *"Golden Shield"*, in 2002, Mr Li decreed the *"Information Technology for China's Public Security"* to a national audience of Chinese law enforcement, during an annual meeting in Beijing.

China's "*Golden Shield*" is also referred to as the "*Great Firewall of China*" (GFW), although it is more popularly known by its perhaps sinister nom de guerre.^{dlxvii} The Ministry of Public Security (MPS) operates this censorship and Internet surveillance initiative. The People's Republic of China spent approximately $800 million on the "*Golden Shield*" infrastructure. Essentially, its purpose is to block and restrict Chinese Internet users and anyone else inside of China filtering material from accessing unauthorized Chinese-provided content. The "*Golden Shield*" performs admirably, via three types of content blocking technology:

1 .The first is a domain name system (DNS) -based blackhole list (DNSBL), also known as a block list or black list. The Chinese Internet censors have created a master countrywide zone file that has domain names, key word searches and specific IP addresses, which are forbidden from access. DNSBL is a DNS filtering and redirection method, which does not resolve domain names, or returns incorrect IP addresses. This affects all IP protocols, such as hypertext transmission protocol (HTTP), file transfer protocol (FTP), or post office protocol (POP). A typical circumvention method is to find a domain name server that resolves domain names correctly, but domain name servers are also subject to blockage, especially IP blocking. Another workaround is to bypass DNS, if the IP address is obtainable from other sources and is not blocked. Examples are modifying the hosts file or typing the IP address instead of the domain name in a web browser.^{dlxviii}

2. IP Blocking is achieved when access to a certain IP address is denied. If the target website is hosted in a shared hosting server, all websites on the same server will be blocked. This affects all IP protocols, primarily transmission control protocols (TCP), such as HTTP, FTP or POP. A typical method of circumventing these restrictions is to find proxies that have access to the target websites; however, some related proxies may be jammed or blocked. A few larger websites allocated additional IP addresses to circumvent the block, but the block was later extended to cover the new addresses.^{dlxix}

3. A third type of method used by the MPS is uniform resource locator (URL) filtering. MPS' URL filtering technology scans the requested URL string for target keywords regardless of the domain name specified in the URL. This affects the Hypertext Transfer Protocol. Both Chinese and

foreign Internet users in the People's Republic of China have utilized typical circumvention methods, such as using escaped characters in the URL, or to use encrypted protocols, such as a virtual private network (VPN) with a secure socket layer (SSL) encryption method.[dlxx] The URL keyword block can block an entire site with the blacklisted keyword, or only a part of the site or an article with the blacklisted keyword. With URL filtering, Internet users are punished with broken connections and web browser display message indicating, "*the connection has been reset.*" The broken connections can last more than an hour if a user repeatedly tries to access a certain blacklisted keyword. If the Internet user continues to attempt the keyword search, the MPS Internet police will be alerted and make an attempt to define the location of the offending Internet user.[dlxxi]

By searching the Internet whilst in China, using specific word searches on websites will bring the Internet police to your screen. This content filtering blocking by the People's Republic of China is accomplished by blocking access to sites with specific keywords that the Chinese Government deems as a threat to public safety and security under the auspices of the MPS. Examples of forbidden and, of course, blocked keywords and phrases, include "Amnesty International" "Dalai Lama", "democracy", "Falun Gong" , "human rights", "Tibet", "Tiananmen Square", "Taiwan independence" and, of course, any items related to either sex or pornography.

Much of the blocking of the Internet by the Chinese Government's MPS is accomplished by technology which disrupts the "connect phase,2 and with the URL keyword block, the filtering and blocking is further accomplished when 1) a user enters a URL (address) to a browser; 2) the monitoring system checks whether the URL is on a blacklist (if it is, the user is sent an error message); 3) filtering systems check whether the text on the URL requested contains flagged terms (again, if it does, the user is sent an error message). There are also filters that screen e-mail and search engine requests, seeking anti-Chinese Government words, phrases or sentiments.[dlxxii]

The "*Golden Shield*" surveillance system is constantly being updated by the authorities at the MPS, as they add new keywords, constantly based upon perceived and real threats to the Communist Party of China.

MPS also uses sophisticated Huawei core Internet routers, to accomplish blocking and surveillance within the "*Golden Shield*". MPS has located these core switches at all three Internet Network Access Points (NAP), where fiber optic cables cross international borders into the People's Republic of China.

The main Internet connections between China and the outside world are routed through optic cables at one of three NAPs. The first NAP is located at the Beijing-Tianjin Qingdao connection in the northern part of China, where undersea cables come in from Japan. The second NAP is located in Shanghai, where the International Internet connection is on the central coast of China; here, the undersea cables also originate from Japan. The third is the Guangzhou NAP connection in southern China. The Guangzhou cables come in from Hong Kong, PRC. Although some lines exist, that run through Central Asia and Russia, the Internet traffic brought into China is insignificant when compared with the three major undersea cables. When Taiwan was hit with a 7.1 magnitude earthquake on the 27th of December, 2006, major sea cables into China were cut by the damage, with Internet access, and connectivity in and out of China, negatively affected for over a month.

The Chinese are able to monitor Internet traffic by installing monitoring devises at the "*international gateways*" into China. Using a technique called "*mirroring*" that incorporates extremely small mirrors, information that travels through the gateways is copied and sent with mirroring routers to "Golden Shield" computers, which sort through the data and determine if anything should be blocked.

MPS also uses mirror routers to block and restrict Internet content; in fact, many of these types of routers are designed by Cisco®. Cisco actually saw the "*Golden Shield*" as a fantastic opportunity by which to increase corporate sales.[dlxxiii] The mirror routers which Cisco sold to China's MPS "*Golden Shield Project*", were used to listen to Internet traffic. If MPS listening efforts heard unauthorized or illegal transmission, such as a banned key word, then the mirror router would block the offending Internet traffic. Some of the systems are quite sophisticated, and block only certain parts of transmissions and let others through. With a site such as CNN or the BBC, sports may be allowed to pass through, while the news is blocked. When a site is blocked, an error message appears.[dlxxiv], [dlxxv]

The Chinese Government requires Internet users to register using their real names, and prevents them from using anonymous names, which Internet users traditionally rely upon to keep their true identities hidden from the watchful gaze of the MPS monitoring staff. China's MPS Internet & Security teams are using Cisco's proprietary network monitoring software, allowing tracking of Internet user's work histories and political tendencies.[dlxxvi]

The surveillance software is developed by the Chinese, at various educational institutions and corporations throughout China, such as Brainwave in Hebei. The People's Liberation Army also has software engineering cadre at their disposal, to design and use network user monitoring software.

Political censorship is built into all layers of China's Internet infrastructure. Internet censorship in the PRC is overseen technically by the Ministry of Information Industry (MII). Policy, regarding exactly what substantive content is to be censored, is largely directed by the State Council Information Office (SCIO), and the Chinese Communist Party's Propaganda Department, with input from other government and public security organs.[dlxxvii]

Physical access to the Internet is provided via nine state-licensed Internet Access Providers (IAP); each has at least one connection to a foreign Internet backbone. Via these high-speed connections, Chinese Internet users access Internet websites hosted outside of China.[dlxxviii] Chinese Internet users purchase Internet access from one of several thousand Internet Service Providers (ISPs), who are, in effect, retail sellers of Internet access; this is in turn, purchased wholesale from the nine IAPs. Internet routers, devices that deliver and direct packets of data back and forth between networks, are an essential part of Internet networks. Most of the modern Internet core routers also allow network administrators to censor or block – or, as the Internet industry refers to it, "filter" data going through these routers. The ISPs will program the router to block certain kinds of data from passing in or out of a network. This filtering capability was initially intended so that Internet Service Providers could control viruses, worms and spam. This same filtering technology can also be easily employed to block political, religious and pornographic material, or indeed any category of content that the person programming the router seeks to block.[dlxxix]

Chinese Internet censorship takes place at the Internet router level. According to the 2005 technical analysis of Chinese Internet filtering, conducted by the Open Net Initiative, IAP administrators have entered thousands of URLs (Internet website addresses) and keywords into the Internet routers, which enable data to flow back and forth between ISPs in China and Internet servers around the world. Forbidden keywords and URLs are also plugged into Internet routers at the ISP level, thus controlling data flows between the user and the IAP. Router-level censorship, configured into the hardware of the Chinese Internet, is reinforced by software programs deployed at the backbone and ISP level that conducts additional "filtering" of political content. Many countries use a product called SmartFilter that offers censorship via software deployed at the Internet backbone and ISP level. SmartFilter was developed by Secure Computing, and is sold currently by McAfee®.

The People's Republic of China has architected and implemented an organic Internet content blocking and filtering program.[dlxxx] The Internet content filtering infrastructure in China is very complex, sophistically elegant and successful in achieving its official aim, of preventing Chinese citizens from accessing Internet information they should not be privy or have access to according to the People's Republic of China MPS organization. It is this type of censorship, or blocking, which causes an error message to appear in the Chinese Internet user's browser when they type, for example, *http://www.facebook.com* (the popular social networking website) into the address field of their web browser.

Figure 10: greatfirewallofchina.org test of facebook.com[dlxxxi]

During June 1998, the PRC's China Education and Research Network (CERNET) participated in the trial network of the next generation IP (IPv6) – 6bone. CERNET found it useful to co-operate and participate with Cisco Systems.[dlxxxii] The China Information Technology Security Certification Center (CNITSEC) initiated its trial operation for controlling access to the Internet within China, after obtaining the acceptance of the Informatization Leading Group Office of the State Council, during July 1998. In August 1998, the Ministry of Public Security officially formed the Public Information Network Security Supervision Bureau. It takes responsibility for maintaining computer network securities, striking against crime in cyberspace, and supervising the security protection of computer information systems.

On February 3, 1999, "*the Certification System of Electronic Business Information Security*" – one of the Key Technological R&D Programs of China's 9th five-year planning (powered by the China International E-Commerce Center), passed the technical achievement appraisal by the Ministry of Science and Technology and the National Pass-code Administrative Commission. It also obtained the license for selling information security products from relevant departments, and became the first purely self-developed and copyright self-owned CA security certification system for E-commerce. This system was successful in administrating the quota licenses of domestic textile.

In February 1999, the China National Information Security Testing Evaluation & Certification Center (CNISTEC) was established. On April 15, 1999, 23 influential domestic websites gathered together for the first time, to discuss the development of the press media of Chinese websites. "*Chinese Journalistic Circles Network Media Joint Pledge*" was approved in principle.

The participants called for the recognition and protection of information property on the Internet. In May 1999, CCERT (CERNET Computer Emergency Response Team) was formed in the Network Engineering Research Center of Tsinghua University. It is the first organization formed to deal with network emergencies in China. On July 12, 1999, ChinaNet went public on National Association of Securities Dealers Automated Quotations (NASDAQ), thus becoming the first Chinese Internet network company listed on an international stock exchange. It is perhaps interesting that Chinese state-owned enterprise would be financially mature enough to be listed on a Western stock exchange.

On January 1, 2000, "*Regulations for the Protection of National Computer Networks*" were announced by the National Administration for the Protection of State Secrets, and was put into force on the same day. On August 21, 2000, the World Computer Congress 2000 was held in Beijing International Conference Center. President Jiang Zemin gave an important lecture, during this conference, stressing Internet information within the People's Republic of China, and a focus on an administration of Chinese information security through the full measure of the Internet.

In September 2000, the State Council issued "*the Telecommunication Regulation of the People's Republic of China*". This is the first integrated regulation for administering the industry of telecommunications in China, marking the development of China's telecommunication industry, and the extent to which it had marched down the legal system track. The State

Council also implemented "*Rules for Administering the Internet Information Services*".^{dlxxxiii}

The State Council News Office, part of the (MII), issued further regulations and control, regarding news items on the Chinese Internet, with its edict entitled "*Interim Regulations for the Administration of Publishing News Materials on Websites*"; this was officially known as "*Order No.17 of the General Administration of Press and Publication of China and the Ministry of Information Industry of China*".^{dlxxxiv} On December 24, 2001, MII also issued "*Regulations for the Administration of the Internet Electronic Bulletin Services*" during the twentieth ministerial meeting of the General Administration of Press and Publication (GAPP).^{dlxxxv}

Several Chinese media outlets also joined the Internet regulation bandwagon, including the Ministry of Culture, the Central Committee of Communist Youth League, the State Administration of Radio Film and Television, the National Students' Federation, the State Office of Informatization Promotion, Guangming Daily, China Telecom and China Mobile. This Chinese Internet content committee on self-regulation issued "*the Internet Manners and Culture Project*", which fundamentally controlled website access, Internet networks, and the design of a controlled Internet environment for media content within the People's Republic of China.^{dlxxxvi}

During December 2000, *the People's Daily*, XinhuaNet, ChinaNet, CCTV International Website, International Online Website, *China Daily* and CYCNET obtained approval from the State Council News Office for press publication, and became the preliminary group of press websites to obtain official authorization to go online. During the 19th session of the Standing Committee of the 9th National People's Congress, they approved the Standing Committee of Communist Party of China's "*Decision on Protecting the Internet Security*".^{dlxxxvii}

During the Spring of 2001, the People's Republic of China enacted several Internet laws and regulations. The first of these Internet controls took place in April 2001; three State ministries: the Ministry of Information Industry (MII), the Ministry of Public Security, and the Ministry of Culture and the

State Administration for Industry & Commerce jointly announced, "*Measures for the Management of Internet Cafés*".[dlxxxviii] Ten days later, on April 13, 2001, the Ministry of Information Industry (MII), the Ministry of Public Security, the Ministry of Culture and the State Administration for Industry & Commerce started the special Rectification of "*Internet café*" policy, further regulating who accesses the Internet from an Internet café, together with what they access and what they download.

During July 2001, the Bank of China (BOC) announced financial regulations for Chinese Internet banking, publishing "*the Interim Rules for the Administration of Online Banking Business*".[dlxxxix] This document contains 18 distinct articles governing Internet Banking in China; covering very unique aspects of online banking, for example, article four states:

"The operator of a corporate customer shall pay attention to the following matters when making use of the online banking corporate services of BOC for the first time:

1. The operator who applied for CA digital certificate shall download the CA authentication (SIC) certificate according to the reference number and authorized code printed on the sealed password envelope.

2. Please customize the online banking user name after logging on the system with the user login name printed on the password envelop(e) or printed on the service slip.

3. Please change the initial logon password printed on the sealed password envelop(e) or sent by short messaging service of mobile phone to a new logon password pursuant to the requirements of User Security Mechanism (8-20 digit combination of numbers and letters).

4. Please customize the reserved information in time."[dxc]

Clearly the BOC had security and regulations in mind when they issued this code of online banking rules. Interestingly, again approximately 10 days later, on July 10th, 2001, the Communist Party of China (CPC) held a conference, on the legalities of protecting information on the Chinese

Internet, at the traditional Communist Party Meeting Hall in Zhongnanhai, Beijing at Huairentang Hall.[dxci] Jiang Zemin, the secretary general of the CPC chaired this conference. The CPC emphasis was on ensuring that China took advantage of all the opportunities the Internet offered, expediting development of information and network technologies, and applying these in practice toward all the spheres of Chinese economy, society, technology, national defense, education, culture and law.[dxcii]

During September and October 2001, MII announced two key pieces of Chinese Internet control policy. The first was the "*Interim Regulations for Connecting Services of the Internet Backbone Networks*"[dxciii] . The second set of regulations published "*the Interim Regulation for the Management of the Connection of Backbone Networks*".

During the last few days of October, the 24th session of the Standing Committee of the 9th National People's Congress, announced "*the Information Network Dissemination Right*", which was formally included in the revised version of "*The Copyright Law of People's Republic of China*". Relevant regulations would protect copyrights by legal means of material posted to the Internet. A month later, on November 22, 2001, the Central Committee of Communist Youth League, the Ministries of Education and Culture, the State Council News Office, the All China Youth Federation, the National Students' Federation, the National Working Committee on Young Pioneer, and the China Youth Network Association, jointly presented to the CPC their own version of Internet self-regulation "*the Civilized Internet Pact of All Country Teenagers*", which established a definition of rules and regulations for youth who access the Internet.[dxciv]

In early 2002, MII approved "*Rules for the Administration of Internet Domain Names in China*" during its 9th session; curiously, this regulation was not enforced until nearly the end of 2002. Also in 2002, the Internet Society of China (ISC) in Beijing issued "*Self-Discipline Treaty of Internet Industry in China*"; essentially establishing a foundation of domestic self-discipline, regarding Internet access among Chinese users.[dxcv] Further Internet rules and regulations came from the Ministry of Culture as they issued the "*Notification on Strengthen the Market Supervision of Internet Culture*".[dxcvi] MII and the State Administration of Press and Publication jointly issued further policies for Chinese Internet users, with an edict called *"Interim Regulations for the Administration of the Internet Publications"*.[dxcvii] Additionally, in May 2003, the Ministry of Culture issued *"Provisional Regulations for Administering Internet Culture"*.[dxcviii]

The Internet Society of China (ISC) announced another blacklist of servers creating and sending spam; this was appropriately entitled the *"Spam Server Name List"*. Coincidentally, the same month, the computer virus WORM_MSBlast.A infected a majority of domestic Chinese Internet users so rapidly that the worm virus broke the world record for infections and became one of the most notorious computer viruses.[dxcix]

The People's Daily attributes the Internet worm to having started in the US:

"A computer virus known as "WORM-MSBlast.A" that began spreading over the Internet since Aug 11 from US wrecked a PC havoc in Europe, South America, Oceania and SE Asia. As reported, 250,000 computers worldwide were hit by the worm up to Aug 14. From Aug 11 to 13, the worm also crashed tens of thousands of computers in the Chinese metropolises of Beijing, Shanghai, Guangzhou, Wuhan and Hangzhou with of over 4,100 enterprises and institutions of local area networks (LAN) infected, and over 2,000 LANs put to a standstill. This has greatly hindered the development of e-government and e-business, incurring great economic losses"[dc]

Created by the Internet News & Information Service Working Committee (INISWC) of the Internet Society of China, the website of net.china.cn was launched in Beijing on June 10, 2004. The website was named the *"Illegal and Inappropriate Information Report Center"*, providing a channel for the public to report suspected illegal or offensive Internet activity and material, and to maintain public interests. The opening of the website is another essential step to strengthening self-discipline and public supervision of the Internet industry. On July 16, 2004, a national teleconference on the crackdown against pornographic websites was held, marking the launch of a nationwide campaign against such sites.

The following day, the Publicity Department of the Communist Party of China (CPC) Central Committee, and some other 13 governmental organizations, jointly published a notice to launch a nationwide crackdown project against pornographic websites according to the laws. On September 6, 2004, China's Supreme People's Court and Supreme People's Procuratorate jointly issued a new judicial interpretation for criminal cases concerning the production, duplication, publication, sale and dissemination of pornographic material via the Internet, mobile communications terminals and fixed-line telephone networks.

The Internet Trust and Self-discipline Alliance, with Internet Content Providers Sina, Sohu and Netease, announced self-disciplinary regulations for China's Internet wireless service providers (WISPs), indicating that they were willing to self-regulate before the Central Government's MII stepped in and imposed regulation.[dci]

The Network Copyright Alliance of Self-Discipline Steering Committee of the Internet Society of China (ISC) was established in Beijing in January 2005. This was an organization aimed at strengthening self-discipline of the Internet industry within the People's Republic of China; this was again, an attempt at industry self-regulation.[dcii]

The Ministry of Information Industry (MII) issued "*Administration Rules for Making Files of Non-profit Internet Information Services*". According to the rule, MII, jointly with 13 additional Ministries, including the Chinese Central Propaganda Department, the News Office of the State Council, the Ministry of Education, and the Ministry of Public Security, agreed to launch a centralized website for filing projects through the People's Republic of China. This project would establish three basic databases of ICP information, IP address information and domain name information, for filing information of ICPs, and laying a foundation for strengthening regulation and policy enforcement administration of the Internet in China.[dciii] Also in February, MII issued "*Administrative Rules for Electronic Authentication Services*".

This "*Administrative Rules for Electronic Authentication Services*" regulation was implemented in consonance with "*Electronic Signature Law*", and laid the foundation for the development of China's electronic authentication service industry. Both of these Chinese Internet regulations would later become very important to the online banking industry in China.[dciv]

Green Dam

In June 2009, an unsuccessful policy of Internet control was implemented by the People's Republic of China: the "*Green Dam Program*" was essentially implemented to further control access to the Internet in China, as an extension of the "*Golden Shield*" program.

The original requirement was for computers sold in China to have pre-installed Internet filtering software called "*Green Dam – Youth Escort,*" which was designed to "*effectively filter the Internet bad text and image content*", and to make it possible to combine punishment and prevention, whilst promoting healthy and orderly development of the Internet.

The Chinese Ministry of Industry and Information Technology, stated "*that in order to build a green, healthy and harmonious network environment, to avoid negative information*" Central Government funds were provided to develop and provide "*Green Dam – Youth Escort*" Green Internet filtering software, and the right to use the product for one year, plus related services for the whole community free of charge.

Specific requirements were set out for the software provider bidding for the government contract for this work:

First, production and sales in China should have the latest applicable version of the "*Green Dam – Youth Escort*" software pre-installed at the computer factory; imports for domestic sales should also have the latest version of the software pre-installed.

Second, the "*Green Dam – Youth Escort*" software should be pre-installed on the computer hard disk or CD-ROM inside, and in the recovery partition and recovery CD-ROM as a backup file.

Third, the "*Green Dam – Youth Escort*" software provider should take active measures to support enterprises to carry out pre-production computer-related work.

The "*Green Dam Program*" was designed to control and filter Internet search capabilities, all the way to the Chinese Internet network edge, via pre-installed software on computers, both desktop and laptop, sold in the People's Republic of China.

From the outset, "*Green Dam*" was a failure. The poorly designed software, while designed to protect children from supposedly questionable websites (such as those associated with pornography, online gaming, homosexual themes, religious sites such as Falun Gong, and those websites with anti-Communist political material), actually did a lot more. "*Green Dam*" actively monitors individual computer behavior; as a result, the wide range of computer programs, such as spreadsheets, Internet browsers or even e-mail, could unexpectedly close, should the "*Green Dam*" content filtering algorithm detect unacceptable word patterns, or questionable sentences.[dcv]

By May 2011, the Chinese Government's State Council Information Office (SCIO) created a new sub agency for regulating the Internet in China called the State Internet Information Office, essentially creating another bureaucracy within the Chinese Internet regulatory landscape.[dcvi] Its sole purpose is to control, regulate and monitor Chinese civilian access to, and use of, the Internet.

The Department, known as the State Internet Information Office, will direct, co-ordinate and supervise online content management, and handle administrative approval of businesses related to online news reporting. The State Council approved the appointment of four senior officials for the State Internet Information Office. Director of the State Council's Information Office, Wang Chen, was appointed as Director of the State Internet Information Office.

The SCIO directs development of online gaming, online video and online publication industries, and is engaged in promoting construction of major news websites and managing government online publicity work. The SCIO is assigned duties of investigating and adjudicating violators of China's website publication laws and regulations.

SCIO also oversees telecommunication service providers, specifically related to efforts of improving management of domain names registration, distribution of IP addresses, websites registration and Internet access, throughout the People's Republic of China.

Conclusions and thoughts …

In conclusion, the People's Republic of China has a very developed and robust Internet network within China, which connects the 'Middle Kingdom' very efficiently and redundantly to the rest of the world. The PRC also has a significant and growing community of Internet users, who are both accomplished and sophisticated in their use of the Internet. Conversely, the Chinese Government has a technically-effective and mature public safety and Internet control effort called the "*Golden Shield*" which prohibits unauthorized keyword searches by Internet users which are considered unfaithful to the CPC. Interestingly, the same Chinese authorities who block access within China, also perhaps have the ability to allow certain groups and organizations access through this massive internet filtering system, to carry out state-sponsored cyberattacks. The most important conclusion to be made regarding Chinese Internet regulation maturity, is that the rules, legislation and controlling authorities have developed such a robust Internet system for China, which effectively curtails foreign cyberintrusions.

APPENDIX B: CHINESE CYBERACTIVISM IN THE SPOTLIGHT

History of Chinese Cyberwarfare Attacks

1999

According to *The Washington Times*, *"Chinese hackers raid U.S. computers – Chinese hackers have attacked U.S. government information systems, including the White House network, in response to the errant bombing of the Chinese Embassy in Yugoslavia, according to an FBI report."*[dcvii]

2000

July 21: The People's Republic of China builds an information industry base to battle invasions by hackers and other illegal cyberspace activities over the next three to five years. The ground-breaking ceremony for the national information security base was held on Thursday in Chengdu, the capital of southwest China's Sichuan Province, with participants from the Ministry of Science and Technology, and other related departments

2001

Following a US Navy Orion P-3 collision with a People's Liberation Army Air Force (PLAAF) fighter jet on April 1st, 2001, Chinese hackers launch cyberattacks on several US Government websites, including both the Department of Labor, and Department of Health and Human Services.[dcviii]

Chinese hackers promise to launch cyberattacks on the United States. According to a BBC News story *"US officials and corporate computer security firms have put the nation on alert as Chinese hackers have promised to step up their attacks in the coming week. The FBI's National Infrastructure Protection Centre (NIPC) said that the attacks will coincide with several dates of historical significance including May Day, Youth Day on 4 May and the second anniversary of the accidental bombing by US forces of the Chinese Embassy in Belgrade."*[dcix]

May 8, 2001: Chinese hackers have a very long memory. Nationalistic patriotic Chinese hackers continue to launch cyberattacks on the US because of the Chinese Embassy in Belgrade cruise missile attack.[dcx]

2003

The US Government designates '*Operation Titan Rain*' as a series of co-ordinated attacks on American computer systems since 2003. The attacks are labeled as Chinese in origin, although their precise nature (i.e. state-sponsored espionage, corporate espionage or random hacker attacks) and their real identities (i.e. masked by proxy, zombie computer, spyware/virus infected) remain unknown. The activity known as '*Titan Rain*' is believed to be associated with an Advanced Persistent Threat (APT).[dcxi]

August: Reports of Chinese hackers against Taiwanese Government and commercial sites.[dcxii]

The Chinese Government grants licenses to open Internet cafe chains to just 10 firms; three affiliated to the Ministry of Culture, one linked to the politically powerful Central Committee of China Youth League, and six state-owned telecom operators.[dcxiii]

2004

Chinese hackers hit Japan Government website, over dispute over Diaoyu Island.

July: Chinese hacker attacks, aimed against Taiwan continues.

November: Media reports of attacks against several US military installations.

2005

Honker Union of China reforms.[dcxiv]

March: Several attacks from sites allegedly in China, against multiple sites in Japan.[dcxv]

August: Media reporting of Chinese Espionage condemns '*Titan Rain*.'

August 29: The SANS Institute, a security institute in the US, says that the '*Titan Rain*' attacks were "*most likely the result of Chinese military hackers attempting to gather information on U.S. systems.*"[dcxvi]

September: According to media staff in Taiwan, the National Security Council is targeted via social engineering e-mails.[dcxvii]

China purchases over 200 routers from Cisco Systems, an American company, that allow the Government more sophisticated technological censoring capabilities.

October: The Chinese Government blocks access to Wikipedia.[dcxviii]

2006

British MPs allegedly targeted by Chinese hacking attempts.[dcxix]

June: Chinese hackers strike at Taiwan MoD.[dcxx]

July 10: Claims of Congressional computers being hacked are made.[dcxxi]

US Representative Frank Wolf (R-10th, one of the most outspoken lawmakers on Chinese human rights issues), reports to the US House of Representatives that "*four of the computers in my personal office were compromised by an outside source. This source first hacked into the computer of my foreign policy and human rights staff person, then the computers of my chief of staff, my legislative director, and my judiciary staff person. On these computers was information about all of the casework I have done on behalf of political dissidents and human rights activists around the world. That kind of information, as well as everything else on my office computers – e-mails, memos, correspondence and district casework – was open for outside eyes to see."*[dcxxii]

July 11: An unwitting US State Department employee in the organization's East Asian Bureau opens an e-mail with malware payload, enabling Chinese cyberwarriors to freely navigate the e-mail and network systems.[dcxxiii]

November: US Naval War College computers infrastructure reportedly attacked.[dcxxiv]

January: A group of former senior Communist party officials in China criticize the internet censorship, warning that it could "*sow the seeds of disaster*" for China's political transition.[dcxxv]

February: Google agrees to block websites that the Chinese Government deems illegal, in exchange for a license to operate on Chinese soil. The search engine responds to international criticism by protesting that it has to obey local laws.[dcxxvi]

May: Chinese Internet users encountered difficulties when connecting to Hotmail, Microsoft's popular e-mail service. Microsoft says the break in service is caused by technical problems, but there is widespread speculation that the incident is linked to state censorship. In the last week of May, Google and many of its services also became unreachable.[dcxxvii]

July: Researchers at Cambridge University claim to have broken through the "*Great Firewall of China*", in response, the People's Republic of China Government impose blocks on large portions of the web.[dcxxviii]

October: A cyberincursion, originating from within the PRC, violates the computers of the Bureau of Industry and Security (BIS). The malware infection was so heinous that even re-installing the computer operating system is ineffective. The result? Throw the PCs away and buy new ones.[dcxxix]

November: The Chinese language version of Wikipedia is briefly unblocked before being shut down again the same month.[dcxxx]

November 15: A Chinese cyberattack on the US Naval War College network brings down the college's entire information infrastructure.[dcxxxi]

2007

The Chinese Government hacks a noncritical DoD computer system in June.[dcxxxii] Pentagon investigators are unable to definitively link the cyberattack to the Chinese military, but the technology was sophisticated enough that it indicated to Pentagon officials – as well as those in charge of computer security – that it came from within the Chinese Government.[dcxxxiii]

July: German Chancellery compromised and China accused of being the perpetrator.[dcxxxiv]

July 26: US Pentagon e-mail servers compromised for an extended period, with the cost to recover reported as $100 million.[dcxxxv]

Oak Ridge National Laboratory targeted by Chinese hackers.[dcxxxvi]

June: Office of the Secretary of Defense (OSD) computers attacked via malicious e-mail.[dcxxxvii]

January: President Hu Jintao, the People's Republic of China President, pledges to "*purify*" the Internet. He makes no specific mention of censorship, saying China needs to "*strengthen administration and development of our country's Internet culture*."[dcxxxviii]

March: Access to the LiveJournal, Xanga, Blogger and Blogspot blogging services from within China become blocked. Blogger and Blogspot become accessible again later the same month.[dcxxxix]

June: American military warn that China is gearing up to launch a cyberwar on the US, and has plans to hack US networks for trade and defense secrets.[dcxl]

2008

December: French Embassy website attacked in protest over meeting with the Dali Lama.[dcxli]

April: MI5 writes to more than 300 senior executives at banks, accountants and legal firms, warning them that the Chinese Army is using Internet spyware to steal confidential information.[dcxlii]

June: Hu Jintao, the Chinese President, makes his first tentative steps online, by answering questions on a web forum.[dcxliii]

August: China faces widespread criticism for Internet censorship in the run-up to the Beijing Olympics. The Government surprises critics by lifting some of the restrictions, making the websites of human rights organizations, such as Amnesty International, accessible for the first time.[dcxliv]

November 4: The networked servers hosting both US Presidential hopefuls Senator McCain and Obama are hacked by Chinese-based cyberwarriors.[dcxlv]

2009

March: *'Operation Ghost Net'* is detected: A vast Chinese cyberespionage network, codenamed *'Ghost Net'*, has penetrated 103 countries and infects at least a dozen new computers every week, according to researchers.[dcxlvi]

The three largest natural resource companies in Australia, including Rio Tinto, are compromised via Chinese based hackers.

April: Compromising of systems across 103 countries by Chinese cyberspies while Chinese Government denies enrollment in '*Ghost Net*'.[dcxlvii]

April: "*The Wall Street Journal reported that China was suspected of being behind a major theft of data from Lockheed Martin's F-35 fighter program, the most advanced airplane ever designed. Multiple cyberinfiltrations of the F-35 program apparently went on for years.*"[dcxlviii]

April: Daily attacks reported against German Government.[dcxlix]

April: The Chinese Government denies reports of hacking the Australian Prime Minister's e-mail.[dcl]

April: Chinese hackers target South Korea official, with social engineered e-mail.[dcli]

March: Bill Gates, Chairman of Microsoft, weighs into the Internet censorship argument, declaring that "*Chinese efforts to censor the Internet have been very limited*" and that the "*Great Firewall of China*" is "*easy to go around*". His comments are met with scorn by commentators on the web.[dclii]

March: The People's Republic of China Government blocks the video-sharing website YouTube, after footage appearing to show police beating Tibetan monks is posted on the site.[dcliii]

March 20: Hackers based in the PRC hack into computer systems of US Senator Bill Nelson. According to Senator Nelson's official Senate website: "*Nelson is a member of the Senate's Intelligence, Armed Services and*

Finance committees; and, he heads a Senate subcommittee that oversees NASA. "I have had my office computers invaded three times in the last month. One of them, we think, is serious," Nelson acknowledged Thursday, during a Senate Armed Services hearing that touched upon the subject of hackers trying to invade U.S. military computer networks."[dcliv]

June: China imposes an information black-out in the lead up to the anniversary of the Tiananmen Square massacre, blocking access to networking sites such as Twitter, as well as BBC television reports.[dclv]

June: China faces a storm of criticism over plans to force all computer users to install *"Green Dam"* Internet monitoring software. The plan is dropped in August.

June: Lord West, the British security minister, warns that Britain faces the threat of a *"cyber cold war"* with China, amid fears that hackers could gain the technology to shut down the computer systems that control Britain's power stations, water companies, air traffic, government and financial markets.[dclvi]

August: The US Government begins covertly testing technology, to allow people in China and Iran to bypass Internet censorship firewalls set up by their own governments.

December: MI5 Issues warring on Chinese cyberattacks.[dclvii]

December: The People's Republic of China Government offers rewards of up to 10,000 Yuan (£888) to users who report websites featuring pornography. The number of pornography-related searches in China skyrockets.[dclviii]

2010

'Shadows in the Cloud' report from the SecDev Group

on successful attacks against India's military networks.^{dclix}

January: The *'Operation Aurora'* attack, aimed at dozens of other organizations; Adobe Systems, Juniper Networks and Rackspace publicly confirm that they were targeted. According to media reports, Yahoo, Symantec, Northrop Grumman, Morgan Stanley and Dow Chemical also among the targets.^{dclx}

January: China announces plans to force its 400 million Internet users to register their real names before making comments on China's many chat rooms and discussion forums.

January: Around 5,000 people in the PRC are arrested for viewing Internet pornography, and 9,000 websites are deleted for containing sexual images and other "*harmful information*".^{dclxi}

January: Google threatens to pull out of China if it is not allowed to operate without censorship. The search engine blames the Government for "*highly sophisticated*" attacks on its servers, and attempts to target the Gmail accounts of human rights activists.^{dclxii}

March: Google shuts down its China-based search engine, redirecting users to an uncensored site based in Hong Kong.^{dclxiii}

April: Chinese state-owned telecommunications firm "*hijacks*" 15 per cent of the world's Internet traffic, including highly sensitive US Government and military exchanges, raising security fears.^{dclxiv}

June: The People's Republic of China Government restricts access to Foursquare, after players used the geo-location service to draw attention to the 21st anniversary of the Tiananmen Square massacre.^{dclxv}

July: Google stops automatically redirecting users of its Chinese search engine to its Hong Kong site, but continues to allow users to access the uncensored search engine by clicking a separate tab. The following week, the row between the search giant and the superpower seems to have drawn to a close as the Chinese Government renews Google's licensed to operate its business in China.[dclxvi]

August 2: Chinese telecommunications manufacturer Huawei announces that the former UK Chief Information Officer (CIO) John Suffolk will become the company's global cybersecurity officer, reporting directly to CEO, Mr Ren Zhengfei.[dclxvii]

August 19: Associated Press reports *"the People's Liberation Army, the Pentagon said, is using "information warfare units" to develop viruses to attack enemy computer systems and networks, and those units include civilian computer professionals."*[dclxviii]

October 4: Stuxnet in China. The official Xinhua News Agency, on Friday quoted Wang Zhantao, an engineer at the Beijing-based Rising International Software Co Ltd as saying that Stuxnet *"can break into computers and steal private information, especially from industrial firms, sending it back to a server in the United States."*[dclxix]

November: A security report to the US Congress warns that the hijacking of 15 per cent of the world's Internet traffic by a Chinese telecommunications firm may have been *"malicious"* including data from US military, civilian organizations, and those of other US allies.[dclxx]

December: Amid growing fears by Government officials, the People's Republic of China arrests Chinese hackers as the People's Liberation Army states *"that China fears that its own computer experts, nationalist hackers and social media could turn against the government."*[dclxxi]

2011

January 14: US warns on China cyber, anti-satellite capability. "*Advances by China's military in cyber and anti-satellite warfare technology could challenge the ability of U.S. forces to operate in the Pacific*", US Defense Secretary Robert Gates said during a visit to Japan.[dclxxii]

February 4: China attacks British Government computers. William Hague, British Foreign Secretary and First Secretary of State, told a security conference in Munich that the Foreign Office repelled the attack last month from "*a hostile state intelligence agency*". Although the Foreign Secretary did not name the country behind the attacks, intelligence sources familiar with the incidents made it clear that he was referring to China. The sources did not want to be identified because of the sensitive nature of the issue.

February 9: It is reported that "*Oil Firm Hit by Hackers From China*" and that Western energy firms have specifically been targeted in cyberespionage attacks, apparently orchestrated by hackers working from inside China.[dclxxiii]

February 17: "*In March, Andrew Jacobs, a correspondent working for The New York Times in Beijing, peered for the first time into the obscure corners of his Yahoo e-mail account settings. Under the "mail forwarding" tab was an e-mail address he had never seen before. That other e-mail address had been receiving copies of all of his incoming e-mails for months. His account had been hacked.*"[dclxxiv]

February 17: Foreign hackers attack Canadian Government an "*unprecedented*" cyberattack on government computers, and were traced back to computers in China. From CBC: The attack, apparently from China, also gave foreign hackers access to highly classified federal information and also forced the Finance Department and Treasury Board – the Federal government's two main economic nerve centers – off the Internet.[dclxxv]

March 10: China's growing capabilities in cyberwarfare and intelligence gathering are a *"formidable concern"* to the United States, the top US intelligence official told a Senate panel.[dclxxvi]

March 19: EMC–RSA In an open letter, RSA executive chairman Art Coviello revealed that the information was stolen via an APT (advanced persistent threat) attack. He stated specifically *"while at this time we are confident that the information extracted does not enable a successful direct attack on any of our RSA SecurID customers, [it] could potentially be used to reduce the effectiveness of a current two-factor authentication implementation as part of a broader attack."*[dclxxvii]

April 5: Toronto spy hunters not only learn what kinds of material has been stolen, but are able to see some of the documents, including classified assessments about security in several Indian states, and confidential embassy documents about India's relationships in West Africa, Russia and the Middle East. The intruders breached the systems of independent analysts, taking reports on several Indian missile systems. Spying on computer systems traces data theft to China. They also obtained a year's worth of the Dalai Lama's personal e-mail messages.[dclxxviii]

April 19: Rio, BHP, Fortescue Hit by China Computer Hackers[dclxxix], Rio Tinto Group faces cyberattacks from China at about the time of the arrest of four executives in the country, while BHP Billiton Ltd and Fortescue Metals Group Ltd are also hit, the Australian Broadcasting Corp reports.[dclxxx]

April 29: Kaspersky Labs' Threat Post reports *"Glass Dragon: China's Cyber Offensive Obscures Woeful Defense"*; this outlines that China's online defenses have failed to keep pace with its widely-hyped offensive capabilities.[dclxxxi] For the last 18 months, Dillon Beresford (a security researcher with testing firm NSS Labs) has spent up to seven hours a day of his spare time crawling the networks of China's state and provincial governments, as well as stealthier networks belonging to the PLA and the country's top universities. Armed with free tools, such as Metasploit and Netcat, as well as Google Translate, he has revealed much about the state of cybersecurity in China.[dclxxxii]

May 5: Lockheed Martin, the largest provider of IT services to the US Government and military, suffers a network intrusion stemming from data stolen pertaining to RSA. It seems that the cyberthieves managed to compromise the algorithm used by RSA to generate security keys. RSA will have to replace the SecurID tokens of more than 40 million customers around the world, including those of some of the world's biggest companies.[dclxxxiii]

May 7: China is ramping up espionage efforts in the US. One key component of their strategy is to recruit US citizens to join clandestine defense organizations and pass along information to Chinese handlers. In a specific incident, reported by the Associated Press, a recruit was said to be "*a seemingly all-American, clean-cut guy: No criminal record. Engaged to be married. A job teaching English overseas. In letters to the judge, loved ones described the 29-year-old Midwesterner as honest and caring – a good citizen. His fiancée called him "Mr Patriot".*"[dclxxxiv]

May 25: China sets up a specialized online '*Blue Army*' unit that it claims will protect the People's Liberation Army from outside attacks, prompting fears that the crack team is being used to infiltrate foreign governments' systems.[dclxxxv]

May 30: During an infrequent and rare briefing reported by the Beijing News, China's defense ministry spokesman, Geng Yansheng, announces that a 30-strong team, China's cybersquad for defense ('Blue Army'), has been formed to improve the military's cybersecurity.[dclxxxvi]

May: Citigroup reveal that information for more than 360,000 US credit card accounts has been compromised by a website hack. The data thieves did not even have to hack a server.[dclxxxvii]

June 22: China restricts a popular report-a-bribe website: Chen's website, http://www.ibribery.com – drew 200,000 unique visitors in two weeks. Its anonymous posts listed all sorts of bribes: from officials who demanded luxury cars and villas, to police officers who needed inducements not to issue traffic tickets; some ousted doctors received cash under the table to ensure safe surgical procedures. Mainstream media spread the word about the site, amplifying the outrage among netizens.[dclxxxviii]

June 24: Since 2008, the Chinese Government has opened a string of National Intelligence Colleges on campuses around the country, in an effort to improve the skills of the nation's spies. *"The Telegraph"* reports that *"the move comes amid growing worries in the West at the scale and breadth of Chinese intelligence-gathering, with MI5 saying that the Chinese government "represents one of the most significant espionage threats to the UK".*"[dclxxxix]

June: The International Monetary Fund says it has been targeted by a sophisticated cyberattack for months, even though the organization has made no public statement about the motivation behind it. The nature of the information stored by the institution would seem to indicate that this was a targeted attack made public. Data included user names, FTP accounts and even FTP login details, stored in plain text files.[dcxc]

June 30: *The Diplomat* reports on the advanced, persistent threat of cyberattacks and incursions on foreign governments, military and defense contractors from the People's Republic of China.[dcxci]

August 2: 'Operation Shady RAT' announced by McAfee – besides Google and its users (who promote anti-Chinese human rights issues), 49 US companies, 13 defense contractors and a host of international organizations in countries around the globe, are targeted by hackers based in the PRC.[dcxcii]

August 23: Chinese Military TV Channel CCTV-7 surreptitiously broadcasts PLA hacking capability – target University of Arkansas.

September 21: Chinese language used to hack Mitsubishi Heavy Industries and Kawasaki Heavy Industries in Japan – both companies are significant defense contractors for the Japanese Self Defense Forces (JDF).[dcxciii]

September 23: Predator and Reaper Drones, piloted by the US Air Force are infected by malware, rendering their mission in Afghanistan not mission capable.

October 5: The Chinese Hacking organization Honker Union, known for its patriotic hacks of US Government websites, announces it will recommence cyberattacks.[dcxciv]

October 6: China is reported responsible for an unprecedented theft of intellectual property (IP), as the new form of espionage against the US.[dcxcv]

October 13: The Chinese state-owned enterprise, the Nanhao Group, based in the city of Hengshui just southwest of Beijing, has military aged males operating as part of a People's Liberation Army cyberunit.[dcxcvi]

October 28: Reported Chinese hacking of US Government satellites: "*a Landsat-7 Earth observation satellite system had 12 or more minutes of interference in October 2007 and July 2008. Furthermore, a Terra AM-1 Earth observation satellite experienced two minutes of interference in June 2008 and nine minutes in October 2008.*"[dcxcvii]

October 28: The Japanese Parliament and overseas embassies attacked by hackers based in the People's Republic of China.[dcxcviii]

November 3: The US Office of the Counterintelligence Executive (ONCIX) releases a report, "*Foreign Spies Stealing U.S. Economic Secrets*" – documenting the billions of dollars in IP and classified information lost every year to cyberespionage.[dcxcix]

November 21: The US-China Economic and Security Review Commission releases a report to the US Congress detailing cyberattacks directed at US satellites; the Chinese motivation for conducting these extra-terrestrial attacks is that they "*currently have a significant competitive disadvantage in the area of satellite technology.*"[dcc]

November 28: General Martin Dempsey, the newly-appointed Chairman of the US military Joint Chiefs of Staff, cautions on the constant threat posed by the PRC to the "*nation's cyber security and continued vulnerability to cyber-terrorism*".[dcci]

December 12: Associated Press reports analysis, showing the majority of cyberbased attacks and network infrastructure intrusions originating from China to be conducted by perhaps just a dozen hacker groups, many in co-ordination with or under Chinese government direction.[dccii]

December 27: The Council on Foreign Relations posts an insightful article detailing China's cybercommand.[dcciii]

December 28: The East-West Institute posts an article illustrating parallels between the Cold War and the current cyberwar between the US and China. NB This is reported by the Arab news agency, Al Jazeera, not the Western press.[dcciv]

December 28: The concept of Chinese "*cyber war mobilization*" is analyzed and reported by "*The Atlantic*" after reviewing the "*China Defense Daily*" article about cyberwarfare in China.[dccv]

December 30: *Time Magazine* reports on how Afghanistan is the latest battleground between the US and China, over the natural resource – oil.[dccvi]

2012

January 4: China's targeting of the US drone fleet is reported by InfoSecIsland and Alien Vault Labs. "*The computer incident response team at defense contractor Lockheed recently reported they detected an active exploitation of vulnerabilities in Adobe's Reader and Acrobat applications, and the alert has been confirmed by the Defense Security Information Exchange.*"[dccvii]

January 11: Cyberdeterrence from the Chinese is a difficult issue.[dccviii]

January 12: After offering the world the US Defense Department's "*Strategy for Operating in Cyberspace*" Adam Segal of *The Diplomat* asks "*Can the U.S. Deter Cyber War?*"[dccix]

January 13: US Army General Gen Keith Alexander, head of the National Security Agency and the United States military's new 'Cyber Command', "*has tens of thousands of hackers, cryptologists, and system administrators serving under him.*" Yet he says the Pentagon's haphazard information infrastructure of 15,000 different networks is too haphazard to defend adequately.[dccx]

January 13: US military identity and authentication technologies, such as the Common Access Card (CAC), are compromised by malicious software attacks based in the PRC.[dccxi]

January 16: The People's Liberation Army readies for cyberwar. See Appendix H.

January 24: "*Popular Mechanics*" article "*Digital Spies: The Alarming Rise of Electronic Espionage*" details how" *foreign agents are stealing stealth technology, hacking heads of state, and sabotaging American companies ... an accelerating scourge that knows no national boundaries.*"[dccxii]

January 26: Symantec Corporation details insight in to the Sykipot Operations, including the use of vulnerabilities in Adobe products that date to 2006. The attacks were an advanced command and control operation, with IP addresses traced irrefutably to the City of Beijing. Efforts were focused on data exfiltration of sensitive information from US defense contractors, with

Mandarin Chinese used within the threat tool delivered as part of the Adobe vulnerability.[dccxiii]

January 30: Mr Pierluigi Paganini writes of the evidence of Chinese-based cyberattacks against US Defense contractors, particularly Symantec.[dccxiv]

January 31: Director of US National Intelligence, Mr James Clapper indicates that, not only Iran & Russia, but also the PRC, pose a significant national security threat to the US.[dccxv]

APPENDIX C: CHINA'S INFORMIZATION CAMPAIGN

In 2006, the People's Republic of China (PRC) mandated an "*informatization development strategy*" known more simply by the term "*informatization*".

Here is the complete text of the official State Informatization Development Strategy (2006-20), as decreed and published by General Office of the CPC Central Committee and General Office of the State Council:

"*The goals for informatization development in the next 15 years are: providing information infrastructure nationwide; strengthening capacities of independent innovation of information technology; optimizing the information industry structure; improving information security; making effective progress on building more information-oriented national economy and society; establishing the new type of industrialization model; building a perfect national policy and system for the informatization process; enhancing the capability of applying the information technology among the public.*

In the Strategy, nine key aspects are emphasized: promoting informatization of the national economy; popularizing e-government; establishing advanced Internet culture; pushing ahead social informatization; popularizing information infrastructure; exploiting information resources more efficiently; improving information industry competition; building national information security system; improving people's ability in using information technology and cultivating more talents in information technology.

Implementation of the Strategy will lay a good foundation for China which is striding toward the information society.

After years of development, China has stepped into an all-around, multi-level period of informatization development. As China is in the process of building a moderately prosperous society in all respects, vigorously pushing forward informatization development will be crucial in promoting social and economic development.

The informatization development is advocated when China urgently needs to grasp opportunity and meet challenges as well as the requirements for the change of the pattern of economic growth, upgrading development concept."[dccxvi]

The Chinese *"informatization"* strategy sets forth China's goals in informatization development for the next 15 years. Since the People's Republic of China has emerged as a global power in information and communications technology (ICT), the State Informatization Development Strategy (2006–20) provides further distinct guidance within China, in as much as this 15-year (2006–20) development strategy is a priority of both the Communist Party of Chinese (CPC) and PRC government. The key tenant of this forward thinking and planned state-sponsored Internet strategy is the notion of *"informatization"*, 信息化, pronounced in Pin Yin as Xìnxī huà. The intent of信息化 is to encourage and support both the military infrastructure and national civilian economic; to grow economically through capitalization of the Internet, as both a vector of ensuring military superiority through cyberoffensive capabilities, and economically, by exfiltrating necessary competitive information, to ensure the economic information needs of Chinese state-owned enterprises (SOE) are met. Both of these military and civilian economic Internet-based methods of信息化 will ensure sustained economic growth, compete globally in the ICT realm, and ensure national security. Information dominance, whether for political, economic, or military purposes, requires mastery of both the electromagnetic spectrum and the global cybersphere. The People's Liberation Army General Staff Directorate (GSD) – both the Third Department, in Mandarin Chinese, 总参三部 with a Pin Yin pronunciation of Zǒngcān sān bù, and Fourth Department represented Mandarin Chinese as 总参四部with a Pin Yin pronunciation of Zǒngcān sìbù – are indeed the two most significant and important military prime movers in China's developing cyberoffensive infrastructure capability.

APPENDIX D: GENERAL WANG PUFENG'S CHALLENGE OF INFORMATION WARFARE

The Challenge of Information Warfare

"Courtesy of the Federation of American Scientists (*www.fas.org*)"

Major General Wang Pufeng is a former Director of the Strategy Department, Academy of Military Science, People's Liberation Army, Beijing, People's Republic of China. The following paper was written for the China Military Science during the Spring of 1995. General Wang presents several carefully articulated core beliefs, with accompanying historical antecedents. His core IW ideas include Cultivating Talent, Strengths to Attack Weaknesses, Organize Offensive and Defensive Information Warfare, Preparation and Defense with Attacking and Fighting, Firm Control of Battlefield Information, Computer Technology and Battlefield Information Networks, Information Weapons Systems, A Reliable Reconnaissance and Remote-Sensing System, Improving Weapons and Equipment Through Information Technology, and Establishing Concepts of Victory in Future Information Warfare.

It is within these following ideas of General Wang's that we begin to get an idea of how China has formulated, and will continue to mature, her cyberwarfare tactics and strategies. Major General Wang's article starts with following passage:

"Andrew Marshall of the Pentagon believes the information era will touch off a revolution in military affairs, just as the cannon in the 15th century and the machine in the past 150 years of the industrial era touched off revolutions. U.S. Army Chief of Staff General Gordon Sullivan holds that the information era is changing the army and will change the means of war fundamentally. U.S. Secretary of the Army Togo West says, "We place the stakes of winning a victory in the next century on digitization." The U.S. Army believes that the assessment of an army's combat capability used to depend on how good its munitions were, but in the 21st century, it will depend on the operational capability of the C3I system based on information technology. The U.S. Army has presented the concept of Force 21 and makes it clear that it should be armed for information warfare and become a digitized army. Its plan is to

build a digitized brigade in 1996 and expand it to a division in 1997. The U.S. Army has taken these actions to prepare for future information warfare.

In the near future, information warfare will control the form and future of war. We recognize this developmental trend of information warfare and see it as a driving force in the modernization of China's military and combat readiness. This trend will be highly critical to achieving victory in future wars.

Establishing Concepts of Victory in Future Information Warfare

Looking at the current situation, it can be seen that the authorized strength and equipment, strategy, tactics, and military theory of China's military are still basically the products of the industrial era and are far from satisfying the demands of information warfare. We have much work to do to shrink this gap, and our first task is to clarify our war preparation concepts. We have already made it clear that the basis of war preparation is to achieve victory in modern warfare, especially high-tech warfare, and this is quite correct. High-tech warfare, however, has already developed from an emphasis on guided missiles to an emphasis on information. Firepower superiority depends on information superiority. This has been a phased transition. In keeping with the demands of information warfare, we must base our war preparations on achieving victory in this area and use it to plan China's military and national defense modernization. When we engage in war with strong enemies in the future, we will face comprehensive and powerful information suppression.

There is a question of how to use weakness to defeat strength and how to conduct war against weak enemies in order to use information superiority to achieve greater victories at a smaller cost. It must be confirmed that information and weapons are all controlled by people. People are the main factor in combat power. However, it must also be confirmed that the functions of people and weapons will primarily be determined by the control of information, because information can play an important role in warfare. Hence, the flow of information, under the control of people, is injected into the flow of manpower, capacity, and materials, and will influence the form of warfare and determine victory or defeat. During the industrial age, the combat power of a military was measured primarily by how much capacity that military held and could utilize. During the information age, the efficiency of capacity utilization is even more important. Generally speaking, a military with capacity but no means to use it cannot become a true combat power. If capacity is used to no effect, it will only cause unnecessary damage and waste and will not have practical significance to victory or defeat in the war. A military can become a truly effective combat power only if it can use its capacity effectively. Capacity utilization controlled by information technology can successfully solve this problem. In this way, the thrust of China's military construction and development of weapons and equipment will no longer be toward strengthening the "firepower antipersonnel system" of the industrial age, but toward the strengthening of information technology, information weapons systems, and information networking. Our sights must not be fixed on the firepower warfare of the industrial age; rather they must be trained on the information warfare of the information age. This must be the starting point from which to propel China's military construction forward and raise that construction to a higher grade and standard.

Theory is the new guide to action, and information warfare theory is a new warfare theory. We must understand it, study it, and use it to guide military construction and combat. China's military, which has always had advanced Marxist and Maoist warfare theory, absolutely must not fall behind the times. We must use a practical combination of information warfare and Marxist and Maoist military thought to guide information warfare and issues in military construction. In light of the fact that the military lags behind its strong enemies in information technology and information weapons, the military must emphasize the study of ways to use inferior equipment to achieve victory over enemies with superior equipment. "Using the inferior to overcome the superior" is a tradition of China's military. However, "using the inferior to overcome the superior" in information warfare is definitely much different in content and form from the techniques of war used in the past. The question of how to conduct a people's war in information warfare also requires study. The people's war of the past was conducted in tangible space, but information warfare, in addition to occurring in tangible space on the ground, on the sea, and in the air, is conducted even more in intangible space, such as in electromagnetic fields. It is not only a battlefield in which guns and bombs proliferate, but also a 'computer battlefield' in sheltered laboratories and control rooms. There are many new issues here we need to explore.

Improving Weapons and Equipment through Information Technology

We must put effort into information technology, information weapons systems, and information networking. These are the important aspects of hardware construction for the military when adapting to information warfare. Information is a material good, and information sources, information channels, and information storage are all material goods. The gathering, transmission, processing, and use of information and the development of information into combat power all depend on certain material goods, energy, and technology carriers. Information technology itself is a pinnacle of high technology. The key technologies are remote-sensing technology, communications technology, and computer technology. Key information weapons include precision-guided weapons systems and electronic warfare weapons systems as well as C4I systems (communications, guidance, control, computers, and intelligence) which form the central nervous system. These hardware items are necessary and essential to adapt to and achieve victory in information warfare, and we must make efforts here. Developing this hardware, however, is not easy. It will be restricted by the level of our information technology base and funds. Hence, comprehensive consideration must be given to the direction, goals, and emphases of this development. The overarching demand, for long-term planning as well as short-term arrangements, is to consider fully the threat faced by China, the possible warfare tasks of the near future, the battle regions and battlefield conditions, the state of China's defense technology development, as well as the possible support for military funding. Thus, it appears that we should emphasize in our development the following aspects of information technology.

A Reliable Reconnaissance and Remote-Sensing System

The goal is to obtain timely information, to understand the enemy and ourselves, and to achieve clarity about our situation with great determination. It is especially necessary to establish a strategic reconnaissance warning and air defense system to achieve a capacity for early detection of enemy movements, in order to be forewarned and ready.

Information Weapons Systems

The most important of these are air defense weapons systems, offensive tactical guided missile attack systems, landing and touchdown operations equipment systems, electronic warfare equipment systems, and underwater minelaying systems. These will give China over-the-horizon, high-precision, concealed, sudden defensive attack capability and a stronger survival capacity and make the enemy terrified and worried, providing an effective threat.

Appendix D: General Wang Pufeng's Challenge of Information warfare

Computer Technology and Battlefield Information Networks

First, we should establish battlefield information networks and battlefield databases for the battlefields in priority strategic directions. By bringing all branches of the military into an information network, information may be shared on the network. Near-real-time communication can be gained in all directions and a better solution can be achieved for the problem of vertical and horizontal coordination in warfare.

Firm Control of Battlefield Information

To achieve victory in information warfare, the central issue is control of information.

Preparation and Defense with Attacking and Fighting

In comparison with the strength of potential enemies, the information technology and information weapons of China's military may all be inferior for quite some time. When China's enemies mainly use their air forces and navies to conduct strategic information warfare, China will be in the strategic position of engaging in defensive warfare along interior lines. The progress and outcome of the war will be determined by the state of China's advance preparations and defensive situation during the war. In defensive warfare, China should still thoroughly implement an active defensive strategy. In addition to hiding and concealing forces, in combat, especially during key phases in key areas, we must engage even more actively in air defense warfare and intercept and attack enemy weapons as they arrive in surprise attack. When conditions permit, we should also engage in counterattacks against the enemy and interfere with or misguide their guided weapons, thus damaging or destroying their equipment. Strategically, we should use preparation and defense, and in combat we should use attacking and fighting to achieve victory.

Organize Offensive and Defensive Information Warfare

Information warfare includes engaging in an active offense of information suppression and attack, as well as in the reactive defense of information counter-reconnaissance, resistance to interference, and defense against destruction. The issue of an information offensive can only be discussed if one has superior technology for information suppression. In a strategic defense situation, sometimes information offensives can be undertaken during warfare actions in limited areas. In that case, information technology suppression superiority must first be achieved in warfare actions in that limited area. Under the conditions of modern high technology, an information offensive is often a prelude to a strategic offensive. Take, for example, the surprise attack on Libya by the United States. Before the attack, 18 electronic-warfare aircraft were sent to Libya to engage in powerful interference.

Fighter aircraft were then sent to launch counter radiation guided missiles to destroy Libya's air defense radar stations, then fighter aircraft were sent to launch precision-guided bombs to attack five important targets.

The information offensives in this raid included:

1) Information reconnaissance to gain information on targets of the raid and to study the target in detail;
2) Electronic interference to paralyze the opponent's communications and blind the opponent's air defense guided missiles;
3) Information suppression by using counter radiation guided missiles to destroy air defense radar stations; and
4) Information attack by using precision-guided warheads to attack pre-set targets.

During the Gulf War, the information offensives of the multilateral forces were even more representative. In addition to the four types listed above at least the following should be added:

1) Computer viruses were used to destroy the computer systems of Iraq's air defense system and thus paralyze it.
2) Stealth aircraft were used to launch precision-guided bombs against the communications building and the command center, thus achieving information suppression.

In situations of information defense, we must strive for an active approach in a reactive situation and use every means possible to destroy the opponent's information superiority and transform our inferior position in information.

We must pay attention to:

Counter reconnaissance to prevent the opponent from obtaining information about the true situation. For example, secret falsification can be used to plant false intelligence and false targets in the place of true intelligence and true targets to confuse the real and the false and muddle the opponent's perceptions and inspire false assessments. When conditions exist, active methods may be used to engage in interference to blind or even destroy the opponent's reconnaissance instruments.

Resistance to interference to maintain one's own channels of information

By using defense advantages, multiple-communication methods can be used to weaken the impact of the enemy's interference.

Resist viruses to protect the normal operations of information processing in computer systems.

Information counterattack

This is an important action to be carried out according to the general strategic plan and in coordination with strategic and combat counterattacks. The specific content and form is the same as that of information offensives.

The information offenses and defenses outlined above, in addition to using information technology extensively, also use information weapons extensively. Thus, during the process of a war, these do not exist alone but accompany strategic offenses and defenses and are consistent with the overall situation of strategic offenses and defenses. Before and after war, information hassling never stops for a moment but usually does not involve the use of information weapons.

"You Do Your Fighting and I'll Do Mine" Using Strengths to Attack Weaknesses

This is the basic warfare style which Mao Zedong taught us, and it is an excellent tradition of China's military. Strengths and weaknesses are in comparison with those of the enemy. What then will China's strengths be in future wars? What will be China's weaknesses? Politically speaking, China's military has the advantage of justness, which is conducive to gaining international sympathy and support, and it has the support of the people domestically. In terms of warfare space, when China's military engages in war on China's soil, it will have the advantages of topography and position. In air, sea, space, and electronic warfare, however, the enemy will have the advantage. In terms of the choice of timing for warfare, because the enemy will have more advanced night-vision instruments, the advantage will not be China's, especially in air and sea warfare at night. The enemy will have advantages in instrumentation. China will have advantages in familiarity with the topography. Each will have half the advantages. In terms of warfare techniques, China's military has a tradition of flexible fighting methods and is more adapted to nonlinear warfare, but lacks practical battle experience in information warfare with high technology. In terms of weapons and equipment, generally speaking the enemy will have the advantage, but in some areas, such as guided missiles and submarines, China can still shock the enemy to a certain degree. China is strong in close warfare; the enemy is strong in distant warfare.

In wars of the future, China will face the enemy's more complete information technology with incomplete information technology. Because sometimes superior tactics can make up for inferior technology, China will still carry out its traditional warfare method of "you fight your way, I'll fight my way," and use its strengths to attack the enemy's weaknesses and adhere to an active role in warfare. To do this, it appears that we must pay even more attention to:

Fully utilizing the advantages of national territory and front information facilities to carry out reconnaissance on the enemy's situation and protect ourselves and attack the enemy.

Developing, improving, and utilizing China's information weapons in a concentrated way to carry out raids on enemy operation platforms and bases and damage and foil the enemy's offensive.

Emphasizing mobile war in the context of information warfare

Conscientiously organizing sabotage operations by the Army, Navy, and Air Force, grasp exploitable opportunities, and make continuous raids to exhaust and wear down the enemy.

Organizing specialized combined special warfare troops and equip these with information technology weapons to carry out powerful special warfare.

In summary, our warfare methods must adapt to the needs of information warfare. We must use all types, forms, and methods of force, and especially make more use of nonlinear warfare and many types of information warfare methods which combine native and Western elements to use our strengths in order to attack the enemy's weaknesses, avoid being reactive, and strive for being active. In this way, it will be entirely possible for China to achieve comprehensive victory over the enemy even under the conditions of inferiority in information technology.

Cultivating Talent

In the final analysis, information warfare is conducted by people. The basic great plan is to cultivate talented people suited to information warfare. One aspect is to cultivate talent in information science and technology. The development and resolution of information warfare can be predicted to a great degree in the laboratory. Information science and technology talent is the forerunners of science and technology talent is the forerunner of science and technology research. The achievements and practical use of their research will play a key role in the development and advancement of society and military construction and warfare. The second aspect is talented people in command and control. They especially need to have the ability to conduct comprehensive analysis and policy-information processing, to understand themselves and the enemy, as well as the battlefield, and also to have a capacity for scientific strategic thinking and a comprehensive point of view. Senior command personnel especially need to have information knowledge and the ability to control information warfare and must be adept at using information technology to organize and command warfare. They must be very knowledgeable, brave, and talented people.

Combat personnel must also be familiar with the technical and strategic aspects of the weapons and equipment in their hands and must be very well versed in the operation of those weapons and equipment. They must be able to understand accurately the combat plan and resolutely and flexibly utilize weapons and equipment to wipe out the enemy. The combat personnel of information warfare are not only the warriors who charge enemy lines for face to face struggles of life or death, but sometimes are the operating technical personnel who sit before computers and instruments. They stand at the first line in electronic warfare and in the resistance against C4I systems and on the front line in information technology conflicts.

Rear support and technical support are very important in information warfare. Information technology relates to a number of high-technology groups of people and touches on new energy, new materials, artificial intelligence, space travel, marine engineering, systems engineering, and other high-technology subjects. The demands for the technical level of support personnel are quite high. They are required to be able to guarantee that weapons and equipment are always kept in excellent condition. While carrying out rear and front-line support, the use of information technology is a support method just like other methods. In information warfare, the support of information technology penetrates the contents of information resistance and is also one method of warfare support.

The main methods of cultivating talent are study and training. In addition to conducting training in politics, ethics, and psychology, there must also be study of high-tech knowledge and the fundamental knowledge of and warfare techniques related to information warfare. If conditions permit, we want to create as much as possible the conditions necessary for implementing simulation training. We can first consider creating stimulated battlefields with information in key areas of the army, navy, air force, and artillery, and, second, conducting rotational training of cadres and key troops. Colleges and universities should also establish curricula in information warfare. Scientific research institutions should also engage in research on information warfare.

The large-scale importation of information technology deep into the field of warfare will inevitably bring about a military revolution. This revolution has actually already started. Those who perceive it first will swiftly rise to the top and have the advantage of the first opportunities. Those who perceive it late will unavoidably also be caught up in the vortex of this revolution. Every military will receive this baptism. This revolution is first a revolution in concepts, and then it is a revolution in science and technology, equipment, troop strength, strategy, and tactics as well as a revolution in training. Thus, the issue of how to adapt to and achieve victory in the information warfare which we will face from now on is an important question which we need to study carefully."[dccxvii]

APPENDIX E: 'THROUGH THE NIGHT OF THE LANTERN'

Through the night of the Lantern: the Second Board of the Central Military Commission.

This is an article detailing the PLA's current CMC understanding of today's modern information warfighting efforts in the context of Mao's Long March.

It was published on July 4, 2011, in the *Beijing Daily*.

It is an extensive article, the core of which is that, during Mao's Long March, the Red Army was able to prepare in advance for attacks by the Russians and by the Kuomintang, because of the effectiveness of their reconnaissance brigades, which had intercepted enemy telegrams and other sensitive intelligence material a month or more ahead of planned attacks. The value of this intelligence, to the ultimate victory of the PLA, was incalculable and, in the same way, advance intelligence would be of incalculable value to the PLA in modern warfare.

APPENDIX F: CHINESE HACKER WEBSITE RESOURCES

There are a number of Chinese hacking websites, all of which can be visited – carefully – online.

The first website for Chinese hackers to gain hacking knowledge about hacking, and discuss their methodologies with one other, is www.chinaeagle.org

The next site comes with a Communist Party of China message on it, and can be found at: *www.neteasy.cn*

The Evil Octal forum is another popular Chinese hacking information site: *http://forum.eviloctal.com/*.

Figure 11: Translated page 2 of EvilOctal Chinese hacking forum

Other Chinese hacking websites worth reviewing include: *http://netxeyes.com/main.html*

http://www.hackerxfiles.net/forum.php

http://www.hackbase.com/

An interesting blog is to be found at: *http://hhacker.com/*

The website from the Red and Black Alliance *http://bbs.2cto.com/* is as interesting and compelling as the previous examples. In this particular example, it describes "*how to track network attacks*".

What are the Chinese Hacker motives & goals?

So where do Chinese hackers get their cyberintrusion tradecraft? What specific hacking tools do they use? There are a number of websites that specialise in providing hacking tools, an example of which follows:

Figure 12: Chinese hacker's automated tool website [dccxviii]

APPENDIX G: HUAWEI'S STATEMENT ON ESTABLISHING A GLOBAL CYBERSECURITY ASSURANCE SYSTEM

The following statement by the CEO of Huawei, on establishing a global cybersecurity assurance system, is quite compelling; it relates to a Chinese company and what they intend to with the products that they produce worldwide and intend on supporting, with a global, cyberassurance dominance in the marketplace.

The statement is provided courtesy of Huawei's corporate communications website via Red-DragonRising; it can be found at:

http://red-dragonrising.com/blog/53-statement-on-establishing-a-global-cyber-security-assurance-system

As a global leading telecom solutions provider, Huawei Technologies Co. Ltd. ("Huawei") is fully aware of the importance of cyber security and understands the concerns of various governments and customers about security. With the constant evolution and development of the telecom industry and information technology, security threats and challenges are increasing, which intensify our concerns about cyber security.

Huawei will therefore pay a great deal more attention to this issue and has long been dedicated to adopting feasible and effective measures to improve the security of its products and services, thus helping customers to reduce and avoid security risks and building trust and confidence in Huawei's business. Huawei believes that the establishment of an open, transparent and visible security assurance framework will be conducive to the sound and sustainable development of industry chains and technological innovation; it will also facilitate smooth and secure communications among people.

In light of the foregoing, Huawei hereby undertakes that as a crucial company strategy, based on compliance with the applicable laws,

*regulations, standards of relevant countries and regions, and by reference to
the industry best practice, it has established and will constantly optimize an
end-to-end cyber security assurance system. Such a system will incorporate
aspects from corporate policies, organizational structure, business processes,
technology and standard practice. Huawei has been actively tackling the
challenges of cyber security through partnerships with governments,
customers, and partners in an open and transparent manner.*

*In addition, Huawei guarantees that its commitment to cyber security will
never be outweighed by the consideration of commercial interests.*

*From an organizational perspective, the Global Cyber Security Committee
(GCSC), as the top-level cyber security management body of Huawei, is
responsible for ratifying the strategy of cyber security assurance. The Global
Cyber Security Officer (GCSO) is a significantly important member of
GCSC, in charge of developing this strategy and managing and supervising
its implementation. The system will be adopted globally by all departments
within Huawei to ensure consistency of implementation. The GCSO shall also
endeavor to facilitate effective communication between Huawei and all
stakeholders, including governments, customers, partners and employees.
The GCSO reports directly to the CEO of Huawei.*

*In terms of business processes, security assurance shall be integrated into all
business processes relating to R&D, the supply chain, sales and marketing,
delivery, and technical services. Such integration, as the fundamental
requirement of the quality management system, will be implemented under
the guidance of management regulations and technical specifications. In
addition, Huawei will reinforce the implementation of the cyber security
assurance system by conducting internal auditing and receiving external
certification and auditing from security authorities or independent third-
party agencies. Furthermore, Huawei has already been certified to BS7799-
2/ISO27001 accreditation since 2004.*

*In connection with personnel management, our employees, partners and
consultants are required to comply with cyber security policies and*

requirements made by Huawei and receive appropriate training so that the concept of security is deeply rooted throughout Huawei. To promote cyber security, Huawei will reward employees who take an active part in cyber security assurance and will take appropriate action against those who violate cyber assurance policies. Employees may also incur personal legal liability for violation of relevant laws and regulations.

Taking on an open, transparent and sincere attitude, Huawei is willing to work with all governments, customers and partners through various channels to jointly cope with cyber security threats and challenges from cyber security. Huawei will set up regional security certification centers if necessary. These certification centers will be made highly transparent to local governments and customers, and Huawei will allow its products to be inspected by people authorized by local governments to ensure the security of Huawei's products and delivery service. Meanwhile, Huawei has been proactively involved in the telecom cyber security standardization activities led by ITU-T, 3GPP, and IETF etc., and has joined security organizations such as FIRST and partnered with mainstream security companies to ensure the cyber security of its customers and promote the healthy development of industries.

This cybersecurity assurance system applies to Shenzhen Huawei Investment Holding Co., Ltd., and all subsidiaries and affiliates which are under its direct or indirect control. This statement is made on behalf of all the above entities.

This statement should comply with local laws and regulations. In the event of any conflict between this statement and local laws and regulations, the latter shall prevail. Huawei will review this statement on an annual basis, and shall keep it in line with laws and regulations.

Huawei Technologies Co, Ltd.
CEO Ren Zhengfei

APPENDIX H: PLA'S NATIONAL DEFENSE UNIVERSITY CHINA'S CYBERWAR PREPARATIONS

The following statement is provided to illustrate the seriousness of China and her military, the PLA, with their intent to prepare for and carry out cyberwarfare operations of an offensive nature.

The post of the original story is provided courtesy of reporter Su Jie of ECNS.com and can be located at the original source: *http://ecns.cn/2012/01-16/6254.shtml* or saved for posterity also at: *http://red-dragonrising.com/blog/58-chinas-peoples-liberation-army-pla-gets-ready-for-cyber-warfare*

"PLA 'Online Blue Army' gets ready for cyber warfare"

The People's Liberation Army (PLA) confirmed in May 2011 that it has established an "Online Blue Army" to improve China's defense capability and ensure the security of the country's military network. The announcement drew close attention from military watchers and experts worldwide.

Zhang Shaozhong, a military expert and a professor from PLA National Defense University, told the People's Daily that China is increasingly dependent on the Internet, but makes no domestic root servers, and various other types of software and Internet hardware are U.S. made. In this sense, China can be described as merely a computer user with a fairly fragile Internet security system. These are circumstances that cry out for the build up of Internet security forces.

Throughout 2010, 480,000 Trojans viruses and 13,782 Zombie viruses were detected, with 221,000 Trojan and 6,531 Zombie remote control clients found to originate in foreign countries.

Appendix H: PLA's National Defense University China's Cyberwar Preparations

Websites of Chinese governmental departments, including the Ministries of National Defense (MND),Water Resources, Land and Resources, and Supreme People's Procuratorate, have been attacked 4,635 times.

Moreover, of the 505 million Internet users in China (a figure reported by Xinhua News Agency citing the China Internet Network Information Center or CNNIC as of November 2011), 217 million or 44.7 percent of them were attacked by malware in the first half of 2011. The assaults included viruses or Trojan horses, but the accounts of 121 million specifically had their accounts hacked and passwords stolen, causing a direct economic loss of tens of billion yuan.

The case raised concerns about web security and triggered widespread panic. "China faces a grim situation in maintaining web security," pointed out the Southern Weekend.

Li Li, a military expert at the National Defense University, told the People's Daily that compared with the online military units of Western countries, China's 'Online Blue Army' is currently at its fledging stage, and applied more in online maneuver mode than as an organic, large-scale online army.

China is a defender in the cyber war battlefield, fending off the 'information warfare' and 'media warfare' of others added the Southern Weekend.

According to the People's Daily, online military units were established in other countries some time ago. The U.S. destroyed Iraq's air defense system using PC viruses during the Gulf War in 1991. Its online army also played a major role in the war in Kosovo and the second Iraq conflict. The UK, Russia, Japan and India all have established online military units.

The Pentagon pointed out in its report Military and Security Developments Involving the People's Republic of China 2011, that "Cyber warfare capabilities could serve PRC military operations in three key areas. First and foremost, they allow data collection through exfiltration. Second, they can be employed to constrain an adversary's actions or slow response time by targeting network-based logistics, communications, and commercial activities. Third, they can serve as a force multiplier when coupled with kinetic attacks during times of crisis or conflict."

Some Western media suspect that China's 'Online Blue Army' is actually "hackers" aiming to carry out attacks on other countries' Internet systems.

At this, Defense Ministry spokesman Geng Yansheng explained during the ministry's news conference in Beijing on May 25, 2011 that launching the 'Online Blue Army' was based on the PLA's needs, and enforcing Internet security protection is critical to military programs.

Though Western countries habitually call attack forces the 'red side,' and in military drills, the opposing sides are often designated as 'red side' and 'blue side,' Teng Jianqun, a research fellow at the China Institute of International Studies asserts that the MND name for the force 'Online Blue Army' has no special meaning, and thus nothing should be read into the 'color' selected for China's online military unit.

"Besides fighting skills of the soldiers in the battlefield, the modern war focuses more on technology and the Internet. Strengthening the national defense Internet construction is another new requirement of the national security. Therefore, the government should attach great importance to the Internet national defense," the People's Daily quoted a fan's comment on hngov.cn.

ITG RESOURCES

IT Governance Ltd sources, creates and delivers products and services to meet the real-world, evolving IT governance needs of today's organizations, directors, managers and practitioners. The ITG website (*www.itgovernance.co.uk*) is the international one-stop-shop for corporate and IT governance information, advice, guidance, books, tools, training and consultancy.

http://www.itgovernance.co.uk/cybersecurity-standards.aspx is the information page on our website for cybersecurity resources.

Other Websites

Books and tools published by IT Governance Publishing (ITGP) are available from all business booksellers and are also immediately available from the following websites:

www.itgovernance.co.uk/catalog/355 provides information and online purchasing facilities for every currently available book published by ITGP.

http://www.itgovernance.eu is our euro-denominated website which ships from Benelux and has a growing range of books in European languages other than English.

www.itgovernanceusa.com is a US$-based website that delivers the full range of IT Governance products to North America, and ships from within the continental US.

www.itgovernanceasia.com provides a selected range of ITGP products specifically for customers in South Asia.

www.27001.com is the IT Governance Ltd. website that deals specifically with information security management, and ships from within the continental US.

Pocket Guides

For full details of the entire range of pocket guides, simply follow the links at *www.itgovernance.co.uk/publishing.aspx*.

Toolkits

ITG's unique range of toolkits includes the IT Governance Framework Toolkit, which contains all the tools and guidance that you will need in order to develop and implement an appropriate IT governance framework for your organization. Full details can be found at *www.itgovernance.co.uk/ products/519*.

For a free paper on how to use the proprietary Calder-Moir IT Governance Framework, and for a free trial version of the toolkit, see *www.itgovernance.co.uk/calder_moir.aspx*.

There is also a wide range of toolkits to simplify implementation of management systems, such as an ISO/IEC 27001 ISMS or a BS25999 BCMS, and these can all be viewed and purchased online at: *http://www.itgovernance.co.uk/catalog/1*.

Best Practice Reports

ITG's range of Best Practice Reports is now at *www.itgovernance.co.uk/best-practice-reports.aspx*. These offer you essential, pertinent, expertly researched information on a number of key issues including Web 2.0 and Green IT.

Training and Consultancy

IT Governance also offers training and consultancy services across the entire spectrum of disciplines in the information governance arena. Details of training courses can be accessed at *www.itgovernance.co.uk/training.aspx* and descriptions of our consultancy services can be found at *http://www.itgovernance.co.uk/consulting.aspx*. Why not contact us to see how we could help you and your organization?

Newsletter

IT governance is one of the hottest topics in business today, not least because it is also the fastest moving; so what better way to keep up than by subscribing to ITG's free monthly newsletter *Sentinel*? It provides monthly updates and resources across the whole spectrum of IT governance subject matter, including risk management, information security, ITIL and IT service management, project governance, compliance and so much more. Subscribe for your free copy at: *www.itgovernance.co.uk/newsletter.aspx*.

BIBLIOGRAPHY

i Greta A. Marlatt. U.S. Naval Postgraduate School. "Information Warfare and Information Operations (IW/IO): A Bibliography".[2008]. [Online]. Available: http://edocs.nps.edu/npspubs/scholarly/biblio/Jan08-IWall_biblio.pdf

ii DOD Dictionary of Military Terms. "Definition of Cyber Warfare". [2011]. [Online]. Available: *http://www.dtic.mil/doctrine/dod_dictionary/*

iii Alford, Lionel D., Jr. *"Cyber Attack: Protecting Military Systems."* Acquisition Review Quarterly, Spring 2000, v. 7, no. 2, p. 105.

iv Ibid.

v Ibid.

vi Borden, Andrew. Chronicles Online Journal. *"What is Information Warfare?"*. [1999]. [Online].Available: *http://www.airpower.maxwell.af.mil/airchronicles/cc/borden.html*

vii Military Operations Research Society [MORS]. [2011]. [Online]. Available: *http://www.mors.org/meetings/oa_nco/oa_definition.htm*

viii Alford, Lionel D., Jr. *"Cyber Attack: Protecting Military Systems."* Acquisition Review Quarterly, Spring 2000, v. 7, no. 2, p. 105.

ix Ibid.

x See both *http://www.uscert.gov/control_systems/csthreats.html* and *http://professionalhackers.webs.com/whatishacking.htm*

xi David S. Alberts and David S. Papp. Information Age Anthology: Volume II, Page 78. DoD C4ISR Cooperative Research Program (CCRP), August 2000.

xii Office of the National Counterintelligence Executive. "Foreign Spies Stealing US Economic Secrets in Cyberspace". October 2011.

xiii John Leyden. "NATO members warned over Anonymous threat". [2011]. [Online]. Available: *http://www.theregister.co.uk/2011/06/02/nato_warned_over_anonymous/*

xiv Andy Greenberg. "LulzSec says goodbye, dumping NAT, AT&T, Gmer data". [2011]. [Online]. Available: *http://www.forbes.com/sites/andygreenberg/2011/06/25/lulzsec-says-goodbye-dumping-nato-att-gamer-data/*

xv Agence France-Presse. "Norway army says faced cyber attack after Libya bombing". [2011]. [Online]. Available: *http://www.abs-cbnnews.com/global-filipino/world/05/19/11/norway-army-says-faced-cyber-attack-after-libya-bombing*

xvi Angela Moscaritolo, Report: Cyber attacks against the U.S. "rising sharply".[2011]. [Online]. Available: *http://www.scmagazineus.com/report-cyberattacks-against-the-us-rising-sharply/article/158236/*

xvii Ibid.

xviii Ibid.

xix John D. Banusiewciz, Deputy Secretary Lynn Details Anti-Cyber Threat Strategy.[2011]. [Online]. Available: *http://www.defense.gov/news/newsarticle.aspx?id=64351*

xx Angela Moscaritolo, Report: Cyberattacks against the U.S. "rising sharply", accessed 16 DEC 2011 via the World Wide Web at *http://www.scmagazineus.com/report-cyberattacks-against-the-us-rising-sharply/article/158236/*

xxi John J. Kruzel, Cybersecurity Seizes More Attention, Budget Dollars. [2011]. [Online]. Available: *http://www.defense.gov/news/newsarticle.aspx?id=57871*

xxii INFO SECURITY Website, No Byline, Hackers sell access to military and government websites. [2011]. [Online]. Available: *http://www.infosecurity-magazine.com/view/15365/hackers-sell-access-to-military-and-government-websites/*

xxiii INFO SECURITY Website, No Byline, NATO begins implementation of cyber shield plan accessed. [2011]. [Online]. Available: *http://www.infosecurity-us.com/view/15410/nato-begins-implementation-of-cyber-shield-plan/*

xxiv Nathan Thornburgh, "Inside the Chinese Hack Attack". [2005}. [Online]. Available: *http://www.time.com/time/nation/article/0,8599,1098371,00.html*

xxv Associated Press. "Computer Hackers Attack State Dept." [2006]. [Online]. Available: *http://www.nytimes.com/2006/07/12/washington/12hacker.html*

xxvi Siobahn Gorman, August Cole and Yochi Dreazen. "Computer Spies Breach Fighter-Jet Project". [2009]. [Online]. Available: *http://online.wsj.com/article/SB124027491029837401.html*

xxvii BBC News. "China rejects claims of cyber attacks on Google". [2010]. [Online]. Available: *http://news.bbc.co.uk/2/hi/8478005.stm*

xxviii Agence France-Presse. Defense minister denies China behind cyber attacks. [2011]. [Online]. Available: *http://newsinfo.inquirer.net/12277/defense-minister-denies-china-behind-cyber-attacks*

xxix Jennifer LeClaire. "China Denies Launching Shady Rat Cyberattacks". [2011]. [Online]. Available: *http://www.newsfactor.com/story.xhtml?story_id=79668&full_skip=1*

xxx Sui-Lee Wee, Ken illia and Yoko Niskikawa. "China denies it si behind hacking of U.S. satellites". [2011]. [Online]. Available:

http://www.reuters.com/article/2011/10/31/us-china-us-hacking-idUSTRE79U1YI20111031

xxxi The JAMESTOWN FOUNDATION Website, No Byline, Mission Statement & Origins [2010]. [Online]. Available: *http://www.jamestown.org/aboutus/*

xxxii Phil Muncaster, Night Dragon Chinese hackers go after energy firms. [2011]. [Online]. Available: *http://krypt3ia.wordpress.com/2011/02/28/operation-night-dragon-nothing-new-but-it-bears-some-repeating/*

xxxiii McAfee Labs Website, Night Dragon Overview. [2011]. [Online]. Available: *http://www.mcafee.com/es/about/night-dragon.aspx*

xxxiv Kelly Jackson Higgins, Spear-Phishing Attacks Out Of China Targeted Source Code, Intellectual Property. [2011]. [Online]. Available: *http://www.darkreading.com/database-security/167901020/security/attacks-breaches/222300840/index.html*

xxxv PCMAG.COM Website, Definition of: zero-day exploit. [2011]. [Online]. Available: *http://www.pcmag.com/encyclopedia_term/0,2542,t=zero-day+exploit&i=55204,00.asp*

xxxvi Kelly Jackson Higgins, Spear-Phishing Attacks Out Of China Targeted Source Code, Intellectual Property. [2010]. [Online]. Available: *http://www.darkreading.com/database-security/167901020/security/attacks-breaches/222300840/index.html*

xxxvii Kim Zetter, Google Hack Attack Was Ultra Sophisticated, New Details Show
accessed on 16 JAN 2010 via the World Wide Web at
http://www.wired.com/threatlevel/2010/01/operation-aurora/

xxxviii Chris Buckley, China military paper urges steps against U.S. cyber war threat (Reuters)
accessed on 17 JUN 2011 via the World Wide Web at *http://wallstreetrun.com/china-military-paper-urges-steps-against-u-s-cyber-war-threat-reuters.htm*

xxxix Ibid.

xl Jeremy Reimer, Report: Chinese conduct "aggressive and large-scale" espionage against US
accessed on 7 JUL 2011 via the World Wide Web at
http://arstechnica.com/security/news/2007/11/report-chinese-conduct-aggressive-and-large-scale-espionage-against-us.ars

xli Ibid.

xlii Brian Grow and Mark Hosenball, Special report: In cyberspy vs. cyberspy, China has the edge
accessed on 14 APR 2011 via the World Wide Web at
http://www.reuters.com/article/2011/04/14/us-china-usa-cyberespionage-idUSTRE73D24220110414

xliii Ibid.

xliv Lucas Constantin, MI5 Accuses China of Cyber-Espionage accessed on 7 JUL 2011 via the World Wide Web at http://news.softpedia.com/news/MI5-Accuses-China-of-Cyber-Espionage-133681.shtml

xlv Rhys Blakely, Jonathan Richards, James Rossiter and Richard Beeston, MI5 alert on China's cyberspace spy threat accessed on 7 JUL 2011 via the World Wide Web at http://business.timesonline.co.uk/tol/business/industry_sectors/technology/article2980250.ec e

xlvi Ibid.

xlvii Don Durfee, China says no cyber warfare with U.S. accessed on 22 JUN 2011 via the World Wide Web at *http://www.reuters.com/article/2011/06/22/us-china-usa-cyberwar-idUKTRE75L1VJ20110622*

xlviii JOHN MARKOFF and DAVID BARBOZA, Academic Paper in China Sets Off Alarms in U.S.
accessed on 15 JAN 2011 via the World Wide Web at
http://www.nytimes.com/2010/03/21/world/asia/21grid.html

xlix AKAMAI Website. No Byline, accessed on 25 JAN 2011 via the World Wide Web at
http://www.akamai.com/html/technology/dataviz1.html

l FOX NEWS Website, NewsCore, No ByLine, accessed on 31 May 2011 via the World Wide Web at *http://www.foxnews.com/scitech/2011/05/26/china-confirms-existence-blue-army-elite-cyber-warfare-outfit/*

li China, The World Factbook, CIA Website, accessed 15 AUG 2011 via the World Wide Web at *https://www.cia.gov/library/publications/the-world-factbook/geos/ch.html*

lii SIOBHAN GORMAN And JULIAN E. BARNES, Cyber Combat: Act of War Pentagon Sets Stage for U.S. to Respond to Computer Sabotage With Military Force, accessed on 14 JUL 2011 via the World Wide Web at
http://online.wsj.com/article/SB10001424052702304563104576355623135782718.html

liii Report of the Defense Science Board Task Force on Information Warfare-Defense (IW-D), November 1996, Office of the Under Secretary of Defense for Acquisition & Technology accessed 14 JUL 2011 via the World Wide Web at *http://cryptome.org/iwd.htm*

liv Marlyn Williams, China pledges to step up administration of Internet The government is expanding control of the Internet to keep pace with new services accessed on 8 MAR 2011 via the World Wide Web at *http://www.networkworld.com/news/2011/030711-china-pledges-to-step-up.html?page=1*

lv Wayne M. Morrison, Marc Labonte, China's Holdings of U.S. Securities: Implications for the U.S. Economy Congressional Research Service accessed on 21 JUN 2011 via the World Wide Web at *http://www.fas.org/sgp/crs/row/RL34314.pdf*

lvi Department of the Treasury/Federal Reserve Board, MAJOR FOREIGN HOLDERS OF TREASURY SECURITIES (in billions of dollars) HOLDINGS 1/ AT END OF PERIOD accessed on 21 JUN 2011 via the World Wide Web at
http://www.treasury.gov/resource-center/data-chart-center/tic/Documents/mfh.txt

lvii Willy Lam, 'Crown prince' Xi consolidates his position with PLA generals and fellow 'princelings'
 accessed on 25 JAN 2011 via the World Wide Web at
http://www.freepressers.com/2011/01/crown-prince-xi-consolidates-his-position-with-pla-generals-and-fellow-princelings/
lviii Jonathon Fenby, Xi Jinping: The man who'll lead China into a new age, accessed 7 NOV 2010 via the World Wide Web at
http://www.guardian.co.uk/theobserver/2010/nov/07/xi-jinping-china-david-cameron
lix Tony Capaccio and Viola Gienger, China Suspends U.S. Military Ties on Taiwan Arms Sale (Update3), accessed 30 JAN 2010 via the World Wide Web at
http://www.businessweek.com/news/2010-01-30/u-s-seeks-to-sell-taiwan-weapons-worth-more-than-6-billion.html
lx Bruce Enhorn, Airbus May Beat Boeing in China's Aviation Market, accessed 2 FEB 2010 via the World Wide Web at
http://www.businessweek.com/globalbiz/content/feb2010/gb2010022_703055.htm
lxi Jon E. Doughterty, China: Debt Deals Unlikely to Salvage U.S., Europe, accessed 5 AUG 2011 via the World Wide Web at
http://www.newsroomamerica.com/story/157496.html
lxii Ibid.
lxiii *"Chinese Military Overview"*. SinoDefence.com. [2011]. [Online]. Available:
http://www.sinodefence.com/overview/default.asp
lxiv Dorothy E. Denning. *"Activism, Hacktivism, and Cyberterrorism: The Internet as a Tool for Influencing Foreign Policy"*. [2011]. [Online]. Available:
http://www.nautilus.org/info-policy/workshop/papers/denning.html
lxv CNN World News Website, No Byline accessed on 7 JUL 2001 via the World Wide Web at *http://articles.cnn.com/2001-05-03/world/china.hack_1_cyber-war-chinese-cyber-chinese-hackers?_s=PM:asiapcf*
lxvi Office of the Secretary of Defense, Military and Security Developments Involving the People's Republic of China
2010 accessed on 28 NOV 2010 via the World Wide Web at
http://www.defense.gov/pubs/pdfs/2010_CMPR_Final.pdf
lxvii Scribd Document Server, No Byline accessed on 30 MAR 2009 via the World Wide Web at *http://www.scribd.com/doc/13731776/Tracking-GhostNet-Investigating-a-Cyber-Espionage-Network*
lxviii Nathan Thornburgh, Inside the Chinese Hack Attack accessed on 26 AUG 2005 via the World Wide Web at
http://www.time.com/time/nation/article/0,8599,1098371,00.html
lxix Vivian Yeo, Asian web surfers top for time spent online, **Internet users in China aged below 25 spend on average 50 percent of their leisure time online, according to a survey** accessed on 14 DEC 2008 via the World Wide Web at

http://www.zdnet.co.uk/news/networking/2008/12/01/asian-web-surfers-top-for-time-spent-online-39568096/

lxx Eric Chabrow, Pentagon: China Cyber Weaponry Poses Threat accessed on 27 MAR 2007 via the World Wide Web at
http://www.govinfosecurity.com/articles.php?art_id=1322

lxxi Ibid.

lxxii Dancho Danchev, China's 'secure' OS Kylin – a threat to U.S offensive cyber capabilities?
accessed on 13 MAY 2009 via the World Wide Web at
http://www.zdnet.com/blog/security/chinas-secure-os-kylin-a-threat-to-us-offensive-cyber-capabilities/3385

lxxiii Bruce Schneier, Kylin: New Chinese Operating System accessed on 19 MAY 2009 via the World Wide Web at
http://www.schneier.com/blog/archives/2009/05/kylin_new_chine.html

lxxiv Map of Hai Nan Island, Hainan Island – Lingshui Area [Topographic Map] Original scale 1:250,000. Portion of AMS series L500, sheet NE 49-6, U.S. Army Map Service, 1961. (474K). 1UpTravel Website accessed on 16 DEC 2010 via the World Wide Web at
http://www.1uptravel.com/worldmaps/china30.html

lxxv Travel Map of Hainan Island, China, Maps Of China accessed 21 JUN 2011 via the World Wide Web at *http://www.maps-of-china.net/province/hainanm.htm*

lxxvi Ralph D. Sawyer. *"Sun Tzu – The Art of War"*. Oxford, England: Westview Press, 1994.

lxxvii Kevin McCauley. *"Noncommissioned Officers and the Creation of a Volunteer Force.* China Brief Volume: 11 Issue: 18, September 30, 2011

lxxviii Qiao Liang and Wang Xiangsui. *"Unrestricted Warfare"*. Beijing: PLA Literature and Arts Publishing House, 1999

lxxix Richard Lawless. *"Testimony before the House of Representatives Committee on Armed Services"*. [2007]. [Online]. Avaialble:
http://armedservices.house.gov/pdfs/FC061307/Lawless_Testimony061307.pdf.

lxxx Jason Fritz. *"HOW CHINA WILL USE CYBER WARFARE TO LEAPFROG IN MILITARY COMPETITIVENESS "*. Culture Mandala, Vol. 8, No. 1, October 2008, pp.28-80

lxxxi Brian M. Mazanec. The Journal of International Security Affairs. *" The Art of (Cyber War)"*. Spring 2009 – Number 16. [209]. [Online]. Available:
http://www.securityaffairs.org/issues/2009/16/mazanec.php#footnotes

lxxxii AFP via Breitbart. *"Hacker attacks in US linked to Chinese military: researchers"*. [2005]. [Online]. Available:
http://www.breitbart.com/article.php?id=051212224756.jwmkvntb&show_article=1

lxxxiii Nathan Thornburgh. Time Magazine. *"Inside the Chinese Hack Attack"*. [2005]. [Online]. Available:
http://www.time.com/time/nation/article/0,8599,1098371,00.html

lxxxiv Brian M. Mazanec. The Journal of International Security Affairs. *" The Art of (Cyber War)"*. Spring 2009 – Number 16. [209]. [Online]. Available: *http://www.securityaffairs.org/issues/2009/16/mazanec.php#footnotes*

lxxxv James Mulvenon. "PLA Computer Network Operations: Scenarios, Doctrine, Organizations, and Capability" in: Roy Kamphausen, David Lai, and Andrew Scobell (eds.), Beyond the Strait: PLA Missions Other Than Taiwan (Carlisle, PA: Strategic Studies Institute, U.S. Army War College, 2009), 257–259.

lxxxvi Brian M. Mazanec. The Journal of International Security Affairs. *" The Art of (Cyber War)"*. Spring 2009 – Number 16. [209]. [Online]. Available: *http://www.securityaffairs.org/issues/2009/16/mazanec.php#footnotes*

lxxxvii Ibid.

lxxxviii Ibid.

lxxxix Ibid.

xc Xiaoming Zhang. Colonel Sean D. McClung, USAF. *"The Art of Military Discovery Chinese Air and Space Power Implications for the USAF"*. [2010]. [Online]. Available: *http://www.au.af.mil/au/ssq/2010/spring/spring10.pdf*

xci James Mulvenon, Testimony before the U.S.-China Economic and Security Review Commission, May 20, 2008

xcii Jeffrey Lewis. Arms Control Wonk Blog. *"China and No First Use"*. [2011]. [Online]. Available: *http://lewis.armscontrolwonk.com/archive/3446/china-and-no-first-use-3*

xciii Wang Houqing and Zhang Xingye, eds., *Science of Campaigns* (Beijing: National Defense University Press, 2000

xciv Peng Pu. *"PLA unveils nation's first cyber center"*. [2010]. [Online]. Available: *http://www.globaltimes.cn/military/china/2010-07/554647.html*

xcv "The PRC's Cyber Command". [2010]. [Online]. Available at: *http://www.thechinatimes.com/online/2010/07/397.html*

xcvi Ibid.

xcvii Peng Pu. *PLA unveils nation's first cyber center*. [2010]. [Online]. Available at: *http://www.globaltimes.cn/military/china/2010-07/554647.html*

xcviii Larry Wortzel. *China's Cyber Offensive*. [2010]. [Online]. Available at: *http://online.wsj.com/article/SB10001424052748703399204574508413849779406.html*

xcix PLA Generals Greet New Cyber base. [2010]. [Online]. Available at: *http://www.chinamil.com.cn/site1/jfjbmap/2010-07/20/jfjbmap.htm*

c China Vitae. Zhang Qinsheng □□□. [2011]. [Online]. Available at: *http://www.chinavitae.com/biography/Zhang_Qinsheng|3971*

ci "President Hu Jintao Greets CPC Personalities". [2010]. [Online]. Available at: *http://news.xinhuanet.com/english2010/china/2011-07/02/c_13962339.htm*

cii "Establishment of US cyber command may start online arms race (3). [2010]. [Online] Available at: *http://english.peopledaily.com.cn/90001/90780/91343/6998833.html*

309

ciii Russell Hsiao, *"China's Cyber Command?*.[2010]. [Online]. Available: *http://www.jamestown.org/programs/chinabrief/single/?tx_ttnews%5btt_new s%5d=36658&tx_ttnews%5bbackPid%5d=414&no_cache=1*
civ Ibid.
cv Qiao Liang, PRC Scholar Discusses China-West Soft Power 'War', May 2008 Beijing Xiandai Guoji Guanxi in Chinese -- monthly journal of the State Council's Chinese Institute of Contemporary International Relations, publishing articles on international relations with an emphasis on the Asia Pacific Region .
cvi Qiao Liang and Wang Xiang sui, *Unrestricted Warfare*, 1995, pp. 228
cvii Qiao Liang and Wang Xiangsui. *"Unrestricted Warfare"*. Beijing: PLA Literature and Arts Publishing House, February 1999
cviii Ibid.
cix Ibid.
cx Ibid.
cxi Ibid.
cxii Ibid.
cxiii Ibid.
cxiv Ibid.
cxv Ibid.
cxvi Ibid.
cxvii Ibid.
cxviii Ibid.
cxix Ibid.
cxx Ibid.
cxxi Ibid.
cxxii *"Chinese Information Operations Capabilities"*. [2003]. [Online]. Available: *http://www.iwar.org.uk/iwar/resources/news/china-io-2003.htm*
cxxiii Theresa Payton. *"Cyber Warfare and the Conflict in Iraq"*. [2010]. [Online]. Avaialble: *https://www.infosecisland.com/blogview/6750-Cyber-Warfare-and-the-Conflict-in-Iraq.html*
cxxiv Chang MengXiong. *"The Revolution in Military Affairs Weapons of the 21st Century"*. [2011]. [Online]. Available: *http://www.au.af.mil/au/awc/awcgate/ndu/chinview/chinapt4.html*
cxxv U.S. Army. Field Manual FM-3 Military Operations. *"Principles of War"*.
cxxvi Ibid.
cxxvii Ibid.
cxxviii Ibid.
cxxix Ibid.
cxxx Ibid.
cxxxi Ibid.
cxxxii Ibid.
cxxxiii Ibid.
cxxxiv Ralph D. Sawyer. *"Sun Tzu Art of War"*. Westview Press: Oxford, England, 1994

cxxxv Chinese-Wiki.com. *"Sun Tzu Art of War"*. [2011]. [Online]. Available: *http://www.chinese-wiki.com/Sun_Tzu_Art_of_War_Chapter_2*

cxxxvi Ibid. *http://www.chinese-wiki.com/Sun_Tzu_Art_of_War_Chapter_3*

cxxxvii Ibid. *http://www.chinese-wiki.com/Sun_Tzu_Art_of_War_Chapter_4*

cxxxviii Ibid. *http://www.chinese-wiki.com/Sun_Tzu_Art_of_War_Chapter_5*

cxxxix Ibid. *http://www.chinese-wiki.com/Sun_Tzu_Art_of_War_Chapter_6*

cxl Ibid. *http://www.chinese-wiki.com/Sun_Tzu_Art_of_War_Chapter_7*

cxli Ibid. *http://www.chinese-wiki.com/Sun_Tzu_Art_of_War_Chapter_8*

cxlii Ibid. *http://www.chinese-wiki.com/Sun_Tzu_Art_of_War_Chapter_9*

cxliii Ibid. *http://www.chinese-wiki.com/Types_of_Terrain-Sun_Tzu*

cxliv Ibid. *http://www.chinese-wiki.com/What_are_the_Nine_Battlegrounds-Sun_Tzu*

cxlv Ibid. *http://www.chinese-wiki.com/Ways_of_Attacking_With_Fire-Sun_Tzu*

cxlvi *"The Thirty-Six Strategies of Ancient China"*. [2011]. [Online]. Available: *http://www.chinastrategies.com/List.htm#Strategy%201*

cxlvii Harod Von Senger. *"The Book of Stratagems"*. Penguin Group, New York, NY, 1991. Pp.13.

cxlviii *"The Thirty-Six Strategies of Ancient China"*. [2011]. [Online]. Available: *http://www.chinastrategies.com/List.htm#Strategy%201*

cxlix Harod Von Senger. *"The Book of Stratagems"*. Penguin Group, New York, NY, 1991. Pp.33.

cl *"The Thirty-Six Strategies of Ancient China"*. [2011]. [Online]. Available: *http://www.chinastrategies.com/List.htm#Strategy%201*

cli Harod Von Senger. *"The Book of Stratagems"*. Penguin Group, New York, NY, 1991. Pp.41.

clii "Host Multiple Domains: Setting Up Virtual Hosts with Webmin." [2011]. [Online]. Avaialble: *http://rimuhosting.com/howto/virtualhosting.jsp*

cliii *"The Thirty-Six Strategies of Ancient China"*. [2011]. [Online]. Available: *http://www.chinastrategies.com/List.htm#Strategy%201*

cliv Harod Von Senger. *"The Book of Stratagems"*. Penguin Group, New York, NY, 1991. Pp.59.

clv Harod Von Senger. *"The Book of Stratagems"*. Penguin Group, New York, NY, 1991. Pp.67.

clvi *"The Thirty-Six Strategies of Ancient China"*. [2011]. [Online]. Available: *http://www.chinastrategies.com/List.htm#Strategy%201*

clvii Harod Von Senger. "The Book of Stratagems". Penguin Group, New York, NY, 1991. Pp.75.

clviii *"The Thirty-Six Strategies of Ancient China"*. [2011]. [Online]. Available: *http://www.chinastrategies.com/List.htm#Strategy%201*

clix Harod Von Senger. *"The Book of Stratagems"*. Penguin Group, New York, NY, 1991. Pp.75.

clx Ed Flangan. NBC News. *"Chinese cyber-hacking caught on camera?* [2011]. [Online].
Available: *http://behindthewall.msnbc.msn.com/_news/2011/08/25/7470817-chinese-cyber-hacking-caught-on-camera*

clxi *"Thirty-six Strategies".* [2011].[Online]. Available:
http://banglacricket.com/alochona/showthread.php?t=30598

clxii *"The Thirty-Six Strategies of Ancient China".* [2011]. [Online]. Available:
http://www.chinastrategies.com/List.htm#Strategy%201

clxiii *"The Thirty-Six Strategies of Ancient China".* [2011]. [Online]. Available:
http://www.chinastrategies.com/List.htm#Strategy%201

clxiv Harod Von Senger. *"The Book of Stratagems".* Penguin Group, New York, NY, 1991.
Pp.135.

clxv Agence France-Presse. *"Official Military Build-Up No Threat: Official".* [2011].
[Online]. Available: *http://www.defensenews.com/story.php?i=6688765*

clxvi *"The Thirty-Six Strategies of Ancient China".* [2011]. [Online]. Available:
http://www.chinastrategies.com/List.htm#Strategy%201

clxvii "三 十 六 計 36 Ji– Thirty-Six Strategies". [2011]. [Online].
Available: *http://wengu.tartarie.com/wg/wengu.php?l=36ji&lang=en&no=12*

clxviii Harod Von Senger. *"The Book of Stratagems".* Penguin Group, New York, NY,
1991. Pp.171.

clxix Robert McMillan. IDG News. *"Report Says China Ready for Cyber-war, Espionage.*
[2009]. [Online]. Avaialble:
http://www.pcworld.com/article/174210/report_says_china_ready_for_cyber_war_espionage.html

clxx *"The Thirty-Six Strategies of Ancient China".* [2011]. [Online]. Available:
http://www.chinastrategies.com/list%202.htm

clxxi "三 十 六 計 36 Ji– Thirty-Six Strategies". [2011]. [Online].
Available: *http://wengu.tartarie.com/wg/wengu.php?l=36ji&lang=en&no=14*

clxxii Harod Von Senger. *"The Book of Stratagems".* Penguin Group, New York, NY, 1991.
Pp.215.

clxxiii Ibid.

clxxiv "三 十 六 計 *36 Ji– Thirty-Six Strategies".* [2011]. [Online].
Available:
http://wengu.tartarie.com/wg/wengu.php?l=36ji&lang=en&no=15&m=NOzh

clxxv Harod Von Senger. *"The Book of Stratagems".* Penguin Group, New York, NY, 1991.
Pp.233.

clxxvi "三 十 六 計 36 Ji– Thirty-Six Strategies". [2011]. [Online].
Available: *http://wengu.tartarie.com/wg/wengu.php?l=36ji&lang=en&no=16*

clxxvii Ibid. Number 17.

clxxviii "三 十 六 計 36 Ji– Thirty-Six Strategies". [2011]. [Online].
Available: *http://wengu.tartarie.com/wg/wengu.php?l=36ji&lang=en&no=18*

clxxix *"The Thirty-Six Strategies of Ancient China".* [2011]. [Online]. Available: *http://www.chinastrategies.com/list%202.htm*

clxxx U.S. Department of Defense Press Release. *"DOD Announces First U.S. Cyber Command and First U.S. CYBERCOM Commander"*. [2010]. [Online]. Available: *http://www.defense.gov/releases/release.aspx?releaseid=13551*

clxxxi David E. Sanger and Elisabeth Bumiller. *"Pentagon to Consider Cyberattacks Acts of War."* [2011]. [Online]. Available: *http://www.nytimes.com/2011/06/01/us/politics/01cyber.html?_r=1*

clxxxii "三 十 六 計 36 Ji– Thirty-Six Strategies". [2011]. [Online]. Available: *http://wengu.tartarie.com/wg/wengu.php?l=36ji&lang=en&no=20*

clxxxiii *"The Thirty-Six Strategies of Ancient China"*. [2011]. [Online]. Available: *http://www.chinastrategies.com/table.htm*

clxxxiv *"Chinese Cyber Attacks on US Called Staggering."* Whiteout Press. [2011]. [Online]. Available: *http://www.whiteoutpress.com/articles/q42011/chinese-cyber-attacks-on-us-called-staggering485/*

clxxxv "三 十 六 計 36 Ji– Thirty-Six Strategies". [2011]. [Online]. Available: *http://wengu.tartarie.com/wg/wengu.php?l=36ji&lang=en&no=22*

clxxxvi Siobahn Gorman. "Electricity Grid in U.S. Penetrated by Spies. [2009]. [Online]. Available: *http://online.wsj.com/article/SB123914805204099085.html*

clxxxvii Ibid.

clxxxviii *"The Thirty-Six Strategies of Ancient China"*. [2011]. [Online]. Available: *http://www.chinastrategies.com/table.htm*

clxxxix People's Daily editorial. *"Why China established 'Online Blue Army' "*. [2011]. [online}. Available: *http://www.china.org.cn/opinion/2011-06/29/content_22881772.htm*

cxc "三 十 六 計 36 Ji– Thirty-Six Strategies". [2011]. [Online]. Available: *http://wengu.tartarie.com/wg/wengu.php?l=36ji&lang=en&no=24*

cxci Robert Collier. *"China moves fast to claim oil sands."* [2005]. [Online]. Available: *http://www.sfgate.com/cgi-bin/article.cgi?f=/c/a/2005/05/22/CHINA.TMP*

cxcii *"The Thirty-Six Strategies of Ancient China"*. [2011]. [Online]. Available: *http://www.chinastrategies.com/table.htm*

cxciii AGENCE FRANCE-PRESSE.*"China: Japan's Defense Comments 'Irresponsible '"*. [2011]. [Online]. Available: *http://www.defensenews.com/story.php?i=7304002*

cxciv Chinmoy Kanjilal. "Mitsubishi Heavy- Japan's Top Defense Contractor, Gets Hacked". [2011]. [Onlline]. Available: *http://techie-buzz.com/online-security/mitsubishi-heavy-japan-defense-contractor-hacked.html*

cxcv *Chinese War Strategies.* [2008]. [Online]. Available: *http://chinesewarstrategies.blogspot.com/2008/11/36-strategies-of-ancient-china-overview.html*

313

cxcvi C. S. Kuppuswamy ."MYANMAR: *Sandwiched between China & India and gaining from both".* [2008]. [Online]. Available:
http://www.southasiaanalysis.org/%5Cpapers26%5Cpaper2574.html

cxcvii "三 十 六 計 36 Ji– Thirty-Six Strategies". [2011]. [Online].
Available: *http://wengu.tartarie.com/wg/wengu.php?l=36ji&lang=en&no=27*

cxcviii Holly Williams. SkyNews HD. *"China: We Didn't Hack into Foreign PCs".* [2009].
[Online]. Available: *http://news.sky.com/home/world-news/article/15251712*

cxcix *"The Thirty-Six Strategies of Ancient China".* [2011]. [Online]. Available:
http://www.chinastrategies.com/table.htm

cc"三 十 六 計 36 Ji– Thirty-Six Strategies". [2011]. [Online].
Available: *http://wengu.tartarie.com/wg/wengu.php?l=36ji&lang=en&no=29*

cci ZHOU Yonglin, et al. National Computer Emergency Response Team/Coordination
Center, Beijing, China and Institute of Computer Science and Technology, Peking
University, Beijing, China. "Matrix, a Distributed Honeynet and its Applications". [2008].
[online]. Available:
http://netsec.ccert.edu.cn/zhugejw/files/2011/01/2008.FIRST_.Matrix-a-
Distributed-Honeynet-and-its-Applications.pdf

ccii Visoottiviseth, V. Jaralrungroj, U. , et al., Faculty of Information & Community
Technology, Mahidol University, Nakhon Pathom, Thailand. *"Distributed Honeypot log
management and visualization of attacker geographical distribution".* [2011]. [Online].
Available:
http://ieeexplore.ieee.org/Xplore/login.jsp?url=http%3A%2F%2Fieeexplore.
ieee.org%2Fiel5%2F5876042%2F5930073%2F05930083.pdf%3Farnumber
%3D5930083&authDecision=-203

cciii *"The Thirty-Six Strategies of Ancient China".* [2011]. [Online]. Available:
http://www.chinastrategies.com/table.htm

cciv Rocky Barker. Idaho Department of Commerce. *"Chinese Company Eyes Idaho".*
[2010]. [Online} Available: *http://commerce.idaho.gov/news/2010/12/chinese-*
company-eyes-idaho.aspx

ccv Sara Haimowitz. *"China Wants To Construct A 50 Square Mile Self-Sustaining City
South Of Boise, Idaho".* [2011]. [Online].
http://www.tradereform.org/2011/06/china-wants-to-construct-a-50-square-
mile-self-sustaining-city-south-of-boise-idaho/

ccvi *"三 十 六 計 36 Ji– Thirty-Six Strategies".* [2011]. [Online].
Available: *http://wengu.tartarie.com/wg/wengu.php?l=36ji&lang=en&no=31*

ccvii *"The Thirty-Six Strategies of Ancient China".* [2011]. [Online]. Available:
http://www.chinastrategies.com/table.htm

ccviii"三 十 六 計 36 Ji– Thirty-Six Strategies". [2011]. [Online].
Available: *http://wengu.tartarie.com/wg/wengu.php?l=36ji&lang=en&no=33*

ccix *"The Thirty-Six Strategies of Ancient China".* [2011]. [Online]. Available:
http://www.chinastrategies.com/table.htm

ccx *Chinese War Strategies*. [2008]. [Online]. Available: *http://chinesewarstrategies.blogspot.com/2008/11/36-strategies-of-ancient-china-overview.html*

ccxi "三 十 六 計 36 Ji– Thirty-Six Strategies". [2011]. [Online]. Available: *http://wengu.tartarie.com/wg/wengu.php?l=36ji&lang=en&no=36*

ccxii Arindam, et al. "*Trojans Think in Mandarin*". [2010]. [Online]. Available: *http://www.outlookindia.com/article.aspx?265073*

ccxiii Senior Colonel Wang Baocun and Li Fei. "*Information Warfare*". [2011]. [Online]. Available: *http://www.au.af.mil/au/awc/awcgate/ndu/chinview/chinapt4.html#8*

ccxiv Wei Jincheng, *Information War: A new form of People's War*, Military Forum column, Liberation Army Daily, June 25, 1996. [2010]. [Online]. Available: *http://www.fas.org/irp/world/china/docs/iw_wei.htm*

ccxv Dennis J. Blasko. "*Chinese Strategic Thinking: People's War in the 21ˢᵗ Century*". The Jamestown Foundation. China Brief Volume: 10 Issue 6.

ccxvi Ibid.

ccxvii James Mulvenon and David M. Finkelstein. "*China's Revolution in Doctrinal Affairs. Emerging Trends in the Operational Art of the Chinese People's Liberation Army*".

ccxviii"*China's National Defense in 2004. Chapter III, Revolution in Military Affairs with Chinese Characteristics*". [2004]. [Online]. Available: *http://english.people.com.cn/whitepaper/defense2004/defense2004.html*

ccxix "*Chapter III, Revolution in Military Affairs with Chinese Characteristics*". China's National Defense in 2004. [2004]. [Online]. Available: *http://english.people.com.cn/whitepaper/defense2004/defense2004.html*

ccxx Magnus Hjortdal. Journal of Strategic Security. "*China's Use of Cyber Warfare: Espionage Meets Strategic Deterrence*". Volume IV Issue 2 2011, pp 1-24.

ccxxi Information Office of the State Council of the People's Republic of China. "*China's National Defense in 2010*". March 31, 2011

ccxxii Ibid.

ccxxiii Timothy L. Thomas. Foreign Military Studies Office. "Like Adding Wings to the Tiger: Chinese Information War Theory and Practice". [2011]. [Online]. Available: *http://www.iwar.org.uk/iwar/resources/china/iw/chinaiw.htm*

ccxxiv Ibid.

ccxxv Wang Pufeng, "*Challenge of Information Warfare*" in Michael Pillsbury (ed.), Chinese Views of Future Warfare, National Defense University Press, Washington D.C., [1997]. [Online]. Available: *http://www.au.af.mil/au/awc/awcgate/ndu/chinview/chinacont.html*

ccxxvi Magnus Hjortdal. Journal of Strategic Security. "*China's Use of Cyber Warfare: Espionage Meets Strategic Deterrence*". Volume IV Issue 2 2011, pp 1-24

ccxxvii John Oakley. University of Minnesota. "*Cyber Warfare: China's Strategy to Dominate in Cyber Space*". [1993]. [Online]. Available: *http://dodreports.com/pdf/ada547718.pdf*

ccxxviii Timothy L. Thomas. Foreign Military Studies Office. "*Behind the Great Firewall of China: A Look at RMA/IW Theory From 1996-1998*". [1998]. [Online]. Available: *http://fmso.leavenworth.army.mil/documents/chinarma.htm*

ccxxix Magnus Hjortdal. Journal of Strategic Security. "*China's Use of Cyber Warfare: Espionage Meets Strategic Deterrence*". Volume IV Issue 2 2011, pp 1-24

ccxxx Ibid.

ccxxxi Wei Jincheng, "*Information War: A New Form of People's War*". Michael Pillsbury (ed.), "Chinese Views of Future Warfare, Part Four". [2011]. [Online]. Available: *http://www.au.af.mil/au/awc/awcgate/ndu/chinview/chinacont.html*

ccxxxii Timothy L. Thomas. "*Like Adding Wings to Tiger: Chinese Information War Theory and Practice*". [2011]. [Online]. Available: *http://www.iwar.org.uk/iwar/resources/china/iw/chinaiw.htm*

ccxxxiii Cryptome. Org. [2011]. [Online]. Available: *http://cryptome.org/cuw.htm*

ccxxxiv Magnus Hjortdal. Journal of Strategic Security. "*China's Use of Cyber Warfare: Espionage Meets Strategic Deterrence*". Volume IV Issue 2 2011, pp 1-24

ccxxxv Dr. Sheo Nandan Pandey. "*Hacktivism with Chinese Characteristics and the Google Inc. Cyber Attack Episode*". [2010]. [Online]. Available: *http://www.southasiaanalysis.org/%5Cpapers37%5Cpaper3683.html*

ccxxxvi Bill Hickey. "NRT-0129 Covert Chinese Cyber Warfare Capability:" [2007]. [Online]. Available: *http://www.usncva.org/nrt/nrt-0129.shtml*

ccxxxvii Dr. Sheo Nandan Pandey. "*Hacktivism with Chinese Characteristics and the Google Inc. Cyber Attack Episode*". [2010]. [Online]. Available: *http://www.southasiaanalysis.org/%5Cpapers37%5Cpaper3683.html*

ccxxxviii Vinod Anand, "*Chinese Concepts and Capabilities of Information Warfare*", [2006]. [Online]. Available: *http://www.idsa.in/strategicanalysis/ChineseConceptsandCapabilitiesofInformationWarfare_vanand_1006*

ccxxxix PLA Daily. "Over 500 Information Professionals Enrolled into Militia Organization". [2004]. [Online]. Available: *http://english.chinamil.com.cn/site2/militarydatabase/2004-09/17/content_19439.htm*

ccxl Timothy L. Thomas. "*Like Adding Wings to Tiger: Chinese Information War Theory and Practice*". [2011]. [Online]. Available: *http://www.iwar.org.uk/iwar/resources/china/iw/chinaiw.htm*

ccxli Vinod Anand, "*Chinese Concepts and Capabilities of Information Warfare*", [2006]. [Online]. Available: *http://www.idsa.in/strategicanalysis/ChineseConceptsandCapabilitiesofInformationWarfare_vanand_1006*

ccxlii Magnus Hjortdal. Journal of Strategic Security. "*China's Use of Cyber Warfare: Espionage Meets Strategic Deterrence*". Volume IV Issue 2 2011, pp 1-24

ccxliii Qiao Liang and Wang Xiang Sui. "*Unrestricted Warfare*". PLA Literature and Arts Publishing House, Beijing, February 1999.

ccxliv M. Taylor Fravel. "The Evolution of China's Military Strategy". [2011]. [Online].
Available:
http://mit.academia.edu/MTaylorFravel/Papers/8478/The_Evolution_of_Chinas_Military_Strategy#

ccxlv Dai Qingmin, "Innovating and Developing Views on Information Operations," Beijing Zhongguo, August 20, 2000, article reviewed by Timothy L. Thomas in "China's Electronic Strategies," Military Review, May-June 2001, pp. 72-77.

ccxlvi Timothy L. Thomas. *"China's Comprehensive IW-Strategy Link"*. [2008]. [Online].
Available: *http://www.au.af.mil/info-ops/iosphere/08special/iosphere_special08_thomas2.pdf*

ccxlvii Richard A. Clarke and Robert K. Knake. *"Cyber War"*. New York, NY., Harper Collins, 2010.

ccxlviii Timothy L. Thomas. *"Like Adding Wings to Tiger: Chinese Information War Theory and Practice"*. [2011]. [Online]. Available:
http://www.iwar.org.uk/iwar/resources/china/iw/chinaiw.htm

ccxlix Major General Dai Qingmin. Dai Qingmin, *"Innovating and Developing Views on Information Operations,"* Beijing China, August 20, 2000. Translated by FBIS. In *Beijing Zhonguo Junshi Kexue* (20 Aug): 72-77.

ccl Ibid.

ccli *"Integrated Network Electronic Warfare"*. [2011]. [Online]. Avaialble:
http://itlaw.wikia.com/wiki/Integrated_Network_Electronic_Warfare

cclii Clay Wilson. CRS Report for Congress, Order Code RL32411. *"Network Centric Operations: Background and Oversight Issues for Congress"*. [2007]. [Online]. Available:
http://www.fas.org/sgp/crs/natsec/RL32411.pdf

ccliii Timothy L. Thomas. Joint Forces Quarterly, issue thirty-eight. *"Chinese and American Network Warfare"*.

ccliv Ibid, page 77

cclv Ibid.

cclvi Steve Dewees, Bryan Krekel, George Barkos and Christopher Barnett. *"Capability of the People's Republic of China to Conduct Cyber Warfare and Computer Network Exploitation"* [2009]. [Online]. Available:
http://www.uscc.gov/researchpapers/2009/NorthropGrumman_PRC_Cyber_Paper_FINAL_Approved%20Report_16Oct2009.pdf

cclvii Department of Defense. *"Military and Security Developments Involving the People's Republic of China* 2011". [2011]. [Online]. Available:
http://www.defense.gov/pubs/pdfs/2011_cmpr_final.pdf

cclviii Gordon Housworth. Intellectual Capital Group. *"Informationalization in Chinese military doctrine affects foreign commercial and military assets"*. [2007]. [Online].
Available:
http://spaces.icgpartners.com/index2.asp?NGuid=E2605D41B8DC46A58813E69E976EC8A1

cclix Steve Dewees, Bryan Krekel, George Barkos and Christopher Barnett. *"Capability of the People's Republic of China to Conduct Cyber Warfare and Computer Network Exploitation"* [2009]. [Online]. Available:

http://www.uscc.gov/researchpapers/2009/NorthropGrumman_PRC_Cyber_Paper_FINAL_Approved%20Report_16Oct2009.pdf

cclx Timothy Walton. *"Treble Spyglass, Treble Spear: China's "Three Warfares"*. Defense Concepts. December 2009 Volume 4, Edition 4, page 58.

cclxi Military Power of the People's Republic of China 2009. Annual Report to Congress. Office of the Secretary of Defense.

cclxii The Science of Military Strategy. EDITED BY PENG GUANGQIAN AND YAO YOUZHI. Beijing: Military Science Publishing House, 2005.

cclxiii Kathrin Hille. *'China hits out at US 'illegal' intrusion'*. [2009]. [Online]. Available: *http://www.ft.com/intl/cms/s/0/ed68fb76-0ddb-11de-8ea3-0000779fd2ac.html*

cclxiv Minitry of Foreign Affairs for the People's Republic of China. "China, Russia and Other Countries Submit the Document of International Code of Conduct for Information Security to the United Nations". [2011]. [Online]. Available: *http://www.fmprc.gov.cn/eng/zxxx/t858978.htm*

cclxv Sun Tzu. *"The Art of War"*.

cclxvi *"Chapter VI Weaknesses and Strengths To Avoid What is Strong and Strike at What is Weak"*. [2011]. [Online]. Available: *http://www.mod.gov.cn/affair/2011-07/31/content_4286873_12.htm*

cclxvii China Military and Armed Forces (People's Liberation Army, PLA). [2011]. [Online]. Available: *http://www.chinatoday.com/arm/*

cclxviii ANNUAL REPORT TO CONGRESS Military Power of the People's Republic of China 2008, 华人民共和国军事力量2008年度报告. [2008]. [Online]. Available: *http://www.xfjs.org/simple/?t26743.html*

cclxix Internet query [2011]. [Online]. Available: *http://www.quora.com/Is-the-US-in-a-cyberwar-with-China-and-we-dont-even-know-it/answer/Don-White-2/comment/524014*

cclxx Ibid.

cclxxi Qingmin Dai, "Innovating and Developing Views on Information Operations," Beijing *Zhongguo Junshi Kexue*, 20 August 2000, 72-77. Translated and downloaded from Foreign Broadcast Information Service (FBIS), 9 November 2000, *http://sun3.lib/uci.edu/~slca/microform/resources/f-g/f_049.htm*

cclxxii Thomas, Timothy L., *China's Electronic Strategies*. [2001]. [Online]. Available: *http://www.au.af.mil/au/awc/awcgate/milreview/thomas.htm*

cclxxiii Dai, *Innovating and Developing Views on Information Operations*.

cclxxiv Thomas, *China's Electronic Strategies*.

cclxxv Dai, *Innovating and Developing Views on Information Operations*.

cclxxvi Thomas, *China's Electronic Strategies*.

cclxxvii Wang Pufeng, "Meeting the Challenge of Information Warfare," *Zhongguo Junshi Kexue* (China Military Science), 20 February 1995, 8-18. Translated and reported in FBIS-CHI-95-129, 6 July 1995, 29 and 30.

cclxxviii Thomas, *China's Electronic Strategies*.

cclxxix Jacqueline E. Sharkey. *"When Pictures Drive Foreign Policy"*. [1993]. [Online].
Available: *http://www.ajr.org/article.asp?id=1579*

cclxxx Senior Colonels Qiao Liang and Wang Xiang Sui. *"Unrestricted Warfare"*. PLA
Literature and Arts Publishing House, Beijing, February 1999

cclxxxi House Select Committee. "The Cox Report -- PRC Acquisition of U.S. Technology".
[1999]. [Online]. Available:
http://archive.newsmax.com/articles/?a=1999/5/25/125459

cclxxxii United States Department of Defense. "*ANNUAL REPORT TO CONGRESS.*
Military and Security Developments Involving the People's Republic of China 2011". [2011].
[Online]. Available: *http://www.defense.gov/pubs/pdfs/2011_cmpr_final.pdf*

cclxxxiii Magnus Hjortdal. Journal of Strategic Security. "China's Use of Cyber Warfare:
Espionage Meets Strategic Deterrence*". Volume IV Issue 2 2011, pp 1-24*

cclxxxiv Richard M. Crowell.*"War in the Information Age:A Primer for Cyberspace*
Operations in 21st Century Warfare". [2011]. [Online]. Available:
www.carlisle.army.mil/dime/CyberSpace.cfm

cclxxxv Jim Bussert, 'PRC Improves Electronic Warfare Capability', Defense
Electronics, November 1987, pp.146-154.

cclxxxvi Ngok Lee, China's Defence Modernisation and Military Leadership,
(Australian National University Press, Sydney, 1989), pp.34-39.

cclxxxvii James Mulvenon, *'The PLA and Information Warfare'*, in James C.
Mulvenon and Richard H. Yang (eds.), The People's Liberation Army in the Information
Age, (The RAND Corporation, Santa Monica, California, 1999), p.177.

cclxxxviii Jim Bussert, 'PRC Improves Electronic Warfare Capability', Defense
Electronics, November 1987, pp.146-149; and Ngok Lee, China's Defence Modernisation
and Military Leadership, p.39.

cclxxxix James Mulvenon, 'The PLA and Information Warfare', p.178.

ccxc Bill Gertz, 'China Snooped on Allied Forces During Gulf War', The Washington Times,
10 April 1997, p.A10.

ccxci Bradley Martin, 'China for Real: Embassy Bombing "Part of Espionage War"', Asia
Times Online, 23 July 1999, at http://www.atimes.com/china/AG23Ad01.html.

ccxcii Damon Bristow, 'Information Warfare Grips China', Jane's Pointers, November 1998,
pp.8-9.

ccxciii *"Chinese Views of Future Warfare"*. (National Defense University Press,
Washington, D.C., revised edition, September 1998). See also James Mulvenon, *'The PLA*
and Information Warfare', in James C. Mulvenon and Richard H. Yang (eds.), The People's
Liberation Army in the Information Age, chapter 9.

ccxciv Aarti Anhal, 'China Erects "Great Firewall" in Effort to Regulate
Internet', Jane's Intelligence Review, May 2002, pp.52-53.

ccxcv NATO's Role in Kosovo, *Operation Allied Force*. [1999]. [Online]. Available:
http://www.nato.int/kosovo/all-frce.htm

ccxcvi Bradley Martin, 'China for Real: Embassy Bombing "Part of
Espionage War"', Asia Times Online, 23 July 1999, at
http://www.atimes.com/china/AG23Ad01.html ; 'The Chinese Embassy Bombing:
Truth Behind America's Raid on Belgrade', The Observer (London), 28 November 1999; and

Joel Bleifuss, 'A Tragic Mistake?', In These Times.Com, 12 December 1999, at *http://www.inthesetimes.com/issues/24/01/bleifuss2401.html*.
ccxcvii Desmond Ball, 'Signals Intelligence in China', Jane's Intelligence Review, (Vol. 7, No. 8), August 1995, pp.365-370; Jeffrey Richelson, Foreign Intelligence Organizations, (Ballinger, Cambridge, Massachusetts, 1988), p.291; Sid Balman, Jr., 'Key U.S. Listening Posts Jeopardized in China', Air Force Times, 19 June 1989, p.8; and Bill Gertz, 'Diplomatic Shield Protects Espionage Agents On Occasion', The Washington Times, 8 July 1988, p.7.
ccxcviii Manuel Cerejo, *"China, Cuba and Information Warfare, Signal Intelligence, Electronic Warfare and Cyber Warfare"*. [2011]. [Online]. Available: *http://www.futurodecuba.org/ChinaandInformationWarfare4.htm*
ccxcix Lieutenant General Abe. C. Lin. *"COMPARISON OF THE INFORMATION WARFARE CAPABILITIES OF THE ROC AND PRC"*. [2000]. [Online]. Available: *http://www.dsis.org.tw/pubs/seminars/2000-02-19/s_ciw00-0219-003e.pdf*
ccc Mark Stokes, China's Strategic Modernization: Implications for the United States, (US Army War College, Carlisle, Pennsylvania, 1999), p.33.
ccci Kissinger, Henry, *On China*. The Penguin Press, New York, NY, First Edition, 2011, page 211
cccii The approximate locations of several Chinese SIGINT sites are given in Jim Bussert, *China's C3I Efforts Show Progress*, in Fred D. Byers (ed.), C3I Handbook, (EW Communications, Inc., Palo Alto, California, First Edition, 1986), p.173
ccciii 'Tachiu Electronic Intercept Facility, China', Photographic Interpretation Report, (National Photographic Interpretation Centre, NPIC/R-130/68, Washington, D.C., January 1969)
ccciv Federation of American Scientists (FAS), 'Hainan Island', Intelligence Resource Program, 26 November 1997, at *http://www.fas.org/irp/world/china/facilities/hainan.htm*
cccv Robert Windrem, 'The Lingshui Intelligence Base', Mario's Cyberspace Station, at *http://mprofaca.cro.net/lingshui1.html*
cccvi Bill Gertz and Rowan Scarborough, 'Inside the Ring: China Eavesdropping', The Washington Times, 5 May 2000, p.A10.
cccvii 'Accommodation Dies, But Is Resurrected in China', Electronic Warfare/Defense Electronics, January 1979, p.19
cccviii Philip Taubman, 'U.S. and Peking Jointly Monitor Russian Missiles', New York Times, 18 June 1981, pp.1,4; and Murrey Marder, 'Monitoring Not So-Secret Secret', The Washington Post, 19 June 1981, p.10
cccix Robert Toth, *'U.S., China Jointly Track Firings of Soviet Missiles'*, Los Angeles Times, 18 June 1981, pp.1,9; David Bonavia, 'Radar Post Leak May Be Warning to Soviet Union', The Times (London), 19 June 1981, p.5; and Philip Taubman, 'U.S. and Peking Jointly Monitor Russian Missiles', New York Times, 18 June 1991, pp.1,14. See also Sid Balman, Jr., 'Key U.S. Listening Posts Jeopardized in China', Air Force Times, 19 June 1989, p.8; and George Lardner, Jr. and R. Jeffrey Smith, 'Inteligence Ties Endure Despite U.S.-China Strain', The Washington Post, 25 June 1989, p.1
cccx Duncan Campbell, 'They've Got It Taped', New Statesman & Society, (Vol.1, No.10), 12 August 1988, p.12

cccxi Marwyn S. Samuels, Contest for the South China Sea, (Methuen, New York, 1982), p.184; and Chi-Kin Lo, China's Policy Towards Territorial Disputes: The Case of the South China Sea Islands, (Routledge, London, 1989), p.119

cccxii David Lague and Nayan Chandra, 'China-United States: The Spying Game Heats Up', Far Eastern Economic Review, 3 May 2001, p.23

cccxiii Desmond Ball, Burma's Military Secrets: Signals Intelligence (SIGINT) from the Second World War to Civil War and Cyber Warfare, (White Lotus, Bangkok, 1998), pp.221-222

cccxiv 'China is Potential Threat Number One', The Indian Express, 4 May 1998. [Online] Available: *http://www.expressindia.com/fe/daily/19980504/12455554.html*

cccxv Desmond Ball, Burma's Military Secrets: Signals Intelligence (SIGINT) from the Second World War to Civil War and Cyber Warfare, pp.222-224; and Bertil Lintner, '. But Stay on Guard', Far Eastern Economic Review, 16 July 1998, p.21

cccxvi Robert Karniol, 'China Sets Up Border SIGINT Bases in Laos', Jane's Defence Weekly, 19 November 1994, p.5

cccxvii Benjamin F. Schemmer, The Raid, (Harper and Row, New York,1976), p.137

cccxviii Manuel Cerejo, *"China, Cuba and Information Warfare, Signal Intelligence, Electronic Warfare and Cyber Warfare"* [2011]/ [Online]. Available: *http://www.futurodecuba.org/ChinaandInformationWarfare4.htm*

cccxix Al Santoli (ed.), 'China, Russia Add New Biological-Weapons; China's New Electronic Intel Bases in Cuba Threaten U.S.', China Reform Monitor, No.217, 28 June 1999. [Online]. Available: *http://www.afpc.org/crm217.htm* ; Pablo Alfonso, 'China Installs Two Communication Bases in Cuba', El Nuevo Herald (Miami), 24 June 1999. [Online]. Available *http://www.schechi.de/crw/crw031.html* ; Nancy San Martin and Jane Bussey, 'Secret Arms Shipments from China to Cuba Reported', Miami Herald, 13 June 2001. [Onlne]. Available: *http://www.nocastro.com/archives/china_cuba.htm* ; Al Santoli (ed.), 'China Replaces Russia in Electronic Spy Operations in Cuba', China Reform Monitor, No. 449, 23 May 2002. [Online]. Available: *http://www.afpc.org/crm/crm449.htm*

cccxx 'China Can Eavesdrop on US Satellites', New Scientist, 19 December 1968, p.655

cccxxi Robert Windrem, 'The Lingshui Intelligence Base', Mario's Cyberspace Station. [2011]. [Online]. Available: *http://mprofaca.cro.net/lingshui1.htm*

cccxxii 'TV Network Furious Over Film Intercept', The Australian, 13 June 1989, p.7

cccxxiii Bill Gertz and Rowan Scarborough, 'Inside the Ring: China Eavesdropping', The Washington Times, 5 May 2000, p.A10

cccxxiv Pablo Alfonso, 'China Installs Two Communication Bases in Cuba', El Nuevo Herald (Miami), 24 June 1999. [Online]. Available: *http://www.schoechi.de/crw/crw031.html* Edward Timperlake and William C. Triplett, Red Dragon Rising: Communist China's Military Threat to America, (Regnery, Washington, D.C., 1999), p.128; and Al Santoli (ed.), 'China, Russia Add New Biological-Weapons; China's New Electronic Intel Bases in Cuba Threaten U.S.', China Reform Monitor, No. 217, 28 June 1999. [Online]. Available: *http://www.afpc.org/crm217.htm*

cccxxv Bruce Gilley, 'Pacific Outpost: China's Satellite Station in Kiribati has Military Purposes', Far Eastern Economic Review, 30 April 1998, pp.26-27; Michael Field, 'The

Mystery of Kiribati', The Dominion (Wellington), 27 August 1999, p.6; and Barbara Opall-Rome, 'PLA Pursues Acupuncture Warfare', Defense News, 1 March 1999, pp.4, 19

cccxxvi Jeffrey Richelson, Foreign Intelligence Organizations, p.292; Stephen Ladd, 'The Chinese Naval Sigint Threat', Naval Intelligence Quarterly, (Vol.7, No.4), 1986, pp.30-34; and Captain Richard Sharpe, RN (ed.), Jane's Fighting Ships, 2000-2001, p.143

cccxxvii Manuel Cerejo, *"China, Cuba and Information Warfare, Signal Intelligence, Electronic Warfare and Cyber Warfare"*. [2011]. [Online]. Available:
http://www.futurodecuba.org/ChinaandInformationWarfare4.htm

cccxxviii 'Chinese Military Aviation: Surveillance Aircraft'. [2011]. [Online]. Available:
http://www.stormpages.com/jetfight/y-8x_sh-5_a-50i.htm

cccxxix Manuel Cerejo, "China, Cuba and Information Warfare, Signal Intelligence, Electronic Warfare and Cyber Warfare". [2011]. [Online]. Available:
http://www.futurodecuba.org/ChinaandInformationWarfare4.htm

cccxxx Doug Richardson, 'China Unveils Aircraft SIGINT/EW Systems', Miltronics, October/November 1989, p.35; and Bernard Blake (ed.), Jane's Radar and Electronic Warfare Systems, 1990-91, (Jane's Information Group, Coulsdon, Surrey, Second Edition, 1990), p.424

cccxxxi Norman Friedman, The Naval Institute Guide to World Naval Weapons Systems, 1997-1998, Naval Institute Press, Annapolis, Maryland, 1997, pp.492-493

cccxxxii International Institute for Strategic Studies (IISS), The Military Balance, 2001-2002, (Oxford University Press, Oxford, 2001), p.190; and Martin Streetly, 'Asia Pacific Boosts Airborne Surveillance', Jane's Defence Weekly, 13 February 2002, p.27

cccxxxiii 'Chinese Tu-154M ELINT'. [2011]. [Online]. Avaiable:
http://www.aeronautics.ru/tu154melint.htm ; and Peter Wang, 'Equipment Matchups: Air Support', 30 August 2002. [Online]. Available:
http://www.emeraldesigns.com/matchup/support.htm

cccxxxiv Charles R. Smith, 'Chinese Airlines Serve PLA military', NewsMax.Com, 16 April 2002. [2002]. [Online]. Available:
http://www.newsmax.com/archives/articles/2002/4/15/172400.shtml

cccxxxv Major Kenneth W. Allen, USAF, People's Republic of China: People's Liberation Army Air Force, 15 April 1991, p.19.2

cccxxxvi *'New Ships for the PLAN'*, Jane's Defence Weekly, 18 January 1992, pp.88-89; and Captain Richard Sharpe, RN (ed.), Jane's Fighting Ships, 2000-2001, (Jane's Information Group, Coulsdon, Surrey, 103rd edition, 2000), pp.142-144

cccxxxvii Ibid., p.142

cccxxxviii Jeffrey Richelson, Foreign Intelligence Organizations, p.292; Stephen Ladd, 'The Chinese Naval Sigint Threat', Naval Intelligence Quarterly, (Vol.7, No.4), 1986, pp.30-34; and Captain Richard Sharpe, RN (ed.), Jane's Fighting Ships, 2000-2001, p.143

cccxxxix You Ji, *The PLA Navy in the Changing World Order: The South China Sea Theatre*, p.21

cccxl David Lague and Nayan Chanda, *China-United States: The Spying Game Heats Up*, Far Eastern Economic Review, 3 May 2001, p.23

cccxli 'Editorial: Japan Responds to China Threat', Taiwan News.Com, 11 August 2001. [Online]. Available:
http://www.etaiwannews.com/Editorial/2001/08/11/997498010.htm

cccxlii Ibid.

cccxliii Charles R. Smith, 'Chinese Spy Ships Breach Japanese and Philippine Waters', NewsMax.Com, 9 April 2001. [Online]. Available: *http://www.newsmax.com/archives/articles/2001/4/8/195441.shtml*

cccxliv Manuel Cerejo, *"China, Cuba and Information Warfare, Signal Intelligence, Electronic Warfare and Cyber Warfare"*. [2011]. [Online]. Available: *http://www.futurodecuba.org/ChinaandInformationWarfare4.htm*

cccxlv 'Taipei Protests Intrusion of Chinese Spy Ship', Channel News Asia.Com, 4 November 2002. [Online]. Available: *http://www.channelnewsasia.com/stories/eastasia/view/23629/1/.html*

cccxlvi Manuel Cerejo, *"China, Cuba and Information Warfare, Signal Intelligence, Electronic Warfare and Cyber Warfare"*. [2011]. [Online]. Available: *http://www.futurodecuba.org/ChinaandInformationWarfare4.htm*

cccxlvii Jim Bussert, *PRC Improves Electronic Warfare Capability*, Defense Electronics, November 1987, pp.146-149

cccxlviii Ngok Lee, China's Defence Modernisation and MilitaryLeadership, (Australian National University Press, Sydney, 1989), p.3

cccxlix Ibid.

cccl Martin Streetly (ed.), Jane's Radar and Electronic Warfare Systems, 2002-2003, (Jane's Information Group, Coulsdon, Surrey, 14 edition, 2002), p.326

cccli Ibid., p.327

ccclii Ibid., p.401

cccliii Ibid.

cccliv John A. Thacker, Jr., *China's Secret Weapon for Information Warfare*. [Online]. Avaiable: *http://www.specialoperations.com/Foreign/China/IW.htm*

ccclv Richard D. Fisher, Jr., 'Chapter 3: Seeking Information Dominance', draft manuscript, 2002, p.4

ccclvi John A. Thacker, Jr., *China's Secret Weapon for Information Warfare*. [Online]. Avaialble: *http://www.specialoperations.com/Foreign/China/IW.htm*

ccclvii Richard D. Fisher, Jr., 'Chapter 3: Seeking Information Dominance', draft manuscript, 2002, p.4

ccclviii Norman Friedman, The Naval Institute Guide to World Naval Weapons Systems, 1997-1998, p.493

ccclix 'The PLA Air Force Build-Up', Asian Defence Journal, 11/92, p.46

ccclx Edward T. Pound, 'U.S. Sees New Signs Israel Resells Its Arms to China, South Africa', Wall Street Journal, 13 March 1992, p.1

ccclxi Major General Wang Pufeng, 'The Challenge of Information Warfare', in Michael Pillsbury (ed.), Chinese Views of Future Warfare, p.325

ccclxii Senior Colonel Wang Baocun and Li Fei, 'Information Warfare', in Michael Pillsbury (ed.), Chinese Views of Future Warfare, pp.332-333

ccclxiii Ibid., p.331

ccclxiv Major General Wu Guoging, *Future Trends of Modern Operations*, in Michael Pillsbury (ed.), Chinese Views of Future Warfare, p.350

ccclxv Ibid.

ccclxvi Bill Gertz, *Chinese Missile Moves Near Taiwan Worry U.S..* The Washington Times, 7 June 2001 [Online]. [2010]. Available: *http://www.taiwandc.org/washt2001-10.htm*

ccclxvii *Falun Gong group hijacked Chinese satellite.* [Online]. [2002]. Available: *http://www.computerweekly.com/Articles/2002/07/09/188269/Falun-Gong-group-hijacked-Chinese-satellite.htm*

ccclxviii Manuel Cerejo, *"China, Cuba and Information Warfare, Signal Intelligence, Electronic Warfare and Cyber Warfare".* [2011]. [Online]. Available: *http://www.futurodecuba.org/ChinaandInformationWarfare4.htm*

ccclxix *Falun Gong group hijacked Chinese satellite.* [Online]. [2002]. Available: *http://www.computerweekly.com/Articles/2002/07/09/188269/Falun-Gong-group-hijacked-Chinese-satellite.htm*

ccclxx James Mulvenon, 'The PLA and Information Warfare', pp.175, 176, 184-185.

ccclxxi *"Capability of the People's Republic of China to Conduct Cyber Warfare and Computer Network Exploitation".* [2009]. [Online]. Available: *http://www.uscc.gov/annual_report/2009/09report_chapters.php*

ccclxxii Ibid.

ccclxxiii *China's National Defense in 2008,* Information Office of the State Council of the People's Republic of China, Beijing, 29 December 2008. [Online]. Available: *http://www.chinadaily.com.cn/china/2009-01/20/content_74133294.htm*

ccclxxiv *China's National Defense in 2004,* Information Office of the State Council of the People's Republic of China, Beijing, 27 December 2004. [Online]. Available: *http://english.peopledaily.com.cn/whitepaper/defense2004/defense2004.html*; *China's National Defense in 2006,* Information Office of the State Council of the People's Republic of China, Beijing, 29 December 2006.[Online]. Available: *http://english.chinamil.com.cn/site2/newschannels/2006-12/29/content_691844.htm*

ccclxxv "PRC Establishes New Military Schools Per Jiang Decree,"Xinhua, 2 July, 1999 | "China Establishes New Military Schools," People's Daily, 7 March,1999. [Online]. Available: *http://english.peopledaily.com.cn/english/199907/03/enc_19990703001001_TopNews.html*

ccclxxvi Ibid.

ccclxxvii "Rising Releases 2010 Report on Threats to Corporate Security" □□发□2010□业□□报□ □□□□□业□□□□. *China Rising*, [2011]. [Online]. Available: *http://www.rising.com.cn/about/news/rising/2011-03-11/9056.html*

ccclxxviii HK Journal Details History, Structure, Functions of PRC Intelligence Agencies," Hong Kong Chien Shao, No 179, 1January, 2006.

ccclxxix *"China – China Civil War 1945-49".* Encyclopedia Britannica Online. [2011]. [Online]. Available: *http://www.britannica.com/EBchecked/topic/111803/China/71834/Civil-war-1945-49*

ccclxxx Tony Capaccio and Jeff Bliss. Bloomberg. "Chinese Military Suspected in Hacker Attacks on U.S. Satellites". [2011]. [Online]. Available: *http://www.bloomberg.com/news/2011-10-27/chinese-military-suspected-in-hacker-attacks-on-u-s-satellites.html*

ccclxxxi Compass Navigation Satellite System (Beidou 20).SinoDefence.com. [2011]. [Online]. Available: *http://www.sinodefence.com/satellites/compass-beidou.asp*

ccclxxxii *"Rising Releases 2010 Report on Threats to Corporate Security* 瑞星发布2010企业安全报告 企业信息安全威胁分析. *China Rising.* [2011]. Available: *http://www.rising.com.cn/about/news/rising/2011-03-11/9056.html*

ccclxxxiii Bryan Krekel, *"Capability of the People's Republic of China to Conduct Cyber Warfare and Computer Network Exploitation".* Northrop Grumman Corporation Information Systems Sector Report for the US-China Economic and Security Review Commission. [2010]. [Online]. Available: *http://www.uscc.gov/researchpapers/2010/NorthropGrumman_PRC_Cyber_Paper_FINAL_Approved%20Report_2010.pdf*

ccclxxxiv You Ming and Zhou Xiyuan. *"Analysis of Attack and Defense Mechanisms in Information Network War".*信息网络对抗机制的攻防分析. *Network Security Technology and Application,* December 6, 2004. [2011]. [Online]. Available: *http://tech.ccidnet.com/art/1101/20041206/185771_1.html*

ccclxxxv Jiang Mingyuan, Ning Bo, and Yong Jing, *"Five Characteristics of Air Force Equipment Informatization"*信息化空军武器装备的五大特征. *Aeronautical Science and Technology,* 2004(6). [2011]. [Online]. Avaialble: *http://d.wanfangdata.com.cn/Periodical_hkkxjs200406009.aspx*

ccclxxxvi *"PLAAF Su-27 Chased U-2 Into Taiwan Airspace".* DEFENSETECH.org.[2011]. [Online]. Available: *http://defensetech.org/2011/07/26/plaaf-su-2-into-taiwan-airspace/*

ccclxxxvii Roger Cliff. "The Development of China's Air Force Capabilities". Rand Corporation. [2010]. [Online]. Available: *http://www.rand.org/pubs/testimonies/2010/RAND_CT346.pdf*

ccclxxxviii Andrew S. Erickson. "Satellites Support Growing PLA Maritime Monitoring and Targeting Capabilities". [2010]. [Online]. Available: *http://www.jamestown.org/single/?no_cache=1&tx_ttnews%5Btt_news%5D=37490*

ccclxxxix The approximate locations of several Chinese SIGINT sites are given in Jim Bussert, 'China's C^{3}I Efforts Show Progress', in Fred D. Byers (ed.), *C^{3}I Handbook,* (EW Communications, Inc., Palo Alto, California, First Edition, 1986), p.173.

cccxc Republic of China National Defense Report. Chapter 7 *"Solid Defense Capabilities".* [2011]. [Online]. Available; *http://163.29.3.66/english/index_01.html*

cccxci Jim Bussert, 'China's C^{3}I Efforts Show Progress', in Fred D. Byers (ed.), *C^{3}I Handbook,* (EW Communications, Inc., Palo Alto, California, First Edition, 1986), p.173.

cccxcii Bernard Blake (ed.), *"Jane's Radar and Electronic Warfare Systems, 1990-91",* (Jane's Information Group, Coulsdon, Surrey, Second Edition, 1990), p.398; and Norman Friedman, *"The Naval Institute Guide to World Naval Weapons Systems, 1997-1998",* p.512

cccxciii *"Strategic Missile Force"*. SinoDefence.com. [2011]. [Online]. Available: *http://www.sinodefence.com/strategic/default.asp*

cccxciv Wendell Minnick. *"China's PLA Involved in Cyber Espionage: Report"*. Defense News. [2011]. [Online]. Available: *http://www.defensenews.com/story.php?i=8207991*

cccxcv *"Technology Co., Ltd Jinan military record"*. [2011]. [Online]. Available: *http://cn.made-in-china.com/showroom/ccmm200/companyinfo*

cccxcvi Mark A. Stokes, et al.

cccxcvii Gong Liangliang, Wang Yunliang, and Luo Jingqing, *"Radar Electromagnetic Environment Simulation in Satellite Reconnaissance"* 基于卫星侦察的雷达电磁环境仿真. Modern Defense Technology. [2011]. [Online]. Available: *http://d.wanfangdata.com.cn/periodical_xdfyjs200803031.aspx*

cccxcviii China's National Defense in 2004, Information Office of China's State Council, December 2004. [Online]. Available: *http://english.peopledaily.com.cn/whitepaper/defense2004/defense2004.html* China's National Defense in 2006, Information Office of the State Council of the People's Republic of China, December 2006, Beijing. [Online]. Available: *http://english.chinamil.com.cn/site2/newschannels/2006 12/29/content_691844.htm* "Telecom Experts in Guangzhou Doubling As Militia Information Warfare Elements," Guofang, Academy of Military Science, 15 September, 2003

cccxcix Lu Qiang, *"Focus On The Characteristics Of Information Warfare To Strengthen The City Militia Construction"* China Militia Magazine, August 2003. [Online]. Available: *http://www.chinamil.com.cn/item/zgmb/200308/txt/16.htmZ*

cd Nicholas Eftimiades. *"Chinese Intelligence Operations"*. Naval Institute Press: Annapolis, MD, pp. 17

cdi David Finklestein. "THE GENERAL STAFF DEPARTMENT OF THE CHINESE PEOPLE'S LIBERATION ARMY: ORGANIZATION, ROLES, & MISSIONS". [2011]. [Online]. Available: *http://www.rand.org/pubs/conf_proceedings/CF182/CF182.ch4.pdf*

cdii Ibid.

cdiii Mark A. Stokes."China's strategic modernization: implications for the United States". Army War College (U.S.). Strategic Studies Institute

cdiv Mr. Cox. *"HOUSE REPORT 105-851. SELECT COMMITTEE ON U.S. NATIONAL SECURITY AND MILITARY/COMMERCIAL CONCERNS WITH THE PEOPLE'S REPUBLIC OF CHINA"* . [2011]. [Online]. Available: *http://www.access.gpo.gov/congress/house/hr105851-html/index.html*

cdv Nicholas Eftimiades. *"Chinese Intelligence Operations"*. Naval Institute Press: Annapolis, MD, pp. 75.

cdvi Ibid, pages 76 -77.

cdvii *"People's Liberation Army"*. [2011]. [Online]. Available: *http://forum.globaltimes.cn/forum/archive/index.php/t-164.html*

cdviii Second [Intelligence] Department, GlobalSecurity.org. [2010].[Online] Available:
http://www.globalsecurity.org/intell/world/china/pla-dept_2.htm
cdixEftimiades. *"Chinese Intelligence Operations"*, pp.79
cdx Huang Yung-nien ."Intelligence Background of Zhou Borong, deputy commander of Hong Kong Garrison" by [Hong Kong], 01 April 1996 No 4, pp 48-51
cdxi Chen Pei-chiung in Washington Ho Yung-hsiung in Hong Kong Yu Hui-hsin in Beijing "*Red Agents Infiltrate Celebrity Circles.* No 255, 27 Jan 95 pp 48-50, 52, 54-5
cdxii Dan Dietrle. InfoSecIsland.com. *"Chinese Hackers Spear-Phishing for US Military Secrets"*. [2011]. [Online]. Available:
https://www.infosecisland.com/blogview/13308-Chinese-Hackers-Spear-Phishing-for-US-Military-Secrets.html
cdxiii Brian Grow and Mark Hosenball ,Reuters. *"China is moving aggressively ahead of US in cyber-spying"*. [2011]. [Online]. Available:
http://www.chinapost.com.tw/commentary/reuters/2011/04/16/298821/China-is.htm
cdxiv Third Department, GlobalSecurity.org. [2010].[Online] Available:
http://www.globalsecurity.org/intell/world/china/pla-dept_3.htm
cdxv HEARING BEFORE THE U.S.-CHINA ECONOMIC AND SECURITY REVIEW COMMISSION *"CHINA'S NARRATIVES REGARDING NATIONAL SECURITY POLICY"*. [2011]. [Onlline]. Available:
http://www.uscc.gov/hearings/2011hearings/transcripts/11_03_10_trans/11_03_10_final_transcript.pdf
cdxvi Cheng Li. *"China's Economic Deciosnmakers"*. [2008]. [Online]. Available:
http://www.brookings.edu/~/media/Files/rc/articles/2008/03_china_li/03_china_li.pdf
cdxviiIbid.
cdxviii National Bureau of Statistics of China. *"Communiqué on Major Data of the Second National Economic Census (No.1)"*. [2009]. [Online]. Available:
http://www.stats.gov.cn/english/newsandcomingevents/t20091225_402610168.htm
cdxix Hoovers. *"Chery Automobile Co. Ltd."*. [2011]. [Online]. Available:
http://www.hoovers.com/company/Chery_Automobile_Co_Ltd/rhkkcri-1.html
cdxx Jason Miks. *"China's Tight Rare Earth Grip"*. [2011]. [Online]. Available: *http://the-diplomat.com/china-power/2011/09/17/chinas-tight-rare-earth-grip/*
cdxxi Jack Dini. Canada free Press. *"China's Monopoly on Rare Earth Metals"*. [2011]. [Online]. Available: *http://canadafreepress.com/index.php/article/41856*
cdxxii Bonner R. Cohen, "China cuts back on rare earth exports, jeopardizing wind and solar power, Environment & Climate News, February 2011
cdxxiii Ronald Bailey, "Rare earth ruckus," Reason Magazine, November 23, 2010
cdxxiv Joe McDonald, *"China rare earth supplier suspends production"*. [2011]. [Online]. Available:

http://old.news.yahoo.com/s/ap/20111020/ap_on_hi_te/as_china_rare_earth s

cdxxv Geoffrey York and Branda Bouw, "Chasing China," The Globe and Mail, July 16, 2011, Page B6

cdxxvi Aziz Huq. Foreign Policy. "*Chinese Takeout*". [2010]. [Online]. Available: *http://www.foreignpolicy.com/articles/2010/06/15/chinese_takeout*

cdxxvii Mahmood Elahi. Letter to the editor. New York Times. "Afghan Mineral Wealth". [2010]. [Online]. Available: *http://www.nytimes.com/2010/06/18/opinion/lweb18afghan.html*

cdxxviii Joe McDonald, "*China rare earth supplier suspends production*". [2011]. [Online]. Available: *http://old.news.yahoo.com/s/ap/20111020/ap_on_hi_te/as_china_rare_earth s*

cdxxix Sinomach Website. "*About*". [2011]. [Online]. Available: *http://www.sinomach.com.cn/templates/T_common_en/index.aspx?nodeid=1 47*

cdxxx Jason Douglass. Infowars. "*Chinese Company Sinomach Poised To Takeover Boise*". [2011]. [Online]. Available: *http://www.infowars.com/chinese-company-sinomach-poised-to-takeover-boise/*

cdxxxi Nicklas Norling. Central Asia-Caucasus Institute Analyst. "*The Emerging China-Afghanistan Relationship*". [2008]. [Online]. Available: *http://www.cacianalyst.org/?q=node/4858*

cdxxxii Shuan Waterman. The Washington Times. "Chinese firm 'owns' telephone system in Iraq". [2011]. [Online]. Available: *http://www.washingtontimes.com/news/2011/feb/21/chinese-telecom-end-ties-us-high-tech-start-/print/*

cdxxxiii Steven Musil. "*Lenovo completes buy of IBM's PC business*". [2005]. [Online]. Available: *http://news.cnet.com/Lenovo-completes-buy-of-IBMs-PC-business/2100-1042_3-5691487.html*

cdxxxiv Lenovo Website. "*Investor Relations – Investor Fact Sheet*". [2011]. [Online]. Available: *http://www.lenovo.com/ww/lenovo/investor_factsheet.html*

cdxxxv BaiDu Slideshare portal. "*HuaWei-Symantec Corporate Briefing*". [2008]. [Online]. Available: *http://wenku.baidu.com/view/fc43f52de2bd960590c677b5.html*

cdxxxvi Ibid.

cdxxxvii Deepika Mala. "*DNS – Huawei, SYNNEX Partner for Distribution of IT, DNS Security Services*". [2010]. [Online]. Available: *http://dns-news.tmcnet.com/topics/internet-security/articles/129193-huawei-synnex-partner-distribution-it-dns-security-services.htm*

cdxxxviii Karl Bode. "*U.S. Blocks Huawei Emergency Network Build Bid U.S. Again Hints at Supposed Chinese Government Ties*". [2011]. [Online]. Available:

http://www.dslreports.com/shownews/US-Blocks-Huawei-Emergency-Network-Build-Bid-116575
cdxxxix Force10 Networks Government Solutions webpage. [2011]. [Online]. Available:
http://www.force10networks.com/solutions/government.asp
cdxl Matthew Forney. TIME Specials. *"Ren Zhengfei"*. [2005]. [Online]. Avaialble:
http://www.time.com/time/specials/packages/article/0,28804,1972656_1972707_1973574,00.html
cdxli Ray Le Maistre. Light Reading. *"Is Huawei in at Level 3?"* [2009]. [Online]. Available:
http://www.lightreading.com/document.asp?doc_id=179384
cdxlii Right Web. *"U.S.- China Commission"*. [2011]. [Online}. Available:
http://rightweb.irc-online.org/profile/US-China_Commission
cdxliii John Markoff. *"Vast Spy System Loots Computers in 103 Countries"*. [2009] [Online]. Available:
http://www.nytimes.com/2009/03/29/technology/29spy.html?pagewanted=all
cdxliv Ibid.
cdxlv Information Warfare Monitor. *"Tracking GhostNet: Investigating a Cyber Espionage Network"*. [2009]. [Online]. Available: *http://www.infowar-monitor.net/research/*
cdxlvi Ibid. [2011]. [Online]. Available: *http://www.infowar-monitor.net/about/*
cdxlvii Scott Henderson. The Dark Visitor website. *"Hunting the GhostNet Hacker"*. [2009]. [Online]. Available: *http://www.thedarkvisitor.com/2009/04/hunting-the-ghostnet-hacker/*
cdxlviii Infowar Monitor, Munk School of Global Affairs and the SecDevGroup. *"Shadows in the Cloud: An investigation into cyber espionage 2.0"*. [2010]. [Online]. Available: *http://www.infowar-monitor.net/2010/04/shadows-in-the-cloud-an-investigation-into-cyber-espionage-2-0/*
cdxlix Ibid.
cdl John Markoff and David Barboza. *"Researchers Trace Data Theft to Intruders in China"*. [2010]. [Online]. Available:
http://www.nytimes.com/2010/04/06/science/06cyber.html?adxnnl=1&adxnnlx=1319975777-UIaHRKDfUhTQLB6knOFWUA
cdli The Official Google Blog. *"A new approach to China"*. [2010]. [Online]. Available:
http://googleblog.blogspot.com/2010/01/new-approach-to-china.html
cdlii Pallab De. "Google hack Attack (Operation Aurora): What We Know". [2010]. [Online]. Available: *http://techie-buzz.com/tech-news/google-hack-attack-operation-aurora.html*
cdliii Ibid.
cdliv Brandon Hill. *"Google Kills Google.cn, Redirect Traffic to Hong Kong"*. [2010]. [Online]. Available:
http://www.dailytech.com/Google+Kills+Googlecn+Redirects+Traffic+to+Hong+Kong/article17950.htm

329

cdlv Shanghai Jaio Tong University. "*School Introduction*". [2011]. [Online]. Available: *http://www.sie.sjtu.edu.cn/ctrler.asp?action=list_en&tp=00047*

cdlvi Jonathon Watts. "*Gmail hack: phishing finger pointed at China's Lanxiang vocational school*". [2011]. [Online]. Available: *http://www.guardian.co.uk/technology/2011/jun/02/chinese-school-implicated-cyber-attacks*

cdlvii McAfee Foundtsone Professional Services and McAfee Labs. "*Global Energy Cyberattacks: "Night Dragon*". [2011]. [Online]. Available: *http://www.mcafee.com/us/resources/white-papers/wp-global-energy-cyberattacks-night-dragon.pdf*

cdlviii Sara Forden. Bloomberg News. "Hacking of DuPont, J&J, GE Were Google-Type Attacks That Weren't Disclosed. [2011]. [Online]. Available: *http://www.bloomberg.com/news/2011-03-08/hacking-of-dupont-j-j-ge-were-google-type-attacks-that-weren-t-disclosed.html*

cdlix Ibid.

cdlx Dimitri Alperovitch. "*Revealed: Operation Shady RAT*". [2011]. [Online]. Available: *http://blogs.mcafee.com/mcafee-labs/revealed-operation-shady-rat*

cdlxi Ibid.

cdlxii Michael Joseph Gross. Vanity Fair. "*Exclusive: Operation Shady RAT—Unprecedented Cyber-espionage Campaign and Intellectual-Property Bonanza*". [2011]. [Online]. Available: *http://www.vanityfair.com/culture/features/2011/09/operation-shady-rat-201109*

cdlxiii Desire Athow. ItProPortal. "*Fake Apple Stores Mushrooming In China; No iPhone 5 Inside*". [2011]. [Online]. Available: *http://www.itproportal.com/2011/07/20/fake-apple-stores-mushrooming-china-no-iphone-5-inside/*

cdlxiv Ibid.

cdlxv Kathrin Hille in Beijing and Patti Waldmeir in Shanghai. "*Apple secures patents on China stores*". [2011]. [Online]. Available: "*http://www.ft.com/intl/cms/s/2/eb1b831c-e42e-11e0-b4e9-00144feabdc0.html*"

cdlxvi Ibid

cdlxvii Reuters. "*Chinese city orders closure of two fake Apple shops.*" [2011]. [Online]. Available: *http://www.reuters.com/article/2011/07/25/uk-apple-china-fake-idUSLNE76O02K20110725*

cdlxviii Dave Smith. "*Apple Wins 40 Patents in China to Counter Piracy*". [20011]. [Online]. Available: *http://www.ibtimes.com/articles/217724/20110921/apple-patent-apple-china-apple-samsung-lawsuit.htm*

cdlxix Ibid.

cdlxx Top Employers. "*China's Top Employers*". [2011]. [Online]. Available: *http://www.topemployers.com.cn/en/ChinasTopEmployers/ChinasTopEmployers2011/C/tabid/5333/C/422/AstraZeneca.aspx*

cdlxxi China CSR Map. [2011]. [Online]. Available:
http://www.chinacsrmap.org/E_Default.asp
cdlxxii Speigel Staff. *"Merkel's China Visit Marred by Hacking Allegations"*.
[2007].[Online]. Available:
http://www.spiegel.de/international/world/0,1518,502169,00.html
cdlxxiii Ibid.
cdlxxiv Cyber Wars Staff Writers. *"Germany Reports 'sharp rise' in cyberattacks"*.
[2010].[Online]. Available:
http://www.spacewar.com/reports/Germany_reports_sharp_rise_in_cyberatt acks_999.html
cdlxxv Chris Kirsch. *"Chinese agencies double cyber attacks on Germany"*. [2011].
[Online]. Available:
https://community.rapid7.com/community/infosec/blog/2011/01/04/chinese-agencies-double-cyber-attacks-on-germany
cdlxxvi Ibid.
cdlxxvii The Local. "Chinese cyber attacks target German ministers". [2011].[Online].
Available : *http://www.thelocal.de/sci-tech/20110629-35947.html*
cdlxxviii Ibid.
cdlxxix BBC News Businesss. *"Cyber attack on France targeted Paris G20 files"*. [2011].
[Online]. Available: *http://www.bbc.co.uk/news/business-12662596*
cdlxxx Ibid.
cdlxxxi Nick Farrell, TechEYE.net. *"Hackers Break into French Defence industry"*. [2011].
[Online]. Available: *http://news.techeye.net/security/hackers-break-into-french-defence-industry*
cdlxxxii Ibid.
cdlxxxiii Stephen Fidler and Maija Palmer. FT.com. " MI5 warns banks of
Chinese hackers". [2007]. [Online}. Available:
http://www.ft.com/intl/cms/s/0/b3e357b8-9fa3-11dc-8031-0000779fd2ac.html
cdlxxxiv Sophie Borland. The Telegraph. "MI5 warns firms over China's
internet spying". [2008]. [Online]. Available:
http://www.telegraph.co.uk/news/worldnews/1571172/MI5-warns-firms-over-Chinas-internet-spying.html
cdlxxxv Michael Smith. The Times. "Spy chiefs fear Chinese cyber attack.".
[2009]. [Online]. Available:
http://www.thesundaytimes.co.uk/sto/news/uk_news/article158319.ece
cdlxxxvi Rosalie Marshall. MI5 warns of Chinese hacks on UK businesses"
[2010]. [Online]. Available: *http://www.v3.co.uk/v3-uk/news/1962328/mi5-warns-chinese-hacks-uk-businesses*
cdlxxxvii Jim Kouri. Examiner. " Chinese espionage remains threat to UK,
says MI5". [2011]. [Online]. Available: *http://www.examiner.com/public-safety-in-national/chinese-espionage-remains-threat-to-uk-says-mi5*

cdlxxxviii Thomas, *China's Electronic Strategies.*

cdlxxxix Ibid.

cdxc Baldor, Lolita C., *Pentagon warns public about cyber-attacks by China.* [Online]. [August 20, 2010.] Available: *http://articles.boston.com/2010-08-20/news/29299438_1_pentagon-report-cyber-attacks-computer-systems*

cdxci *Pentagon takes aim at China cyber threat.* [2010]. [Online]. Avaiable: *http://www.hackerjournals.com/?p=12055*

cdxcii *US takes aim at China cyber threat.* [2010]. [Online]. Available: *http://www.technologyreview.com/wire/26100/*

cdxciii Baldor, Lolita C., *Pentagon warns public about cyber-attacks by China.* [Online]. [August 19, 2010.] Available: *http://investorshub.advfn.com/boards/read_msg.aspx?message_id=53579245*

cdxciv Dennis Dwyer. *Chinese Hackers Talk Hacking.* [2009]. [Online]. Available: *http://www.secureworks.com/research/blog/general/20833/*

cdxcv Ibid.; Military and Security Developments Involving the People's Republic of China 2010. [2010]. [Online]. Available; *http://www.defense.gov/pubs/pdfs/2010_CMPR_Final.pdf*

cdxcvi . Edward Cody. *Chinese Official Accuses Nations of Hacking.* Wall Street Journal. [2007]. [Online]. Available: *http://www.washingtonpost.com/wp-dyn/content/article/2007/09/12/AR2007091200791.html?nav=rss_technology*

cdxcvii Ibid.

cdxcviii Ibid.

cdxcix Baldor, Lolita C., *"Pentagon warns public about cyber-attacks by China".* [Online]. [August 20, 2010.] Available: *http://articles.boston.com/2010-08-20/news/29299438_1_pentagon-report-cyber-attacks-computer-systems*

d U.S. Government Accounting Office. "CYBERCRIME: Public and Private Entities Face Challenges in Addressing Cyber Threats". *[2007]. [Online]. Available: http://www.gao.gov/new.items/d07705.pdf*

di *"THE A-Z GUIDE FOR ISO 27001 AND ISO17799 / ISO27002 ISO 27000 CENTRAL".* [20100]. [Online]. Available: *http://www.17799central.com/*

dii U.S. Department of Defense. "Annual Report on the Military Power of the People's Republic of China. [2010]. [Online]. Available: *www.defense.gov/pubs/pdfs/2010_CMPR_Final.pdf*

diii DoD Instruction 5220.22 March 18, 2011."*National Security Program (NISP)".* [2011]. [Online]. Available: *http://www.dtic.mil/whs/directives/corres/pdf/522022p.pdf*

div U.S. Department of Defense. Defense Security Service. "National Industrial Security Program". [2011]. [Online]. Available: *http://www.dss.mil/about_dss/fact_sheets/nisp_faqsheet.html*

dv *http://www.foreignaffairs.com/articles/53020/donald-zagoria/china-in-the-information-age-telecommunications-and-the-dilemmas* accessed 1997-06-07

dvi *http://news.bbc.co.uk/2/hi/technology/3699820.stm* accessed 2004-10-06 dvii *http://www.foreignaffairs.com/articles/53020/donald-zagoria/china-in-the-information-age-telecommunications-and-the-dilemmas* accessed 1997-06-28

dviii Liu, C., (1995), "Some tentative ideas and recommended guidelines for construction of China's information infrastructure", *China Telecommunications Construction*, Vol. 7, No. 3, pp. 5 – 9

dix Lovelock, Peter; Clark, Theodore C.; *Petrazzini, Ben A.*. The "Golden Projects": China's National Networking Initiative, IOS Press, Van Diemenstraat 94, 1013 CN Amsterdam, Netherlands, pp 265 – 267.

dx PRC State Council. "Interim Regulation on International Interconnection of Computer Networks in PRC." Order No. 195, Feb. 1, 1996.
http://som.csudh.edu/fac/lpress/devnat/nations/china/chinah.html accessed 8 JUL 2011

dxi PRC State Council. "The Regulations of Safety Protection for Computer Information Systems in the PRC." Order No. 147, Feb. 18, 1994.
http://www.cernet.edu.cn/LAW/qry_law2.html accessed 8 JUL 2011

dxii Daniel Bardsley, Chinese tighten web access even more with wi-fi clampdown in cafes and hotels accessed 26 JUL 2011 via the World Wide Web at
http://www.thenational.ae/news/worldwide/asia-pacific/chinese-tighten-web-access-even-more-with-wi-fi-clampdown-in-cafes-and-hotels

dxiii Ravi Mandalia, China Intensifies Internet Censorship Drive, Sets Up Web Monitoring , accessed 26 JUL 2011 via the World Wide Web at
http://www.itproportal.com/2011/07/26/china-intensifies-internet-censorship-drive-sets-up-web-monitoring/

dxiv XE Universal Currency Convertor accessed 3 AUG 2011 va the World Wide Web at
http://www.xe.com/ucc/convert/?Amount=1&From=CNY&To=USD

dxv Statistical Reports on the Internet Development in China, China Internet Network Information Center accessed 27 JUL 2011 via the World Wide Web at
http://www.cnnic.net.cn/en/index/0O/02/index.htm

dxvi Ibid.

dxvii Rainysia's cloverfield blog, CANET:Across the Great Wall we can reach every corner in the world., accessed on 10 MAR 2011 via the World Wide Web at
http://rainysia.wordpress.com/2011/03/08/canetacross-the-great-wall-we-can-reach-every-corner-in-the-world/

dxviii People's daily Online, China's first internet user- Prof. Qian Tianbai of Peking University accesed 05 JUL 2011 via the World Wide Web at
http://english.peopledaily.com.cn/90002/95607/6526583.html

dxix Ibid.

dxx Eric Harwit and Duncan Clark, Shaping the Internet in China: Evolution of Political Control over Network Infrastructure and Content, Asian Survey 41, Number 3, (2002) pp 383.

dxxi Ibid.

dxxii R. L. A. Cottrell, Charles Granieri, Lan Fan, Rongsheng Xu, Yukio Karita, Networking with China, Conference on Computing in High Energy Physics San Francisco, CA, April 21–27, 1994, pp 4- 5.

dxxiii Network Research Center of Tsinghua University, Campus Network of Tsinghua University (TUNET) accessed 27 JUL 2011 via the World Wide Web at *http://www.nrc.tsinghua.edu.cn/7_english/Situation2.htm*

dxxiv Ibid.

dxxv R. L. A. Cottrell, Charles Granieri, Lan Fan, Rongsheng Xu, Yukio Karita, Networking with China, Conference on Computing in High Energy Physics San Francisco, CA, April 21–27, 1994, pp 4- 5.

dxxvi China Internet Chronology 2: Public Networks and Network Regulation accessed 5 AUG 2011 via the World Wide Web at *http://china-wired.com/pubs/ch/ChIntChronology2.htm*

dxxvii Statistical Reports on the Internet Development in China, China Internet Network Information Center accessed 27 JUL 2011 via the World Wide Web at *http://www.cnnic.net.cn/en/index/0O/02/index.htm*

dxxviii Ann Zhang, GOLDEN BRIDGE PROJECT –*Connect China and Finland and Make Your Biz Easier in Finland* Accessed 21 JUN 2011 via the World Wide Web at *http://www.prizz.fi/linkkitiedosto.aspx?taso=4&id=576&sid=503*

dxxix Statistical Reports on the Internet Development in China, China Internet Network Information Center accessed 27 JUL 2011 via the World Wide Web at *http://www.cnnic.net.cn/en/index/0O/02/index.htm*

dxxx People's daily Newspaper online version accessed 9 AUG 2011 via the World Wide Web at *http://www.people.com.cn/*

dxxxi Introduction to People's Daily, accessed 18 JUL 2011 via the World Wide Web at *http://english.peopledaily.com.cn/other/about.shtml*

dxxxii Zhenyu Liu, Albert-Ludwigs-University, Freiburg, Germany China's Information Super Highway: Its Goal, Architecture and Problems, Focus Asia, Volume 7, Number 4, 1997, pp. 45 – 46.

dxxxiii Ibid.

dxxxiv China Information and Statistics China IT and Internet accessed 7 AUG 2011 via the World Wide Web at *http://www.chinatoday.com/it/it.htm*

dxxxv Statistical Report of the Development of Chinese Internet, accessed 21 JUL 2011 via the World Wide Web at *http://www.cnnic.net.cn/download/manual/en-reports/1.pdf*

dxxxvi The Internet Timeline of China 1987~1996, Beijing Instracc Networks Science and Technology Co. Ltd., accessed 6 AUG 2011 via the World Wide Web at *http://www.instracc.com/news_xx.asp?id=137*

dxxxvii Jian ping wu, China Next Generation Internet CNBI Project Presentation, 25 SPET 2003

dxxxviii China Internet Network Information Center (CNNIC), 16th Statistical Survey Report on the Internet Development in China, July 2001 accessed 17 JUL 2011 via the World Wide Web at *http://www.cnnic.net.cn*

dxxxix China Internet Network Information Center (CNNIC), 16th Statistical Survey Report on the Internet Development in China, July 2002 accessed 17 JUL 2011 via the World Wide Web at *http://www.cnnic.net.cn*

dxl China's Broadband 169 Network, C114 Website, accessed 14 JUL 2011 via the World Wide Web at *http://www.cn-c114.net/575.html*

dxli China Internet Network Information Center (CNNIC), 16th Statistical Survey Report on the Internet Development in China, July 2003 accessed 18 JUL 2011 via the World Wide Web at *http://www.cnnic.net.cn*

dxlii Ibid.

dxliii China Science & Technology website, ,accessed via the World Wide Web on 21 JUL 2011 at
http://www.cstnet.cn/english/internationalexchangesandooperation/gloriad.htm

dxlivGLOBAL RING NETWORK FOR ADVANCED APPLICATIONS DEVELOPMENT, accessed 27 JUL 2011 via the World Wide Web at
http://www.gloriad.org/gloriaddrupal/

dxlvStatistical Reports on the Internet Development in China, China Internet Network Information Center accessed 27 JUL 2011 via the World Wide Web at
http://www.cnnic.net.cn/en/index/0O/02/index.htm

dxlvi Ibid.

dxlvii K. Konishi,K. Huang, H. Qian and Y. Ko, Joint Engineering Team (JET) Guidelines for Internationalized Domain Names (IDN) Registration and Administration for Chinese, Japanese, and Korean, Request for Comments: 3743, RFC 3743 JET Guidelines for IDN April 2004, Accessed 13 JUL 2011 via the World Wide Web at
http://www.ietf.org/rfc/rfc3743.txt

dxlviii Ibid.

dxlix Statistical Reports on the Internet Development in China, China Internet Network Information Center accessed 27 JUL 2011 via the World Wide Web at
http://www.cnnic.net.cn/en/index/0O/02/index.htm

dl The Central People's Government of China, The People's Republic of China accessed 10 AUG 2011 via the World Wide web at *http://www.gov.cn/english/*

dli Ibid.

dlii Government and Policy. "*White Paper on the Internet in China. IV. Basic Principles and Practices of Internet Administration*". [2010]. [Online]. Available:
http://www.chinadaily.com.cn/china/2010-06/08/content_9950198_6.htm

dliii William Foster and Seymour Goodman, The Diffusion of the Internet in China, September 12, 2000 accessed 18 JUL 2011 via the Wporld Wide Web at
http://www.fosterandbrahm.com/docs/chinainternet.pdf

dliv工业和信息化部英文译名确定 新网站将上线 accessed 8 AUG 2011 via the World Wide Web at *http://news.xinhuanet.com/tech/2008-06/27/content_8450738.htm*

dlv Ministry of Industry and Information Technology (MIIT) website accessed 8 AUG 2011 via the World Wide Web at *http://www.miit.gov.cn/n11293472/index.html*

dlvi The U.S.-China Business Council, Ministry of Industry and Information Technology (MIIT) briefing page accessed 7 AUG 2011 via the World Wide Web at *https://www.uschina.org/public/china/govstructure/govstructure_part5/12.html*

dlvii Zhang Mo, China Issues New Rules Strengthening Regulatory Structure Over Internet, , East Asian Executive Reports Novemeber 15, 2007 accessed 15 JUL 2011 via the World Wide Web at *http://journalseek.net/journalseek/journalseek_v1060.txt*

dlviii Taubman, G., A not-so world wide web: the Internet, China, and the challenges to non-democratic rule.'1998, Political Communication. 15, 255–272.

dlix OpenNet Initiative, "China Tightens Controls on Internet News Content Through Additional Regulations," Bulletin 012, July 6, 2006 accessed 23 JUL 2011 via the World Wide Web at *http://www.opennet.net/bulletins/012/*

dlx Statistical Reports on the Internet Development in China, China Internet Network Information Center accessed 27 JUL 2011 via the World Wide Web at *http://www.cnnic.net.cn/en/index/0O/02/index.htm*

dlxi The Provisional Regulations of the People's Republic of China Governing the Management of Computer Information Networks Hooked Up With International Networks, accessed 19 JUL 2011 via the World Wide Web at *http://www.fas.org/irp/world/china/docs/internet_960201.htm*

dlxii Harwit, Eric. "China's Telecommunications Revolution." New York: Oxford University Press, 2008

dlxiii Interim Regulations on the Management of International networking of Computer Information (Amended), World Intellectual Property Organization website accessed 2 AUG 2011 via the World Wide Web at *http://www.wipo.int/wipolex/en/text.jsp?file_id=199607*

dlxiv Chris Chang, 'Father' of China's Great Firewall Has Six VPNs on his PC, accessed 23 FEB 2011 via the World Wide Web at *http://micgadget.com/11370/father-of-chinas-great-firewall-has-six-vpns-on-his-pc/*

dlxv Ibid.

dlxvi China Security & Surveillance Technology Inc. Company Information, Business Section, The New York Times online accessed 10 AUG 2011 via the World Wide Web at *http://topics.nytimes.com/topics/news/business/companies/china-security-and-surveillance-technology-inc/index.html*

dlxvii Richard Koman, Inside China's Golden Shield, ZDNet Government, accessed 16 JAN 2011 via the World Wide Web at *http://www.zdnet.com/blog/government/inside-chinas-golden-shield/3726*

dlxviii What is a DNSBL?, DNSBL.info at Spam Database Lookup website accessed 8 AUG 2011 via the World Wide Web at *http://www.dnsbl.info/dnsbl-database-check.php*

dlxix YAHOO! Help, IP Blocking Overview, accessed 8 AUG 2011 via the World Wide Web at *http://help.yahoo.com/l/us/yahoo/smallbusiness/store/risk/risk-17.html*

dlxx Web URL Filtering Service Description, Symantec Cloud, MessageLabs website accessed 8 AUG 2011 via the World Wide Web at *http://www.symanteccloud.com/products/web-security-services/web_urlfiltering*

dlxxi Andy Greenberg, China's Golden Cyber-Shield, Forbes.com, 07.31.01, 6:00AM ET accessed 8 AUG 2011 via the World Wide Web at

http://www.forbes.com/2007/07/30/china-cybercrime-war-tech-cx_ag_0730internet.html

dlxxii James Fallows, The Connection Has Been Reset, the Atlantivc, March 2008 accessed on 10 AUG 2011 via the World Wide Web at

http://www.theatlantic.com/magazine/archive/2008/03/-ldquo-the-connection-has-been-reset-rdquo/6650/

dlxxiii Sarah Lai Stirland, Cisco Leak: 'Great Firewall' of China Was a Chance to Sell More Routers, WIRED Magazine, May 20, 2008 accessed 8 AUG 2011 via the World Wide Web at *http://www.wired.com/threatlevel/2008/05/leaked-cisco-do/*

dlxxiv Kevin Poulsen, Critics Squeeze Cisco Over China, Wired Magazine, 07.29.05 accessed 9 AUG 2011 via the World Wide Web at

http://www.wired.com/techbiz/media/news/2005/07/68326

dlxxv Jim Duffy, Cisco can't live down selling gear to China for censorship, NetworkWorld, 05/12/08 accessed 10 AUG 2011 via the World Wide Web at

http://www.networkworld.com/community/node/27713

dlxxvi John Markoff, Surveillance of Skype Messages Found in China, The New York Times, Internet, accessed 7 AUG 2011 via the World Wide Web at

http://www.nytimes.com/2008/10/02/technology/internet/02skype.html

dlxxvii Eric Harwit and Duncan Clark, "Shaping the Internet in China: Evolution of Political Control Over Network Infrastructure and Content," *Asian Survey*, 41:3, May-June 2001, pp. 337-408.

dlxxviii Open Net Initiative, Internet Filtering in China in 2004-2005: A Country Study accessed 18 JUL 2011 via the World Wide Web at *http://opennet.net/studies/china*

dlxxix Steven Cherry, The Net Effect, As China's internet gets a much needed make-over, will the new network promote freedom or curtail it? *IEEE Spectrum*, June 2005 accessed 21 JUN 2011 via the World Wide Web at

http://spectrum.ieee.org/computing/networks/the-net-effect

dlxxx Internet Filtering in China in 2004-2005: A Country Study accessed 18 JUL 2011 via the World Wide Web at *http://opennet.net/studies/china#toc4e*

dlxxxi Greatfire wallof china.org test of Facebook.com accessed 2 AUG 2011 via the World Wide Web at

http://www.greatfirewallofchina.org/index.php?siteurl=facebook.com

dlxxxii Cisco Systems White Paper, THE COMING INTERNET EVOLUTION: IPv6 AND ITS
IMPLICATIONS FOR THE SERVICE PROVIDER MARKETPLACE, 2004,pp.8.

dlxxxiii Jesse TH Chuang, Phillip Qu and Isabelle IH Wan, China's Internet Policy & Legislation, TransAsia Lawyers, 1999

dlxxxiv Interim Administrative Provisions on Internet Publishing, Order No.17 of the General Administration of Press and Publication of China and the Ministry of Information

Industry of China accessed 12 JUL 2011 via the World Wide Web at
http://www.chinaitlaw.org/?p1=print&p2=050611165049
dlxxxv Ibid.
dlxxxvi Internet Manners and Culture Project launched in Beijing, China.ORG.CN, accessed via the World Wide Web at *http://china.org.cn/english/5071.htm*
dlxxxvii The Internet in China (White Paper), CPC Encyclopedia repost from
http://www.chinahumanrights.org/
2010-12-22 accessed 7 AUG 2011 via the World Wide Web at
http://cpcchina.chinadaily.com.cn/issues/2010-12/22/content_11741396.htm
dlxxxviii Bruce Einhorn, How China Controls the Internet, accessed 11 DEC 2010 via the World Wide Web at
http://www.businessweek.com/bwdaily/dnflash/jan2006/nf20060113_6735_d b053.htm
dlxxxix Rules for Online Banking Corporate Services of Bank of China Limited, accessed via the World Wide Web on 18 JUL 2011 at
www.boc.cn/bocinfo/bi2/201002/P020100210649214522899.doc
dxc Ibid.
dxci Wikimapia website Aerial Photograph of Huairentang Hall (Beijing) accessed 10 JUN 2011 via the World Wide Web at
http://wikimapia.org/3914792/Huairentang-Hall
dxcii Statistical Reports on the Internet Development in China, China Internet Network Information Center accessed 27 JUL 2011 via the World Wide Web at
http://www.cnnic.net.cn/en/index/0O/index.htm
dxciii Ibid
dxciv Internet Users and Regulation in the People's Republic of China accessed 19 JUL 2011 via the World Wide Web at *http://chinadigitaltimes.net/china/internet-users*
October 7, 2005, accessed via BBC Monitoring Media.
dxcv Ian Weber and Lu Jia, Internet and self-regulation in China: the cultural logic of controlled commodification, Media Culture Society September 2007 vol. 29 no. 5 772-789
dxcvi Statistical Reports on the Internet Development in China, China Internet Network Information Center accessed 27 JUL 2011 via the World Wide Web at
http://www.cnnic.net.cn/en/index/0O/index.htm
dxcvii Jesse TH Chuang, Phillip Qu and Isabelle IH Wan, China's Internet Policy & Legislation, TransAsia Lawyers, 2001
dxcviii Jesse TH Chuang, Phillip Qu and Isabelle IH Wan, China's Internet Policy & Legislation, TransAsia Lawyers, 2003
dxcix TREND Micro Threat Encyclopedia, Worm MSBLAST.A , accessed 19 JUL 2011 via the World Wide Web at *http://about-threats.trendmicro.com/ArchiveMalware.aspx?language=us&name=WORM_MSBLAST.A*
dc Liu Wei, Computer Viruses: Archenemy of China's Informationization, accessed 17 JUL 2011 via the World Wide Web at
http://english.peopledaily.com.cn/200308/22/eng20030822_122868.shtml

dci Internet Filtering in China in 2006-2007, OpenNet Initiative, accessed 7 JUL 2011 via the World Wide Web at *http://opennet.net/studies/china2007*

dcii IP News & Publications, East IP, accessed 11 JUL 2011 via the World Wide Web at *http://www.eastip.com/news/ip/index_html_v2*

dciiiJesse TH Chuang, Phillip Qu and Isabelle IH Wan, China's Internet Policy & Legislation, TransAsia Lawyers, 2003

dciv Electronic Signature Law of the People's Republic of China, China Trade in Services, accessed 9 JUL 2011 via the World Wide Web at *http://tradeinservices.mofcom.gov.cn/en/b/2007-11-29/13694.shtml*

dcv *"China's Green Dam: The Implications of Government Control Encroaching on the Home PC"*. OpenNet Initiative, [2011]. [Online]. Available: *http://opennet.net/chinas-green-dam-the-implications-government-control-encroaching-home-pc*

dcvi Michael Wines, China Creates New Agency for Patrolling the Internet, The New York Times, Asia Pacific, accessed 15 JUN 2011 via the World Wide Web at *http://www.nytimes.com/2011/05/05/world/asia/05china.html?_r=1*

dcvii Bill Gertz. *The Washington Times. "Chinese hackers raid U.S. computers"*. [1999]. [Online]. Available: *http://www.industrialdefender.com/general_downloads/incidents/1999.05.16%5Bisn%5Dchinese_hackers_%20raid_us_computers.pdf*

dcviii China Internet Information Center. *"Pro-China Hackers Invade US Govt Websites"* . [2001]. [Online]. Available: *http://www.china.org.cn/english/12150.htm*

dcix BBC News Online. *"US fears Chinese hack attack"*. [2001]. [Online]. Available: *http://news.bbc.co.uk/2/hi/americas/1301327.stm*

dcx Carrie Kirby. *"Click and bicker / U.S. and Chinese hackers explain their online war of words"*. [2001]. [Online]. Available: *http://articles.sfgate.com/2001-05-08/business/17596865_1_hackers-web-sites-dead-cow*

dcxi Bradley Graham, Hackers Attack Via Chinese Web Sites, accessed 29 JUL 2011 via the World Wide Web at *http://www.washingtonpost.com/wp-dyn/content/article/2005/08/24/AR2005082402318.html*

dcxii Michael Richardson, Taiwan is cyber warfare battlefield and Chinese target says security study, accessed on 24 JUL 2011 via the World Wide Web at *http://www.examiner.com/taiwan-policy-in-national/taiwan-is-cyber-warfare-battlefield-and-chinese-target-says-security-study*

dcxiii Heidi Blake, Timeline of Chinese web censorship and cyber attacks, accessed 29 JUL 2011 via the World Wide Web at *http://www.independent.ie/business/technology/timeline-of-chinese-web-censorship-and-cyber-attacks-2426210.html*

dcxiv Amit Grower, Cyber War's Final Frontier: Network Centric Warfare Framework, pp. 20 – 21, Identity Theft and Financial Fraud Research and Operations Center

dcxv Robin Ghandi, et al, Dimensions of Cyber Attacks, IEEE Technology AND SOCIETY MAGAZINE, pp 15.

dcxvi Ibid.

dcxvii Ibid, pp 18.

dcxviii Heidi Blake, China hijacks internet traffic: timeline of Chinese web censorship and cyber-attacks, accessed 18 NOV 2010 via the World Wide Web at
http://www.telegraph.co.uk/news/worldnews/asia/china/8142328/China-hijacks-internet-traffic-timeline-of-Chinese-web-censorship-and-cyber-attacks.html

dcxix Peter Warren, Smash and grab, the hi-tech way, accessed 25 JUL 2011 via the World Wide Web at
http://www.guardian.co.uk/politics/2006/jan/19/technology.security

dcxx AFP, The Straits Times, Chinese plan to hack into Taiwan websites, No Byline, accessed 29 JUL 2011 via the World Wide Web at *http://www.hartford-hwp.com/archives/55/105.html*

dcxxi Daniel W. Reilly, Lawmakers say congressional computers hacked by Chinese, accessed 23 JUL 2011 via the World Wide Web at
http://www.politico.com/blogs/thecrypt/0608/AP_Lawmakers_say_congressional_computers_hacked_by_Chinese.html

dcxxii Congressman Frank Wolf. *"Wolf Reveals House Computers Compromised by Outside Source"*. [2008]. [Online]. Available:
http://wolf.house.gov/index.cfm?sectionid=34&parentid=6&sectiontree=6,34&itemid=1174

dcxxiii The Washington Times by Associated Press. *"Computer Hackers Attack State Dept."*. [2006]. [Online]. Available:
http://www.nytimes.com/2006/07/12/washington/12hacker.html

dcxxiv Siobahn Gorman, China Expands Cyberspying in U.S., Report Says, accessed on 22 JUL 2011 via the World Wide web at
http://online.wsj.com/article/SB125616872684400273.html

dcxxv Heidi Blake, China hijacks internet traffic: timeline of Chinese web censorship and cyber-attacks, accessed 18 NOV 2010 via the World Wide Web at
http://www.telegraph.co.uk/news/worldnews/asia/china/8142328/China-hijacks-internet-traffic-timeline-of-Chinese-web-censorship-and-cyber-attacks.html

dcxxvi GOOGLE AND INTERNET CONTROL IN CHINA:A NEXUS BETWEEN HUMAN RIGHTS AND TRADE?, HEARING before the CONGRESSIONAL-EXECUTIVE COMMISSION ON CHINA
ONE HUNDRED ELEVENTH CONGRESS SECOND SESSION, U.S. GOVERNMENT PRINTING OFFICE, Washington DC March 2010

dcxxvii Yi Heng, China Internet Censorship, accessed 29 JUL 2011 via the World Wide Web at *http://www.facebook.com/topic.php?uid=64863896079&topic=7889*

dcxxviii Tom Espiner, Academics break the Great Firewall of China, accessed 29 JUL 2011 via the World Wide Web at *http://news.cnet.com/2100-7348_3-6090437.html*

dcxxix Information Week. *"Chinese Hackers Hit Commerce Department"*. [2006]. [Online]. Available: *www.informationweek.com/news/193105227*

dcxxx Simon Burns, Wikipedia partly unblocked in China, accessed 30 JUL 2011 via the World Wide Web at *http://www.pcauthority.com.au/News/84044,wikipedia-partly-unblocked-in-china.aspx*

dcxxxi Josh Rogin. *"China is suspected of hacking into Navy site"*. [2006]. [Online]. Available: *http://fcw.com/articles/2006/12/04/china-is-suspected-of-hacking-into-navy-site.aspx?sc_lang=en*

dcxxxii Jennifer Griffin, Pentagon Source Says China Hacked Defense Department Computers, accessed 22 JUL 2011 via the World Wide Web at *http://www.foxnews.com/story/0,2933,295640,00.html*

dcxxxiii Fox News.com from Financial Times, No ByLine, Pentagon Source Says China Hacked Defense Department Computers, accessed 21 JUL 2011 via the World Wide Web at *http://www.foxnews.com/story/0,2933,295640,00.html*

dcxxxiv Speigel Staff, Merkel's China Visit Marred by Hacking Allegations, accessed 30 JUL 2011 via the World Wide Web at *http://www.spiegel.de/international/world/0,1518,502169,00.html*

dcxxxv Richard Stiennon, Haephrati technique used to crack US research lab, accessed 26 JUL 2011 via the World Wide Web at *http://www.zdnet.com/blog/threatchaos/haephrati-technique-used-to-crack-us-research-lab/497*

dcxxxvi Ibid.

dcxxxvii Robert McMillan, Pentagon Shuts Down Systems After Cyber-Attack, accessed via the World Wide Web on 24 JUL 2011 at *http://www.pcworld.com/article/133301/pentagon_shuts_down_systems_after_cyberattack.html*

dcxxxviii China's Communists Seek to 'Purify' The Net, No ByLine, Status of Chinese People (中国人状况) Website accessed 23 JUL 2011 via the World Wide Web at *http://chinaview.wordpress.com/2007/01/27/chinas-communists-seek-to-purify-the-net/*

dcxxxix Kelley Beyer, Jumping the Great Firewall: Social Media Among China's Youth, accessed on 25 JUL 2011 via the World Wide Web at *http://www.datelineshanghai.com/scaling-the-great-internet-wall/*

dcxl Webster G. Tarpley, *US Readies Cyberwar, Virtual-Flag Terrorism*, accessed 23 JUL 2011 via the World Wide Web at *http://rockcreekfreepress.tumblr.com/post/465992689/us-readies-cyberwar-virtual-flag-terrorism*

dcxli CHINESE CYBERNATIONLISTS AND HACKERS AND THEIR ACTIVITIES IN CHINA AND ABROAD website, No Byline, accessed 26 JUL 2011 via the World Wide Web at *http://factsanddetails.com/china.php?itemid=1636&catid=7&subcatid=43*

dcxlii Ibid.

dcxliii Richard Spencer, China: Internet debut for leader Hu Jintao, accessed on 21 JUL 2011 via the World Wide Web at *http://www.telegraph.co.uk/news/worldnews/asia/china/2164637/China-Internet-debut-for-leader-Hu-Jintao.html*

dcxliv CHINESE CYBERNATIONLISTS AND HACKERS AND THEIR ACTIVITIES IN CHINA AND ABROAD website, No Byline, accessed 26 JUL 2011 via the World Wide Web at *http://factsanddetails.com/china.php?itemid=1636&catid=7&subcatid=43*

dcxlv Newsweek. "Hackers and Spending Sprees". [2008]. [Online]. Available: *http://www.thedailybeast.com/newsweek/2008/11/04/hackers-and-spending-sprees.html*

dcxlvi Malcolm Moore, China's global cyber-espionage network GhostNet penetrates 103 countries, accessed 16 JAN 2011 via the World Wide Web at *http://www.telegraph.co.uk/news/worldnews/asia/china/5071124/Chinas-global-cyber-espionage-network-GhostNet-penetrates-103-countries.html*

dcxlvii Ibid.

dcxlviii Siobhan Gorman et al. The Wall Street Journal. *"Computer Spies Breach Fighter-Jet Project"*. [2009]. [Online]. Avaialble: *http://online.wsj.com/article/SB124027491029837401.html*

dcxlix Marcel Fürstenau, Andreas Illmer, Germany shores up defenses against Internet attacks accessed 26 JUL 2011 via the World Wide Web at *http://www.dw-world.de/dw/article/0,,14870892,00.html*

dcl Chinese Cyberwar Attacks Canadian and Australian Governments, No Byline, accessed 30 MAR 2011 via the World Wide Web at *http://beforeitsnews.com/story/522/258/Chinese_Cyberwar_Attacks_Canadian_and_Australian_Governments.html*

dcli Ricardo Gatomalo, Chinese Hacker TimeLine, accessed 24 JUL 2011 via the World Wide Web at *http://uscyberlabs.com/blog/?p=6*

dclii Robert McMahon and Isabela Bennett, U.S. Internet Providers and the 'Great Firewall of China' accessed 24 FEB 2011 via the World Wide Web at *http://www.cfr.org/china/us-internet-providers-great-firewall-china/p9856*

dcliii MSNBC via the associated Press, No Byline, China blasts video claiming Tibet violence, accessed via 25 JUL 2011 via the World Wide Web at *http://www.msnbc.msn.com/id/29863003/ns/world_news-asia_pacific/t/china-blasts-video-claiming-tibet-violence/*

dcliv Senator Bill Nelson. *"Lawmaker hacked off over cyber invasions"*. [2009]. [Online]. Available: *http://billnelson.senate.gov/news/details.cfm?id=310162*

dclv Peter Foster, China begins internet 'blackout' ahead of Tiananmen anniversary, accessed via the World Wide Web at *http://www.telegraph.co.uk/news/worldnews/asia/china/5429152/China-begins-internet-blackout-ahead-of-Tiananmen-anniversary.html*

dclvi Duncan Gardham, Al-Qaeda, China and Russia 'pose cyber war threat to Britain', warns Lord West, accessed 29 JUL 2011 via the World Wide Web at *http://www.telegraph.co.uk/news/uknews/law-and-order/5634820/Al-Qaeda-China-and-Russia-pose-cyber-war-threat-to-Britain-warns-Lord-West.html*

dclvii Michael Smith. "*Spy chiefs fear Chinese cyber attack*". [2009]. [Online]. Available: *http://www.timesonline.co.uk/tol/news/uk/article5993156.ece*

dclviii Heidi Blake, China hijacks internet traffic: timeline of Chinese web censorship and cyber-attacks, accessed 18 NOV 2010 via the World Wide Web at *http://www.telegraph.co.uk/news/worldnews/asia/china/8142328/China-hijacks-internet-traffic-timeline-of-Chinese-web-censorship-and-cyber-attacks.html*

dclix Joint Report, Information Monitor and ShadowServer Foundation, Shadows in The Cloud: Investigating Cyber Espionage 2.0 Report accessed on 29 JUL 2011 via the World Wide Web at *http://www.nartv.org/mirror/shadows-in-the-cloud.pdf*

dclx Kelly Jackson Higgins, 'Fog of War' Led To Operation Aurora Malware Mistake, accessed 31 MAR 2010 via the World Wide Web at *http://www.darkreading.com/database-security/167901020/security/attacks-breaches/224200972/fog-of-war-led-to-operation-aurora-malware-mistake.html*

dclxi ZiXue Tai, The Internet in China Cyberspace and Civil Society, Routledge, 2006, pp. 99, 133, and 156.

dclxii Edmund Conway, Google threatens to quit China over censorship, accessed 13 JAN 2010 via the World Wide Web at *http://www.telegraph.co.uk/technology/google/6977756/Google-threatens-to-quit-China-over-censorship.html*

dclxiii Miguel Helft and David Barboza, Google Shuts China Site in Dispute Over Censorship, accessed 22 MAR 2010 via the World Wide Web at *http://www.nytimes.com/2010/03/23/technology/23google.html*

dclxiv Heidi Blake, China 'hijacks' 15 per cent of world's internet traffic , accessed 18 NOV 2010 via the World Wide Web at *http://www.telegraph.co.uk/news/worldnews/asia/china/8142267/China-hijacks-15-per-cent-of-worlds-internet-traffic.html*

dclxv Claudine Beaumont, Foursquare blocked in China, accessed 29 JUL 2011 via the World Wide Web at *http://www.telegraph.co.uk/technology/social-media/7802992/Foursquare-blocked-in-China.html*

dclxvi BBC News Business website, No ByLine, Google says China licence renewed by government accessed via the World Wide Web on 10 JUL 2010 at *http://www.bbc.co.uk/news/10566318*

dclxvii Michael Kan. Computerworld. " Huawei appoints former UK CIO to head cyber security post". [2011]. [Online]. Available: *http://www.computerworld.com/s/article/9218793/Huawei_appoints_former_UK_CIO_to_head_cyber_security_post*

dclxviii Technology review by MIT via Associated Press. *"US takes aim at China cyber threat"*. [2010]. [Online]. Available: *http://www.technologyreview.com/wire/26100/*
dclxix Jason Miks. The Diplomat. "Stuxnet in China". [2010]. [Online]. Available: *http://the-diplomat.com/china-power/2010/10/04/stuxnet-in-china/*, and, *http://news.xinhuanet.com/english2010/china/2010-10/01/c_13538835.htm*
dclxx European Times, No ByLine, accessed 20 NOV 2010 via the World Wide Web at *http://www.eutimes.net/2010/11/china-has-hijacked-us-based-internet-traffic/*
dclxxi Sean Noonan. *"China and its Double-edged Cyber-sword"*. [2010]. [Online]. Available: *http://www.stratfor.com/weekly/20101208-china-and-its-double-edged-cyber-sword*
dclxxii TAIPEI TIMES, No ByLine, China's military advances challenge US power: Gates accessed on 15 JAN 2011 via the World Wide Web at *http://www.taipeitimes.com/News/front/archives/2011/01/15/2003493537*
dclxxiii Nathan Hodge and Adam Entous, Oil Firms Hit by Hackers From China, Report Says, accessed on 10 FEB 2011 via the World Wide Web at *http://online.wsj.com/article/SB10001424052748703716904576134661111518864.html*
dclxxiv Samuel Wade, Journalists Under Online Attack, in China and Beyond, accessed 17 FEB 2011 via the World Wide Web at *http://chinadigitaltimes.net/2011/02/journalists-under-online-attack-in-china-and-beyond/*
dclxxv David Ljunggren and Peter Cooney, Canada hit by cyber-attack from China computers: CBC accessed 17 FEB 2011 via the World Wide Web at *http://www.reuters.com/article/2011/02/17/idUSN1623272920110217*
dclxxvi Paul Eckert and John Whitesides, China's cyber abilities worry U.S. – spy chief, accessed on 10 MAR 2011 via the World Wide Web at *http://uk.reuters.com/article/2011/03/10/oukin-uk-china-usa-cyber-idUKTRE7295XF20110310*
dclxxvii Adam Vincent, RSA hacked by Advanced Persistent Threat (APT) accessed on 19 MAR 2011 via the World Wide Web at *http://www.cybersquared.com/rsa-hacked-by-advanced-persistent-threat-apt/*
dclxxviii John Markoff and David Barboza, Researchers Trace Data Theft to Intruders in China accessed 5 APR 2010 on the World Wide Web at *http://www.nytimes.com/2010/04/06/science/06cyber.html*
dclxxix *Jesse Riseborough,* Rio Tinto, BHP Billiton, Fortescue Hit by China Computer Hackers, ABC Says accessed 20 APR 2010 via the World Wide Web at *http://www.bloomberg.com/news/2010-04-19/rio-tinto-bhp-billiton-fortescue-hit-by-china-computer-hackers-abc-says.html*
dclxxx Ibid.
dclxxxi Paul Roberts, Glass Dragon: China's Cyber Offense Obscures Woeful Defense accessed on27 APR 2011 via the World Wide Web at

http://threatpost.com/en_us/blogs/glass-dragon-chinas-cyber-offense-obscures-woeful-defense-042711

dclxxxii Ibid.

dclxxxiii Matt Liebowitz, Lockheed Martin Suffering 'Major' Network Disruption, accessed 27 MAY 2011 via the World Wide Web at

http://www.securitynewsdaily.com/lockheed-martin-suffering-major-network-disruption-0828/

dclxxxiv Pauline Arrillaga, AP IMPACT: China's spying seeks secret US info, accessed 7 MAY 2011 via the World Wide Web at

http://www.cbsnews.com/stories/2011/05/07/ap/business/main20060765.shtml

dclxxxv Robert Cazares, China Confirms Existence of Elite Cyber-Warfare Outfit the 'Blue Army', accessed 26 MAY 2011 via the World Wide Web at

www.foxnews.com/scitech/2011/05/26/china-confirms-existence-blue-army-elite-cyber-warfare-outfit/?test=latestnews

dclxxxvi Li Hong, China's cyber squad is for defense – Blue Army, accessed 31 MAY 2011 via the World Wide Web at

http://english.peopledaily.com.cn/90002/96743/7395784.html

dclxxxvii AFP News Website, No ByLine, Citigroup says 360,000 US credit card accounts hacked, almost double original estimate,

http://www.theaustralian.com.au/australian-it/citigroup-says-360000-us-credit-card-accounts-hacked-almost-double-original-estimate/story-e6frgakx-1226076520086

dclxxxviii Chi-Chi Zhang, China restricts popular report-a-bribe websites, accessed 22 JUN 2011 via the World Wide Web at

http://seattletimes.nwsource.com/html/nationworld/2015389255_apaschinabriberybattle.html?syndication=rss

dclxxxix Malcolm Moore, China opens string of spy schools, accessed on 29 JUL 2011 via the World Wide Web at

http://www.telegraph.co.uk/news/worldnews/asia/china/8596647/China-opens-string-of-spy-schools.html

dcxc Rory Cellan-Jones, IMF hit by 'very major' cyber security attack, accessed 12 JUN 2011 via the World Wide Web at *http://www.bbc.co.uk/news/world-us-canada-13740591*

dcxci Jeffrey Carr. The Diplomat. "World's Biggest Cyber Threat". [2011]. [online]. Available: *http://the-diplomat.com/china-power/2011/06/30/worlds-biggest-cyber-threat/*

dcxcii Michael Joseph Goss. Vanity Fair Magazine. "*Exclusive: Operation Shady RAT—Unprecedented Cyber-espionage Campaign and Intellectual-Property Bonanza*". [2011]. [Online]. Available:

http://www.vanityfair.com/culture/features/2011/09/operation-shady-rat-201109

dcxciii Daily Yomiuri Online. *"Chinese used in MHI cyber-attack"*. [2011]. [Online]. Available: *http://www.yomiuri.co.jp/dy/national/T110920006087.htm*

dcxciv Owen Fletcher. The Wall Street Journal. *"Patriotic Chinese Hacking Group Reboots"*. [2011]. [Online]. Available: http://blogs.wsj.com/chinarealtime/2011/10/05/patriotic-chinese-hacking-group-reboots/

dcxcv Jason Miks. The Diplomat. "China's Brazen Cyber Theft?". [2011]. [Online]. Available: *http://the-diplomat.com/china-power/2011/10/06/chinas-brazen-cyber-theft/*

dcxcvi Kathrin Hille. FT.com. "Chinese military mobilises cybermilitias". [2011]. [Online]. Available: *http://www.ft.com/intl/cms/s/0/33dc83e4-c800-11e0-9501-00144feabdc0.html#axzz1afoeUXEh*

dcxcvii Elinor Mills. CNET news. *"Report: Hackers interfered with US satellites"*. [2011]. [Online]]. Available: *http://www.zdnet.co.uk/news/security-threats/2011/10/28/report-hackers-interfered-with-us-satellites-40094303/?s_cid=938*

dcxcviii Leo Chen. TheEpochTimes. "Japanese Parliament Hacked, China Suspected". [011]. [Online]. Available: *http://www.theepochtimes.com/n2/china-news/chinese-hack-attack-suspected-at-japanese-diet-63389.html*

dcxcix Office of the National Counterintelligence Executive. [2011]. [Online]. Available: *http://www.ncix.gov/publications/reports/fecie_all/index.html*; and, *http://www.ncix.gov/publications/reports/fecie_all/Foreign_Economic_Collection_2011.pdf*

dcc U.S.-China Economic and Security review Commission. "2011 Report to Congress". [2011]. [Online]. Available: *http://www.uscc.gov/annual_report/2011/annual_report_full_11.pdf*

dcci Cynthia Hodges. " U.S. Military Chief: "We're under constant attack every day". [2011]. [Online]. Available: *http://www.examiner.com/homeland-security-in-chicago/u-s-military-chief-we-re-under-constant-attack-every-day*

dccii Associated Press. [2011]. [Online]. Available: *http://abcnews.go.com/US/wireStory/chinese-hacker-teams-us-data-theft-15135854#.TuZA41Ypr-9*

dcciii Adam Segal. Council on Foreign Relations. "Ideas about China's Cyber Comman". [2011]. [Online]. Available; *http://red-dragonrising.com/blog/42-ideas-about-the-peoples-republic-of-chinas-cyber-command*

dcciv Graham Webster. "Cyber Cold War rhetoric haunts the US and China ". [2011]. [Online].Available:

http://www.aljazeera.com/indepth/opinion/2011/12/20111221134038875151. html?mid=565558

dccv Adam Segal. The Atlantic. "How China Thinks About the Future of Cyberspace Conflict". [2011]. [Online]. Available: *http://www.theatlantic.com/international/archive/2011/12/how-china-thinks-about-the-future-of-cyberspace-conflict/250589/*

dccvi Mark Thompson, Time Magazine – Battleland. "(U.S.) Blood For (Chinese) Oil". [2011]. [Online]. Available: *http://battleland.blogs.time.com/2011/12/30/u-s-blood-for-chinese-oil/*

dccvii InfoSecIsland. Chinese Cyber Espionage Targeting Drone Technology". [2012]. [Online]. Available: *http://www.infosecisland.com/blogview/19163-Chinese-Cyber-Espionage-Targeting-Drone-Technology.html*

dccviii Adam Segal. Council on Foreign Relations. " A Chinese View on Why Cyber Deterrence Is So Hard". [2012]. [Online]. Available: *http://blogs.cfr.org/asia/2012/01/11/a-chinese-view-on-why-cyber-deterrence-is-so-hard/*

dccix Adam Segal. The Diplomat. "Can U.S. Deter Cyber war?". [2012]. [Online]. Available: *http://the-diplomat.com/flashpoints-blog/2012/01/12/can-u-s-deter-cyber-war/?*

dccx Noah Schachtman. Wired. " Military Networks 'Not Defensible,' Says General Who Defends Them". [2012]. [Online]. Available: *http://www.wired.com/dangerroom/2012/01/nsa-cant-defend/*

dccxi Niciole Perlroth. The New York Times. " Malicious Software Attacks Security Cards Used by Pentagon". [2012]. [Online]. Available: *http://bits.blogs.nytimes.com/2012/01/12/malicious-software-attacks-security-cards-used-by-pentagon/*

dccxii Adam Picre. Popular Mechanics. " Digital Spies: The Alarming Rise of Electronic Espionage". [2012]. [Online]. Available: *http://www.popularmechanics.com/technology/how-to/computer-security/digital-spies-the-alarming-rise-of-electronic-espionage*

dccxiii Vikram Thakur. Symantec Corporation. "The Sykipot Attacks" [2012]. [Online]. Available: *http://www.symantec.com/connect/blogs/sykipot-attacks* and, *http://www.symantec.com/connect/blogs/insight-sykipot-operations-0*

dccxiv Pierluigi Paganini. " Evidence of Chinese Attacks on US Defense Contractors" [2012]. [Online]. Available:

http://www.infosecisland.com/blogview/19772-Evidence-of-Chinese-Attacks-on-US-Defense-Contractors.html

dccxv Shaun Waterman. The Washington Times. " Intelligence chief: Iran, Russia, China top intel threats to U.S." [2012]. [Online]. Available:
http://www.washingtontimes.com/news/2012/jan/31/intelligence-chief-iran-russia-china-top-threat-us/

dccxvi *"China maps out informatization development strategy(05/11/06)"*. Embassy of the People's Republic of China in the United States of America". [2006]. [Online]. Available:
http://www.china-embassy.org/eng/xw/t251756.htm

dccxvii Major General Wang Pufeng, *The Challenge of Information Warfare,* China Military Science (Spring 1995)
http://www.fas.org/irp/world/china/docs/iw_mg_wang.htm

dccxviii China Brand Consulting Limited. *"Adavnaced Strategies of Anti-Counterfeiting in China"*. [2011]. [Online]. Available:
http://www.stopfakes.gov/presentations/ACF_Strategies.pdf

Lightning Source UK Ltd.
Milton Keynes UK
UKOW040928020312

188218UK00001B/39/P

9 781849 283342